(D22)

D0718431

Dr ... spent thirty years studying the prehistory of the Fens. He has excavated ... as diverse as Bronze ... farms, field systems and ... Iron Age v... From 1980 he turned his attention to pre-Roman religion and has excavated barrows, 'henges', and a large ceremonial centre dating to 3800 BC. In 1982, while working in a drainage dyke at Flag Fen, on the outskirts of Peterborough, he discovered the waterlogged timbers of a Bronze Age religious site. In 1987, with his wife Maisie Taylor, he set up the Fenland Archaeological Trust, which opened Flag Fen to the public. He frequently appears on Channel 4's popular archaeology programme *Time Team*, and in 2003 he wrote and presented a two-part television series on *Britain BC*. His latest book, *Britain AD: A Quest for Arthur, England and the Anglo-Saxons*, accompanies his new Channel 4 series.

From the reviews of *Britain BC*

'A book as successful and exciting as its ambition is huge: a prehistory of Britain that incorporates the perspectives of time and the most stimulating of new thought. Although the book is written ostensibly for the lay reader, Pryor's style is so lucid and engaging ... that people of every level of interest and proficiency will be informed by his insights. Above all, it is his headlong enthusiasm and willingness to speculate, combined with his authority, that are so impressive, and which make *Britain BC* a bedrock for the working future'

ALAN GARNER, *The Times* Books of the Year

'Pryor's great skill lies in his careful choice of case studies of excavations to illuminate his vision of prehistory. He gives us vivid vignettes, complete with character sketches of the personalities involved ... Each is presented from the author's particular viewpoint, underscored with a good measure of shrewd personal comment ... The result is a compulsive narrative intertwining prehistory, the excitement of discovery and personalities. It

bounds along, wonderfully enlivened by Pryor's earthy enthusiasm'
BARRY CUNLIFFE, *New Scientiest*

'Beautifully written, exciting and extremely good ~~~~~~~~~~ssential
read'
British Archaeology

'The author has great enthusiasm for his subject, and all the skill
of a storyteller, so he's done a sterling job of condensing the
considerable body of knowledge and theory on our prehistoric
past into one highly readable account ... Brimming with information ... You'll be hard-pressed to find a more convincing
and readable introduction to the subject than this'
Living History

By the same author

Seahenge
Britain AD

BRITAIN B.C.

Life in Britain and Ireland
Before the Romans

FRANCIS PRYOR

HARPER PERENNIAL

Harper Perennial
An imprint of HarperCollins*Publishers*
77–85 Fulham Palace Road
Hammersmith
London w6 8jb

www.harpercollins.co.uk/harperperennial

This edition published by Harper Perennial 2004
8

First published by HarperCollins*Publishers* 2003

Francis Pryor asserts the moral right to
be identified as the author of this work

Maps and diagrams by Leslie Robinson and Rex Nicholls

A catalogue record for this book
is available from the British Library

ISBN 978-0-00-712693-4

Set in PostScript Linotype Minion and Photina display by
Rowland Phototypesetting Limited,
Bury St Edmunds, Suffolk

Printed and bound in Great Britain by
Clays Limited, St Ives plc

For
TOBY FOX
and
MALCOLM GIBB

CONTENTS

PART III: The Tyranny of Technology

PLATES

The main chamber of the passage tomb of Maes Howe, Orkney (about 2800 BC). (© *Crown copyright. Reproduced Courtesy of Historic Scotland*)

A view of the standing stones of the Ring of Brodgar, Orkney (about 2800 BC).

The Stones of Stenness, Orkney (about 2800 BC).

An outcrop of the local stone on a beach in the Orkney Islands. This stone fractures naturally into flat slabs that are ideally suited for use in buildings.

A house belonging to the Neolithic settlement at Skara Brae, Orkney (3100–2500 BC).

A view of the short entrance passageway into the larger of the two Earlier Neolithic houses at Knap of Howar on the small Orkney island of Papa Westray (3600–3100 BC).

Interior of the smaller house at Knap of Howar, Orkney (3600–3100 BC).

Silbury Hill, near Avebury, Wiltshire (about 2500 BC). This man-made Later Neolithic hill is believed to be the largest artificial mound in prehistoric Europe.

The stones of Stonehenge, Wiltshire. The encircling ditch was dug around 3000 BC, but the stones themselves were not erected for another five hundred years (between 2550 and 1600 BC).

Two views of the great henge monument at Avebury, Wiltshire (about 2100 BC).

The wooden Sweet Track, Somerset. This timber footpath has been precisely dated by tree-rings to the winter of 3806–07 BC. (© *J.M. Coles*)

A small selection of the many hundreds of oak woodchips found in the bedding-trench of the timber circle known as 'Seahenge' at

Holme-next-the-Sea, Norfolk. This site has been dated by tree-rings to the year 2049 BC (Early Bronze Age).

Seahenge. At the centre of a roughly circular arrangement of fifty-five oak posts is an upside-down oak tree which had been sunk into the ground in a tightly-fitting pit.

One of the timbers of Seahenge.

Two views of the lower, cut, ends of Seahenge timbers.

Wooden haft for a polished stone axe from the Earlier Neolithic causewayed enclosure ditch at Etton, Cambridgeshire (3800 BC).

Polished stone axe placed alongside a woodchip that it produced some six thousand years ago, when last used. From the ditch of an Earlier Neolithic long barrow at Stanwick, near Raunds, Northamptonshire (3800 BC).

Producing a parallel-sided, or tangentially-split, oak plank using wooden wedges, a technique that was frequently employed in Britain from the Neolithic to the Iron Age.

Meticulous excavation of the Old Stone Age or Palaeolithic site at Boxgrove, West Sussex (500,000 years ago). (© The Boxgrove Project)

Caves on the shore at Paviland on the Gower Peninsula, south Wales, viewed from the low-tide mark. (© Stephen Aldhouse-Green)

The great grass-covered mound of the Later Neolithic passage grave at Knowth, County Meath, Ireland (3200 BC). (© The Irish Image Collection)

A view inside the Newgrange passage grave, County Meath (3200 BC). (© The Office of Public Works, Ireland)

Perhaps the greatest artwork from the British Neolithic, the carved flint ceremonial macehead from the Knowth passage tomb.

Timbers of the Later Bronze Age post alignment or causeway at Flag Fen, Peterborough, looking west.

Another view of timbers at Flag Fen, looking east.

A bronze 'flesh-hook' found beneath the lowest timbers of the post alignment at Flag Fen.

Bronze shears and their ash 'shoe' box, Early Iron Age (possibly 500 or 600 BC), from Flag Fen.

A group of bronze objects (1100–900 BC) from Flag Fen.

A Bronze Age tripartite wheel (about 1300 BC) from Flag Fen.

Two views of the sharpened tips of oak posts from Flag Fen.

A complete axe haft for a bronze socketed axe, in oak (about 1000 BC), from Flag Fen.

View of the traces of the foundations of a Bronze Age roundhouse at Fengate, near Flag Fen (about 1500 BC).

Reconstructing the Fengate Bronze Age house.

Four views of the reconstruction of the Fengate Bronze Age house.

A general view of the reconstructed Bronze Age farmstead within its fields and paddocks at Flag Fen.

Later Bronze Age wattle-lined well at Fengate (1430–1010 BC).

Another example of a Bronze Age sock well at Fengate.

A small flock of Soay sheep grazing in one of the paddocks of the reconstructed Bronze Age farmstead at Flag Fen.

A Soay ewe of about three years old.

A newly born Soay lamb keeping up with its mother.

Exmoor pony. This animal is typical of British prehistoric horses, with a characteristic loose coat and pale muzzle.

A so-called 'Iron Age pig' at Flag Fen, the result of crossing a Tamworth with a domesticated wild boar.

The Great Orme copper mines, Llandudno, north Wales (about 1900–900 BC).

An Iron Age logboat from a course of the River Trent, found in a gravel quarry near Shardlow, in Derbyshire.

Posts of a Middle Bronze Age timber causeway on the south bank of the Thames near Vauxhall Bridge.

Bronze Age timber excavated and removed by *Time Team* archaeologists from the causeway at Vauxhall Bridge.

A view of the Fengate field system (in use between 2500 and 500 BC).

Aerial view of the Iron Age hill-fort defences (fifth–second centuries BC) at Maiden Castle, Dorset. (© *Angelo Hornak/Corbis*)

An aerial view of the cairn surface of Site B at Navan Fort, County Armagh, Northern Ireland. (© *Crown copyright. Reproduced with the permission of the Controller of Her Majesty's Stationery Office*)

Three crouched Iron Age burials from Fengate, showing the variation encountered.

Two views of the reconstruction of a thatched Iron Age-style roundhouse at Fengate.

The excavation of three Bronze Age roundhouses at Cladh Hallan, South Uist, by a team from Sheffield University under the direction of Dr Mike Parker Pearson.

A close-up of one of the roundhouses at Cladh Hallan.

The late Peter Reynolds leads a team of two Dexter cows at his famous experimental Iron Age farm at Little Butser, Hampshire.

The underside of an Iron Age logboat from the River Witham at Fiskerton, Lincolnshire.

An aerial view of the low stone walls that are so characteristic of the Bronze Age fields on Dartmoor, known as reaves. (© *Andrew Fleming*)

Aerial view of the Cat's Water Iron Age village or hamlet at Fengate.

Excavation of the Fiskerton Iron Age causeway near Lincoln.

Reconstruction of the prehistoric Oakbank crannog at Loch Tay, Scotland. The crannog on which this superb reconstruction is based was excavated by a team of divers under the direction of Dr Nick Dixon. (© *Doug Houghton/ePicscotland*)

The Iron Age Broch of Mousa, Shetland, the tallest surviving pre-Roman structure in Britain. (© *Crown copyright. Reproduced courtesy of Historic Scotland*)

TEXT ILLUSTRATIONS AND MAPS

ACKNOWLEDGEMENTS

This book has profited enormously from comments by Richard Johnson and my editor Robert Lacey, both at HarperCollins. My agent Bill Hamilton, together with Roy Ackerman and Nick Hornby of Diverse Production, helped me turn preliminary outlines of the idea into something that could actually be achieved. Roy had the cheek to suggest the main title, and I had the good grace to accept it. The line drawings in the text are the work of Rex Nicholls, who also did such a superb job (regrettably unacknowledged by me) for my previous book, *Seahenge*; the maps are by Leslie Robinson. The excellent index is the work of Douglas Matthews. Best thanks go to Professor Ian Shennan (University of Durham), who kindly sent me a copy of his paper on the modelling of western North Sea palaeogeographies. Mark Knight sent me a potted account of his dig at Bradley Fen in advance of his own definitive report. I also owe special thanks to Richard Bradley, Mike Parker Pearson, Maisie Taylor and Edward Pank for reading the first draft of the manuscript and for their very useful comments, corrections and insights. Tims Schadla-Hall and Reynolds made helpful comments on some of the earlier chapters.

It's customary to end the acknowledgements to non-fiction books with a formulaic statement to the effect that the errors, biases and omissions owe nothing to the various people mentioned, and are entirely the author's responsibility. But in this particular instance, I really *do* mean it.

FRANCIS PRYOR
Flag Fen
Peterborough
Cambridgeshire
May 2003

Preface

British 'Peculiarity'

I decided to write this book because I am fascinated by the story that British prehistory has to tell. By 'prehistory' I mean the half-million or so years that elapsed before the Romans introduced written records to the British Isles in AD 43. I could add here that I was tempted to give the book a subtitle suggested to me by Mike Parker Pearson: 'The Missing 99 Per Cent of British and Irish History' – but I resisted. In any case, when the Roman Conquest happened, British prehistory did not simply hit the buffers. Soldiers alone cannot bring a culture to a full stop, as Hitler was to discover two millennia later. It is my contention that the influences of British pre-Roman cultures are still of fundamental importance to modern British society. If this sounds far-fetched, we will see that Britain and Ireland's prehistoric populations had over six thousand years in which to develop their special insular characteristics.

I regard the nations of the British Isles as having more that unites than divides them, and as being culturally peculiar when compared with other European states. I believe that this peculiarity can be traced back to the time when Britain became a series of offshore islands, around 6000 BC. Those six millennia of insular development gave British culture a unique identity and strength that was able to survive the tribulations posed by the Roman Conquest, and the folk movements of the post-Roman Migration Period, culminating in the Danish raids, the Danelaw and of course the Norman Conquest of 1066. It's in the very nature of British culture to be flexible and to absorb, and sometimes to enliven or transform, influences from outside. Nowhere is this better illustrated than by the historical hybrid that is the English language, which many regard as Britain's greatest contribution to world culture.

The English language is of course a post-Roman phenomenon that owes much to influences from across the North Sea. Very recent research carried out by a team of scientists from University College (London University) Centre for Genetic Anthropology has shown that the genetic make-up of men now living in English towns mentioned in the Domesday Survey of 1086 is closely similar to that of men from Norway and the Province of Friesland in northern Holland.[1] By contrast, Welshmen from towns on the other side of Offa's Dyke are genetically very different from English, Dutch and Norwegian males. Does this mean (as some have claimed) that the Anglo-Saxon 'invasions' of the early post-Roman centuries wiped out all the native Britons in what was later to become England? I suppose that on the face of it, it could, although I'd like to see more supporting data, because there's very little actual archaeological evidence for the type of wholesale slaughter such a theory demands. Besides, people have always had to live in settlements and landscapes, which over the centuries acquire their own myths, legends and histories. These in turn may have a profound effect on the incoming component of the local population. It's not by any means a simple business of one lot in and another lot out.

It is difficult to accept that the entire British cultural heritage of England was wiped out by the Anglo-Saxons. Why, for example, did the newcomers continue to live in the same places as the people they are supposed to have ousted, retaining the earlier place-names? It simply doesn't make sense, and we should be cautious before adopting all the findings of molecular biology holus-bolus. Culture and population are not synonymous.

Stories have plots and themes, and I have fashioned this book around what I think are the most important. But inevitably I have had to omit an enormous amount of significant material, simply because it fell outside the immediate scope of the story. However, *Britain B.C.* is not intended to be a textbook, nor is it in any way comprehensive. It's essentially a narrative – and a personal one at that. This is how I see the story of British prehistory unfolding, and I hold the view that a good narrative should be clear-cut, and not cluttered with fascinating but inessential detail.

*   *   *

What is it about archaeology that fascinates so many people? My own theory is that it's because it is a tactile, hands-on subject. It isn't something that exists in the mind alone. Unlike archaeologists, historians rarely get the opportunity to hold something that was last touched by a human hand thousands of years ago. Archaeology is a vivid and direct link to the past, which I believe accounts for the immediacy of its appeal – and to a wide cross-section of society. Over twenty years ago my wife was on a train from London to Huntingdon and found herself sitting next to the British heavyweight boxer Joe Bugner. He was charming and impeccably mannered. At the time he was a national celebrity, but when he discovered that Maisie was an archaeologist he confided that that was something he had always wanted to be. Then this morning I opened *The Times* to read that the most famous (or infamous) heavyweight of them all, Mike Tyson, had stated: 'I would like to be an archaeologist.'[2] I would imagine that both of them could wield a mattock quite effectively.

Many archaeological books which purport to be non-technical are written as impersonal descriptions of places and objects that are seldom explained, and are united only by the thinnest of themes. As a result, the public may be forgiven for wondering why so much money is currently being spent on a subject that seems to produce such dreary results. 'Does it really matter?' is a question I've been asked many times in recent years. Of course I think it does. I believe passionately that archaeology is *vitally* important. Without an informed understanding of our origins and history, we will never place our personal and national lives in a true context. And if we cannot do that, then we are prey to nationalists, fundamentalists and bigots of all sorts, who assert that the revelations or half-truths to which they subscribe are an integral part of human history. It needs to be stated quite clearly: they're not. In my view, the main lesson of prehistory is that humanity is generally humane, but from time to time is subject to bouts of extreme and unpleasant ruthlessness. Of course one cannot be sure, but I wonder whether this ruthlessness is perhaps a relict survival mechanism that goes back to our origins as a distinct and separate species, known as *Homo sapiens*. Whatever the cause, the important thing is that it exists, and we should recognise it, not just in others, but within ourselves as well.

Archaeology as an academic discipline is a humanity, and while there are accepted rules for 'doing' the subject, it is both impossible and, I believe, undesirable to pretend that archaeologists can provide unbiased and objective truth. We all have our own hobby-horses to bestride, and we might as well ride them in public. So I'll come clean. My own background is as a field archaeologist – what in the States they refer to as a 'dirt archaeologist'. It's a badge I wear with pride, and this book will inevitably reflect that background. Also, for what it's worth, my views on Creation, religion, ideology and the other related topics I'll be addressing in this book are essentially pragmatic. I don't believe in revealed truth, and if I'm forced to seek justification for our existence on this planet, I would turn to Darwin before scripture. He at least provided explanations, even if some of them have been superseded by later findings.

Has its insular peculiarity excluded Britain from other, more important relationships with mainland Europe? In 1972, in his book *Britain and the Western Seaways*, Professor E.G. Bowen attempted to explain the cultures of western Britain and Ireland in essentially maritime terms.[3] He saw close ties between those regions and neighbouring parts of Europe, especially Brittany, Spain and Portugal. In a masterly reworking of the subject, *Facing the Ocean: The Atlantic and its Peoples* (2001), Professor Barry Cunliffe has arrived at much the same view, but revised and extensively enlarged.[4] I wouldn't contest the observations of these two distinguished authors, but I would emphasise the many features that are unique to British and Irish prehistory, ranging from roundhouses and henges to the massive livestock landscapes of the Bronze Age. I would also stress the strong ties that unite east and south-east England to the Low Countries and north-western France; and north-eastern England and eastern Scotland to Scandinavia and the North Sea shores of Germany. I would further suggest that the natural overseas communication routes of at least half of England and Scotland lie to the east, to the North Sea basin and the mainland of north-western Europe.[5]

This east–west division of Britain also broadly coincides with the lowland and upland zones (respectively) that the great mid-twentieth-century archaeologist Sir Cyril Fox saw as being fundamental to the development of British landscape and culture – what he referred to as the 'personality of Britain'.[6] I tend towards a less closely defined view of these zones. I do not see them as inward-looking or self-referential. Quite the opposite, in fact. To me, the Atlantic/North Sea contrast is just that: it's a cultural contrast, not a divide, and is one of the key characteristics of the British Isles. It's a long-term stimulus that has fired the social boilers of Britain and helped ward off complacency.

Before I start in earnest, I'd like to express the hope that by the end of this book you will be as convinced as I am that their pre-Roman cultures have made a distinct contribution to the various national identities of the people of the British Isles. I hope you will also agree that the Ancient Britons have lurked in the twilight zone of history for far too long.

DATES AND PERIODS

Date*	Period	British Isles: main events
Fifth century AD	Early (or Pagan) Saxon	Main period of folk movements from the Continent
AD 410	Roman	Official withdrawal of Rome from Britain
AD 43		Roman legions land near Richborough, Kent
150 BC	Late Iron Age	Rise of larger tribal 'kingdoms'
450 BC	Middle Iron Age	Population growth
	Early Iron Age	Fiskerton
750 BC	Late Bronze Age	
1250 BC		
1500 BC	Middle Bronze Age	Flag Fen built
	Early Bronze Age	
2150 BC		
2500 BC	Metal-using Neolithic	
3000 BC	Late Neolithic	Stonehenge, Avebury, Orcadian and Boyne passage tombs
3500 BC	Middle Neolithic	Causewayed enclosures, long barrows etc.
	Early Neolithic	Sweet Track and first farmers
5000 BC		Britain separates from mainland Europe (6500 BC)
	Mesolithic	'Cheddar Man'
10,000 BP	Late Upper Palaeolithic	Ice Age ends
13,000 BP	Early Upper Palaeolithic	Burial of the Red 'Lady' of Paviland Cave
40,000 BP		
	Middle Palaeolithic	Mousterian culture
130,000 BP	Lower Palaeolithic	
500,000 BP		First humans in what was to become Britain
2,500,000 BP		

*Note that 'BP' refers to *Before Present*.

British Isles: technological innovations	Events and innovations elsewhere	Chapter in this book
	Migration period in Europe (fourth and fifth centuries AD)	
Factory production		Afterword
Wheel-made pottery	Caesar conquers Gaul (60–50 BC)	12
Widespread use of iron		
	Classical Greece flourishes	11
First use of iron		
		10
	Tutankhamen (1333–1323 BC)	
Earliest use of metal	Indus Valley civilisation	
		9
Stone axe 'trade'		8
		7
First use of pottery. Polished flint and stone tools		6
		5
Introduction of microlithic flint tools and weapons		4
	Neolithic Jericho (7500 BC)	
	Jomon culture in Japan makes first pottery (12000 BC)	
	Very cold. Northern Europe abandoned Modern man (Crô-Magnon man)	3
Introduction and widespread use of blade-based tools	Transition between Neanderthals and modern man	2
Sophisticated, flat-based hand-axes	Era of the Neanderthals	
	Evolution of various forms of hominids	1
Boxgrove, West Sussex. Hand-axes		
	Earliest humans (in Africa)	

PART I

Another Country

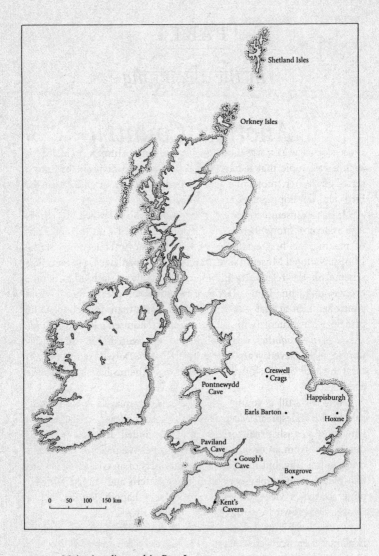

FIG 1   *Main sites discussed in Part I.*

CHAPTER ONE

In the Beginning

OUR STORY WILL BE about people and time. Human prehistory is such a vast topic that it has proved necessary to divide it up into a series of shorter, more manageable periods. Their origins lie in the birth and development of archaeology itself.

It was a museum curator, C.J. Thomsen, who proposed the Three-Age System of Stone, Bronze and Iron when faced with the challenge of making the first catalogue of the prehistoric collections of the Danish National Museum of Antiquities in Copenhagen. He based his scheme on the relative technological difficulty of fashioning stone, bronze and iron. Iron, of course, requires far greater heat – and controlled heat at that – to smelt and to work than does copper, the principal constituent (with tin) of bronze. Thomsen's book, *A Guide to Northern Antiquities*, was published in 1836, with an English translation in 1848. Eleven years later (1859) Charles Darwin published *On the Origin of Species*; by then Thomsen's scheme had gained wide acceptance.

Although still a young subject, prehistory played an important role in the widespread acceptance of Darwin's ideas.[1] Perhaps that's why most English prehistorians, myself included, tend to approach our subject from an evolutionary perspective. We probably shouldn't think in this way, but most of us are products of an education system that places great emphasis on structure, pattern and analytical discipline. Darwin's views on evolution sit very happily within such a rigorous yet down-to-earth conceptual framework.

In the early and mid-nineteenth century archaeologists in both Britain and France were caught up in the great debate around Noah's Flood. Working on material found in the gravels of the river Somme, the great French archaeologist Boucher de Perthes published evidence in 1841 that linked stone tools with the bones of extinct animals. He argued that these remains had to predate the biblical Flood by a very long time. It was revolutionary stuff a full eighteen years before the appearance of *On the Origin of Species*.

I said that Boucher de Perthes published evidence that *linked* stone tools with the bones of extinct animals. I should have said he published evidence that *associated* stone tools with the bones of extinct animals. 'Associated' is a very important word to archaeologists. It's code for more than just a link; it can imply something altogether tighter and more intimate. An example might help.

A few years ago we built our house, and whenever I dig the vegetable garden I find pieces of brick and roof-tile in the topsoil. I also find sherds of Victorian willow-pattern plate and fragments of land-drainage pipe which date to the 1920s. Like most topsoils, that in my vegetable garden is a jumble of material that has accumulated over the past few centuries. In archaeological terms these things are only very loosely associated. However, when work eventually finished on the house, I used a digger to excavate a soakaway for a drain, and filled the hole with all manner of builders' debris left over from the actual building of the house: bricks, tiles, mortar, bent nails and so on. In archaeological terms, my soakaway is a 'closed group', and the items found within it are therefore closely associated. To return to the Somme gravels, Boucher de Perthes was able to prove that the bones and the flint tools were from a closed group. This tight association gave his discoveries enormous importance.

It was not long before gravel deposits elsewhere in Europe, including Britain, were producing heavy flint implements like those found in the Somme. They are known as hand-axes, and are the most characteristic artefacts of the earliest age of mankind, the Palaeolithic or Old Stone Age.

Initially, archaeologists, and many others too, were more interested in what these finds stood for – evidence for the true antiquity of mankind – than in the finds themselves. Alliances were formed with pioneering geologists such as Sir Charles Lyell, whose book *Principles of Geology*, published in 1833, had established the fundamentally important 'doctrine of uniformity'. This sounds daunting, but isn't. It's a grand-sounding way of saying that the natural processes of geology were the same in the past as they are today. So, even ten million years ago rivers wore away at their banks, glaciers scoured out their valleys and every so often volcanoes erupted, covering the countryside around with thick layers of ash and pumice, just as they do today. Put another way, after Lyell nobody could argue that, for example, the highest mountains on earth were covered by the waters of a vast flood just because that accorded with their beliefs.

If one accepted Lyell's idea of uniformity, it became impossible to deny that the extinct animal bones and the flint tools found by Boucher de Perthes were in existence at precisely the same time – and a very long time ago. By the mid-nineteenth century, Palaeolithic archaeology was on something of a popular roll. No educated household could afford to ignore it. John Lubbock's book *Pre-Historic Times* (1865) became a best-seller. Indeed, it was so popular that it's still possible to pick up a copy quite cheaply. Mine is the fifth edition of 1890, and it cost me a fiver in 1980. It introduced the word 'prehistory' to a general audience, albeit with a hyphen, and it didn't stop short at the Palaeolithic (or Old Stone Age). Lubbock also discussed the later Ages with considerable learning and not a little gusto. I find his enthusiasm infectious, and it isn't surprising that some of his other books had titles such as *The Pleasures of Life* (in two volumes, no less). Like many of his contemporaries, Lubbock was able to turn his hand to subjects other than archaeology: his other works include books on insects and flowers aimed at both popular and scientific readers. He was a diverse and extraordinary man.

The first three chapters of this book will be about the earliest archaeological period, the Palaeolithic, or Old Stone Age. The archaeologists and anthropologists who study the Old Stone Age are grappling with concepts of universal, or fundamental, importance. What, for example, are the characteristics that define us as human beings? When and how did we acquire culture, and with it language? Let's start with the first question; we can deal with the next one in the chapters that follow. I'll begin by restating it in more archaeological terms: when and where did humankind originate?

The study of genetics has been transformed by molecular biology, but it isn't always realised just how profound that transformation has been.[2] I studied these things in the 1960s, as an undergraduate at university, where I learned that human beings and the great apes were descended from a common ancestor over twenty million years ago. But molecular science has shown this to be wrong. For a start, the time-scale has been compressed, and it is now known that mankind and two of the African great apes, the chimpanzee and the bonobo (a species of pygmy chimp found in the Congo basin),[3] share a common ancestor who lived around five million years ago. However, you have to go back thirteen million years to find a common ancestor for man and all the great apes, which include the orang and the gorilla.

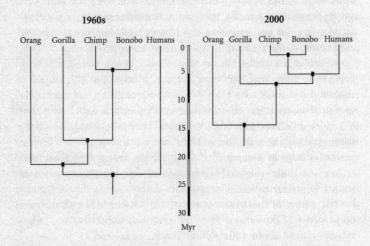

FIG 2   *A comparison of the descent of humans and the great apes, as understood by science in the 1960s and today (2000). The transformation in our understanding is largely a result of molecular genetics.*

There is now a growing body of evidence to suggest that recognisably human beings had evolved in Africa over two and a half million years ago. By 'recognisably human' I mean that if one dressed an early hominid, such as *Homo rudolfensis* (named after a site near Lake Rudolf in Kenya), in a suit and tie, and gave him a shave and a haircut he would, as the old saying goes, probably frighten the children, but not necessarily the horses, should he then decide to take a stroll along Oxford Street. His gait and facial appearance would certainly attract strange looks from those too ill-bred to conceal them; but such frightened sidelong glances aside, he might just be able to complete his shopping unmolested. His appearance in modern clothes would not be as undignified and inappropriate, for example, as that of those poor chimpanzees who until very recently were used to advertise teabags; he was no Frankenstein's monster. He died out less than two million years ago, and his place was immediately taken by other hominids, including the remarkable *Homo erectus*, a late form of whose bones were found at a site in Italy dating to a mere 700,000 years ago.[4] If *Homo erectus* took a stroll along Oxford Street, his appearance would attract far less attention than *Homo rudolfensis*, even if his size and stature would cause most men to step respectfully aside.

When I was a student, the descent of man (people were less twitchy then about using 'man' to mean 'mankind') was seen as essentially a smooth course, with one branch leading naturally to another. More recently it has become clear that the development actually happened in a more disjointed fashion, with many more false starts and wrong turnings along the way. We now realise that our roots don't mimic those of a dock or a dandelion, with a single strong central taproot, but are more like those of grasses and shrubs, with many separate strands of greater or lesser length.

The dating of these early bones and the rocks in which they are found depends on various scientific techniques, but not on radiocarbon – more about which later – which is ineffective on samples over about forty thousand years old. Palaeolithic archaeology relies more on the dating of geological deposits, or the contexts in which finds are made, than in dating the finds themselves, as is frequently the case in later prehistory. This often means that dates are established by a number of different, unrelated routes, and that in turn leads to a degree of independence and robustness. So it is possible to say, for example, that early hominids had begun to move out of Africa and into parts of Asia about 1.8 million years ago. When did they move into Europe? That is a very vexed question, involving many hotly disputed sites, dates and theories. But it is probably safe to suggest that man appeared in Mediterranean Europe somewhere around

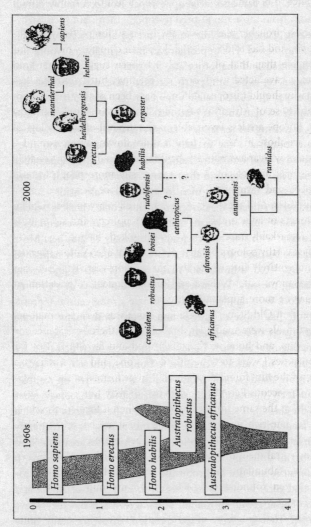

FIG 3   *Two plans which compare the human family tree as it was understood in the 1960s and today (2000). The tree on the left shows many fewer branches and 'false starts' than the more diverse tree on the right, which is itself constantly being changed and modified as new fossil bones come to light.*

800,000 years ago, but did not reach northern Europe and the place that was later to become the British Isles until just over half a million years ago.

The most probable reason why there was so long a delay is relatively simple, and has to do with the European climate, which was far less hospitable than that of Africa. It has been suggested that wild animals may have acted as another disincentive, but I find that less plausible: why should European animals have been so very much more fierce than those of Africa? We should also bear in mind that conditions in Europe are less favourable to the survival of archaeological sites than are those in Africa. There is more flowing water around – rivers ceaselessly wear away at their banks; there is a disproportionately larger coastline; and of course there are vastly more people, whose towns, roads and farmlands must have buried or destroyed many Palaeolithic sites. And these very early sites aren't easy to spot. Unlike the settlements of later prehistory, there's no pottery, and stone tools are both remarkably rare and easily overlooked, having frequently been stained earthy colours because of their great age. All this suggests that it's not entirely impossible that the million-year 'gap' between the original move out of Africa and the subsequent colonisation of Europe may be more apparent than real.

As the term Old Stone Age implies, stone was the main material from which tools were made. Having said that, there is evidence for wooden spears, and bone was certainly used and fashioned. But for present purposes I want to concentrate on stone, and particularly on flint. Most of the flint found in northern Europe formed in the geological Upper Cretaceous Period (one hundred to sixty-four million years ago), usually at the same time as the chalk. When it formed, the chalk was a deep, lime-rich mud on the seabed. In it are countless fossils, including the bones of marine dinosaurs, but more often one finds straight and spiral shells of squid-like creatures, which must have been extraordinarily abundant. Flint is found in the chalk both as nodules, which are often rounded and knobbly (to my mind they closely resemble Henry Moore sculptures), and as a near-continuous tabular deposit which was mined in later prehistory at places such as Grimes Graves in Norfolk (see Chapter 6). It is also frequently found in much later Ice Age gravels, which are composed of stones that have been worn down from much earlier rocks, including the chalk. It's probably fair to say that most prehistoric flint tools in Britain were made from flint pebbles found in gravel deposits at or close to the surface.

The stone tools used by the earliest people in Africa were fashioned from flakes and pebbles, and were probably used as choppers to break bones and to sever tendons to remove the meat. They are simple but effective, with a series of sharp cutting edges which were formed by removing flakes of flint from one side of a rounded pebble, using a hard stone as a hammer. The part of the pebble that was to be gripped when it was in use was left smooth and unworked. They may have been simple tools, but they weren't *that* simple: if I were to ask an educated modern person with no experience of such things to make one, I strongly suspect that he or she would fail. For a start, the stone-toolmaker must know how to select the right sort of stone for both the tool and the hammer. If the stone for the tool isn't flint, it should be as fine-grained as possible. The hammer should be hard, but not brittle; plainly, it should be resilient too. It's also important to check that the stone to be used for the tool isn't run through with hidden planes of weakness, perhaps caused by heat, compression or severe Ice Age frost, as these will cause it to disintegrate when struck even a light blow.

Now we come to the process of removing flakes. Again, this is far from straightforward. Put yourself in the toolmaker's position: in one hand is a rounded, fist-sized pebble, and in the other is a hammerstone of similar size. Both are rounded, with no obvious points, bumps or protuberances. So how do you knock a flake off? A hard hit at the centre will either achieve nothing, or will simply break the stone in half. A softer blow around the edge will just glance off, rather like a bullet striking the rounded edges of a Sherman tank. I know that first blow is far from straightforward, because I've delivered it many times myself. I've spent hours and hours trying to perfect and then replicate its force and angle. It's not easy to detach those all-important initial flakes cleanly. After that, it gets a little less difficult, because the removal of the first flakes leaves behind ridges, which make better targets and result in larger flakes that are simpler to remove.

Flint-working – or knapping, to use the correct term – is an art, a craft.[5] Even the crudest of pebble chopping-tools require considerable

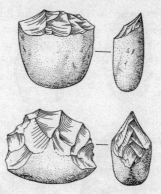

FIG 4   *Pebble chopper-tools worked from one side (above) and two sides (below).*

skill to make. Tools of this, the earliest tradition of flint-working, are remarkably similar from one site to another, which would suggest that the people who made them told each other about good sources of potential raw material, and passed on technological improvements as they happened. Alternatively, perhaps they communicated by example. Either way, the communication took place, which is all that really matters, because these tools were not only extraordinarily effective, they were important.

To my mind there is a vast divide between our earliest hominid ancestors and the closest of our African great ape cousins, the chimp and the bonobo.[6] It is true that apes can learn to use and even fashion tools; it is also true, as I have noted, that we arose from a common genetic stock. But the widespread adoption of something as complex as a stone-using technology could only have been accomplished by creatures who were both physically adaptive and who possessed mental capabilities that bear comparison with our own. Make no mistake, the earliest tool-using hominids were almost fully human: cross-bred ape-men they were not.

Pebble choppers were the main component of the earliest tool-using groups, but around 1.6 million years ago a new style of tool began to appear in Africa. Very soon it would be the tool of choice

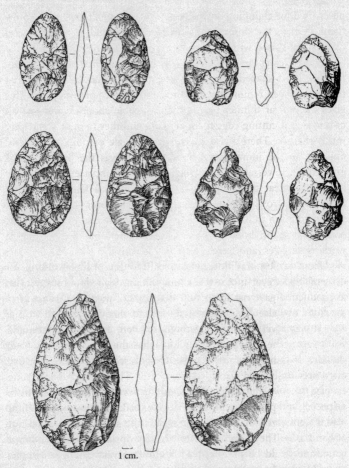

FIG 5   *Hand-axes from the Lower Palaeolithic (500,000 years ago) site at Boxgrove, West Sussex. (Drawings by Julian Cross and Perry Hardacre.)*

across the world. Possibly the best-known of all ancient archaeological artefacts, it's known as the 'hand-axe'. Like many archaeological objects it acquired its name early on, and we've been regretting it ever since. These tools may have been used in the hand, but they were never used for chopping down trees. So they weren't axes as we know them. Perhaps the closest modern equivalent would be the light steel cleaver that's used with such skill by chefs in Chinese kitchens.

Hand-axes come in a variety of shapes and sizes, but most are roughly heart-shaped. Their most distinctive characteristic is that flakes have been removed across the entire surface of both sides. This gives them a far thinner profile than a pebble chopper, and instead of one jagged cutting edge there are two, and they're finer – and very much sharper. There's also a very useful angle or point at the end opposite to the more rounded butt, which was the part that was gripped. These versatile tools, which were commonplace in the Palaeolithic, take great skill to produce: I could make a fairly convincing Bronze Age arrowhead out of flint, but I could never achieve a hand-axe. In addition to hand-axes, people at this time also made tools for scraping flesh off bone or hide. These scrapers had strong, angled working surfaces, and were also highly effective.

These earliest traditions of stone tools gave rise to a series of descendants of ever-increasing sophistication. Stone tool technologies in production gave rise to tens of thousands of waste flakes that litter the floor of Palaeolithic habitation sites to this day. Viewed in one way, it was a very wasteful technology. Then, about forty thousand years ago, some anonymous genius (I use the word advisedly) had the idea of fashioning a new range of tools from the flakes that had often previously been discarded as rubbish.[7] The new technology soon evolved ways whereby long, thin, sharp blades could be removed from a specially prepared piece of stone or flint, known as a core. These blades were razor sharp, but they lacked the strength and durability of hand-axes. They were, however, the appropriate tool for the job at hand, and could be produced with just one, very carefully directed blow. Mankind was taking the first tentative steps towards specialisation, and also – perhaps more worrying – he was acquiring a taste for lightweight, disposable implements. Our throwaway culture has roots that extend back a very long way indeed.

The final stages of the long prehistoric tradition of flint-working happened in Britain a mere six thousand years ago, with the introduction of polishing in the earlier Neolithic. This technology was very labour intensive. First, a rough-out for the axe or knife was flaked in the conventional way, then the cutting edge and any other surfaces that seemed appropriate were polished using a sand-and-water grinding paste or a finely grained polishing stone, known as a polissoir. Flint is very hard, and the process of grinding took a long time. The end result was, however, very decorative, and there can be little doubt that many polished flint axes were produced to be admired rather than used. Some indeed are made from beautiful 'marbled' or veined flint, which polishes up superbly but is so full of internal planes of weakness that it shatters on impact. An axe that broke when it first encountered a tree would not be selected by even the most inexperienced prehistoric lumberjack.

In Britain, the half-million-year-old tradition of making stone tools came to an end around 500 BC, in the first centuries of the Early Iron Age. By then the long, thin blades of the Neolithic to Palaeolithic periods had long gone out of use. Indeed, I suspect that the ability to produce them started to die out rapidly after about 1200 BC. The last flint tools reflect the widespread adoption of metal, which supplied people's need for cutting implements. So flint was used to provide scrapers and strange faceted piercing implements, which were produced by bashing gravel flint of poor quality that partially shattered, leaving a series of hard, sharp points. These points were probably used to score bone and scour leather. At first glance these odd-looking tools of bad flint seem strangely 'degenerate' when compared with the hand-axes and blades of much earlier times. But in fact they were good tools for certain purposes – and they were cheap (in terms of effort) and easy to produce.

I'm often asked how effective flint tools were, possibly because many people, especially those used to working with sharpened steel edge-tools such as axes, billhooks and knives, cannot believe that a flint blade could be of much practical use. I recall an incident in the early 1970s, when I was directing a large excavation at Fengate, on the eastern side of Peterborough. It was in the days before the planning regulations changed, and there was no friendly developer waiting to fund us, so we were working on a very tight budget indeed. One of our main costs then, as now, was staff, and in order to keep expenses down I came to an agreement with the authorities at North Sea Camp Prison, at that time a training establishment for young offenders, close by The Wash. They supplied me with labour, and I supplied them with work and training.

One day we discovered a multiple burial in a pit dating to the Neolithic period, and I took a party of North Sea Camp trainees to erect a scaffold shelter over it.[8] In the distance to the north-west the clouds were growing darker, and I knew that rain would be with us soon; I also knew that the fragile bones in the pit – which included the remains of children – would be seriously damaged by the heavy thunderstorm that was heading our way. So we had to move fast. Six lads headed off to collect scaffold poles and the shackles that held them together, while I and the others went to choose a small used tarpaulin from the stock I kept on site for such emergencies. We soon had an A-frame erected, using the poles and shackles, then it came to fitting the tarpaulin cover.

By now a thin scatter of those warm, large drops that so often precede a thunderstorm was just starting to hit the ground. Already the wind was beginning to get up, and there were occasional squalls of much heavier rain. We dragged the tarpaulin over the frame, but it was far too large, and there was no way we could secure all of its billowing folds in place. The rest of the team had taken shelter in the site huts two hundred metres away, so we couldn't summon help. I felt in my pocket for my knife, but it wasn't there. I asked the lads if any of them had a knife, which of course they hadn't.

After a very short pause, one of them sarcastically suggested I make one from flint. Stung by this, I reached down and happened to find a largish pebble at the edge of the grave. I rapped it firmly on one of the steel shackles, and it broke cleanly in half. I then gave it a series of lighter taps with the long handle of the wrench we'd used to tighten the shackles. These taps removed half a dozen sharp blades, and in no time at all we'd cut the tarpaulin to size and trimmed the long rope we'd used to tie it to the A-frame. After that there were no more sarcastic remarks.

Any discussion of northern Europe in the Old Stone Age has to approach the question of Ice Ages. The term was coined by the geologist Edward Forbes in 1846, when writing about the Pleistocene period of geological time. Victorian books on geology sometimes refer to the

Pleistocene as the Glacial Epoch. As this name implies, the Pleistocene was marked by a series of extremely cold phases, which are known as glacials; these are separated by periods when the climate became very much warmer, known as interglacials. During the warmest of the interglacials it was actually somewhat hotter than it is today. Perhaps I should add here that our own epoch, known as the postglacial or Flandrian, can be seen as a sub-phase within the Pleistocene: it began when the last glacial ended, around ten to twelve thousand years ago. Some (actually most) specialists in the Pleistocene reckon that the *post*glacial is nothing of the sort, that we're living in an extended *inter*glacial, and that there are cold times waiting in the future. There were also smaller oscillations of temperature within the major advances and retreats of the great ice sheets, and the whole cycle of cooling and warming began (with the Pleistocene period itself) around 1.8 million years ago – at least a million years before man penetrated into northern Europe.

When I was at university in the 1960s, study of the Pleistocene period was beginning to be enriched by a series of new sources of information, such as deep-sea core samples. I recall well how analyses of the temperature-sensitive plankton preserved in the Mediterranean muds off the North African coast showed a complex succession of warm and cold phases. Other information, such as deep cores through the Arctic ice, was also coming on stream. Today there are many more science-based sequences of past climates, and it is now clear that although general, global trends can indeed be discerned, the impact of individual glaciations and interglacials varied enormously in both strength and character from one area to another. I'll focus on the area of northern Europe that was later to become Britain, and restrict myself to the last half-million years or so.

Our story starts with a memorial plaque in the chancel of the church at Finningham, a small village in Suffolk. Most tablets of this sort are erected shortly after the person's death, but this one is very different.[9] It commemorates the life of John Frere (1740–1807), and it was dedicated at a special service on Sunday, 8 August 1999. It is plain, uncluttered, but beautifully made. And its message is simple:

JOHN FRERE
FRS.FSA
*who from his discoveries
at Hoxne
was the first to realise the
immense antiquity
of mankind*
1740.1807

The plaque was erected by the local archaeological society, with the aid of money raised from archaeologists and others all over Britain. All involved were agreed that it was high time that the man who has been called the father of scientific archaeology was given some form of public recognition. The decision to place the memorial in the church followed a visit to the villages of Hoxne and Finningham by the Suffolk Institute of Archaeology and History on 22 June 1997,[10] commemorating the reading of a famous paper by Frere to the Society of Antiquaries of London exactly two hundred years before. This paper concerned Frere's observation of flint hand-axes in the brick pit at Hoxne, which he reasoned had been made by people 'who had not the use of metals', and who lived in a very remote period, *'even beyond that of the present world'*.[11] These were extraordinarily prophetic words, given the stranglehold of religious orthodoxy that prevailed in Britain at the time.

Archaeology has given rise to some very disturbing ideas, and certainly there were few people in the late eighteenth century who were prepared publicly to support Frere's radical notion. So life continued much as before. As a profession, archaeologists tend not to make a fuss: we're generally polite and restrained. The 1997 visit to Hoxne and Finningham was no exception. It was organised – indeed inspired – by John Wymer, the leading specialist in the Lower Palaeolithic in Britain, who has himself excavated extensively at Hoxne.

There's one other thing I'd like to mention about that memorial in Finningham church. Above the inscription is a replica of a flint hand-axe found at Hoxne in 1797. It's a superb piece of craftsmanship, made by Phil Harding, who is better known as the member of television's *Time Team* with the broad-brimmed hat and the rich West

Country voice. During the early and mid-1990s Phil and John Wymer travelled the roads of southern Britain, carrying out an extraordinary and comprehensive survey of Lower Palaeolithic finds from the river valleys of the region. This survey resulted in seven specialised reports, which were given to local authorities to help them with planning applications, and an authoritative two-volume overview, published in 1999.[12] This report reflects its author: it is both erudite and remarkably down-to-earth.

From the very outset of the great survey, John Wymer decided on a landscape-based approach. He wanted to see how sites and so-called 'stray' finds (hand-axes and other flint implements that were found on their own, without any other archaeological context) could be related to their ancient surroundings. River valleys were a crucially important component of the ancient landscape – as they are of the present-day one – and they provided a natural framework for the survey. We tend to think of the inhabitants of the Old Stone Age as 'cave-men', but in reality, although caves were indeed used, they don't occur naturally in lowland river valleys, so it is likely that most people constructed shelters in the open air, probably using wood, bone and hides. Convincing archaeological evidence for such shelters has so far eluded us, but this is hardly to be wondered at: ancient equivalents of the New Agers' bender – temporary houses made from hoops of steel pipe or green wood covered with plastic – would leave very few clues to their existence after several hundred thousand years. The uprights used to build such structures would not need to be sunk into the ground, so they would leave no trace of that commonest of all archaeological features, the post-hole. By the same token, there would be no wall foundation trenches. These shelters would not have been occupied over an extended period, as the community, which relied entirely on hunting and gathering their food, would move around the countryside, probably following well-trodden routes.

The earliest period of human settlement in what were later to become the British Isles predates the most extensive glaciation of Britain, known as the Anglian glaciation, which began around 480,000 years ago. Anglian ice covered all of Britain north of a line drawn from south Essex and the Thames estuary, due west across the country to Bristol; thereafter it hugged the southern shore of the Bristol

Channel, but never truly penetrated inland into Somerset, Devon or Cornwall.

Happisburgh (pronounced 'Hazeborough') is about seventy kilometres east of Holme-next-the-Sea, where the so-called 'Seahenge' timber circle was found in 1998. Like Holme, Happisburgh is a very exposed beach, and subject to serious erosion. It has an outcrop of the so-called Cromer Forest Bed, a Pleistocene deposit which was laid down well before the Anglian glaciation. Recently, Palaeolithic flints, including a hand-axe, were found on the beach, and they appeared to be very closely associated with the Cromer Forest Bed. This would place them about 150,000 years earlier than the earliest flints yet found in Britain – i.e. around 650,000 years ago. The site is under such grave threat of destruction by erosion that any passing archaeologist should make a visit, recover anything he sees, and carefully record its position. It's not far from where I live, and it will make an excellent spot for weekend winter expeditions – there's something magical about finding 'the earliest' of anything that appeals to me enormously.

Whatever is, or is not, found at Happisburgh, there are only a handful of sites belonging to this very remote period of prehistory. There are also 'stray' finds of hand-axes and pebble chopping-tools along many of the river valleys of southern Britain, but these cannot always be dated with accuracy.

At this point some readers may query the presence of pebble chopping-tools in Britain, a mere half-million years ago, of a type that supposedly ceased to be made in Africa about a million years ago. Does the existence of these tools indicate that Britain was occupied over a million years ago? I don't think it does. It's inconceivable that large areas of a region so far into northern Europe could have been occupied at so early a date, and there's no other independent evidence to support such an idea. Many pebble choppers are unearthed as 'stray' finds in river gravels, especially in Essex, which is why this British tradition of pebble tools was named the Clactonian.

Most specialists in this field are today agreed that the Clactonian is not a 'tradition' in its own right; in other words, these tools (if that's indeed what they were) were not produced by a separate group of people with their own distinctive culture and identity. Most probably the choppers were made because the gravels routinely produce nice fist-sized, rounded pebbles which were too small to be made into hand-axes, but whose shape simply demanded that they be fashioned into a tool. Some fist-sized and -shaped flints can have that effect when one's brain is in flint-knapping mode. Put another way, Clactonian choppers are examples of local adaptation and inventiveness. It's easy to forget that people in the past weren't aware that their toolmaking activities would later be examined in minute detail by archaeologists. So occasionally they depart from what we expect them to do. Personally, I find this explanation for British pebble tools pretty satisfying, but still a tiny doubt niggles away at the back of my brain: Clactonian-like tools do occur occasionally on later sites of the Palaeolithic, which tends to support the 'local adaptation and inventiveness' theory; but having said that, in general they *are* very early. Even if it is only a half-mystery, it's an intriguing one, and I wonder when, or if, it will be resolved.

It's time now to turn our attention to the south coast of England, and the site at Boxgrove, West Sussex, which is undoubtedly the most important Palaeolithic discovery ever made in Britain. It's hard to exaggerate its significance. When one talks to Palaeolithic archaeologists their eyes light up at the mention of the quarry at Eartham, and their enthusiasm becomes infectious.

Although I only managed to go to the site once, it was almost like a religious experience. To reach the quarry one has to walk down a long, gradually sloping road. Beside me was the then Chairman of English Heritage, Jocelyn Stevens (now Sir Jocelyn), who was visiting Boxgrove to see how his organisation's money was being spent. I was there as a member of the committee which provides English Heritage with independent advice on all sorts of archaeological matters.

Sir Jocelyn is a very snappy dresser: trousers with knife-edge creases, shoes that glisten in the sun, double-breasted coats with a rose at the lapel. He is also a rapid walker, and likes to get to the point in all manner of ways. He was very keen to see the site, which had often featured on the national news. I was keen too, but I was also in the throes of a nasty cold, and was not feeling 100 per cent up to scratch, which is why I found myself stumbling over the small cobbles in my efforts to keep pace with the great man. My shambling gait did little to improve the impression given by my less than immaculate tailoring, which owed rather more to Skid than to Savile Row. We made a strange pair. Around us were the other members of the committee, and various archaeologists and administrators from English Heritage head office in London. It was a fabulous summer morning, crisp and fine, with larks on the wing in the clear coastal air. I was almost feeling better.

I wasn't aware of it as we walked, but the hill leading into the quarry was actually a smoothed-out ancient cliff, and it was this cliff which provided the key to the dating of the finds at Boxgrove. Most archaeological discoveries are associated with a single person. True, he or she almost invariably works with and leads a closely knit team, but it usually requires one person to provide the fire and enthusiasm which fuels the project. At Boxgrove that person was, and is, Mark Roberts.

As I've noted, Boxgrove frequently featured in the news, but unlike some other famous sites, it has also been comprehensively written-up. The learned, heavy-duty report was published by English Heritage in 1999.[13] It's a superb piece of work, but it's fairly heavy-going and technical, aimed at postgraduate students and professional archaeologists rather than the general reader. A far more accessible account of the project, written by Mike Pitts and Mark Roberts, appeared in 1997.[14] This is a landmark of a book that's hard to put down, combining a good, racy narrative with accurate scholarship.

Boxgrove is so important because its very ancient archaeological finds and deposits were preserved *in situ*, precisely as they were left half a million years ago. When I visited, I could almost have believed that the people who made the dozens of hand-axes that still lay in the trenches had only just left, and that they would return shortly to collect one for use, as soon as they had killed the wild horse they were now out stalking. It was an eerie feeling – almost upsetting, were it not so extraordinarily exciting.

The reason Boxgrove became, in effect, a time capsule, is that the original surface on which Palaeolithic people walked was quickly buried below a mantle of quite fine-grained deposits. This material accumulated entirely naturally – as a result of normal processes such as wind-blown sand, water wash, etc. – but the result was an eventual accumulation of some twenty metres (sixty-five feet) of overburden, which protected the hand-axes and other finds which still lay where they had been dropped on the original land surface. Today Boxgrove is fifteen kilometres from the south coast, and forty metres above sea level, on the highest of a series of raised beaches. This gives some indication of what can happen when one is considering a time frame as long as half a million years. You have to think in geological, rather than human, terms – which makes the superb preservation at Boxgrove all the more remarkable.

I was astonished when I saw the condition of the hand-axes. Having knocked up a few of them myself, I'm very familiar with the look of a newly made flint implement. There's an almost unfinished look to the things: edges are incredibly sharp and jagged, and there are clearly defined areas of 'bruising', perhaps where flakes failed to detach, or only partially detached. Knapping flint can also produce a distinctive, slightly sulphurous smell, not dissimilar to that of a freshly struck match. I've no idea what causes it – perhaps an occasional spark, or very fine dust – but it must be familiar to anyone with more than occasional experience of flint-knapping. As I looked at those hand-axes in the ground, I could have sworn I caught a whiff of that smell – which is plainly ridiculous, but it does hint at just how superbly fresh everything was.

Boxgrove would not have featured on national television more than once had it only produced extraordinarily fresh hand-axes. Something more was needed; and what could possibly be better than human remains? The bones in question were part of a shinbone, or tibia, of a left leg, and two front teeth. The shinbone and the teeth must have come from two separate individuals, as the shinbone was found about three feet below the teeth, which were close together, and were almost certainly from the same person. The teeth had distinctive scratch-marks on their surface, suggesting that the person they belonged to had used his or her mouth to grip meat while cutting it with a flint tool. This was consistent with a build-up of tartar-like deposits on the other tooth surfaces, which is typical of people who ate a diet rich in meat. Vegetarians they were not.

The tibia came from a large person, most probably a man to judge from his build, who was about six feet (1.8 metres) tall and weighed twelve and a half stone (eighty kilos). He was muscular, and presumably pretty strong and fit. Evidence for this comes from the great thickness of the bone, which is what one would expect of a person who was used to continuous hard exercise – like, for example, hours spent out on the trail, stalking and hunting.

I've tried to steer clear of hominid classification because it's both complex and constantly changing (incidentally, this is a good sign, as it shows that our knowledge about past people is growing all the time). It would appear that the Boxgrove people were distinctly different not only from modern man, but indeed from Neanderthal man, who came later. The Boxgrove finds are thought to belong to a species of hominids known as *Homo heidelbergensis*, after a well-preserved lower jaw-bone found in a quarry near Heidelberg in 1907. At present, physical anthropologists aren't wholly agreed as to whether *Homo heidelbergensis* was a direct ancestor of modern man (*Homo sapiens*) and Neanderthal man (*Homo neanderthalensis*), or of just one of them, of which Neanderthal seems the most probable. Recent research, however, suggests that *Homo heidelbergensis* may have been one of the many 'blind alley' developments of mankind's history, and that the true ancestor to both Neanderthal and modern man was another African hominid known as *Homo helmei*, who lived some 400,000 years ago.[15]

The large quantities of animal bones found at Boxgrove have an equally fascinating tale to tell as the flints and hand-axes. The material accumulated on flat, mainly open ground very close to the coast, and as I read through the accounts of Boxgrove I was struck by the fact that this could have been a site almost anywhere in inland England: nowhere could I find evidence that fish, seabirds or shellfish were eaten. Mealtimes weren't enlivened by so much as a humble dressed crab: it was meat, meat, meat – and red meat at that. This fits with what we know about other Lower Palaeolithic sites in Europe, where seafood also seems to have been ignored.

Further evidence for the consumption of meat is provided by the hand-axes. They are so superbly preserved that examining their cutting edges under a high-powered microscope reveals traces of so-called microwear – the scratches and polishes left when the tool was used in the Palaeolithic. The project's microwear specialist gave a local butcher several replica hand-axes, made by *Time Team*'s Phil Harding, and asked him to butcher a deer carcass with them.[16] Not surprisingly, the butcher had never used a hand-axe before, but even so he declared them excellent tools for the job. When he had finished, the edges of the replicas were examined microscopically, and the distinctive polish that had been produced by cutting the meat was very similar to that seen on ancient hand-axes from Boxgrove and other Palaeolithic sites.

Most of the animals that lived at or near Boxgrove would have been familiar to us today, but there were also extinct species of wolves, giant deer, bear and rhinoceros. There's no doubt that large mammals such as deer, wild horse and even rhino were being butchered at Boxgrove. There's also evidence to suggest that meat was removed on the bone and taken somewhere else to be eaten, presumably because the butchery sites were foul-smelling and swarming with flies – not a pleasant accompaniment to even a Palaeolithic lunch. It would seem most likely – again, there is some slight evidence to support this – that the meat was taken a short distance up the hill to the edge of the woods, where people would have stayed overnight. It was a sheltered area, protected from sight by trees and shrubs, where there would also have been abundant supplies of firewood. It's worth noting that the butchery areas at Boxgrove did not produce evidence for hearths or fires, as one might have expected had people lived there for a prolonged period of time.

So far I've concentrated on what one might term simple, direct observations: hand-axes were made, animals were butchered and so forth; to what extent can one go further and ask more searching questions, of which the most obvious is: did the people who lived at the Boxgrove site have language? I firmly believe that archaeology can answer such questions, but they often need to be approached indirectly, and from several directions at the same time.

A minimalist view has been proposed by Professor Clive Gamble. This view would have it that these were very simple folk. They lived, after all, half a million years ago, and their brains were far smaller than ours. Gamble has suggested that theirs was essentially an opportunistic 'fifteen-minute culture' that involved an absolute minimum of planning ahead. If they could think in ways that are truly comparable with us, he argues, why on earth did it take them so long to reach northern Europe from Africa? A million years is a long time to pause and admire even the grandest of Alpine views. If we look at the evidence from Boxgrove, the minimalist would challenge whether there was actually any 100 per cent solid evidence even for hunting. One horse shoulderblade had been penetrated by something which left a neat semi-circular wound,[17] which Mark Roberts is convinced is evidence for the use of the sort of pointed wooden spears that have been found at Palaeolithic sites in Britain and Germany, but not at Boxgrove itself (where the conditions of preservation did not favour wood). However, a minimalist wouldn't necessarily agree with this. To my eye that semi-circular wound seems fairly convincing, but minimalists would remind us that other interpretations are also possible. Certainly, it can't be regarded as a piece of 'smoking gun' evidence; it's pretty indicative, but no more than that.

So if they weren't hunting (which I very much doubt), presumably they were simply scavenging animals that had died naturally, or had been killed by a carnivore further up the food chain. If that were the case, there wouldn't be any need for them to plan ahead. And if you don't need to plan ahead, you don't require the sophistication of language that goes with it. Just pause for a moment and reflect on how much of one's conversation, at breakfast, for example, is spent planning for the day to come: if I take the car to do this, then you have to do that until I return; but if you take the car, then I'm left stranded, unless etc., etc. If, on the other hand, we simply bumped along, taking life and food as we found it, then everything, language included, would be so much simpler. That, at least, is the minimalist position.

In my opinion, minimalist views such as this are important because they make us keep our feet on the ground. They prevent us from building academic castles in the air. Had there been a clear-eyed minimalist standing at their elbows, I doubt whether medieval scholars would have wasted their time arguing about the number of angels that could balance on a pinhead. Having said that, I also believe in common sense and informed debate enriched by practical experience. All of which is to say that the totality of the evidence from Boxgrove seems to suggest to me that the people who lived there half a million years ago *did* hunt their prey, which included animals as fearsome as the rhino. This must have taken teamwork, organisation and forethought, and with them some sort of language. Let's examine further the direct evidence for forward planning.

First, consider the distinction between hunting and opportunistic scavenging. I can see no reason why hunting should not have developed quite naturally out of scavenging. It seems a perfectly reasonable progression, just as in later chapters I will argue that stock-keeping and animal husbandry are a logical development from hunting. The problem may lie inside our own heads. In countless books and articles I've seen mankind's relentless march of evolutionary progress illustrated in full colour, with crouching, ape-like hominids gradually being replaced by taller, more erect and intelligent beings until – Glory be! – modern man strides forth, head held erect and not so much as a genital in sight. Steps of progression form an important part of this pattern of evolutionary thought: from scavenging to hunting; from hunting to farming; from farming to urban life; from urban life to literacy, 'Civilisation', the Industrial Revolution and so on. It's a pattern of thought that makes us feel good, but I wonder to what extent it reflects the truth, which was probably more like the way I'm writing this book: two pages forward, then one page deleted, and so on.

So, perhaps one day they hunted, and the next day they scavenged – whichever seemed the appropriate thing to do at the time. Eventually they found that hunting was both more efficient and more effective. It could also be fun – I suspect this was of equal importance as efficiency and effectiveness – and it gave young people a chance to show off their skills. Larger groups would have been needed to catch animals as massive as rhinos, and they would surely have relished not only the thrill of the chase and the reward of food at its completion, but also the teamwork required to co-ordinate so many individuals into an effective unit.

These arguments sound attractive, but are they true? Do they represent what might have happened half a million years ago? Remember, we are not discussing people like ourselves, but people with a very different brain and patterns of thinking. Most of the ideas in the previous paragraphs presuppose that the people of the Lower Palaeolithic thought more or less like ourselves; and we can't assume that – a minimalist certainly wouldn't. A minimalist would argue that their way of thinking differed profoundly from ours. For them thought was more to do with habit; what would seem straightforward to us – for example the logical leaps from one set of unrelated ideas to another – simply didn't happen. I shall discuss this further in Chapter 3, but here I want to note that the way one interprets a site such as Boxgrove depends very much on one's theoretical position. It's no good even attempting to approach such problems with 'an open mind'. One has to have a theoretical position and a particular set of ideas to test out. Otherwise one's analysis lacks purpose and direction. Put another way, for 'open' mind, read 'empty', throughout.

So, what is the evidence for scavenging, or rather for persistent scavenging, at Boxgrove? As we have seen, the *direct* evidence for hunting is still quite slight, but it would be a mistake to assume that killing was necessarily accomplished by a sudden, massive and catastrophic wound that felled the prey on the spot – something like a javelin through the heart. In later periods of the Palaeolithic and in the subsequent Mesolithic there is good evidence that death could be very slow.[18] The prey was wounded badly enough to bleed to death slowly. As the poor beast gradually became weaker, it would be stalked by the hunting party until it either died or was weak enough to be finished off. Certainly this pattern of hunting would help to account for the thickness of the Boxgrove people's shinbones.

One piece of positive evidence for hunting, as opposed to scavenging, at Boxgrove is the evidence for human control of the carcasses found there. If the prey was dragged there from scavenging expeditions, one might reasonably expect to find that the initial hunters – be they bears or wolves – had left their toothmarks on the bones first. Thereafter one might expect to find the scratches left by the hand-axes that detached the meat. But this never happens. Where gnaw-marks and hand-axe marks are found together on the same bone, it is always the gnawing that comes later – presumably when the hunters had no further use for the carcass. I have to say, I find this evidence for hunting fairly convincing. But I can still hear Clive Gamble asking, 'Why? Surely these patterns could equally well have resulted from people arriving at a kill site first, before the other scavengers arrived on the scene.' And he could well be right. After all, there is no direct, incontrovertible evidence for human beings actually killing prey at Boxgrove.

This absence of direct evidence may in part be due to the fact that the wooden spears of the Lower Palaeolithic leave only a slight impression on bone, unlike, say, a broken-off flint arrowhead. We do, however, know that wooden spears of this period did exist. There's a very probable contender made of yew wood which was found at Clacton, but several complete examples have been found across the North Sea at Schönongen, a site in Germany.[19] So the evidence most certainly is out there. But it still seems to be absent from Boxgrove. Maybe I ought to reserve my position until something definite, one way or the other, turns up. But I can't: I still find the cumulative evidence for hunting, especially as presented in the full Boxgrove report by Mark Roberts, convincing. And what is far more significant, John Wymer does too. In his preface to the full report, he is emphatic (the italics are his):

> The people *were* hunters of large mammals; they *did* hunt with spears; they *did* retain useful objects for future use . . . We know that they had craftsmen among them with a concept of symmetry, if not beauty. They performed tasks that involved a division of labour and there is much to imply a social order of groups larger than usually imagined working together.[20]

I'll leave it there for the time being. In Chapter 3 I'll review the evidence for Palaeolithic social organisation, and then Clive Gamble will have a chance to give the reasons why he inclines to a more minimalist view. I find this controversy both stimulating and refreshing – not least because the people concerned are not at each other's throats, but are all far more concerned about the broader issues lying behind Palaeolithic research. As John Wymer put it in the final words of his preface to the Boxgrove report, the topic is alive because it is 'research into what is the most important subject confronting us: ourselves'.

I've tended to emphasise the *quality* of preservation at Boxgrove, simply because it's so extraordinary and, for me at least, affecting. But we shouldn't lose sight of the *quantity* either. Before Boxgrove, discoveries of hand-axes from this period were rare events indeed – perhaps a dozen or two each year, most of which were those archaeologically less-than-useful isolated or 'stray' finds. By contrast, one small area of the Boxgrove excavations revealed over 150 hand-axes, some of which were unused. Mark Roberts has suggested, quite reasonably, that these implements had been made, perhaps when a particularly good source of flint had been found, to be kept to one side and used when needed. If he is right, plainly this is evidence for forethought.

The hand-axes themselves were difficult to make, and in this respect, as we've already seen, they were quite unlike the earlier tools of the pebble-chopper tradition. One doesn't simply select a suitably sized piece of flint and then remove flakes on the off-chance that one can whittle away enough, and in the right places, to produce the desired end-result. There are a number of quite clearly defined stages that have to be gone through before one can produce a finished hand-axe, starting with the removal of the softer, more granular cortex, a type of 'skin' or 'peel' that develops through time and which protects the higher-quality, glass-like flint within.

At Boxgrove there is clear evidence that many of the hand-axes used for butchery were made then and there, on the spot. There are numerous waste flakes along with the finished hand-axes, and in one instance it's possible to see where a person sat on the ground while he knapped a hand-axe. As he worked he allowed the flakes of flint to fall into his lap and then onto the ground, making a characteristically tight pattern (about ten inches across) that can be replicated experimentally. It's as if fifteen minutes of time had been frozen for half a million years.

Each stage of a hand-axe's manufacture requires a great deal of manual skill to start and complete, and it also takes good judgement to know when to move from one stage to another. The hand-axes found at Boxgrove are rarely ever skewed or misshaped, and are nearly always balanced and evenly proportioned, both when laid flat and when viewed edge-on. Speaking again from personal experience, I know that it takes considerable skill and judgement to keep an eye on the proportions of two separate planes simultaneously. It's easy to get slightly carried away when things are going well, only to realise – when it's too late – that one's arrowhead, or whatever else one is making, will never fly straight. I've watched a good flint-knapper make a hand-axe, and a large part of the time he spent turning and inspecting the piece at arm's length, to see that everything was in balance. The discipline required, and the knowledge of the different stages of manufacture, must surely have been taught from one generation to the next – and teaching, of course, requires language of some sort.

Much of the manufacture of hand-axes requires the use of a so-called 'soft' hammer, which in most cases was probably made from a billet or baton of antler, perhaps a foot or slightly less long and with the diameter of, say, a cricket stump. Antler is hard, but it's also very resilient, and doesn't chip or flake even when hit with force. This makes it ideal for flint-working. Before Boxgrove, we suspected that antler was used for soft hammers, but couldn't prove it. But at Boxgrove an antler billet was found with small, sharp fragments of flint still sticking into it. The worn state of that antler hammer suggests that it was used to make more than one hand-axe, and again this provides good evidence for forethought, as presumably whoever it was that owned it carried the hammer around until he needed to use it again.

Where do all these indications of forethought lead us? Did the inhabitants of Boxgrove possess a sophisticated, highly adaptable language, such as English? The evidence from those who understand and study the human brain and the inside of the bone case – the cranium – that protects it suggests that *Homo heidelbergensis* simply didn't have the mental equipment to develop or use a highly sophisticated language. On the other hand, the archaeological record makes it clear that these people must routinely have used a form of language – albeit of a relatively simple type. That, it would appear, is as far as we can take matters at present.

CHAPTER TWO

Neanderthals, the Red 'Lady' and Ages of Ice

BOXGROVE WAS OCCUPIED before the great chill of the Anglian glaciation, whose ice retreated around 423,000 years ago. Then, so far as we know, essentially the same type of lifestyle resumed. Much of the evidence for this comes not from spectacular sites like Boxgrove, but from the discovery of hundreds of hand-axes from the lowland river gravels of England. In the past these hand-axes would generally not have been systematically studied, as they would have been seen as out of context, or 'derived', to use the archaeological term. They were derived because they were found in gravels whose very formation – derivation – had eroded away the original settlement sites where the hand-axes had been deposited. Imagine that a series of rivers had flowed through Boxgrove, churning the material around and around. Would what was left have any archaeological value? It depends, as Professor Joad of *The Brains Trust* would have said, on what one means by archaeological value. And that, in turn, depends on the scale at which one is working.

Boxgrove is remarkable for the detail it provides. It's actually possible to refit flint flakes back together, to reconstruct precisely how a Palaeolithic flint-knapper once worked for fifteen minutes. One might refer to this as the micro-scale of archaeological investigation. But one might also quite reasonably wonder what else was going on at that time so very long ago. Were there, for example, other settlements in the area, and how long did they last? These larger-scale, or macro-level, questions require a different type of information if they're to be answered properly. However remarkable refitting flint flakes might be in itself, it won't take us any further forward in this instance.

I mentioned that the river gravel hand-axes were 'derived' from earlier deposits, and this was due to the down-cutting of rivers and the reworking of the gravels lying in the floodplain. These changes in the rivers' behaviour were caused by fluctuations in climate during the successive glacial, cold, cool and temperate phases of the Ice Ages. There was plenty of fast-flowing water around as the ice melted, then less during temperate times, and none when ice was present. And of course, each of these phases had innumerable sub-phases, which varied from one river valley to another. If you understand how the resulting sequence of gravel terraces within the floodplain formed, then you provide at least a secondary context for the hand-axes and other flints within them.

John Wymer's survey of the river gravels unravelled the sequence of terraces of all the major river valleys of southern Britain, and for that alone it is notable. The results of the survey 'provide incontrovertible evidence for the presence of human groups during intermittent occupations in all the major valleys, over a time span of some half-million years'.[1] The survey also revealed extensive evidence for occupation in areas outside the major river valleys, such as around lakes, on the coastal fringe and in the chalk downland. It's difficult at this stage even to hazard a guess at the British population during a warmer period of an interglacial, but I imagine that a low-level flight across the country would have detected the smoke from at most one or two fires. In 1972, the eminent archaeologist Don Brothwell estimated that the population for Britain as a whole at any one time during the Lower Palaeolithic would have been less than five thousand.[2]

So far we have been dealing with the longest period in British prehistory, the Lower Palaeolithic. Now we must move forward, and rapidly, if we are to keep to our schedule. The next significant stage starts shortly after 250,000 years ago and is known as the Middle Palaeolithic. Initially it would appear that occupation – or the evidence for occupation – during this period is slight, and this was doubtless due to adverse climate conditions. But unlike the previous period, the evidence from elsewhere in Europe is very much better. This is a shame, because it was a time of very considerable interest.

I started the previous chapter with some thoughts about the very earliest recognisable hominids, and perhaps the best way to span the half-million or so years that now confront us is via them (the hominids) and us (modern man, or *Homo sapiens*). In other words, we shall rapidly trace the story of human evolution and development, insofar as it affects what was shortly to become Britain. The other approach would be via the flint implements and other archaeological remains that were left behind.[3] The problem here, however, is that there is a wealth of material which can be discussed and classified in various ways, depending on one's archaeological interests and background.[4] Sometimes one can become too introspective: it's easy to be more concerned with flint implements, and what they may have been used for, than with the people who actually made and used them. I shall stick to flesh and blood – to people.

In the previous chapter we saw how early hominids moved out of Africa, and took a very long time indeed finally to colonise northern Europe. We then took a closer look at the site at Boxgrove, where possible ancestors of modern man and the Neanderthals butchered their meat and made flint tools for the purpose. It's those two descendants – or possible descendants – of the people at Boxgrove who will concern us here. We will start with perhaps the most famous name in archaeology: Neanderthal man (*Homo neanderthalensis*).

The Neanderthals have not always had a good press, and I often wonder how they would have reacted to some of the things that have been said (or worse, painted) about them. A recent (and hugely expensive) television series and its spin-off book were at pains to be objective about them, and they succeeded admirably.[5] But things haven't always been so well done: there's something about the Neanderthals, and our treatment of them, that ultimately mocks ourselves. When it comes to our closest, deceased relatives, historically we can't seem to get it right. Perhaps they're just too close to us.

The story of the finding of bones in the Neander valley (or *thal*) near Düsseldorf in 1856 is well known.[6] It was a discovery that was profoundly to affect the development of archaeological thought, and not always for the better.[7] Quite soon after the initial discoveries at the Feldhover Cave, other, earlier finds were recognised as people of the same type, or species. Neanderthals have been found over most of

Europe and western Asia – but not, interestingly, in Africa; presumably because they had become so well adapted to cooler climates that they didn't fancy crossing the Sahara desert. Actual hard-and-fast evidence for Neanderthals in Britain was only found very recently. They lived in this vast stretch of the globe for a very long time indeed, and during some of the coldest episodes of the Ice Ages, between about 130,000 and thirty thousand years ago. As we will see, the Neanderthals were on the earth for considerably longer than modern man (*Homo sapiens*) has yet managed.

FIG 6   *Restored face of Neanderthal man in modern dress.*

Happily, there's no shortage of Neanderthal bone to work with, and as a result we have a pretty good idea of what they would have looked like. For a start, they were absolutely human, and would not have given rise to those ill-bred stares in Oxford Street, although when first confronted with one, I suspect I might have registered that they came from somewhere a long way away. In the days when such questions were not considered sexist in academic circles, I once asked a colleague who specialised in the Palaeolithic whether he thought he'd fancy a young Neanderthal woman. He replied: 'You bet I would, but I'd make myself scarce when her brother arrived.' They were thick-set and quite heavily built, with stout bones that showed signs of having supported a very active body. The face was characterised by strong brow ridges above the eyes and a forehead that sloped backwards far more than ours. The lower face and jaw was more prominent, which tended to disguise the fact that the chin profile was weak.

Reading this through, I'm struck by the fact that I'm judging the unfortunate Neanderthaler as if he were an aberrant modern man. He might say of us: they have domed, baby-like foreheads which, when combined with a receding jawline and spindly limbs, gives them an awkward, insubstantial and unbalanced appearance.

Neanderthals had a larger brain than modern man, not just in relation to their somewhat larger body mass, but absolutely. I suppose we're bound to say this, but there is no evidence that this larger brain gave them more intelligence. Indeed, the bare fact that they failed to survive the evolutionary rat-race – given no help whatsoever from *Homo sapiens* – tends to support this view. It has been suggested that the principal difference in the way the two species thought was that modern man was able to lump his thoughts together.[8] He was more of a generalist, whereas Neanderthals were 'domain specific', to use a term coined by the cognitive archaeologist Steven Mithen.[9] Put another way, *Homo sapiens* was better at integrating concepts: he could identify similarities in supposedly unrelated spheres (the way that Newton could see how a falling apple and gravity were part of the same phenomenon). I remember reading that remarkable book by Arthur Koestler, *The Act of Creation* (1964), in which he maintained that all great intellectual insights came as a result of making links between different spheres (he termed them 'matrices') of thought. It would now seem that this ability to cross-reference and reintegrate is something unique to our species, and it led directly to the development of sophisticated language. Neanderthals, on the other hand, are believed to have maintained more rigid or impermeable pigeonholes in their brains: different realms of thought stayed apart from each other. In some respects this was good: it gave focus and discipline, as their magnificently executed flintwork attests. But so far as is known it doesn't seem to have given rise to art (as opposed to decoration plain and simple), or to more complex symbolic expression.

There were other things that distinguished Neanderthals from modern humans. Plainly these ideas are tentative, but it's worth noting that drawing conclusions about ancient behaviour from dry bones, flints and, crucially, the contexts of their discovery is a major achievement of Palaeolithic archaeology. The concept of 'context' is fundamentally important to archaeology.[10] Essentially it refers to the way that different artefacts, bones and other finds relate to each other. Thus, the dagger found protruding from a dead man's ribcage tells a very different story to the dagger tucked into a dancing Scotsman's sock. The dagger may be constant, but the context – which provides the meaning – isn't. The word can also be used in a more specific archaeological sense, which loosely correlates with 'layer' or 'deposit'. So, in an ancient settlement, for instance, the soil (and the finds therein) that filled an abandoned ditch would form a different archaeological *context* to the ashes and charcoal in a nearby hearth.

Using such contextual information, it would appear that the children of Neanderthal parents grew up faster, and achieved their independence more rapidly, than their *Homo sapiens* equivalents.[11] Maybe this was a result of their large brains and focused way of thinking, but it could have had a downside, too. Without prolonged exposure to their parents' acquired experience and wisdom, the younger generation would have been forever reinventing and rediscovering things that their parents knew perfectly well. This would undoubtedly have affected the pace and dynamics of social development within the group as a whole. As we will see later, change in *Homo sapiens* society is by its nature slow, but in the case of the Neanderthals it must have been even slower. This would have put them at a considerable disadvantage compared with the more adaptable communities of *Homo sapiens* – especially in periods when the natural environment around them was changing rapidly.

One should resist the temptation always to put theories and observations on past behaviour into modern terms, but I can't help thinking that the Neanderthal thought-process may have been similar to the overfocused approach of obsessive trainspotters or stamp collectors. Their hobbies lack interest or appeal for me, because they are devoid of most social context. Don't get me wrong – I love steam trains, but I'm far more interested in their drivers and firemen and where they would have taken their summer holidays. I have lately observed a certain philatelic tendency creeping into archaeology, both professional and non-professional: an obsession with sites, dates, artefacts and other *minutiae* – at the expense of the original people and the stories that lay behind them. It's all very Neanderthal.

It is clear that the Neanderthals ate a great deal of meat, which they undoubtedly hunted effectively, using a variety of techniques and tactics. As we have seen, their bones were robust and thick-walled, which indicates that their lives were extremely active. Dr Paul Pettitt, a notable authority on the subject, put it well: 'Neanderthals lived fast and died young.'[12] I don't want to give the impression that Neanderthals were thugs, because the facts do not support that. Far from it, there is much evidence (mainly from Europe and the Middle East) to suggest that they cared deeply about death and the dead: burials were deliberately placed in dug graves, and bodies were sometimes accompanied by grave goods and red ochre – a natural powder-based mineral paint. Neanderthals took considerable care over the burial of children and older, physically disabled people, who would not have been able to survive outside what must have been a small, robust but nonetheless caring community. Sadly, as we will see shortly, our Neanderthal cousins were to learn that small, caring communities don't last long when the competition for survival begins to hot up.

The Middle Palaeolithic is the name given to the period dominated by Neanderthal man. As we have noted, Britain was sparsely occupied especially during the earlier years of the period; I know of only one find of Neanderthal-style bones here (teeth and lower jaw fragments from two individuals), from Pontnewydd Cave, in north Wales. I say Neanderthal-*style* bones because although they have Neanderthal characteristics, their date is very early indeed (around 240,000 years ago), so they are perhaps best seen as coming from people who were ancestral to the true Neanderthals. But Pontnewydd Cave also had another, far subtler, archaeological secret to reveal.

The cave was superbly excavated by Dr Stephen Aldhouse-Green of the National Museum of Wales, in Cardiff. I first met Stephen when he was excavating open-air (i.e. non-cave) sites that were threatened by the construction of the New Town at Milton Keynes, in Buckinghamshire. At that time I was also working on open sites threatened by a New Town, at Peterborough, and we kept in close touch. Stephen's

approach was meticulous: everything was carefully planned and plotted, and his excavations were a model of neatness. When I returned
to my own sites, which seemed to spread across acres of eastern
England in an organic, amoeba-like sprawl, I envied his neatness and
precision. Incidentally, it's worth noting that archaeology *can* have
different styles and approaches. In that respect it's like art or design:
there's more than one way to approach a site or a given research
objective, and very often the one chosen will reflect the personality
and academic outlook of the people, or person, concerned. Stephen
has always been meticulous and precise, which is absolutely essential
in his line of Palaeolithic research, and was ideally suited to the excavation of the Palaeolithic caves and rock shelters he became interested
in when he moved to Wales.[13]

He has examined a number of Welsh caves, and has found evidence
for the presence of Palaeolithic people in or near them; but so far there
is no convincing evidence for large-scale occupation in the manner of,
say, Boxgrove. Sadly, Stephen has found no classic Flintstone-style cave
dwellings, complete with hearths, floors and surfaces where families
actually lived their day-to-day domestic lives. One reason for this
might have been that other, rather fiercer animals, such as bears and
hyenas, chose the caves for themselves. They were mainly used in the
short term, as lookout spots during hunting, or as overnight stopping-
off points. Gnawing on prey bones and other telltale signs suggest that
at least one site, Priory Farm Cave, above the Pembroke river, was a
hyenas' den; even so, it produced evidence (in the form of flint tools)
for human beings, albeit from our next period, the Upper Palaeolithic.
Stephen's research at Pontnewydd and other Welsh caves has shown
that the river gravels do not tell the entire story: that large areas of
upland Britain could have been occupied during warmer phases of
the Lower and Middle Palaeolithic, but all the archaeological evidence
has been removed – in effect planed off – by subsequent glaciers.

Neanderthal people would not have arrived here until about sixty
thousand years ago, during the second half of the last glaciation; this
probably reflects the fact that Britain lay close to the northern limit
of their distribution. The trouble is that, with the rather strange exception of Pontnewydd Cave, there was until very recently indeed no
clear evidence for Neanderthal bones in Britain. So Pontnewydd Cave

is potentially very important. Its location is unusual too, as it is currently the most north-westerly Earlier Palaeolithic site in Europe. The European landscape would have been very different then to that of today. It was largely open and treeless, steppe-like, with enormous expanses of grassy plain that extended into Asia. In Britain, as elsewhere, people mainly hunted large mammals, such as mammoth, woolly rhinoceros, bear, spotted hyena, wolf and wild horse. It's no wonder that their own bones often carry signs of injury similar to what a modern rodeo rider might expect. It was a challenging diet.

I mentioned that there was no clear evidence for the presence of Neanderthal people in Britain until 'very recently indeed'. The latest discovery was announced in June 2002, about two months after I had completed the first draft of this book. The site in question is in Thetford, Norfolk, and is one of those commercial excavations that have become such an important part of the modern archaeological scene.[14] Initial reports suggest that the bones and tools from the Thetford quarry are about fifty thousand years old, and were found close to a group of ponds which were used as watering places by Neanderthal people and their animal prey, which consisted of mammoth (bones of three or four animals), woolly rhino (a tooth) and reindeer (antler). Along with the bones, and most probably associated with them (using the word in its strictly archaeological sense), were eight hand-axes and 129 pieces of worked flint. Subsequent excavations have revealed many more bones, flint implements and hand-axes, some of them in mint condition. There are also clear signs that much of the mammoth bone had been cut up with flint tools. Was this a Boxgrove-style butchery site, or perhaps, better still, a settlement of some sort? We don't know at this stage, but David Miles, Geoff Wainwright's successor as Chief Archaeologist at English Heritage, is wildly excited. It's a dream of a site, even if it hasn't (yet) produced human bones.

The Neanderthals were the great survivors of the Ice Age world, and they made a far wider variety of flint tools than are found in the Lower Palaeolithic. Some are most beautiful, and show an extraordinary degree of skill and control. To my eye they also show that Neanderthals could create and appreciate, if not art, then craft of the highest order. The principal archaeological 'culture' of Neanderthal man is known as the Mousterian, after a series of overhanging rock shelters at a place called Le Moustier, in south-western France. Before we go on, perhaps I should say a few words about what I mean by the term archaeological 'culture', and how it differs from what we are used to in our own, living culture.

An archaeological culture is essentially an attempt by archaeologists to define a culturally distinct group of people, using any evidence left to us by the passage of time.[15] Inevitably this means that, for example, Palaeolithic cultures tend to be very much larger and more broadly defined than those of later prehistory, for the simple reason that Old Stone Age artefacts are few and widely dispersed. Clearly there are problems in this: could we, for example, distinguish archaeologically between the different cultures of, say, nineteenth-century Wales and western England? I doubt it, but we could probably discern broad differences between the rural populations of eastern and western Britain. The landscape was different, in particular field systems were different, and people used regionally distinctive styles of tools, ranging from ploughs to bill-hooks.

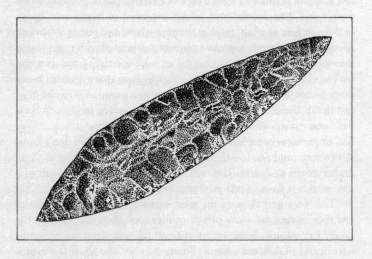

FIG 7   *Neanderthal people were expert craftsmen in flint. This example of a so-called Solutrean point comes from the type site at Le Solutré, in the Dordogne, France.*

This is the fleeting image – the chimera – that we are trying to pin down when we define an archaeological culture from groups of similar finds, animal bones, house types and so on. Ideally there should be a hard core of items that consistently occur together, and there should not be too much blurring at the edges, because by and large true human cultures tend to stop and start, rather than merge. This reflects the fact that societies have internal workings – that marriage, for example, tends to be restricted within a given culture – and that people need to speak languages or dialects that they all understand. Religion also provides barriers that most people find very difficult to cross. As I write these words, the barriers being erected by the world's religions seem to be growing daily. It's depressing, but it brings me to another aspect of archaeological cultures and their behaviour.

Professor Ian Hodder is extraordinarily dynamic, and produces books at the rate of one or two a year. Most tend to be very theoretical – indeed, Ian was one of the pioneers of 'theoretical archaeology', which gained a firm foothold during the latter 1960s and the seventies, and is now a permanent fixture.[16] Ian and his followers steered archaeology away from what had previously been a practical, functional, quasi-scientific way of thinking. That was, they argued, a flawed approach, because it assumed that cultural behaviour could be predicted, and that it followed a series of rules or laws, none of which have yet been successfully defined. One example will suffice. Suppose we excavate a male burial in which we also find a gold-encrusted sword and jewelled spurs. The functional archaeologist would conclude that the person was a warrior prince, and that the society he came from was probably very hierarchical, with powerful warriors and humble, serf-like footsoldiers. Ian and others pointed out that that reading was altogether too simple. It ignored the fact that we often act in a symbolic way, which expresses what we *want* to believe rather than the reality which frames and colours the real world. Thus the aristocracy of England are traditionally buried without grave goods, symbolising the belief that all are equal in the eyes of God. A naïve functionalist archaeologist might interpret English graves as indicating that British society was, and is, egalitarian – which is patently absurd, because it ignores the symbolism that objects and their contexts can express.

By drawing analogies with modern tribal societies, Ian Hodder was able to show that in times of social and economic tension the boundaries between different cultural groups became better defined and more closely guarded.[17] A modern parallel would be the national boundaries of Europe in, say, 1935 compared with today. Before the war, to cross a border meant producing passports, submitting to a customs search, and so on; today, if you are driving, your shoe barely rises off the accelerator. And of course the world of modern European politics is very much more stable than it was in 1935. In archaeological terms, Hodder reasoned that cultures with clearly defined edges – for example, where one style of pottery stops sharply, and another starts with equal abruptness – were possibly co-existing in a state of tension. In times of peace, people would be less worried about maintaining their own identities at the expense of much else, and there would be more cross-border trade; as a result, boundaries would soon lose their clear definition.

This brings us, in a roundabout way, to the relationship between the cultures of Neanderthal and modern man – each of which was defined with stark clarity. It used to be thought that the two groups of humans co-existed in relative harmony, and that the demise of the Neanderthals was a result of external or internal forces – perhaps a failure to adapt to changing environmental conditions, combined with feuding between different groups in the face of declining resources. However, it looks increasingly probable that although the Neanderthals were excellent hunters of the biggest big game imaginable, they were no match for their two-legged foes in the form of *Homo sapiens*. As Paul Pettitt has written:

> For too long we have regarded the extinction of the Neanderthals as a chance historical accident. Rather, where Neanderthals and modern humans could not co-exist, their disappearance may have been the result of the modern human race's first and most success-ful deliberate campaign of genocide.[18]

When feeling depressed, I sometimes wonder whether the ability and instinct to carry out genocide isn't one of the defining character-istics of *Homo sapiens*. The ruthless use of force against the last real competitor we've ever had to face up to gave us the edge to survive in the Later Ice Age world. Without it, who knows – we may well have perished. Seen in the crudest Darwinian terms, it may have been legitimate thirty thousand years ago; but we still can't shake the habit off.

This brings me to a question I am frequently asked. Did modern man and Neanderthals interbreed, or were they too busy fighting to have time for what one might consider to be more human pursuits? Had I been asked that question before 1999, my answer would have been a firm 'no', based on some substantial evidence. But it now appears that the picture is more complex.

The original bones from the Neander valley were scientifically dated to around forty thousand years ago. This made them relatively late, but within the known Neanderthal age-range. Then samples of DNA were extracted, and these showed that the original Neanderthal was by no means a close cousin of modern man. In fact the DNA from the bones, when compared with our own, showed a difference which the scientists considered represented a divergence of some half a million years. In other words, the two groups had a common ancestor who lived at the time of, say, Boxgrove. According to the DNA, there had been no genetic contact since then. This seemed to confirm the theory that the two groups had lived very separate lives, and did not interbreed.

But now we cannot be so certain. In June 1999 Paul Pettitt wrote another article for the popular journal *British Archaeology*, in which he gave the first details of a remarkable burial that had just been excavated at a rock shelter at Lagar Velho, in Portugal.[19] The bones were from a boy who had been buried about twenty-four thousand years ago. In theory this was at least five to six thousand years after the last Neanderthal had settled in the Iberian peninsula. He had been buried with some ceremony: he wore a shell pendant or amulet around his neck, and the edges of the grave were marked out by stones and bones. Also in the grave were articulated bones of red deer and rabbit – presumably placed there as offerings. The grave contained a layer of red ochre, from dye which coloured either the boy's clothes or his shroud. Red ochre burials are known from other sites of this period across Europe and into Russia, and I shall have more to say about one of them, from south Wales, shortly.

The real interest in the Lagar Velho boy lies in the anatomical form of his bones, which are clearly those of *Homo sapiens*, but also reveal a number of distinctively, and very strongly marked, Neanderthal features. Anatomically, there can be no doubt whatsoever: his ancestors had interbred with Neanderthals, and not just once, but regularly and over a long time. It would be impossible to account for so many Neanderthal features any other way. What are the wider implications of this discovery? Did the two groups of humans routinely interbreed everywhere? We don't know, but probably not. Spain and Portugal may be a special case, as there does seem to have been a persistent ecological border zone (known as the Ebro Frontier) between the two groups along the northern edge of the Iberian peninsula.

It would seem that modern humans took their time to penetrate south of the Ebro Frontier, possibly because they were better adapted to the cooler conditions of the north. But whatever the root causes might have been, Neanderthals persisted for some time in Spain and Portugal, and it would appear that even though the end result for one group was extinction, for extended periods relations were more friendly than genocidal. The impression we get is what one might expect of human interactions at any time. In some areas the genocide was swift, efficient and ruthless; in others the two groups continued to live side by side for several millennia, and the 'genocide' may not have been deliberate, but more the sad consequence of an inevitable process. As groups of Neanderthals became more widely separated, mates would be harder to find, and the population would decline further. It was a process that in the end took some ten thousand years to complete.[20]

The evidence provided by a particular form of DNA, known as mitochondrial DNA (see Chapter 5), which is passed on via the female line, suggests strongly that *Homo sapiens* is not a direct descendant of *Homo neanderthalensis*.[21] So how on earth does the Lagar Velho boy fit in with this? The leading authority, Bryan Sykes, Professor of Human Genetics at Oxford University, has suggested that the Lagar Velho boy may be the human equivalent of a mule – a cross between two closely related, but different, species: horse and donkey. The mule is tough, strong and hardy, but sterile, because its parents do not share the same number of chromosomes (horses have sixty-four, donkeys sixty-two). We don't know yet, because the Lagar Velho boy's DNA has not been examined, but Bryan Sykes reckons that if he was indeed a cross between a modern human and a Neanderthal, then he might well have been sterile, like the mule. This, of course, would help explain why Neanderthal genes appear to be absent from our own genetic make-up.

As I have already noted, although *bona fide* Neanderthal bones are so far lacking in Britain, their culture, the Mousterian, was certainly present, and their hand-axes have been found at a number of cave, rock-shelter and open sites, mainly in southern England, but also in East Anglia, south Wales and the midlands.[22]

I want now to move forward to what one might term our own time – the world of the earliest truly modern man, known as Crô-Magnon man, after a rock shelter at Les Eyzies in southern France which produced particularly good collections of bones.[23] Crô-Magnons were not identical to us, and if I may return for one final time to that slightly strained Oxford Street analogy, they would not inspire sideways glances from even the most ill-mannered of passers-by. But they were different from us nonetheless, with slightly larger brains (maybe this reflected their larger body size), larger teeth and somewhat flatter faces. Physical anthropologists, such as Chris Stringer in his *African Exodus*, feel that the tall and relatively thin frames of early *Homo sapiens* betray the fact that they evolved in the warm, tropical climates of Africa, rather than in Europe.[24]

One of the best-known examples of Crô-Magnon man in Britain is the so-called Red 'Lady' of Paviland Cave, on the Gower Peninsula of south-west Wales. I put the word 'lady' in quotes because 'she' was in fact a he. His story is altogether most unusual, and is well worth repeating. Like many archaeological tales it is caught up with contemporary intellectual and political controversies.

Dean William Buckland, the first excavator of the Red 'Lady' of Paviland, came across some of 'her' bones in 1823. He had been invited by the landowner to investigate the cave at a time when he was attempting to reconcile the field evidence of geology with the Biblical account of Creation and Noah's Great Flood – surely a futile pursuit if ever there was one. But in many ways Buckland was a most able and remarkable man. He was the first Reader in Geology at Oxford, and was later appointed Dean of Westminster. Sadly, he took the clerical line, and backed the wrong horse when it came to the Great Flood. Nor was he by any means adept at creating snappy titles: his discovery of bones and other items at the Goat's Hole Cave, Paviland, was published in 1823 as *Reliquiae Diluvianae: or Observations on the Organic Remains contained in Caves, Fissures, and Diluvial Gravel and on other Geological Phenomena attesting the action of an Universal Deluge.*[25] He considered that the Red 'Lady' was Roman, and that the bones of extinct animals found around 'her' dated to a time before the Great Flood. One could say he got it as wrong as it was possible to get it.

It is of course only too easy to take the work of men like Buckland out of the context of their times. True, he failed to find a link of any sort between the lowland river gravels of Britain – patently water-derived deposits – and the Biblical Flood; and he allowed his powers of reason to be overruled by his emotional acceptance of a theological doctrine which was never meant to be taken literally, even when first written. But the fact remains that he *did* go into the field to find empirical evidence to support his views, at a time when most clerics would never have left their libraries. He also took the work of science seriously; and although he certainly didn't intend it, by doing what he did and by promptly publishing his results, he ultimately helped release geology from the grip of the Church. And he did discover a most remarkable burial, complete with loosely associated Palaeolithic flint implements.

What is the modern view of the Red 'Lady' and the archaeological deposits from the Goat's Hole Cave? Stephen Aldhouse-Green has just edited what he himself has entitled *A Definitive Report*, and I'm confident it will survive the test of time rather better than Dean Buckland's *Reliquiae Diluvianae.*[26] (There are also some shorter, and perhaps more accessible, accounts widely available.[27])

Buckland's report concluded that the body was that of a Roman scarlet woman, or 'painted lady', whose business was to look after the carnal needs of Roman soldiers from a camp nearby – which we now know is Iron Age anyway. All round, it was an excellent story for a man of the cloth to concoct. But the truth was more remarkable than fiction. In the words of Stephen Aldhouse-Green, 'When the "Red Lady" skeleton was found, it was the first human fossil recovered anywhere in the world.'[28] The burial of the body recalls that of the Lagar Velho boy. The Paviland body was that of a young Crô-Magnon man aged twenty-five to thirty, about five feet eight inches (1.74 metres) tall, and probably weighing about eleven stone (seventy-three kilos). His build and weight were somewhat smaller than the average for such early *Homo sapiens*, and radiocarbon dates have shown he was alive around twenty-six thousand years ago – again, pretty well contemporary with Lagar Velho.

The molecular biologist Brian Sykes, writing in the definitive report, describes how DNA extracted from the bones can be related to the commonest ancestry extant in Europe. This strongly suggests that the current population of Britain arrived in these islands in the Palaeolithic, and did not spread here seven thousand years ago with the arrival of Neolithic farmers from farther afield. As we will see later, it was most likely the *concept* of farming that reached us, rather than a wholesale migration of farmers.

I'll describe the details of the Red 'Lady's' burial in a moment, but first I must say a few words about radiocarbon dating, which will become a regular feature of our story from now onwards.

Radiocarbon dating was invented by Willard F. Libby, a chemist at Chicago University, in 1949.[29] The idea behind the technique is straightforward enough. Libby was researching into cosmic radiation – the process whereby the earth's outer atmosphere is constantly bombarded by sub-atomic particles. This process produces radioactive carbon, known as carbon-14. Carbon-14 is unstable and is constantly breaking down, but at a known and uniform rate: a gram of carbon-14 will be half broken down after 5730 years, three-quarters broken down in twice that time (11,460 years), and so on. Libby's breakthrough was to link this process to living things, and thence to time itself.

Carbon-14 is present in the earth's atmosphere – in the air we all breathe – in the form of the gas carbon dioxide. Plants take in the gas through their leaves, and plant-eating animals eat the leaves – and carnivores, in turn, eat them. So all plants and animals absorb carbon-14 while they are alive. As soon as they die, they immediately stop taking it in, and the carbon-14 that has accumulated in their bodies – in their bones, their wood or whatever – starts to break down through the normal processes of radioactive decay. So by measuring the amounts of carbon-14 in a bone, or piece of charcoal, fragment of cloth or peat, it is possible to estimate its age.

But there are problems. First of all, cosmic radiation has not been at a uniform rate, as Libby at first believed. Sunspots and solar flares are known to cause sudden upsurges of radiation. Nuclear testing has also filled the atmosphere with unwanted and unquantifiable radiation. If these problems weren't enough, the quantities of radiation being measured in the radiocarbon laboratories around the world are truly minute, especially in older samples, such as those from Paviland Cave. Efforts have been made to quantify the way in which radiocarbon dates deviate from true dates, using ancient wood samples that can be precisely dated to a given year AD or BC. This process is known as calibration, and is now widely accepted in archaeology (I've tried consistently to use calibrated radiocarbon dates in this book). All this uncertainty means that radiocarbon dates are usually expressed in the form of a *range* of years – say 1700 to 2000 BC, rather than a single central spot-date of 1850 BC.

A by-product of radiocarbon dating are the figures known as the 'stable isotope values' of carbon and nitrogen. These provide very useful information on the general nature of an individual's diet when the bone was being formed. It would appear that fish and seafood formed a major part of the Red 'Lady's' diet. Today the sea is close by Goat's Hole Cave, but in the Upper Palaeolithic it was about a hundred kilometres away. Of course, fish could have been caught in rivers closer by, but such a very 'fishy' diet surely suggests regular access to the sea – and with it a way of life that must have involved a great deal of travel. The contrast with Boxgrove, which was closer to the sea, but where there was no evidence for fish-eating, is remarkable; but then, so too is the huge time-span (roughly 480,000 years) that separates these two Palaeolithic sites – it's easy to forget that the Palaeolithic takes up about 98 per cent of British prehistory.

There are remarkable aspects to the Paviland burial which illustrate some of the far-reaching changes that were in the process of transforming humanity. That may sound grandiloquent, but the Upper Palaeolithic was the first period in which many of the defining characteristics of modern civilisation become apparent. Put another way, without the social and intellectual developments of the period, what was subsequently to be known as civilisation would have been impossible. It is difficult to overstate the importance of the achievements made by the people of the Upper Palaeolithic period. We may not always be aware of it, but we owe them an enormous amount.

There is far more to Paviland than just the famous burial. The cave floor also produced numerous flint implements and the by-products of their manufacture, together with charcoal and ash, all of which were found in contexts that must predate the burial. Radiocarbon dates suggest that this earlier occupation preceded the Red 'Lady' by three thousand years (i.e. about twenty-nine thousand years ago), and there is evidence that the cave was intermittently occupied both before and after that date, as well as after the Red 'Lady' burial. This extended use would indicate that the Goat's Hole Cave was well known to people at the time.

The Red 'Lady' burial was accompanied by a mammoth ivory bracelet and a perforated periwinkle pendant, numerous seashells and some fifty broken ivory rods. Marker stones were placed at the head and foot of the grave. The staining, which most people regard as being derived from heavily stained clothes or wrapping, still colours the two ornaments and the bones, but there is a colour difference between the bones of the arms and chest and the hips and legs – which perhaps suggests that the young man was buried in a two-piece garment of some sort. The feet were only lightly stained, which would indicate that he wore shoes. The ochre, a natural product, was obtained locally. The body was headless, and it's quite possible that it was deliberately buried in this way – other headless burials are known from this period – but the removal of the head could also have taken place later: perhaps it was carried away by the sea, which is known to have broken into the cave. The archaeological term for disturbance of this sort, which takes place after a deposit, such as a burial, has been placed in the ground, is 'post-depositional'. It can sometimes take a great deal of skill to distinguish between an action that took place when a body was placed in the ground and a subsequent, post-depositional, effect. It's something I always have in the back of my mind when I'm excavating.

Paviland Cave also revealed three remarkable bone spatulae. They are small things, roughly six inches (fifteen centimetres) long, and are beautifully shaped, with unusual curves and bulges that don't seem to make immediate practical sense. As well as the spatulae, there were

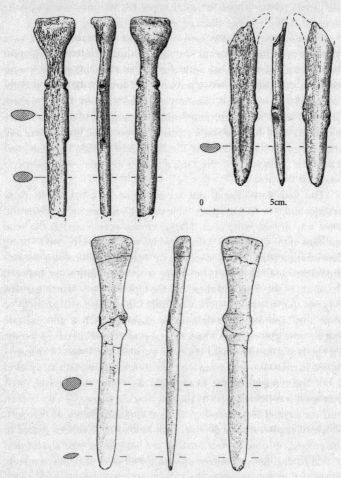

FIG 8   *Three bone spatulae found in the 1830s at Goat's Hole Cave, Paviland, south-west Wales (twenty-four thousand years ago).*

a number of worked pieces of mammoth ivory, including a well-known perforated pendant that was thought to have formed part of the burial assemblage. Radiocarbon now shows that these objects were slightly later than the Red 'Lady' burial, and indicates that the cave was repeatedly used between about twenty-five and twenty-one thousand years ago.

To sum up, there was a main phase of settlement in the cave around twenty-nine thousand years ago, with intermittent occupation both before and after. Then came the burial, at twenty-six thousand, and later use of the cave between twenty-five and twenty-one thousand years ago. It's no wonder that Paviland Cave is the richest Upper Palaeolithic site in Britain – but does this pattern of use and reuse tell us anything more about the site? I believe that the Goat's Hole Cave was a special place of some sort. If archaeologists have a fault it is to describe everything they find as special, unusual or remarkable. That's because it *is* to them personally, who have spent weeks, months or years slaving away at whatever it might be. But is it to the world in general? In the case of Paviland it most certainly is, for the following reasons.

Paviland Cave lies at the extreme northern edge of the Early Upper Palaeolithic world, and it was used remarkably late in the sequence, when the climate was getting very chilly. Those unique bone spatulae and the episode of mammoth-ivory working happened at a time when the climate was rapidly deteriorating and evidence for settlement elsewhere in Britain was virtually unknown. If we also bear in mind that nearly all well-preserved occupied cave sites have extensive living areas outside the cave itself, and that those at Paviland have been removed by the postglacial rise in sea levels, then the use of the cave so far into the developing glaciation, or mini-Ice Age, is truly remarkable – and demands explanation.

Let's look at the artefacts before turning to the burial itself, and first at those strange, red-stained mammoth-ivory rods discovered by Dean Buckland.[30] They don't appear to have any practical purpose, other perhaps than as blanks for ivory beads, but as there's no indication that any had been notched or cut up prior to being more closely worked, that idea can probably be rejected. That leaves us with the archaeologist's catch-all explanation for anything he can't understand: 'ritual', or religion, to use a non-jargon term. If we do decide to invoke religion as an explanation, we shouldn't do so on negative grounds alone; it always helps if we can provide some positive evidence that supports the suggestion. And in the case of these peculiar ivory rods there is a positive suggestion, but it comes from an unexpected source.

In 1981 the anthropologist J.D. Lewis-Williams published a detailed study of the rock paintings of a southern African people known as the San.[31] Like the communities of the Upper Palaeolithic, the San were hunters. Their realm was the Kalahari desert, and they lived in small, mobile groups of a few dozen people. Their houses were light and temporary, as befits a highly mobile lifestyle, and their religion was based around shamans and rock art. The San used ochre-painted rods, very similar to those from Paviland, in their religious ceremonies. This could just be coincidence, but the close similarity of the way that the two sets of people were organised and lived their lives does give it greater weight. The red colour of the ochre plainly recalls blood, and with it the symbolic expression of animal or human life-force. It goes without saying that the sight (and meaning) of blood was an everyday occurrence to a hunting people.

As for those three oddly-shaped, but beautifully made, bone spatulae, they're unique in Britain, and probably in western Europe. The closest parallels for them are in Moravia, or the plains of Russia, where they occur in context dates of twenty-four to twenty thousand ago – precisely contemporary with the later use of Paviland Cave. So what are they? They may have been used to perform a useful purpose of some sort, but then the same can be said, for example, of the Christian paten and chalice – the platter and goblet used in the Eucharist. The workmanship employed on the spatulae is wholly exceptional, and if we compare them with similar items from contemporary sites on the Russian plain it's possible to see links, for example, with highly stylised images of the female form.[32] While not necessarily objects of veneration in their own right, these decorated spatulae could have been closely involved in religious ceremonies. It's certainly very odd that three were found together. This would suggest deliberate disposal, or laying to rest after use, rather than casual loss in the normal course of daily life. As we will discover shortly, by this late time in the Paviland sequence we are drawing ever closer to the last great glacial maximum of eighteen thousand years ago, when conditions outside the cave were becoming extremely cold. It's not unreasonable to suppose that some fairly strong incentive must have been required to tempt people so far north. As Professor Richard Bradley and others have shown,[33] certain places, and the stories attached to them, had extraordinary pulling power for people in the past – and of course in the present too: Lourdes springs immediately to mind.

I find in my own work in the East Anglian fens that the shape and form of the modern landscape can often mask patterns and land-forms that would have been obvious in prehistory. In the fens this has been caused by the wholesale drainage of the past three centuries, which has lowered the land surface and shrunk peats, so that areas that were once high are now low, and *vice versa*. Something similar applies at Paviland Cave, which today sits just above the high-tide mark. In the Upper Palaeolithic the sea level was massively lower than it is today, when the waters of the Bristol Channel have inundated a broad coastal plain. But at low tide it's still possible to stand on the floor of the drowned coastal plain and look up towards Goat's Hole Cave, just as people would have done twenty-six thousand years ago. It's a very striking and affecting sight; but more important than that, it's a setting that accords well with the situation of comparable impor-tant places in the religious and mythological lives of people with shamanistic religions – people like the San.[34]

There's always a danger of delving into ethnographic and anthro-pological literature and doing a Little Jack Horner: inserting a thumb to select a plum, whilst ignoring less palatable fruit that doesn't happen to fit with our ideas. This was the fatal flaw of many late-Victorian writers, who would assiduously comb through a vast range of anthro-pological writing, classical authors and travellers' tales, selecting plums to bolster a particular theoretical view of the world. Sir James Frazer, one of the founding fathers of modern anthropology, was guilty of this academic sin,[35] and today very similar things are done at the weirder extreme of so-called 'alternative' archaeology (the realm of ley lines, Atlantis, aliens, UFOs, etc.). If you pull a huge array of plums out of their original contexts it becomes easy to draw far-fetched conclusions, particularly with regard to things as imprecise as simple landscape features like lines of posts, or stones or pebbles. So the great ceremonial straight 'roads' on the high plains of southern Peru could be compared, for example, with Neolithic cursus monuments in lowland Europe (I shall have more to say about these later). It seems not to matter that each is taken out of context to 'prove' that ancient people were in regular contact over immense distances, or came from the same alien or extra-terrestrial source. To return to the earlier analogy, plums are being pulled out of two quite separate pies, whereas it's the pies themselves that ought to be looked at.

To return to those ivory rods, it's reasonable to seek illustrative parallels from a culture that is comparable in other respects to that at Paviland, but one should also be on the alert for other uses of rods in that culture – perhaps to support a temporary roof, or whatever.[36] More to the point, one should beware of drawing parallels that are too specific – and the use of ochre-stained rods within a ritual might well be such a case. Only time will tell. On the whole, it's safer and ultimately wiser to seek broader parallels that might help explain why and how people chose to do different things. A good, and very relevant, example are the criteria that lie behind the selection of special places by recent societies that practised shamanistic religion. That might help explain why Goat's Hole Cave was selected for special treatment. This takes us back to the low-tide mark at Paviland.

Viewed from here, Goat's Hole Cave 'appears as a south-facing cave clearly visible from some distance and set into the high cliffs of a promontory defined, on either side, by slades or valleys'.[37] It's a very striking landmark, and there are anthropological accounts of shamanistic mythological beliefs that link caves in such striking positions with, for example, the creator of mountains, or the spirits of mountains. In one wonderful Siberian account, caves are seen as the holes left by the great mammoth who created the mountains; caves in mountain or hillsides are particularly interesting because they can be seen as a stage or resting place on a mythical ladder between Heaven, earth and the Netherworld. Shamans would have performed the ceremonial tasks of climbing and solemnising the various stages of this symbolic ladder.[38] Given this context, the Red 'Lady' burial can be seen to fit into an established sequence of possibly regular visits to a very special place.

Clive Gamble has already been mentioned as a prehistorian with an extraordinary ability to stand back from the detail of a subject and see things from an unusual or unexpected angle. Writing about the social context of Upper Palaeolithic art, he pointed out that societies may have been organised in small groups, but this did not mean that their concerns were entirely parochial. Far from it. In a paper written in 1991 he provided convincing evidence that people at this time were in communication over extraordinarily long distances.[39] Those three bone spatulae, with their close parallels on the plains of Russia, surely reinforce his theory. The physical expression of this communication would have been in the form of ceremonial exchange of important objects, such as the spatulae. These ceremonies would have served to reinforce social ranking within the various societies that took part. I would imagine that the spatulae were given to an important person, most probably a senior shaman. It's worth noting that such long-distance communication would have been very much more difficult had Britain not been physically united with mainland Europe.

Earlier I said that the Upper Palaeolithic was the period in which many of the defining characteristics of modern civilisation first become apparent. In his 1991 paper Clive Gamble showed how art in the Upper Palaeolithic was far more than just a matter of beauty, whether of carved objects or painted cave walls. This, of course, was the period of the famous cave paintings at places like Lascaux in France and Altamira in Spain.[40] Sadly, in Britain we still lack such extraordinary finds, but we do know from smaller, portable carved objects (such as those spatulae) that people here used, appreciated and made art. What did art and its appearance in the Upper Palaeolithic signify? To quote from Clive's paper:

> Art for me is . . . a system of communication and includes a wide range of mediums and messages. As an act of social communication it is defined by style which . . . has its behavioural basis in a fundamental human cognitive process: personal and social identification through comparison. Consequently [art] style is not just a means of transmitting information about identity but is an active tool in building social strategies.[41]

This is very important, because it dismisses commonly heard

simplistic views such as, for example, that cave art was merely something done to give good luck in the hunt – the equivalent of tossing a coin in the fountain. That's rather like saying that Michelangelo's masterpiece was painted simply to decorate the ceiling of the Sistine Chapel – classy, hand-painted wallpaper. In part it was, but it was also a great deal more than that: among many other things it was a profound restatement of the aspirations that lay behind the later Renaissance – and that's just scratching the intellectual surface.

What we're witnessing in the Upper Palaeolithic is very complex, but it probably includes the elaboration, if not the development, of languages that were sufficiently sophisticated to express the ideas and symbolism lying behind the art, because an image devoid of any written or spoken textual reference is hard to comprehend. This is particularly true if the image is being introduced to people who are not familiar with the culture or part of society in question. As a European, for example, I can admire the execution of Japanese art, but I find much of its meaning and the philosophy behind it incomprehensible. In such circumstances explanation is essential. Recently the newspapers carried a story of how an installation by Damien Hirst was collected up and thrown away, along with the rubbish, by the gallery's cleaners on the morning after the opening party. It consisted of empty Coca-Cola cans and other debris and, according to the newspaper I read, had a market value of £40,000. The artist, to his credit, thought it all very amusing. The point is that the textual reference, whether written or explicit, was missed by the cleaners. The art had lost its context, and with it its meaning and distinctiveness. Whichever way one looks at it, there had been a failure in communication. So into the bin it went.

The Red 'Lady' of Paviland belonged to the first or earlier part of the Upper Palaeolithic, which is separated from the later part by the last (and hopefully final) great glacial cold period, which began around twenty-five thousand years ago. During its coldest phase, about eighteen thousand years ago, large areas of northern Europe (including what was later to become Britain) were uninhabited. About thirteen thousand years ago, occupation of the areas abandoned to ice and freezing-cold tundra was resumed.

CHAPTER THREE

Hotting up:
Hunters at the End of the Ice Age

I'D LOVE TO TRAVEL to the moon. In stellar terms it's so near, but I know it's somewhere I'll never visit, no matter how much I'd like to. True, I'll probably never visit the Australian Outback either, or certain suburbs of Torquay – but then again, I might. Such journeys aren't impossible, in the way that a trip to the moon is. And that, in a rather roundabout way, is where we find ourselves now, in the later part of the Upper Palaeolithic, with the final glacial maximum just behind us. We're on the archaeological moon, looking out towards earth, with the planets and stars of the Lower and Middle Palaeolithic light years behind us.

We ended the last chapter with the glacial conditions that prevailed eighteen thousand years ago. The best evidence now suggests that the area later to be known as the British Isles was reoccupied around 12,600 years ago, about five hundred years later than nearby parts of the continent.[1] The climate suddenly reached a warm peak around thirteen thousand years ago, when it was actually slightly warmer than today. Then it grew colder again, reaching another near-glacial period which began around eleven thousand years ago and ended a thousand or so years later. This final colder period was by no means as severe as the last glacial maximum, and is known as the Loch Lomond sub-phase. When it ended, around ten thousand years ago, our own, postglacial or Flandrian, period began. During the Loch Lomond sub-phase, glaciers covered areas of the Scottish Highlands. So it was pretty cold, but not nearly as bad as the earlier glacial maximum, which

peaked around eighteen thousand years ago, and ultimately took Paviland Cave out of the picture.

Most late glacial or Later Upper Palaeolithic sites in Britain predate
the Loch Lomond sub-phase, and many are from caves (although open
sites are known) which are found in England south of the Humber and
in south Wales. Although Britain has yet to produce the quantities of
superb art found on the continent, there are one or two examples of
carving on bone, ivory and stone. My personal favourite is a very
confident yet delicately executed horse's head on a fragment of horse
rib, found in a cave at Creswell Crags, Derbyshire.

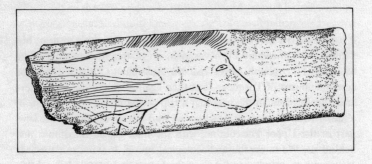

FIG 9   *Engraving of a horse's head on a fragment of horse rib, from Robin
Hood Cave, Creswell Crags, Derbyshire. Late Upper Palaeolithic (c.12–12,500
years ago).*

The Late Upper Palaeolithic is a field that has seen a great deal
of recent activity, with many exciting new excavations; but I shall
confine myself to just one site, Gough's Cave, in Somerset.[2] In a way
it selected itself, because what it has revealed is both extraordinary
and, frankly, a little bizarre.

Gough's Cave is in that spectacular tourist attraction the Cheddar
Gorge, on the southern slopes of the beautiful Mendip Hills. It has
been excavated twice, in the 1890s and the 1980s. The earlier excavations brought the site to public attention, but in the process they
removed most of the important archaeological deposits. Other chance
discoveries were made in the early years of the twentieth century as

Gough's Cave was converted into what it is today, a show cave for visitors. As a result of this earlier activity, the dig of the 1980s was of necessity small, and was partly undertaken to assess the reliability of the earlier work and the extent to which ancient deposits still survived intact within the cave.

I remember the first time I came across a modern account of Gough's Cave. It was in the archaeological journal *Antiquity* for March 1989, which I read from cover to cover for the vainglorious and slightly embarrassing reason that I had published a paper in the same issue on my efforts to turn my own site at Flag Fen, Peterborough, into a visitor attraction.[3] Normally I'd have skipped over the short report on the Natural History Museum's dig at Gough's Cave as being outside my own particular field of study. I'm glad I didn't, because it rekindled a flame that was almost extinguished within me. I don't believe that anyone, least of all a prehistorian – even a specialist in the later periods of prehistory – can ever afford to lose sight of our Palaeolithic roots.

The excavations by the Natural History Museum took place between April and July 1987, following a shorter project the previous year by one of the team, Roger Jacobi, who was then a lecturer at Nottingham University. As I've already noted, Gough's Cave had been a popular visitor attraction for a long time. The basis of its appeal was as a vast, echoing cave rather than an archaeological site, and its preparation for visitors in the early twentieth century involved a great deal of cleaning up and general prettifying, during which numerous human bone fragments and archaeological artefacts were unearthed.[4] All the bone was superbly preserved in the calcareous environment of the limestone cave, which was to prove extremely important when it came to the running of DNA analyses in the 1990s. When I first studied the Palaeolithic in the sixties, Gough's Cave was generally thought to have been rendered archaeologically sterile – or nearly so – by this preparation work. Accordingly, there was much professional interest when Roger Jacobi carried out a short programme of research into a deposit that seemed to have survived the depredations of the last century relatively intact.

Jacobi's dig in 1986 was in a small pocket of archaeological deposits which lay hidden behind a massive fallen rock on the floor of the cave. The meticulous excavation revealed fragments of flint and several isolated human teeth, making it clear that the deposit was indeed archaeological and seemed to have survived intact, and was generally undisturbed – at least in modern times, if not in antiquity. These results, as happens with most good excavations, posed more questions than they answered, and a larger dig was planned for the following year. The aims of the 1987 project were to decide whether the deposit really was undisturbed, how it got there in the first place – and therefore what it signified – and to map its full extent. If it was shown to be at all extensive, measures would be taken to ensure its survival in the future. I'm happy to report that it's still there, and likely to remain there, intact, for a very long time indeed.

I mentioned that bone at Gough's Cave was superbly preserved. In fact it was in such good condition that even the lightest, tiniest of surface scratches survived. These proved extraordinarily revealing. The excavations uncovered the remains of at least three adults and two children, aged from eleven to thirteen and three to five years. The bones at Gough's Cave differed from those at Paviland in that they weren't from deliberately placed or arranged burials. Instead they were loose, disarticulated bones that probably derived from a midden, or refuse deposit, as they were found jumbled in amongst flint tools, pieces of antler, bone and mammoth ivory. Does this mean that human remains in the Later Upper Palaeolithic were treated as mere debris, like the animal bones that lay with them on the floor of the cave? The answer is an emphatic no. And the justification of that denial lies in those light scratches on the bones' surfaces.

The bones were from modern humans: *Homo sapiens sapiens*, to give us our full scientific name. The surface scratches were studied under the microscope by Jill Cook.[5] There was absolutely no indication of healing, so the marks had been made *post mortem*, but probably not very long after death. They had been made by flint knives wielded by a person, or persons, who knew what they were doing and what they meant to achieve. I recall press headlines at the time screaming the case for cannibalism, and there have been better-founded and more considered such claims subsequently.[6] Certainly the marks suggested that the corpses had been carefully dismembered. There was even evidence for skinning, and for the careful removal of a tongue from the mouth. Cannibalism is and has been a widespread phenomenon all over the world, and there's no reason why Britain should not have experienced it several times over in its half-million-year-long prehistory. Maybe it did happen at Gough's Cave. I don't think it matters very much if it did, because this wasn't the casual consumption of human flesh as a lazy substitute for, say, a haunch of venison when the larder was empty. No, it was something ceremonial, symbolic and special. It could have been an act of hostility to a vanquished foe, but more likely it was an act of respect to a departed relative.

What happened to the corpses after their dismemberment? Sadly, we don't know for certain. We do know that they weren't broken open to extract marrow, nor were they smashed, burnt and broken like many of the animal bones found in the cave, which surely *are* the residue of food preparation and consumption. Perhaps soft parts of the head – especially the brain – could have been eaten, as still happened very recently in New Guinea, where it is believed that ceremonial cannibalism of this sort is a means of transferring experience and wisdom from the dead to the living. Maybe. We just don't know.

It is clear, however, that the bones at Gough's Cave were expertly and carefully treated, and this suggests that the way in which the body was disposed of may have involved more than one stage. In many human societies the transition from the world of the living to the next world is a gradual process.[7] There are many reasons for this: it allows the bereaved immediate family more time to mourn their loss, it gives far-flung relatives time to reach the funeral, and it provides a prolonged period of ceremonial during which the myths and legends that bind the community together can be learned, rehearsed and repeated by everyone. Death, like other so-called rites of passage such as birth, puberty and marriage, was a time when societies, tribes and families could meet, celebrate or commiserate, just as we do to this day.

There are many forms of multi-stage burial, cremation or exposure. The latter is the process, sometimes known as excarnation, whereby the flesh is removed by birds or other natural means. The removal of the flesh symbolises the soul's journey to the next world, and the clean bones are often ignored, piled together in ossuaries or, as happened in later prehistoric times, in purpose-built communal tombs. In the case of Gough's Cave, the careful dismemberment of the cadavers suggests that the detached limbs were placed in a special area reserved for bodies or souls that were still in a transitional state, either in the cave or perhaps on a platform outside, in the open. Again, we don't know precisely what was going on, but the general picture – of a two-stage funerary process – seems fairly clear.

What is also abundantly clear is that prolonged and elaborate funeral rites didn't suddenly appear six thousand years later with the arrival of the Neolithic period around 5000 BC. This is when we have the introduction of farming and houses and a more settled style of life; it is also when we find the first large communal tombs, barrows and other evidence for people coming together to mark or celebrate rites of passage. But the social processes, and in particular the human need to mark a person's passing in this special way, have roots which go down very deep. As we will see in the next two chapters, there's a growing body of evidence to suggest that the hard-and-fast barrier that archaeologists have traditionally erected between the distant world of hunter-gathering and our world of farming and settled life simply isn't there.

The Red 'Lady' of Paviland provided evidence for contacts over enormous distances. Of course, those contacts need not have been direct. I'm not suggesting that the people who used the Paviland caves commuted to the plains of Russia; what I am suggesting is that they may well have met people who knew people who did – just as I have met people who knew someone who was a friend of another person who died in the World Trade Center disaster of 11 September 2001. Both are examples of contacts within societies where people move around a great deal.

Gough's Cave also provided evidence for long-distance contact, although this time the distances were not quite so massive; but the evidence was also much stronger, and not based on something as hard to pin down as the style of art used to decorate those three bone spatulae.

So far in this book I have concentrated more on people than on the flint tools they left behind them. This is not because I dislike flint – on the contrary, writing reports on flint artefacts has been my bread and butter for many years. However, to a non-specialist the technological differences between the various types and styles of flint can be hard to remember. Indeed, it took me a long time to master them with any degree of assurance, and when I eventually did so, I found I knew very little extra about the people behind the technology – and that, surely, is what our story is about. But now I have no alternative, because the extraordinary rapidity with which styles of flint-working start to change in the Upper Palaeolithic and subsequent Mesolithic periods surely reflects the hotting up of social evolution that was predicted in the last chapter. It must also reflect increasing opportunities for contacts between different groups, and perhaps too a gradually increasing population. Certainly a warming climate after the cold Loch Lomond sub-phase would have helped, but that was only part of the picture. It was human beings, not the climate or some other external stimulus, who were the main engines of change.

The most important innovation of Upper Palaeolithic flint-working technology was the widespread adoption of tools fashioned from blades that had been struck off a larger block of flint, known as a core. In Chapter 1 I described the person or persons who invented this process as a 'genius', and I stand by that: it takes a very special way of thinking to turn technology back to front in this way. I can see nothing very clever in inventing the wheel, which seems to me a perfectly logical progression from the log rollers that had always been used to move large timbers and rocks. But to work out how to prepare a specially shaped core that would allow the removal of long, thin, razor-sharp blades – now that took real intelligence.

The style of flint-working found in the warmer times before the cooler Loch Lomond sub-phase is known as Creswellian, after cave finds at Creswell Crags on the Nottinghamshire/Derbyshire borders. (Incidentally, one of the pleasures of being a specialist in the Palaeolithic must surely be the location of the sites: the Gower Peninsula, Cheddar Gorge, Creswell Crags – all of them gorgeous places that stir the soul.) But the high-quality, fine-textured flint needed for the carefully prepared cores used in making blade-based tools came from further east, where the landscape is softer and far less dramatic. A good example of this is the flint used for Creswellian flake tools found at Gough's Cave and at contemporary caves in south-west Wales and southern Devon. This occurs naturally in the Vale of Pewsey (Wiltshire), about a hundred miles (160 kilometres) north-east of the Devon findspots.

One of the striking aspects of some Creswellian sites is that in the debris on the cave floors, the early stages of making a flint tool are apparently missing. We saw at Boxgrove how a hand-axe-maker sat on the ground and first removed the outer, cortical or softer parts of the flint nodule. The flakes removed during this initial, roughing out or preparatory, work are known as primary flakes, and they're easily spotted, as they're usually very much paler than the other flakes, due to the cortex of soft, weathered flint on their upper surface. But primary flakes are rare, or just don't occur, on many Creswellian sites. The evidence suggests that first the cores and then the blades were made at the source of the flint, before being carried to the place where they were to be used. Only then were they further modified to be turned into points, piercers, burins (a specialised bone- or antler-scoring tool), knives or scrapers. In conceptual or cognitive terms what we are seeing here is forethought, light years away from the world of the heavy, all-purpose hand-axe.

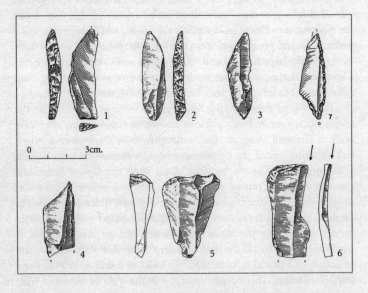

FIG 10   *Examples of Late Upper Palaeolithic blade-based flint tools of the Creswellian tradition (12–12,600 years ago) from sites in south-western England.*

A view of the main chamber of the passage tomb of Maes Howe, Orkney (about 2800 BC). The low entranceway passage is at the centre. Note the high quality of the masonry (made without mortar) and the two large standing stones set back from the entranceway. These stones may once have formed part of a free-standing stone circle constructed before the building of the tomb.

A view of the standing stones of the Ring of Brodgar, Orkney (about 2800 BC). In the foreground are traces of the external bank and ditch, surrounding the stones, which may originally have been intended to hold water.

ABOVE A view of the Stones of Stenness, Orkney (about 2800 BC). These stones, together with the Ring of Brodgar and the passage tomb of Maes Howe, formed the centre of a religious and ceremonial complex on Mainland, Orkney. Originally there were probably twelve stones of Stenness. The sheep are of the hardy local Shetland breed, which may have its origins in Iron Age times.

RIGHT An outcrop of the local stone on a beach in the Orkney Islands. This stone fractures naturally into flat slabs that are ideally suited for use in buildings.

BELOW A house belonging to the Neolithic settlement at Skara Brae, Orkney (3100–2500 BC). Many of the houses feature fine stone 'dressers', such as this example in House 7, which often face towards the single entranceway and may have been used as a special, altar-like focus for the building.

A view of the short entrance passageway into the larger of the two Earlier Neolithic houses at Knap of Howar on the small Orkney island of Papa Westray (3600–3100 BC). The passage was probably intended to provide protection against the all-pervading Orcadian winds.

Interior of the smaller house at Knap of Howar. These houses were more oval than the later round buildings, such as Skara Brae, which were probably connected with the introduction of circular monuments, such as the great chambered tomb of Maes Howe, around 3000 BC.

ABOVE Silbury Hill, near Avebury, Wiltshire (about 2500 BC). This man-made Later Neolithic hill does not appear to cover a burial, so it cannot be considered a barrow. It forms part of the huge Avebury 'ritual landscape' and is believed to be the largest artificial mound in prehistoric Europe.

The stones of Stonehenge, Wiltshire, with the encircling ditch (and the less visible internal bank) visible in the foreground. The ditch was dug around 3000 BC, but the stones themselves were not erected for another five hundred years (between 2550 and 1600 BC).

Two views of the great henge monument at Avebury, Wiltshire (about 2100 BC). The standing stones are arranged around the inner edge of a massive ditch with a high external bank, which may have served as a viewing point for ceremonies taking place within the enclosed arena-like space.

LEFT The wooden Sweet Track, Somerset. This timber footpath was raised off the surface of the surrounding marsh and was constructed early in the Neolithic period. It has been precisely dated by tree rings to the winter of 3806–07 BC.

BELOW A small selection of the many hundreds of oak woodchips found in the bedding-trench of the timber circle known as 'Seahenge' at Holme-next-the-Sea, Norfolk. This site has been dated by tree rings to the year 2049 BC (Early Bronze Age).

Seahenge. At the centre of a roughly circular arrangement of fifty-five oak posts is an upside-down oak tree which had been sunk into the ground in a tightly-fitting pit. In this view the trunk is hidden and the beginnings of the roots can clearly be seen (below and to the left of the figure in yellow). The other timber within the circle is a spar from a nineteenth-century shipwreck.

ABOVE One of the timbers of Seahenge. This timber has rotted off above the ground (to the left in this view). The lower end has been cut obliquely, probably during the process of felling. This near-flat end provides good evidence for the digging of a trench for the posts.

LEFT AND BELOW Two views of the lower, cut, ends of timbers from Seahenge. Note the axe-marks, which clearly show that the oak trees were felled with a broad-bladed bronze axe.

LEFT Wooden haft for a polished stone axe from the Earlier Neolithic causewayed enclosure ditch at Etton, Cambridgeshire (3800 BC). The haft had split during use, the axe-head was removed and the handle abandoned.

BELOW Polished stone axe placed alongside a woodchip that it produced some six thousand years ago, when last used. Small nicks in the cutting edge of this axe precisely match slight ridges on the cut face of the woodchip. From the ditch of an Earlier Neolithic long barrow at Stanwick, near Raunds, Northamptonshire (3800 BC).

BELOW Producing a parallel-sided, or tangentially-split, oak plank using wooden wedges, a technique that was frequently employed in Britain from the Neolithic to the Iron Age. This method of production requires knot-free wood of high quality. The splitting wedges are driven in from the end-grain, which has to be dressed square (or chain-sawed as in this instance!).

These smaller tools were clearly intended to carry out specific tasks, and were used by people with much skill and dexterity. It's apparent from the scratches found on meat bones that the animal carcasses butchered at Gough's Cave were taken apart expertly and with great economy of effort. Animals such as wild horse and red deer not only gave quantities of meat and bone marrow, but also tongue, brain and doubtless offal too. Their hides were removed to provide warm coats, boots and tent coverings – all essential given the cold climate of the time. Their bones were used to make sewing needles, personal adornments (beads and pendants) and parts of spearheads. Sinew was used for thread, and the animal glue used to fix small flint blades into slots in bone spearheads was boiled up from hooves. Nothing was wasted.

The movement of goods apart from flint, over even longer distances, can also be demonstrated. Among the many other items found there, Gough's Cave produced pieces of Baltic amber and non-local seashells which may well have come from beaches of the North Sea coast. But in this instance, are we looking at groups meeting other groups who have visited these far-off places, or at a single group (or groups) that was highly mobile and well adapted to travelling very long distances? Taken together, the evidence tends, somewhat unexpectedly, to suggest the latter. Indeed, Roger Jacobi has suggested that certain finds from caves as far apart as Kent's Cavern (in south Devon) and Robin Hood's Cave in Creswell Crags (Nottinghamshire/Derbyshire) are so extraordinarily alike that they could have belonged to, or been made by, the same group of people.[8] Certainly the distance from Creswell Crags to the North Sea coast would be nothing to a group capable of moving between the north midlands and southern Devon.

It's interesting that Baltic amber was valued in the Upper Palaeolithic and Mesolithic, because in later prehistory, most especially in the Early Bronze Age (around 2000 BC), it was widely traded and was made into some extraordinarily beautiful objects, including a large variety of beads and elaborate multi-stranded necklaces.[9] It's tempting to wonder whether some of the routes whereby this later material found its way to Britain and central parts of mainland Europe were not beginning to emerge as early as late glacial times. But why did people choose to move around in this seemingly restless fashion?

In order to answer this question, one must try to imagine the environment of late glacial Britain during the Creswellian (i.e. between 12,600 and twelve thousand years ago). By this period the Arctic tundra conditions that prevailed after the peak of the last glacial maximum (eighteen thousand years ago) had gradually been replaced by birch woodland. But the climate was already starting to get colder – heading towards the Loch Lomond cold sub-phase – after 12,600 years ago. The main wild animals were horse and red deer, but there were also significant populations of mammoth, wild cattle, elk, wolf, fox, Arctic fox and brown bear. Many of these are animals that move around. The wild horse and red deer, which were the main prey animals, moved through the landscape during the passage of the seasons, and the human population who depended on them would have had to be equally mobile if they were to take advantage of the times, such as when the mares foaled, when their prey was most vulnerable to attack.

Archaeologists often seek to demonstrate seasonality when they suspect that a site was only occupied at a certain time of year. There are many ways of doing this, and it's much easier to demonstrate when a site was occupied than when it wasn't. Absence is invariably harder to pin down. Bearing that in mind, a close examination of the eruption and growth patterns of horse and red-deer teeth found at Gough's Cave suggests that the animals were killed in two seasons: in late winter or spring, and in the summer. This would suggest that the group moved away from the cave in the autumn. Perhaps that was when they went to the North Sea coast.

The final cold period, the Loch Lomond sub-phase, lasted from 10,800 to ten thousand years ago, and thereafter we're in our own postglacial or Flandrian period, which I'll cover in the next chapter. It was very cold in Loch Lomond times: there was ice over the High-lands of Scotland, winter sea-ice as far south as Spain, and most of Britain and north-central Europe was tundra. Scandinavia north of Denmark was under ice, and the Baltic Sea was a seasonally frozen-over lake. Along with the cold came dryness, and this suited the develop-ment of the particular dwarf grasses, mosses and lichens preferred by animals such as wild horse and reindeer. We must imagine that herds of reindeer migrated across the plain that was later to form the North

Sea, between Britain and the continental mainland. Like the Lapps of today, people would have followed behind the herds, taking beasts when the time and place was appropriate. It's an elegant and rather attractive idea, but what is the evidence to support it?

The old road from Peterborough to Northampton is very familiar to me. It twists its way along the Nene valley, swerving randomly from one side to another. Nowadays a soulless dual carriageway bypasses anything of interest, but that old road went through all the villages and hamlets. One of these was the pleasant village of Earls Barton, which nestled in what was still then the remote peace of the Northamptonshire countryside. It was in a low-lying, flat, tranquil and prosperous landscape, quite unlike the more rugged uplands characteristic of places like Creswell Crags and Cheddar Gorge – the natural habitat, as I once believed, of Late Upper Palaeolithic man. The boring reality is that evidence for him (and her) in open and less protected environments has mostly been removed by later geological events.

I used to travel that road to Northampton quite regularly in the 1970s. A few years later, in 1982, an extraordinary discovery would be made that would forever tie Earls Barton into the frozen world of the Loch Lomond cold phase, over ten thousand years ago. Not just that, it would weld this small part of rural Northamptonshire to more distant horizons, far across the North Sea. For me at least, the remote past was coming home. Immediately I could identify with it.

The discovery was made unexpectedly in a gravel quarry in the Nene valley, just outside the village, which is well known to historians and archaeologists because its church boasts one of the finest Saxon towers in Britain. The quarry revealed a strange-looking object made in reindeer antler and known as a 'Lyngby axe'. The antler itself was radiocarbon dated to just over ten thousand years ago – in other words to the very end of the Loch Lomond sub-phase. At this time sea levels were lower because so much water was locked up in ice, and as a consequence the southern North Sea would have been a low-lying plain.

Lyngby axes are strange-looking objects that are fashioned from the main shaft of a reindeer's antler which has been shortened and all the side-pieces trimmed off. The end result more or less resembles a modern policeman's baton. They occur at about forty sites around the edges of what is now the southern North Sea basin, in Denmark, Germany, Poland, Holland and, with the discovery at Earls Barton, Britain. Most have been found on their own, as isolated finds. What were they? Perhaps it's easier to state what they weren't: they weren't axes or wood-working tools of any sort. The name is entirely inappropriate; maybe, like the Red 'Lady', we should refer to them as Lyngby 'axes' – but life's too short.

The Earls Barton example was large, generally well-preserved, and heavily used. There was no evidence that it had ever had an inserted flint or stone cutting edge to act as a blade. So it was made to be

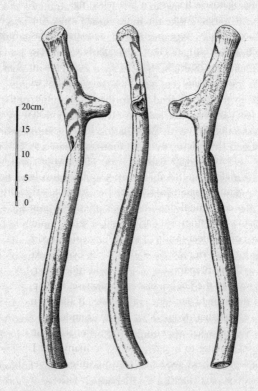

FIG 11   *A Final Upper Palaeolithic (c.ten thousand years ago) 'Lyngby axe' made from reindeer antler, found at Earls Barton, Northamptonshire in 1982.*

used on its own. A number of worked, step-like or scalloped facets distinguished it from some of its continental cousins, and showed that it had been used to work softer materials than stone, or indeed wood. In their study of the Earls Barton piece Jill Cook and Roger Jacobi were also able to rule out its use as a slaughterman's pole-axe, a weapon, or a pick or digging-stick,[10] and suggested that the wear-patterns implied that it had been used to work something like leather, meat, fat or plant material. They thought the scalloped bevels were secondary – i.e. not to do with its actual use – and could have been formed, for example, by being slung from a tent or from wear caused by rubbing against a harness or sledge fitting.

Reindeer were actually killed by hunters using flint-tipped arrow-heads whose shafts were sometimes deliberately fashioned in two pieces, to break on impact. One particularly well-preserved site of this period (about ten thousand years ago), at Stellmoor in north-western Germany, has revealed numerous reindeer bones with flint arrow-heads, or their tips, still in place within them. Some animals appear to have been hit twice, and it has been suggested that the wounds indicate that the hunters worked in groups, and not alone. Evidence from the growth-pattern of the many antlers found suggests too that the hunting took place in autumn or early winter, and that large numbers of people and animals may have been involved. Bodil Brat-lund, who studied the Stellmoor material, suggested that the evidence hints at 'the communal drive-hunts of migrating animals'.[11]

We know that the postglacial climate grew rapidly warmer, but the pattern of reindeer- and horse-hunting continued as during colder times. It would seem reasonable to link the Lyngby axe with reindeer-hunting and the preparation of food and hides after the kill during the final years of the Loch Lomond sub-phase. Perhaps the secondary wear reflects a highly mobile way of life. If that is indeed the case, one can suggest that people followed the reindeer in a large seasonal cycle, starting in what are now the depths of the southern North Sea in summer, moving to north-western Germany and Denmark in the autumn, then perhaps further south in winter, dispersing to Britain and Holland in the spring.[12] Earls Barton would fit well into such a pattern. The Nene valley is wide and open, and very gently dips down into the natural basin of the fens, which at the close of the Ice Age would have formed an integral part of the larger North European Plain.

In terms of elapsed time alone, the reader should now be turning the last half-dozen pages of this book. But our story still has a long way to go. As a prehistorian of later periods, I am all too aware that we have tended to play down the Palaeolithic and the archaeology of the Ice Age in general. I used to think that this simply reflected the fact that specialists in the earlier periods seemed to be more concerned with the classification of flints than with the recreation of ancient societies. From the Neolithic period onwards archaeologists were increasingly involved with social matters, with the organisation of cultures, the transfer and gaining of power, prestige and authority, and latterly with the academic and social politics surrounding different gender perspectives (for 'gender' read 'female' throughout).

Perhaps this variety of approach merely reflected the better information that was then available for the later periods. Perhaps it reflected the prevailing archaeological 'culture'. I don't know. But what I do know is that today this has changed completely. The Palaeolithic is coming alive, and it has even proved possible to carry out successful studies on changing social structure in such extraordinarily ancient times. The key which unlocked these secrets and released those poor isolated, structureless 'cave-men' from their cavernous prisons in our minds came with the simple realisation that they were hunters – and that hunters still exist today.

One of the main pioneers of this new approach was Richard B. Lee. Lee was at the Department of Anthropology at the University of Toronto when I was a young curator at the Royal Ontario Museum there, and I went to several of his lectures on the Bushmen people of the Kalahari desert. He had lived with them, and his lectures were inspiring. He edited a most influential collection of papers, with another anthropologist, Irven DeVore, under the collective title *Man the Hunter*.[13] In Britain we were a little slower to join the *Man the Hunter* revolution, but when we did, we did so with great success – as the contributions by archaeologists like Roger Jacobi and Nick Barton attest. Once again, Clive Gamble has given us some remarkable insights into the way that Palaeolithic people organised their material and social worlds. He has used a variety of sources, including studies made by specialists in later periods, such as the Neolithic and Bronze Age. He has also drawn heavily upon the anthropological literature to produce a thoroughly satisfying explanation of life in the Old Stone Age.

Gamble's arguments are closely reasoned and complex.[14] They are also very convincing, being based on observations of human behaviour and not a little common-sense. The main problem he has had to contend with is that the players in his drama change physically and mentally as hundreds of thousands of years roll by. And, of course, nobody knows for certain what those changes did or did not involve. It's rather like painting a picture with a brush that's constantly mutating as you work: at first it's wider, then narrower, but at the same time it can be thicker, finer or coarser.

Gamble's work is confined to Europe, which as we have seen was mainly colonised by human beings in the last half million years or so. He defines three broad time periods, which he uses to describe the ways people lived and organised their lives. The first is from half a million to 300,000 years ago, and he begins by making the unusual claim that the slow colonisation of Europe wasn't merely a matter of cold climate alone. He believes that 'it was never their intention to colonise Europe', that their lives were lived on a small scale: groups of people were small, and their outlook was essentially vertical; in other words they looked inwards and vertically up, towards the previous generation, and down, towards their own children and grandchildren. In many respects it was a pattern of social behaviour that owed a certain amount to their primate ancestors of five million years previously. It was against this background that Gamble wrote about the short-lived 'fifteen-minute culture' of Boxgrove, a minimalist view with which I have increasing sympathy – despite the proven wonders of Boxgrove and the controversy about whether they did or did not hunt prey there. It's very difficult not to take sides in Palaeolithic archaeology, and in this instance I find myself in the uncomfortable position of being on both sides at the same time.

In Gamble's view, people of the Lower Palaeolithic lived in a small-scale 'landscape of habit', rather than a truly social landscape. Communication was essentially a face-to-face process that happened between two or more people at the same time. Indirect reference to people elsewhere in time and space would not have taken place. Language, in other words, was used 'as an attention device rather than as an organising principle'. He sums up their world thus: 'they had lives of great variety within a small social neighbourhood of possibilities'. I can think of many worse ways to spend one's time on this earth.

His second phase is that of the more complex society of the Neanderthals, between 300,000 and twenty-seven thousand years ago. It is a period which sees the appearance and growth of true social networks. In the previous period, when relationships were essentially one-to-one, and based on close family ties, they were probably very strong, simple and unambiguous. In the Neanderthal world this was to change, largely because communication improved – but not just through language. Objects themselves can communicate. For example, in my family, like many others in England, it is traditional to give children a small engraved mug on their christening. That mug carries the child's name and the date of its christening. Sometimes, as in my case, the mug formerly belonged to a dead relative, whose name and date of christening appears above mine. That mug is communicating all manner of things to me and others. It is telling me that I am part of an established family, that I am a baptised Christian, and that my parents loved me sufficiently to have a mug engraved for me. So symbolically it's expressing my place in society (Church of England) and family. It's also symbolic of me to other people. Its actual function as an object – i.e. a mug to hold liquid – is of minor importance.

There is no evidence to suggest that any of the manmade objects from Boxgrove carried such a burden of communication. They were hand-axes, admittedly beautifully made hand-axes, but they were made to be used. They were not passed on from one community to another, and they didn't express anything more than the need to butcher a carcass. But from 300,000 years ago material things can be perceived as communications: as symbols of individuals, of families and family ties. As Gamble puts it, 'after 300,000 BP [Before Present] chains of connection were extended in all regions of Europe'. With the growth of social networks came more subtle close and long-distance human relationships. The simplicity of the one-to-one, me-to-you, close and unambiguous family relationship was supplemented by a host of new, subtle and ambiguous relationships.

This was a period when there was greater teamwork and co-operation in hunting, which doubtless reflected the larger scale of social networks that were being achieved. But it was not a society that modern people would feel at ease in, still being very restricted in all manner of ways. Clive Gamble sums it up well:

> These Neanderthal societies, the product of large-brained homi-nids, equipped with language to talk about themselves, alive with gestures and incorporating objects, were, for all that variety and creativity, still exclusive, local and complex. Theirs was a most successful hominid society. Well matched to the longer rhythms of the ice ages.[15]

The third of Clive Gamble's Palaeolithic periods is the one we have been concerned with in this and the previous chapter, what he styles 'transition and complicated Crô-Magnon society (sixty to twenty-one thousand years ago)'. The Crô-Magnons, you will recall, were the first examples of our own species, *Homo sapiens*, to appear in Europe. The main innovation of the time was what Gamble has called 'the release of our primate heritage of proximity'. The term may sound daunting, but when that release happened, we were free to develop a truly complex social life. Let's return to 'proximity' for a moment; if we understand what it is, we can appreciate what it is to be without it. The idea is actually quite straightforward: when two primates, such as chimps, meet, they groom each other, communicate in various non-verbal ways, and when they part they effectively cease to exist for each other. Absence really does mean just that. Then, as soon as they meet again, the relationship is continued where it left off. In other words, the relationship only happens when two or more individuals are in proximity.

When we are released from the ties that bind relationships that only happen in proximity, we are able to continue relationships across time and space. You may not see your grandchildren in Australia, but it's possible to have a growing and evolving relationship with them by phone, letter, e-mail, presents, films and photographs, etc. By the same token, in the past it was possible to have relationships at long distance between people who were illiterate, by way of gifts and other material gestures of affection, aided sometimes by a helpful third party.

Modern human beings (and in 'modern' I include the Crô-Magnons) can go even further. They can have loving relationships with objects (Clive Gamble mentions sports cars), pets, or something as bizarre as archaeological theory.

Gamble characterises social life in his third period as being truly complicated, rather than simply complex. I will let him sum up what life at the closing stages of the Ice Ages was about. He is writing about the ability of people to create social, personal and symbolic networks, which for the first time included both human beings and objects. I have no problem in identifying with the lives they led, even if I

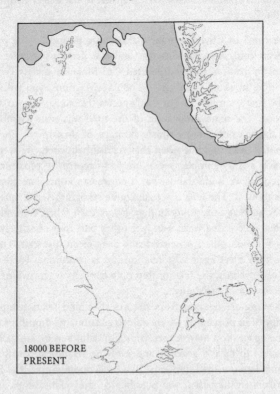

FIG 12   *Map of the southern North Sea area, showing the approximate coastline eighteen thousand years ago, during the coldest part of the last glacial*

couldn't have survived in their world for very long: 'The surrounding environment in the Upper Palaeolithic was now richly layered with meaning and symbolically linked. Social occasions with rituals and resources now structured the seemingly unfettered life of the Palaeolithic person.'[16]

One of the aspects of earlier prehistory that I find the hardest to come to terms with is the extent to which the immediate surroundings of what was shortly to become the British Isles changed. Perhaps my inability to feel at home with the colossal transformations of the entire North European Plain simply reflects the short-lived, ephemeral world

12000 BEFORE
PRESENT

maximum, and twelve thousand years ago, shortly after the peak of the subsequent warmer period.

in which I spend my professional life: a matter of perhaps five millennia. In terms of what had gone before, the Iron Age (700 BC–AD 43) is a mere blink of an eye. In later prehistory we deal with events on a human scale, events we can relate to, such as those years when rivers flooded and farmers were forced to abandon their lowest meadow pastures. These may have been catastrophic events at the time, but in terms of the Upper Palaeolithic they are storms in thimbles, let alone teacups.

During the height of the last glacial maximum, around eighteen thousand years ago, when the climate was at its coldest and vast amounts of fresh and seawater were locked up in ice caps and glaciers, the North European Plain (whose remnants survive in parts of northwestern Germany, the Low Countries and eastern England) extended right across the southern North Sea. A narrow channel was all that separated Scandinavia from Scotland. The Hebrides were part of mainland Britain. The climate then warmed a great deal, reaching a peak about thirteen thousand years ago when, as has been mentioned earlier, the climate of Britain was if anything warmer than today. This is the warm spell that preceded the final or Loch Lomond cold sub-phase. Shortly after the warmest period at twelve thousand years ago, the North Sea extended very much further southwards, and Orkney and Shetland were beginning to look more like islands-to-be. Despite this shrinkage of the North European Plain, there is still a huge width of 'land bridge' available to those settlers who recolonised Britain to set up the Creswellian tradition around 12,600 years ago.

We have reached a turning point in our story. The ice has melted, the climate is suddenly growing warmer. It's ten thousand years ago – and it's that time of year to change the clocks. In this instance we'll pretend it's spring, and we'll turn the clocks forward two thousand years. So, 'ten thousand years ago' will become '8000 BC'. There's no good reason for this, other than the fact that many archaeologists, myself included, are happier working in years BC after the Ice Age. It's also symbolic, and after what has gone before – and the momentous changes that are just around the corner – we ought to do *something* symbolic of the new era we are about to enter.

PART II

An Island People

Shetland Isles

Orkney Isles

Morton

Goodland
Holywood
Mount
Sandel
Ballygalley
Langdale
Street House
Farm
Céide
Fields
Star Carr

Lismore
Fields
Etton/Maxey
Hockwold
Fengate
Grimes
Graves
Little
Paxton
Haddenham
Hazleton
Barrow Hills
Avebury
Thatcham
Sweet Track
Hill
Dorset
Stonehenge
Cissbury
Haldon
Cursus
Harrow
Hill

0   50   100   150 km

FIG 13   *Main sites discussed in Part II.*

CHAPTER FOUR

After the Ice

I'VE LONG BEEN OF THE OPINION that archaeological terminology can get in the way of sense and meaning, which is why so far I've tried to keep matters as straightforward as possible. The trouble is that the Palaeolithic was so long-lived, and the complexities of human physical evolution were such, that any attempt at greater simplification would actually have become misleading. But from now on, the people we are dealing with will be physically identical to us in every respect, and the dates, which will be expressed in years BC, are plain enough. This is just as well, because from here on the pace of our story really does begin to speed up. We will also have a larger canvas available to us, as Scotland emerges from the cold, and Ireland is populated by people who have made the journey west across the channel that was later to become the Irish Sea.

The period we are concerned with in this chapter is known as the Mesolithic or Middle Stone Age, and it begins with the onset of the postglacial some ten thousand years ago, when the Loch Lomond cold snap finished. The climate grew rapidly warmer (the most intense warming lasted a mere fifty years), so that within two or three lifetimes, average temperatures were as high as they are today.[1] This is the background to the final five thousand years of Britain as a realm exclusively inhabited by groups of hunters.

In every way, the Mesolithic was transitional: between the Ice Ages and the postglacial, and between hunting/gathering and farming. It would be a great mistake to view these changes of culture and environment as abrupt steps, because they weren't. The more closely we examine the material record of that period, the more we realise that, the initial postglacial warming aside, change was essentially gradual or evolutionary. There were no sudden and dramatic swerves of direction, just as there was no abrupt break between the Final Upper Palaeolithic and the Mesolithic. They were the same people, doing more or less the same things, in an environment that had grown dramatically warmer. And as it grew warmer, so it grew wetter underfoot, as sea levels began to rise – mainly as a result of melting ice.

When I was a student at Cambridge, my first Professor of Archaeology was a specialist in the Mesolithic, Grahame (later Sir Grahame) Clark.[2] He excavated what is now the most famous Mesolithic site in Britain, at Star Carr, in the flat, open Vale of Pickering, in northeastern Yorkshire. It's a drowned landscape, buried beneath layers of peat, that closely resembles the East Anglian fens, where I've spent most of my professional life. Strangely, I have no recollection of Professor Clark lecturing about Star Carr, but that could well be down to my youthful inability to get up in the morning. Alternatively, it could reflect the fact that the Professor's lectures were *very* dry indeed. They did not linger fondly in the memory, perhaps because they were so very flinty – almost obsessively flinty.[3]

In fairness to Clark, he did view the study of flints as a means of reaching the people who made and used them, but at the time I found his enormous interest in their typology daunting. Typology, incidentally, is an archaeological term that describes how one thing gradually develops into another. An example often used to teach the concept to students is the development of the first railway coaches, which initially resembled horse-drawn carriages on flanged wheels, then were joined together on the same chassis, before finally taking the form of something which resembled the railway coach of today. It was a process that took several decades. The history of archaeology is full of typological studies, of which perhaps the most famous is the development of bronze from stone axes. The succession of Upper Palaeolithic and then Mesolithic flint typologies is, however, truly frightening.

In a vastly simplified nutshell, it is essentially a story of miniaturisation. Many of the tiny flints were used to provide barbs or points for composite bone or antler spears which were used for hunting or fishing. Others were used for other purposes – to do, for example, with working bone, or shaping leather. These so-called microliths were made in a highly developed technique that was ultimately based on the core and blade tradition of the Earlier Upper Palaeolithic. Mesolithic microliths occur in a bewildering variety of geometric shapes that are tailor-made for the detailed typological analyses that have kept many scholars gainfully employed for decades. I shan't attempt to summarise their work here. As I have said previously, life is too short.

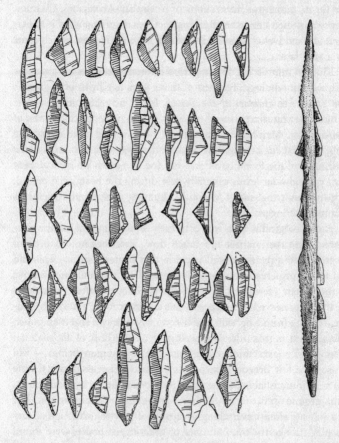

FIG 14   *A selection of flint microliths from Star Carr, near Seamer, Yorkshire (left). A slotted bone spearhead from Sweden with its flint microlith barbs still in place (right).*

Although his lectures were as dry as a charcoal biscuit, and I found him impossible to relate to as a student, Clark was undoubtedly one of the greatest and most innovative prehistorians of the twentieth century. In 1967 he published a short, well-illustrated account of *The Stone Age Hunters*, aimed at a popular readership.[4] It put his own site at Star Carr into the context of living societies, and I found it memorable for its numerous illustrations of Australian Aborigines, Eskimos, Lapps, Bushmen and other hunting societies. In many ways it anticipated Lee and DeVore's more influential *Man the Hunter*, which came out a year later.

Modern approaches to the period have moved on from a narrow study of flint typology. The best of them, such as Christopher Smith's *Late Stone Age Hunters of the British Isles*,[5] view Mesolithic people as hunters who acted out their lives within very specific types of environment. Mesolithic communities often settled near rivers and lakes, not just for fishing, but because that was where animals came to drink, and the forest cover was not too dense. As we have already seen, groundwater levels generally rose during the postglacial period, with the result that many Mesolithic hunting camps and settlements became waterlogged.

Archaeologically, this was extremely important. In certain situations where there is not too much flow, waterlogging can prevent oxygen feeding the fungi and bacteria that promote decay. This can lead to the preservation of organic material which would not survive for more than a few decades under normal circumstances. Sometimes the things preserved by stagnant waterlogging can be amazingly delicate, ranging from hair, skin and hide to wood, leaves and even pollen grains. On a normal, dry site, well over 90 per cent of all 'material culture' – i.e. everything made and used by human beings – will vanish in a few decades, leaving only those archaeological stalwarts and near-imperishables, stone, flint, pottery and fired clay. Sometimes, if the ground isn't too acidic, bone and antler will survive too. But on a wet site almost everything is capable of survival, although acidity can play strange tricks. A number of waterlogged bodies were found within Bronze Age oak coffins in Denmark. In some, clothes and footwear survived, but the skeletons themselves had vanished, eaten away by acid attack.[6]

Waterlogging also preserves the fragile remains of plants, insects and other creatures, large and small, that lived in or near the settlements occupied by prehistoric people. These waterlogged environmental remains can be analysed by various specialists, such as pollen analysts (or palynologists), botanists and experts in ancient molluscs or insects, to reconstruct the environment around the settlement. The principle lying behind these studies is Sir Charles Lyell's doctrine of uniformity, which we encountered in Chapter 1; waterlogged ground often favours plants and creatures that are fussy about where they live. So, the combination in a single deposit of, say, species of water snail, rush and cowslip would indicate not only that it was wet for part of the year, but also that it dried out in summer.

Taking a broad view of the subject, Christopher Smith points out that although Mesolithic people may well have gathered plant foods to supplement their primarily meat-based diet, they were always far more hunters than gatherers, or indeed fishers. With the British climate being what it is, gathered plant foods alone wouldn't even begin to supply the calories people require to stay alive for more than a short period.[7] Having said that, the term 'hunter-gatherer' has been around so long that it has stuck. So I'll continue to use it.

Grahame Clark's excavations at Star Carr took place between 1949 and 1951, and revealed a remarkably well-preserved and partially waterlogged site, on the marshy fringes of a postglacial lake, which was occupied around 7500 BC.[8] Since Clark's excavations, the animal bones from the original dig, plus the area around Star Carr, have been closely examined by archaeologists and archaeological environmentalists, so that it now possible to put the site into a reasonably coherent regional context.[9] This, of course, is necessary if we are to work out how hunters operated. It's no good looking at just one spot in the landscape, because the prey, and with it the hunters, are obliged to move around.

Star Carr produced a wealth of information about hunting. It was also a site where antler – of both native species of British deer, red and roe – was worked to make a variety of barbed spearheads, the vast majority of which were not fitted with small flint barbs. Antler is tough stuff, and requires special tools and techniques to be worked efficiently. Many of the flint tools, borers and burins, were designed to score and bore through the antler in a technique known as groove-and-splinter, which produced long, thin and strong 'blanks'; these could then be further modified to produce the finished spearhead. Most of the raw material for this mini-industry was brought to the site as antlers, rather than as deer on the hoof. So it is best to omit antlers when using bones from an excavation to estimate the range and number of animals that were hunted.

Tony Legge and Pete Rowley-Conwy have analysed the bones from Star Carr and have shown that over half, by weight, of meat came from wild cattle, followed by elk and red deer, with roe deer and wild pig bringing up the rear. It is suggested that the larger animals were hunted by stealth, rather than by large groups of hunters working a 'drive/stampede' system, which we saw at Stellmoor in Germany in the Final Upper Palaeolithic. Evidence to support the idea of stalking is provided by the remarkable discovery on the shoulderbones of two elk and one red deer of lesions produced by a flint-tipped spear or arrowhead. What makes them remarkable is that they had healed over. In other words, the three animals in question had each survived at least one attempt to hunt them before they were finally caught and killed.

The position of the wounds, at the shoulders, suggests that the hunters were aiming for the heart. If they missed, as often would have happened, they would have had to resign themselves to a long period of stalking, as the prey slowly bled to death.[10] And of course sometimes the animals got away – maybe when night fell and the trail went cold. The fact that these three beasts had done so suggests that the animal population around Star Carr and the now-vanished Lake Flixton was more sedentary than usual. Alternatively, it might suggest a somewhat larger human population in the region, perhaps at certain times of the year. But whatever the explanation, it is not the sort of thing one would have expected to encounter much earlier, at places like Paviland or Boxgrove. It's a sign, surely, that the general population was growing.

Smaller animals, including pine marten, red fox and beaver, were also taken, probably for their pelts. The hunters at Star Carr were most remarkable for having domestic dogs, which presumably were used for hunting and rounding up.[11] I find it fascinating to think that my own Border collie sheepdog, Jess, when she rounds up ewes is behaving in a fashion that any Mesolithic hunter would immediately recognise.

I've mentioned that the site was positioned next to a lake, so how can we explain the lack of fishbones? The best theory to account for the absence of fish, particularly pike, a large freshwater fish that one might have expected to be found near Star Carr, is that they hadn't recolonised this part of Britain after the very cold years of the last glaciation.[12] The North Sea would still have been very cold, and it is doubtful whether the small prey fish that pike need to feed on would have been present in anything like adequate numbers. So in this instance the absence of fishbones *may* indicate an absence of fish. Unfortunately, however, the acidity of the peats at Star Carr is sufficient to degrade fishbone, so the question cannot be satisfactorily resolved one way or the other.

Star Carr was waterlogged, and produced large quantities of wood, but evidence for actual wood-working took some time to appear. And when it did appear it lingered on our kitchen draining-board for ages. I should perhaps point out that my wife, Maisie Taylor, is a specialist in prehistoric wood-working, and I have had to grow used to finding black, grimy and rather unpalatable pieces of ancient wood in the sink. It's a part of our life.

The pieces in question were sent to Maisie by Professor Paul Mellars at Cambridge, who was writing up excavations he had carried out at Star Carr with Tim Schadla-Hall in 1985 and 1989. They had come across some pieces of wood they thought had been worked by man. The wood in question seemed to have come from an artificial platform of some sort, but they couldn't be entirely certain, unless it could be shown to have been worked or split by man. Other wood-working specialists had expressed reservations about its possible man-made status.

Maisie looked at it very closely, and at first she too had her doubts; but there were areas where peat still adhered to the surface, and if gently floated off (in our sink) its removal might reveal fresh surfaces, which could be diagnostic. The freshly removed peat did indeed expose cleanly split surfaces, and I spent several happy hours in our barn taking close-up photographs which showed clearly that the wood –

or rather timber, to give it its correct name* – had been worked by humans.[13] This is the earliest evidence for worked timber found anywhere in the world – and it spent a tiny part of its long life in my sink. When he saw Maisie's first results, Paul immediately recalled a series of bevelled red-deer antler tines, illustrated in the original Clark report, which he thought might well have been used as wedges for splitting.

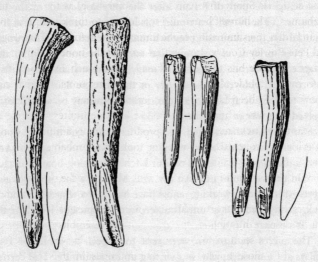

FIG 15   *Three bevelled red-deer antler tines from Star Carr, which may have been used as wedges for splitting timber. Timber rarely stays clean when it is being split, and pieces of soil, sand, gravel or grit would probably account for the abrasion evident at the tips.*

In our story so far we have failed, if that's the right word, to discover a site that we could safely say was a home-base: in other words, somewhere where people stayed and lived. Even at Boxgrove

---

* Timber, a word unique to English, defines a form of wood which has been trimmed up and sometimes split, sawn or further subdivided, with the intention of being used in a structure of some sort. A felled tree is not timber (despite what lumberjacks shout out as a warning), but its trimmed-up trunk is.

we saw how the meat was probably taken away from the smelly, fly-blown butchery site at the bottom of the cliff and up towards the woods on the chalk hill above. None of the Middle and Upper Palaeolithic caves we have looked at could with any certainty be considered a permanent dwelling-place, and Earls Barton wasn't really a site at all.[14] What about Star Carr, which has produced a huge amount of material, including a great variety of things such as antler mattocks and bone scrapers? Surely this represents a home-base, as the excavator, Grahame Clark, himself believed? I would love to think so, but unfortunately that re-examination of the animal bone refuse by Tony Legge and Pete Rowley-Conwy showed that most of the bone found on site comprised those bits that don't actually have much meat on them: lower jaws, shoulderblades and foot bones. The joints, the rich cuts as it were, had been taken away and eaten elsewhere – and wherever it was, that's where home was for those lakeside hunters. Despite its archaeological richness, Star Carr was still essentially a hunting camp, albeit a well-frequented one, and one, moreover, probably quite close to a main home-base.

Work carried out in the Vale of Pickering after the original excavations of Grahame Clark gives a clear impression that there were a number of settlements around the now vanished postglacial Lake Flixton. Some were hunting camps, others more resembled home-bases. But there does seem to be one important respect in which Star Carr differs from those hugely mobile communities in the Late Upper Palaeolithic: it would seem that life near Lake Flixton did not involve much long-distance travel. The area was richly stocked with large mammals, and the human inhabitants knew this well. They probably didn't use the Star Carr hunting camp all year round, but neither did they go hundreds of miles away when they were absent from it. Seasonal movements were most likely small in scale.

Before we leave this remarkable place, which continues to provide the liveliest and most interesting archaeological debate of any prehistoric site in Britain (with the possible exception of Stonehenge), we must pause for a moment to examine its most intriguing finds. These consist of twenty-one red-deer skull fragments, known as frontlets, some of them complete with their antlers. The undersides of the skulls have had the sharper ridges knocked off, and the massive antlers have

FIG 16   *Head-dress made from a red-deer stag frontlet, with the antlers reduced. Both the parietal bones of the skull have been perforated with roughly circular holes (twelve millimetres diameter).*

been reduced in such as way as still to look impressive, and more or less balanced, but not to be so heavy. The skulls have also been perforated with two or four circular holes. Grahame Clark reckoned these extraordinary and rather heavy objects were head-dresses that were secured in place by hide straps through the holes.

Rather surprisingly for someone so down to earth and a self-confessed functionalist, Clark suggested that the antlers had been used in shamanistic-style dances, reminiscent perhaps of the Abbots Bromley horn dance of Staffordshire, a regional version of the traditional English Morris dance.[15] At Abbots Bromley the horns are carried in both hands. Christopher Smith inclines to the view that the Star Carr head-dresses were more likely to have been worn as a disguise when out stalking. He reasons that Star Carr was probably a hunting camp, and that the large number of frontlets found must argue in favour of a practical use.[16] He also suggests that a hard-and-fast distinction between the two forms of use is probably wrong, with which I agree 100 per cent.

We now come to an extraordinary twist in this tale. I recently returned from filming at Star Carr with Tim Schadla-Hall, who you will remember co-directed the dig that discovered the split wood that Maisie examined. I've known Tim for years, and whenever we meet he has a habit of producing new information that completely blows apart my old ideas. I find archaeologists like Tim exciting because not only do they dig, but they also think, in a lateral way. As we talked between 'takes' in the filming, it became clear that after over twenty years' research Tim had quite suddenly abandoned most of his own and many of his colleagues' explanations of what was going on at Star Carr. His new theories didn't accord with the way most people regarded the hunter/gatherer world of the Mesolithic, but would have fitted in better with some much later – say Neolithic or Bronze Age – site. It was as if the artificial boundaries erected by archaeologists between hunter/gatherers and farmers had completely dropped away.

Tim pointed out that Lake Flixton and the land immediately around it was an area of stability: it was wooded, not prone to flooding, and was remarkably protected by the nearby valley-side of the Vale. It was a landscape where small-scale movement was a part of everyday life (the coast was about an hour's walk to the east), but there was no need at all for longer-distance seasonal migrations. It was a naturally protected and gentle landscape, that was ideally suited for hunting – so people stayed put.

Star Carr was close to the edge of the stable landscape, and Tim suggested that the artificial timber platform on the edge of the lake might have been constructed as somewhere set aside for ceremonies to emphasise or mark the special nature of the stable landscape of Lake Flixton. We'll see later that so-called 'liminal' or boundary zones were viewed as being of particular importance to prehistoric communities. Ceremonies in these places 'at the edge' would have protected or reinforced the 'core' or stable area against forces that were thought to threaten it. They were also neutral places where people from outside could safely be met – and maybe gifts and other items be exchanged.

The idea of constructing a timber platform at the fringes of water is something we'll re-encounter in the Bronze Age at Flag Fen (and other sites); moreover, the fact that some care was taken in the platform's construction should not cause any surprise. Religious sites and shrines were, and indeed still are, both well designed and well built. Tim's latest explanation also accounts for the otherwise rather strange collection of bones from the site, and of course for those shamanistic antler head-dresses.

So, if Star Carr is out, where can we look for a site of the early postglacial period, around 8000 BC, where there is evidence that people actually lived on the spot – our elusive so-called 'home-base'? Must we seek out somewhere remote, untouched by the passage of time? Perhaps up in the hills? Or a cave? Far from it. In fact it's in the pleasant rural town of Newbury in Berkshire that we'll meet one of the heroes of this book, the great John Wymer, once again.

The date is 1958, and John is working for Reading Museum. The site he is interested in lies in the valley of the Kennet, a tributary of the Thames, nearly two miles east of Newbury, near Thatcham, the village after which it is named. Like several archaeological sites I am personally familiar with, including my own project at Flag Fen, Peterborough, the Thatcham site lies close to a sewage outfall works; but in this instance there is an additional and more serious threat, and one that we will encounter more often as time passes – namely gravel extraction. Today the site is a large flooded hole. John and his team from Reading and Newbury Museums worked on weekends between 1958 and 1961, and his full report was published with model promptness in 1962.[17]

England has a long and honourable tradition of amateur archaeology, which in the first part of the twentieth century was pretty well indistinguishable from the professional. It was amateurs, mainly, who established many of the county archaeological journals in Victorian times, and it was amateurs who found and then kept an eye on well-known sites in case they came under threat. The Newbury area had its own group of archaeological stalwarts who located a number of Mesolithic flint scatters in fields close to the river Kennet at Thatcham and in Newbury itself. In 1921 a trench through one of the flint scatters was excavated at Thatcham. This produced clear evidence that flint implements were actually being made on site. There were finished implements, but there were also numerous flint waste flakes, the by-products of flint-knapping.

The earlier work made it essential that something be done about the site when the threat of gravel-digging arose in the late 1950s. Today a threat of this sort to an archaeological site would lead to a dig which would be funded by the company that owned the gravel quarry – which is fair, as it is they who stand to profit from the site's destruction. But in those days there was less justice, and the local archaeologists had to find the money, which they managed to do, from the local museums, the Prehistoric Society and Cambridge University. The Prehistoric Society, incidentally, is the national society for the study of all pre-Roman archaeology. Its *Proceedings* is an academic journal of record, and is pretty technical. But it also organises tours of prehistoric landscapes in Britain and Europe, and has regular meetings, a wide non-professional membership, and a lively newsletter, *Past*.[18] The Society helped to excavate Thatcham – and dozens of other sites in Britain.

As a first stage, John Wymer decided to cut a quick reconnaissance or trial trench in December 1957. This produced quantities of flint and scraps of bone which lay beneath nine inches (twenty-three centimetres) of peat and eighteen inches (forty-six centimetres) of peaty topsoil. This depth of material was hugely important, because it meant that the site beneath was sealed intact. It could never have been damaged by ploughing, and the presence of the *in situ* peat bed clearly demonstrated that it hadn't. John immediately realised that he had an extraordinarily important site on his hands.

As work progressed in the seasons that followed that winter exploratory trench, it became evident that Thatcham was not just one site. It was clearly a place where people settled repeatedly, as there were distinct concentrations of flint and other debris on the gravel terrace that ran along the river. Although many flint implements were made there, Thatcham doesn't seem to have been a place where specialised tasks were carried out, like the antler-working at Star Carr. And there was a huge variety of things found: antler and bone, as at Star Carr, hammerstones for flint-working, flint axes or adzes and vast numbers (16,029) of waste flakes, blades (1,207), cores (283) and those tiny, geometrically-shaped microliths (285) that were used to make composite spears and arrowheads. At Thatcham waste flakes formed 96.5 per cent of the entire flint assemblage, even higher than at Star Carr (92.8 per cent).

John's style of excavation was rather like that of Stephen Aldhouse-Green, somewhat more recently. Both are neat and extremely meticulous, and both make a point of recording everything they find three-dimensionally. This takes time and effort; it also only happens if the crew actually doing the work are happy and highly motivated – and that's the real skill of a successful dig director: somehow he must keep people informed and enthusiastic, otherwise they won't willingly do what he asks them.

The most important concentration of occupation debris at Thatcham was unearthed in an area known as Site III, where John had not expected to find much. Like the other settlement sites it was located on the edge of a slope which dipped down to reed beds along an edge of the river floodplain. In Mesolithic times it would have been on the edge of a large lake. The area in question was actually a shallow dip when seen from the surface, and John had quite reasonably expected to find better evidence for settlement on the drier humps than in the damper hollows. But in this case his guess was wrong, which, paradoxically, is why he is such a good field archaeologist. A lesser man would only have put trenches where he expected to make

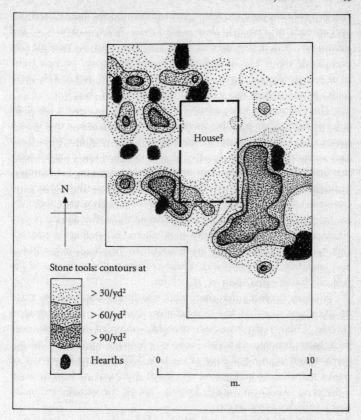

FIG 17   *The early postglacial (about 8000 BC) settlement at Thatcham, Berkshire, produced evidence for a possible house area (within the dashed lines), surrounded by hearths and high densities of flint-working debris.*

discoveries. A good archaeologist, however, is always aware that he must break the mould, destroy the predictable chains of reasoning.

Like other sites at Thatcham, Site III was dug by yard (metre) squares, and flints were recorded to the appropriate square. As the crew worked they were amazed by the density of flints they found: sometimes as many as two to three hundred per square, and in one extraordinary instance a massive 764. In amongst the flints were numerous burnt pebbles, burnt and unburnt bones, burnt hazelnuts and spreads of charcoal, clear evidence for hearths or fires – and indeed for food, both meat and nuts. This was clearly a domestic site, and clearly too it had been occupied more than once, because some of the flints showed signs of having been worked twice. The sheer quantity of material also indicated repeated use of the place.

There were also some areas of Site III where there were low densities of flints. If we plot the densities at Site III, we notice that there's an area near the centre of the site which is relatively free from flints and surrounded also by hearths. If one assumes that flint-working was an activity best carried out in the open (as we saw, for example, at Boxgrove), this could well have been a place where light structures were erected when people returned to the site. It measures about 6.5 by 5.5 metres, and has a floor area of some thirty-five square metres – large enough for a single family. In northern Europe there is evidence that early postglacial people made houses by bending birch saplings and covering them with hides. These are about the same size as the possible house-sized space at Thatcham.

It seems probable that more than one family occupied the ridge at Thatcham, and that, like other communities of the time, they were mobile. Their home-base was probably occupied in the summer months, and analysis of pollen shows it to have been positioned within birch woodland, on the edge of the lake.[19] They hunted a variety of animals, including both native species of deer, and wild pig (a term I prefer to 'wild boar', which implies that all the animals are male) was particularly important.

Once in a while it happens that an archaeologist excavates a site and publishes a report in which he speculates about its date and function, then someone else comes along ten years later, with the improved techniques of the time, and proves him right or wrong. It happened to me a few years ago, and I was proved wrong – but in the nicest possible way.[20] It happened to John Wymer too – and of course he was proved right. Another spread of flint on the same ridge, but about two hundred metres to the north-west, was excavated in 1989.[21] This revealed a pattern of sharp rises and falls in the density of flints found on the ancient surfaces, just as John had done, but the excavators now had available the newer technique of microwear, or use-wear, analysis. Essentially this is a way of examining microscopic damage to the scraping and cutting edges of flint tools, but it requires flints from sealed contexts, such as Thatcham (where the occupation levels were covered by a layer of peat), otherwise it's hard to discount the 'noise' caused by more recent, post-depositional effects, such as plough damage.

The technique relies on the controlled experimental 'use' of flints, which are then examined, and the results compared with the ancient material. The microscopic edge-damage found at kill or butchery sites is very characteristic and includes, as one might expect, evidence for percussion and harsh damage, when joints are severed and bones are broken. There will also be arrowheads and projectile points at such sites. A domestic site – a home-base, in other words – produces a far more diverse pattern of edge-wear. The heavy-duty percussive damage tends to be lacking, as are quantities of arrowheads, and there are more signs of scraping hides and sinews, and of cutting soft materials, such as vegetable matter. The range of flint implements found at Thatcham, and the edge-wear revealed in the microwear analyses, showed that it had indeed been a domestic site. John had been right: it was a true home-base.

It cannot have escaped attention that up till now I have been writing about Britain alone – as if Ireland was floating out over the horizon, miles away in the Atlantic. Of course it wasn't, but neither was it inhabited by human beings in the Ice Age, with the possible exception of the odd visitor or two at the close of the Lower Palaeolithic.[22] For practical purposes Ireland's earliest Stone Age was the Mesolithic. It is a very well-preserved Mesolithic, with some fascinating stories to tell.

I have a soft spot for Ireland and the Irish. My mother came from an old Anglo-Irish family who went to Ireland in the sixteenth century, essentially as English mercenaries to fight in the Desmond Wars of County Wexford. They built a moated tower house, Huntington Castle, on the borders of Counties Wexford and Carlow in 1625, and are living there to this day. My grandmother, Nora Robertson, wrote a wonderful account of the Anglo-Irish Ascendancy which I keep by my bed and dip into regularly.[23] I have never had the privilege of excavating in Ireland, but I would love to do a dig there one day.

It is well known that Ireland has a long tradition of close relations with the United States, and this extends to archaeology, too. I remember when I worked at the Royal Ontario Museum in the early 1970s being recommended to read the reports of the Harvard University Irish Project of the 1930s. Not only were these a model of how to do good field archaeology, but they were published promptly and in sources that were readily accessible to the 'natives', and in a language that they could understand. This was in contrast to what was going on elsewhere in the world, especially in the Near East, Western Asia and South America. I can imagine how indignant I'd feel if the standard reference work on the archaeology of East Anglia was published in Russian.

Ireland was cut off from the rest of Britain by rising sea levels at some time around 7500 BC. Thereafter anyone wishing to settle in what we still assume was an uninhabited island had to come by way of a short sea crossing. Actual physical evidence for Earlier Mesolithic boats has yet to be found in Britain, but dug-out, canoe-style logboats have been found in Denmark,[24] and possible logboats of the Mesolithic to Neolithic transition period are known in Britain.[25] These are generally too rigid and inflexible for long sea-crossings, unless fitted with outriggers or double hulls, and would more likely have plied inland waterways such as Lake Flixton (a possible paddle was found at Star Carr). We also know from rock carvings in Scandinavia and elsewhere that skin-covered craft existed in prehistory. These would have been similar to the curraghs that I remember seeing bobbing about in the Atlantic surf off County Galway as a boy. Such vessels could perfectly well have crossed the narrow channel separating Britain from Ireland in the mid-eighth millennium BC.

For a long time the version of the Irish Mesolithic established by the Harvard expeditions of the 1930s held sway, but then a young archaeologist working close to the river Bann, in County Antrim, changed all that. Peter Woodman's discoveries at Mount Sandel, a settlement on a thirty-metre-high bluff or sandy bank alongside the river, showed that the gap that separated the world of the hunter/gatherers and the very first (Neolithic) farmers was by no means as wide as we used to believe. He has also helped to fill in that central void at Thatcham – the one surrounded by hearths and huge numbers of flints. I remember well when the first pictures of his dig appeared in the archaeological literature. I couldn't believe my eyes: his meticulous excavations had revealed the clearest evidence possible for lightweight, tent-like houses built by these hunters of the Later Mesolithic.

The site has been dated by radiocarbon to about 6500 BC, so it's significantly later than Thatcham or Star Carr, but in many respects it's quite similar.[26] It's positioned near water in woods of birch and hazel, but unlike either English site, Peter Woodman's excavations produced huge quantities of fishbones, of which salmon and sea trout were by far the commonest. This gives us an important clue as to the time of year the site would have been occupied. Both fish are migratory, and enter rivers from the sea to spawn in summer and autumn. It seems most probable that this was when the site was occupied. We don't know where the occupants went for the rest of the year, although the seaside is a possibility. Other evidence shows that their food was not confined to these very delicious fish; they also ate eel, wild pig, various birds including game birds, and hazelnuts. I can think of worse diets.

Mount Sandel is principally famous for its lightweight houses, which are still, I believe, the oldest proven domestic structures in the British Isles. There were two types. Six examples of the first type were found. It consists of a roughly circular or oval arrangement of angled stake- or post-holes, plus a doorway; sometimes there's also evidence for a central hearth. The house was probably built from curved or hooped poles covered with hides, and the average size was just over five metres across, giving a floor area of about thirty square metres, which is broadly comparable with the 'void' area at Thatcham.

The second type of house was more tent-like, and about half the size of the hooped pole structures. It consists of four banana-shaped, shallow ditches or gullies arranged in a rough circle. Presumably these were dug to take the run-off of water from a tent-like structure. There's no evidence for post-holes, so we must assume the framework didn't need to be securely anchored, being structurally stable and able to shed all but the severest of gales. In this instance the hearth was positioned outside, but opposite, the entranceway.

Both styles of structure are lightweight and appropriate to people

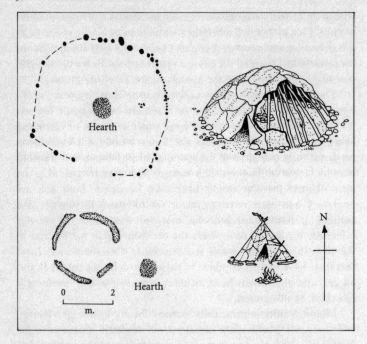

FIG 18   *The earliest evidence for domestic structures in Britain was found at Mount Sandel in County Antrim, dating to about 7000 BC. Two types of buildings were found, a hoop-framed house (upper), and a smaller tent-like structure with an external hearth (below).*

whose pattern of life requires movement through the landscape. Can we call them houses? I don't see why not. A house is where people choose to live. As soon as we start to talk about 'huts' – or worse, 'shacks' – we do these buildings a disservice. The small structure within the four gullies at Mount Sandel is undoubtedly a tent-house, the other is a house, albeit a lightweight one. I strongly dislike the term 'hut', which I see in the archaeological literature far too often. Huts are for wheelbarrows and garden tools, not for people.

We've looked at Mesolithic settlements in England and Ireland, but what was happening further north, in Scotland – was it too cold for settlement in postglacial times? The answer is that it wasn't; Scotland has produced plentiful evidence of life in the period. One of the most revealing sites was excavated by John Coles, who lectured to me on the Palaeolithic at Cambridge and co-authored the standard textbook of the day.[27] He also lectured on the European Bronze Age, and a few years later co-authored another standard work.[28] At the time he was busily engaged in experimental archaeology, and was dipping his toes into the waters of wetland archaeology, which posterity will probably judge to have been his major contribution. So he's a man of many parts, which is perhaps why he was invited to take over an existing Mesolithic excavation at Morton, in the Kingdom of Fife, in 1967. The main dig took place in 1969 and 1970.[29]

I should perhaps note here that we still know of no evidence for postglacial occupation in Scotland before about 9000 BC. To the best of my knowledge the earliest site on the mainland is currently Cramond, near Edinburgh, which has produced radiocarbon dates from hazelnut shells to around 8500 BC.[30] This is remarkably early, given the fact that it is generally agreed that most of Scotland would still have been uninhabitable before around 9600 BC.

Like most other Mesolithic sites, Morton shows clear evidence for more than one episode of occupation, and there are at least two centres of interest, which are known as Sites A and B. Today these are located a short distance inland, but in the fifth millennium BC they would have been very close to the shoreline. Radiocarbon dates indicate the sites were occupied three or four centuries before 4000 BC. So we are now approaching the end of the Mesolithic in this particular part of Scotland. Elsewhere in Britain some formerly Mesolithic communities will already have started to adopt the techniques of farming – to become in effect Neolithic.

Morton isn't far from St Andrews, the home of golf, and the countryside round about reflects this, being gentle and undulating. In the fifth millennium BC the area was cloaked in open oak woodland (with elm) and an under-storey of hazel. These woods probably didn't extend right down to the shoreline, which is where we find our two areas of occupation.

I hesitate to call both Sites A and B settlements, because Site B was very specialised, being in effect a huge dump or midden – a mound no less – of seashells. Mesolithic shell midden mounds are found in many places around the coasts of Britain and Ireland, but the shores of Scotland and the Western Isles boast some of the largest. Some are massive: substantial hillocks you could build a small bungalow on. They demonstrate, among other things, that shellfish were a highly important part of the seasonal round. The shells of shellfish such as the common cockle grow at varying rates at different times of year, in response to a variety of factors including air/water temperature and the salinity of the seawater. Using the information encoded within the shells at Morton, Margaret Deith of Cambridge University was able to demonstrate that a high proportion of them had been harvested high on the beach, and that no particular season seems to have been favoured.[31] If anything, wintertime, when the meat of cockles is less nutritious than in summer, was the most popular period for visiting Morton beach.

The impression gained is of opportunistic visits, the way one 'grabs a bite' whilst busily engaged in something else – at Morton this may have been the collection of suitable beach pebbles from which to fashion implements. The midden did however show clear signs that small temporary squats or camps had been scooped into it, perhaps as refuges from the worst of the wind. The surviving mound of shells was large, gently curving, and about thirty by 3.5 metres; its maximum thickness was 0.78 metres. At one point John Coles was able to identify a succession of five scoops or hollows which were floored with an occupation deposit – essentially crushed shells and an organic 'dark earth' – and showed clear signs of human use, including 'bashed lumps', stones that had been roughly hit to provide usable cutting edges and sharp points. But the signs of settlement on the midden were far less intensive than at Site A, about 150 metres to the south. The midden produced just 372 stone artefacts – compared with over thirteen thousand on Site A – and large quantities of fish and mammal bones, including red and roe deer, wild cattle and pig. By way of numerical compensation, it was composed of some ten million shells.

Why did these vast mounds of shells accumulate? The beach is a very hostile environment, lashed by winds, waves and storms. Heaps of shells wouldn't last for long unless (a) they were carefully positioned to be out of the reach of storms and tides, and (b) people wanted them to build up, and took pains to see that they grew every season. I think it's absurd to suggest that these great mounds were simply piles of rubbish, and had no other role. In any case, if a site was seen merely as being suitable for disposing of food refuse, it would surely not be regarded as appropriate for settlement, as happened at Morton, however short-lived. It seems to me that these great middens also served a symbolic role – perhaps marking out the position of a particular band's stretch of beach – in some respects rather like the similarly-shaped long barrows of the Neolithic, which I'll discuss in Chapter 8. If this idea has any validity at all, it knocks on the head the idea that Mesolithic people didn't construct, or understand, monuments and the symbolism lying behind them. Traditionally the introduction of monuments has been regarded as a strictly Neolithic innovation, but a few hints are beginning to emerge that it was never quite as straight-forward as that. As we will see, some very strange things indeed were happening in the area that was to become the Stonehenge car park. But more on this later.

Site A at Morton didn't produce evidence for lightweight houses, or spaces for them, as convincing as Mount Sandel or Thatcham. Post-holes, even decayed fragments of wood, did survive, but were never arranged in patterns that suggested any sort of permanence. They more resembled windbreaks, or temporary shelters over sleeping places, than dwellings as such.

Bones from Morton revealed that cod, and even sturgeon, were eaten, but the size of these bones suggests that they were caught offshore (what my local fishmonger flags up as 'long shore cod'), most probably from skin boats. Birds were also taken, including guillemot, gannet and cormorant, which nest on cliffs nearby and can be caught in the spring by an intrepid, or hungry, climber.

Morton wasn't a permanent settlement or a home-base. It was a place visited at several times of the year by a mobile band of hunters whose home-base was probably not far distant. Although visited epi-sodically, it gives us an impression of stability: it would have been familiar to the people who used it, part of the seasonal round. Maybe on certain visits, perhaps to collect suitable stone for making tools, only a few people came, possibly for a day and a night, stopping over in temporary shelters on the midden. They would have recognised

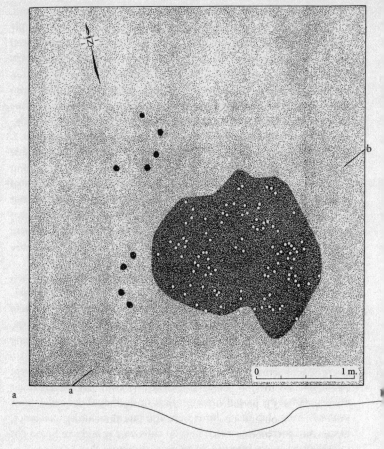

FIG 19   *Plan of two post-built windbreaks near a shallow scoop containing stone artefacts at a coastal hunting and fishing camp near Morton, Fife (about 4300 BC).*

the little headland and its accompanying inlet as 'theirs', and would have been well aware of why they were there. The landscape was becoming sufficiently populated for people to carry clear maps within their heads. The slow process of dividing up Britain was beginning to gather momentum. Soon it would become an irresistible force.

This brings me to the question of population in the Mesolithic period. It will, of course, always be difficult to estimate prehistoric populations, simply because the basic data – the sites and finds – which one has to use are constantly changing. This does not mean that one shouldn't make the effort. One particularly well-thought-out attempt to chart population trends in postglacial Britain (excluding Ireland) was made by Christopher Smith in 1992.[32] He based his calculations not on individual sites, but on the evidence provided by ten-by-ten-kilometre squares, reasoning that in highly mobile societies simply counting sites was probably going to involve a great deal of replication and distortion, because the same band of people would have occupied more than one in a single season, while an area as large as a hundred square kilometres would probably contain all the seasonal stopping-off points of a single group. It may be easy to suggest pitfalls in this hypothesis, but then, it's very much harder to come up with anything better. So I'm happy to stay with it.

Smith's paper was principally concerned with the rate at which population growth happened. He notes a steadily rising British population in the centuries before the Loch Lomond cold episode, then retreat, followed by growth leading to rapid growth thereafter. By 5000 BC he believes growth slowed down or ceased – only to pick up again, as we will shortly see, in the subsequent Neolithic period. He steers clear of actual numbers, but does commit himself to some broad estimates: 1100 to 1200 people at 9000 BC; 1200 to 2400 by 8000 BC. Then there was a period of rapid growth, leading to an estimate of 2500 to five thousand people by 7000 BC. By the end of the period (approximately 5000 BC) the range was 2750 to 5500.[33]

Smith used material he assembled for his *Late Stone Age Hunters of the British Isles* for his paper on population, which was published in the same year (1992). As we noted earlier, in this book he stayed clear of the more usual flinty typological approach to the subject, and instead viewed the people of the Mesolithic for what they were, namely hunters. As time passed they seem to have become somewhat less mobile, and the territories each band controlled became progressively smaller – as, for example, at Morton. Perhaps this more sedentary way of life was accompanied by a slightly greater reliance on gathered and stored vegetable foods, such as hazelnuts. It's remarkable how productive a large stand of hazelnut bushes can be.* I imagine it would not be difficult, in an unrestricted area of mature woodland, for a group of people working full-time in the autumn to fill the equivalent of several wheelbarrows with hazelnuts, which could then be stored above or below ground, in pits.

I concluded the previous chapter with Clive Gamble's thoughts on the nature and structure of Palaeolithic society. How did British society change in the Mesolithic? The consensus of opinion would suggest that structurally it altered very little.[34] Certainly the population grew, and grew quite quickly, but there was plenty of country to absorb this expansion. In other words, people didn't live in such close proximity that disputes and rivalry for scarce resources could give rise to social competition, which might in turn lead to the development of more formally organised, hierarchical communities.

It has been suggested that one of the signs that societies have moved beyond the simple group or band level of organisation is the appearance of cemeteries, which start to appear in the Late Mesolithic right across northern Europe, including the Baltic and Scandinavia. Cemeteries might also be taken to indicate sedentism, as they would make little sense in a highly mobile world. But for some reason they don't appear in Britain at this time.

There are three possible reasons for this. The most obvious is that communication across the ever-wetter North Sea basin was becoming more difficult, and after 7000 BC it effectively became impossible without a sea-going boat. It could also be argued that the British Mesolithic patterns of life were admirably suited to islands with a long and intricate coastline. Societies had to remain mobile in order to exploit the seasonally available marine and land-based sources of food properly. So why change? Indeed, in coastal areas of Scotland and Ireland this pattern of living was so successful that an essentially Mesolithic way of life continued pretty well unaltered until as late as

---

* I planted nine hundred hazel bushes in a 7.5-acre (three-hectare) plantation of native hardwoods in the winter of 1992–93, and in 1999 they yielded a minimum of ten kilos of nuts. I say a minimum because I didn't strip every bush, as I wanted to leave enough lying around to feed the wood mice. Mercifully our area is not (yet) plagued by the introduced grey squirrels that normally denude hazel bushes in Britain.

3000 BC.[35] A third explanation, which I suspect might turn out to be the true one, is that we haven't yet struck lucky. On the mainland of Europe, Mesolithic cemeteries tend to occur outside the areas of settlement, as indicated by scatters of flints on the ground surface. To date in Britain we've tended only to excavate the ground beneath flint scatters, because we know there will be something to reveal there. I think it will take an accident, or a chance find of some sort, to reveal the first hunter/gatherer cemetery.

A fine example of the developing insularity of Britain is provided by the flint implements of the time. The main series of British microliths becomes ever more reduced as time passes, and there are many types which are unique to Britain, and not commonly encountered on the mainland of Europe. As Christopher Smith remarks, 'The initiation of the technique of making geometric microliths on narrow blades may mark the last input, of people or ideas, to Britain from the Continent until the initiation of farming over three thousand years later.'[36]

But in Ireland during the Later Mesolithic we encounter a tradition of flint implements that goes against the trend of miniaturisation entirely. These large tools, known as 'Bann flakes', are characteristic of so-called Larnian industries in Ireland. There's no reason not to suppose that they were very efficient at what they were intended to do: they are made using a specialised technique of direct percussion with a hard stone hammer on a specially prepared core, and have trimmed-up indentations near the base, presumably to make mounting onto a shaft easier. But the fact remains that they fly in the face of what was happening to flint industries outside Ireland.

But why was this? The answer has to be: insularity. Ireland was separated from Britain for a sufficient length of time to allow differences to develop between the types of animals that lived on each island. Red deer, for example, had to be introduced to Ireland from England – and then of course there are those snakes that St Patrick is meant to have banished. We have seen that Ireland had to be colonised, or possibly recolonised, by boat; and as time passed the channel between Britain and Ireland grew progressively wider – in effect it developed from a strait into a sea. The Irish, as they have always done, set about solving the technological problems that confronted them in their own manner, and the result was the unique 'Bann flake'.

In the next chapter I shall briefly describe the processes whereby Britain physically became an island. But this is a book about people, not geomorphology, and I will leave the final words on what Britain's newly acquired insular status was to mean to the development of British society in general to someone else. They're by Christopher Smith, whose ideas have contributed much to this chapter on the Mesolithic, and to my mind they express a recurrent theme of British history and prehistory: 'It is characteristic of societies in large islands that have substantial populations isolated from other groups that they develop rather idiosyncratic responses to social, economic and techno-logical issues.'

That, surely, is the story of Britain and Ireland in a nutshell.

CHAPTER FIVE

DNA and the Adoption of Farming

LIKE MANY CHILDREN, I adored dinosaurs, and by the time I reached the grand old age of sixteen this fascination had evolved into a growing interest in marine biology. I don't know why this was, because it isn't an interest that has lasted – maybe it simply reflected the fact that I enjoyed fishing when we went to Ireland for our summer holidays. Anyhow, by great good fortune I discovered that a teacher at school was planning a trip for teams of two boys each to join the crew of a deep-sea trawler out of Grimsby, and take pot luck: some would go to the fishing grounds of north Norway and the White Sea, others would fetch up somewhere off north-east Iceland. I was assigned a berth in a ship heading for the latter.

I remember the day I arrived at the Fish Quay. It was cold, wet and windy. The sea looked rough and the crew *were* rough, although later I was to learn that theirs was the hardest life going, and you had to be tough just to survive. I also learned not to judge people by their appearance. The cook, an enormous Pole who had worked in the coalmines of his native country, and then as a lumberjack in Canada, had an abiding interest in Chopin, and could fry the best fresh plaice it was possible to eat.

It was April, and as soon as we left the protection of the harbour we hit the north-easterly spring gales of the North Sea. The trip lasted three weeks, and I have never been so cold and sick as I was for the four days it took to acquire my sea legs. The two weeks we spent in the Iceland fishing grounds were largely remarkable for the activities of two Icelandic World War II Catalina flying boats that tried to stop us fishing inside their self-declared twelve-mile limit. Whenever it was stormy, we painted out our identification numbers with fuel oil and went well inside all existing limits, while the Catalinas circled overhead like frustrated gannets.

At night the fishing grounds were a floating city of a thousand disembodied lights that stretched between the invisible horizons. There were hundreds of trawlers from all European nations, and massive Russian factory ships. Even the crew of our ship, some of whom stood to lose their jobs if the 'Cod War' went Iceland's way, admitted that it was absurd, and couldn't continue for long. On our way back I felt excited and hugely invigorated by my first experience of an undiluted adult world. Just outside the Humber Estuary we hit a storm, and perhaps because the sea is relatively shallow there, we had to contend with waves as high as the vessel's bridge. I didn't know it then, but

FIG 20   *Maps showing how the coastline altered as the island of Britain formed (at approximately 5900 BC). The earliest map shows the position at the*

had we been at that precise spot just before Star Carr and Thatcham, around say 8000 BC, we wouldn't have needed a ship. We'd have been on foot, standing on dry land, and perhaps looking anxiously towards the storm raging around the North Sea coast some ten miles to the north.

When I first learned about the relatively recent formation of the southern North Sea I was incredulous – partly, I suppose, because of my trawler experience. How on earth, I wondered, could something as huge, grey and brooding as the North Sea just swamp dry land and swallow it up forever? Even now my head accepts the fact, but something deep inside me retains irrational doubts. Today we have hard and fast proof of the relatively recent advance southwards of the North

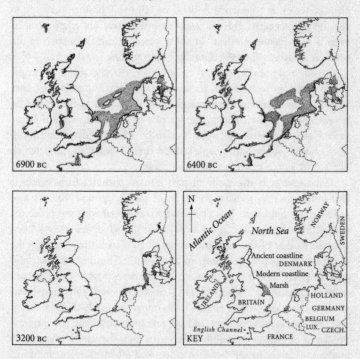

end of the Ice Age (9500 BC). The final map (3200 BC) is similar to the situation today, and shows the state of the coastline in the Neolithic period.

Sea, in the form of offshore borehole records and other scientific data.

A recent paper by a team assembled by Professor Ian Shennan of the Department of Geography at Durham University has collated all this information with some sophisticated computer wizardry, and produced a sequence of authoritative – I hesitate to say definitive – maps showing how and when the process of inundation happened.[1]

The root cause of the sea's triumph over land is ultimately the rise in sea level consequent upon postglacial warming, but there are many other factors that Ian, his team and their computers have had to contend with. For example, as the burden of ice was removed, the land beneath tended to rise, thereby counteracting some of the effects of increasing sea level. It was like taking one's finger off a cork in a glass of water: it (the land) bobbed up. But this bounce-back, or to use the correct term, this 'isostatic recovery', was not a universal or even a homogeneous effect: in some places it didn't happen at all, whereas in others the land actually began to sink.

So the relationship of land to sea level is by no means a simple picture, and as we will see, its consequences in human terms, too, were to prove far from predictable. This is because these important developments in the shrinking geography of the north-western European Plain coincided with what was to be a hugely significant long-term change in the way people gained their livelihoods, after which our world would never be the same again.

Archaeology is the study of past human societies from artefacts and other material remains found in or on the ground. But it's also rather more than that: it is profoundly concerned with the processes of cultural change. We must now confront what has always been considered one of the biggest changes in human history, namely the switch from food acquisition, in the form of hunting, fishing and gathering, to food production, in the form of arable farming and animal husbandry.[2] With hindsight – of course something fundamental to archaeology – this switch looks more dramatic than in fact it was. Its consequences were indeed revolutionary, but the original processes of change probably weren't. In fact, they were remarkably gradual. This confusion between cause and effect, plus an imperfect appreciation of the timescale involved, has led archaeologists in the past to view the period of the Mesolithic/Neolithic transition as somehow special, and even traumatic to people living at the time. Personally, I doubt this.

The *Meso*lithic hunter-gatherers belonged to the *Middle* Stone Age, and the farmers to the *Neo*lithic or *New* Stone Age. It is important not to lose sight, however, of the *lithic*, the '*Stone* Age' suffix of their labels. To my mind both were the same Stone Age people whose roots lay back in the Upper Palaeolithic, at sites like Paviland or Gough's Caves. The fact that they decided to adopt the techniques of farming did not make them culturally different – at least not at first. What it did do was allow them to populate the landscape far more densely, because farming is a vastly more efficient means of producing food calories than hunting or gathering.[3] It allows many more people to live in the landscape, and that in turn means that communities have to live alongside each other. So they must find ways of settling disputes, coping with individual and tribal rivalries, moving goods, animals and people, and dealing with the emergence of what later we would recognise as politics.

All of these social transformations took time: from the beginning to the end of the process, right across Britain, it took centuries – as long as two millennia before the farthest-flung areas acquired a fully Neolithic lifestyle. Despite what some earlier authors would have had us believe, the arrival of farming was not the 'Neolithic Revolution'.[4] It was certainly not comparable with the Industrial or Agricultural Revolutions of recent times, which happened rapidly and had immediate as well as long-term effects. It was a process of change, not a revolution.

Let's examine what was probably going on as the waters of the North Sea spread relentlessly south. To do this I must return to the decks of the trawler in the North Sea that opened this chapter. That trawler was built in 1954, and was powered by a marine-oil engine. It was noisy and smelly, but it was powerful, capable of hauling a large trawl through high seas. But until quite recently, trawlers that worked closer to the shore than my ship from Grimsby were not powered at all. One such vessel was the sailing trawler *Colinda*. In September 1931 she was fishing in nineteen to twenty fathoms of water about twenty-five miles off the Norfolk coast, between the submerged Leman and Ower sandbanks.[5] The 'cod-end' (the toe-like end of the trawl net in which the fish accumulate) floated to the surface, and the men on deck looked keenly out towards it. They could recognise a good catch – and good pay for all of them – by the way the cod-end breaks the surface. If it's full of fish it seems to burst up, then floats proud of the water. If it's a small catch it seems reluctant to float, as if ashamed of the poor payout it promises to deliver. In this case the omens looked bad, and the men went back to their stations crestfallen. It's never much fun gutting fish, but it's even worse if you know the payback is going to be lean.

The trawl was raised in the air on block and tackle, and with a sharp jerk on a line the Mate released the special cod-end knot and the fish hit the deck with a shimmering, silvery, splatter. To the surprise of everyone aboard, it wasn't such a very small catch after all. Soon the reason why the cod-end had failed to bob freely to the surface became apparent: in amongst the fish were large pieces of waterlogged peat, which is known in Holland as 'moorlog'. It wasn't unusual to drag this stuff to the surface, as there were layers of peat on the seabed all around the Dogger, Leman and Ower Banks. The men kicked the lumps into the scuppers, to be washed overboard when the decks were next hosed down. But as they worked on the fish one larger piece of moorlog fell open, and within it the fishermen spotted an unusual object. It was a barbed antler harpoon, and its smooth, wet, polished surfaces glistened in the early autumn sun.

The antler 'harpoon' found by the crew of the *Colinda* was very similar to dozens of spearheads unearthed by Grahame Clark at Star Carr. It was 8.7 inches (218 millimetres) long, and in mint condition.[6] One side had been deeply scored near the base, presumably to provide better grip for the lashing which secured it to the spear shaft. Had it been lost overboard during a prehistoric fishing expedition? The answer must be no. The moorlog in which it was found formed in freshwater conditions, and we know that the spearheads from Star Carr and elsewhere were most probably used to hunt land mammals, such as deer and wild horse. Recently the *Colinda*'s spearhead has been dated by radiocarbon, and it turns out to have been made, and presumably lost, around 11,500 years ago (9500 BC), somewhat earlier than Star Carr, in the closing years of the Ice Age. The *Colinda*'s spearhead is by no means unique: a number of dryland finds, mainly

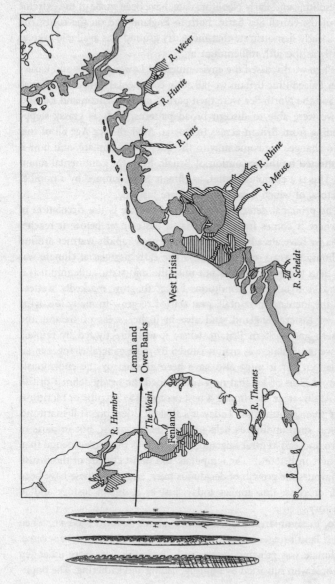

FIG 21   *Three views of a notched Upper Palaeolithic antler spearhead, radiocarbon dated to about 11,500 years ago (9500 BC), dredged from the seabed between the Leman and Ower Banks, twenty-five miles off the Norfolk coast. The map shows the extent of naturally marshy land around the coastline of the southern North Sea basin.*

of Mesolithic and Early Neolithic date, have been made at the extreme edge of the North Sea basin, both in England and on the continent. They clearly demonstrate that more dry ground was available even as recently as the fifth millennium BC.[7]

When we discussed the environment of Lower, Middle and Earlier Upper Palaeolithic Britain we talked in continental terms. The British Isles and the North Sea were then part of northern mainland Europe, and we were able to discern broad patterns, such as grassy steppe extending from Britain across to Russia. After the Ice Age all of that was to change. We come now to the question of climate, and how it was affected by the separation of Britain from the continental mainland. This is a complex matter, as climate is determined by a number of factors, of which local conditions are just one.

The principal determining factor of climate is the circulation of air: where it comes from, and what it passes over before it reaches us.[8] As we have already seen, the climate grew rapidly warmer around ten thousand years ago (8000 BC). The early postglacial climate was drier than today, and it was not until the mid-sixth millennium (i.e. around 5500 BC) that conditions began to grow markedly wetter.[9] With the increase in rainfall, peat started to grow in many low-lying parts of eastern England, and also in higher areas of Ireland and northern and western Britain, where it was directly fed by rainfall. This wetter climate was mainly caused by more general changes in air circulation, but it must also have been affected by the enormously increased areas of sea that now surrounded the newly defined British Isles. At this stage the climate is best described as Atlantic or maritime, rather than continental. Today it's slightly drier, but still maritime. The seas surrounding us help to keep the air moist, but in parts of eastern and east-central England the climate is more continental than elsewhere in Britain.[10] The temperate and moist climate of the British Isles favours the growth of deciduous trees, and when these have been felled, of grass; this applies today, just as it did in history and in prehistory.[11]

So, to summarise the situation at about 6000 to 6500 BC, when the last land bridges between Britain and the continent were severed: the climate was growing wetter, and the British Isles were inhabited by people who subsisted by hunting, fishing and gathering. The population was large enough to be genetically viable; in other words, there must have been intermarriage between different bands of people in order to prevent inbreeding. On the mainland of Europe the structure of Mesolithic societies was subtly changing: disparate bands of people were coming together to form larger tribal groupings, but in Britain this does not appear to have happened before the severance of the last land bridge. As a result, the earliest inhabitants of the new British Isles still had a more isolated and probably a more mobile style of life than their continental counterparts. This, then, was the situation at the time when farming started to be introduced to north-western Europe, in the fifth millennium BC.

There has been much debate about the introduction of farming to Britain. The dispute can be reduced to two simple propositions: was it brought here by people, or was it merely an idea – a concept – that somehow reached us from the continent? Let's examine the 'movement of people' hypothesis first, as this has been the conventional wisdom of the later twentieth century. We now have the molecular biological means to test the hypothesis directly. I refer to the work on human genetics carried out by Professor Bryan Sykes at Oxford, and by other teams around the world.[12]

As we have seen in Chapter 2, we are all descended from the first Crô-Magnon people who arose in Africa at some time around 150,000 years ago. This second African Genesis (following the original development of hominids some two and a half million years ago) explains our light, gracile build, which natural selection preferred because it was more efficient at losing heat in a hot climate. The African mother of the entire *Homo sapiens* tribe has been named Mitochondrial Eve by Bryan Sykes (for reasons that will shortly become clear), but her descendants didn't penetrate into Europe for a hundred thousand years, until about fifty thousand years ago. Whether we like it or not, the DNA residing in our cells shows that the world is indeed a global village; it follows that the barriers we choose to erect between ourselves are all ultimately irrelevant.

The first type of DNA successfully studied by geneticists interested in the history of mankind was found in the mitochondria of human cells. The mitochondria are small bodies that reside outside the cell nucleus, and are the means by which the cell burns biological fuel to produce energy. It's the mitochondria that give off heat when we use our muscles vigorously. Their DNA, which carries the encoded instructions on the way they are to function, is arranged in loops, and is very much smaller than the long strings of DNA found in the nucleus. It is also more stable than the DNA within the nucleus, and changes far less rapidly from one generation to another. In fact it changes at a more or less even rate of approximately one mutation every ten thousand years. Bryan Sykes worked with a short, recurrent length of DNA on the loop, known as the 'control region'. The actual location of any mutation on the control region is random.

The most important aspect of mitochondrial DNA, from the historical geneticist's point of view, is that it is passed down directly through the female line *alone*. So, I and my brother and two sisters share our mother's mitochondrial DNA. My daughter Amy, on the other hand, derives hers from her mother, and not from me. My mother's mitochondrial DNA has been transferred to my nephews and nieces by way of my two sisters, who have had two and four children. Already I have four great-nieces, so my mother's mitochondrial DNA is now to be found in our small but rapidly growing 'tribe' of fourteen individuals. Using this pattern of inheritance, Bryan Sykes and his team were able to discover that almost the entire indigenous population of Europe was derived from just seven women who lived between about forty-five and ten thousand years ago.[13] He named these 'clan mothers' 'the Seven Daughters of Eve', and gave them names whose first letter corresponded with the distinctive mutation that characterised their DNA. For our purposes I will confine my attention to two of these Daughters of Eve: first Ursula, then Jasmine.

Bryan Sykes's team believes that Ursula began her clan about forty-five thousand years ago in Greece, close to what was much later to become the Classical site of Delphi. Today about 11 per cent of all Europeans are the direct maternal descendants of Ursula. They are to be found all over Europe, but most particularly in western Britain and Scandinavia.

Chris Stringer, a leader of the original Natural History Museum team that excavated Gough's Cave in the Cheddar Gorge, Somerset (see Chapter 3), provided Bryan Sykes with two samples from bodies found there. These were dated by radiocarbon to thirteen thousand

and nine thousand years old (11,000 and 7000 BC). DNA extracted from a tooth showed the Cheddar Man was a direct descendant of the clan mother, Ursula. This was a discovery that was to have profoundly important implications for archaeology.

According to the conventional wisdom of later-twentieth-century archaeology, the bones from Gough's Cave should have been genetically different from the modern population, because it was believed that the farmers of the Neolithic period represented an 'invasion' or mass folk-migration into Britain from the continent shortly after 5000 BC. Using a sophisticated argument founded on population statistics and a theoretical model of how soil rapidly became exhausted, archaeologists in the 1960s and 1970s proposed a population 'wave of advance', which took farming across Europe from its origins in the so-called 'fertile crescent' of modern Iraq and Syria. One arm of this advance entered Europe via the Balkans around 6500 BC, then spread into the Danube valley and the fertile loess plains of central Europe.[14] Loess, incidentally, is a light, wind-borne soil that is very easy indeed to cultivate, and was consequently preferred by the earliest arable farmers. A second series of routes leapfrogged along the northern Mediterranean before heading north up the Rhône Valley and across to Britain, either via south-western France[15] or though the Straits of Gibraltar and along the coast of Spain and Portugal.

These 'waves of advance' simply pushed the native hunter-gatherer, Mesolithic populations out of the way – to the hills and fringes, where presumably they eked out a miserable existence for a few generations before they succumbed to cumulative malnutrition or migrated somewhere else – we know not where. I gained the distinct impression that nobody cared much about what had happened to them. They were yesterday's people.

As a consequence, it was argued, the modern population of Europe was descended from the 'wave of advance', and these people were quite distinct from the Mesolithic folk they replaced, who were derived from the indigenous Palaeolithic communities. In an important book, which upset many linguists when it was published, Professor Colin Renfrew of Cambridge University argued further that the Neolithic 'wave of advance' also introduced a new family of languages, known as the Indo-European group, to Europe.[16] If the two theories were correct, the years of the fifth and sixth millennia BC in Europe must have been a time of extraordinary upheaval and turmoil – something far closer to the earlier idea of a Neolithic Revolution. But there were problems.

The first, like many grassroots movements, is hard to define, but many field archaeologists working in Britain found these ideas difficult to accept. We deeply mistrusted talk of prehistoric 'invasions'. Some of us had been taught at university that the Celts had 'invaded' Britain at various times in the Iron Age, each hypothetical invasion bringing with it a new style of pottery that was believed to show strong new continental influences. The trouble was, our digs showed that these so-called invaders lived in the same villages, and sometimes in the same buildings, as the people they were meant to have replaced. Then Professor Roy Hodson of the Institute of Archaeology in London published two papers, in 1962 and 1964, which effectively demolished the various Iron Age invasions.[17] More recently, Simon James has cogently argued that the Celts themselves probably never existed as a distinct cultural entity.[18] Not surprisingly, this has not proved particularly popular in Irish academic circles.

Mindful of the non-incoming Celts and the fiasco of the multiple Iron Age invasions, many of us found it hard to accept the idea of an earlier 'invasion', albeit one dressed up in academically acceptable 'wave of advance' terminology. In the course of thirty years I have excavated at dozens of different places, and nowhere have I seen signs that the Neolithic farmers were intruders of any sort. For a start, they lived in precisely the same places as their supposedly unrelated Mesolithic forebears: in the cases with which I am familiar, they were usually around a metre above sea level and on the sides of low-lying and sandy dryland 'islands' in the marsh. In the earliest Neolithic they seemed to have led a very mobile way of life, just like Mesolithic communities elsewhere in Britain. They also showed an extraordinarily close adaptation to their 'new' watery environment for people who were meant to have arrived hotfoot from the loess plains of Europe.

There were many other things that made me doubtful about the 'wave of advance' as it applied to Britain; but like most of my colleagues I held my peace, not wishing to be blown out of the water by the academic big guns who rumbled ominously in the distance. That didn't stop me, or many of my friends, from publishing our thoughts – we just didn't invite confrontation; besides, I suspect that many of the down-to-earth excavation and survey reports in which we voiced these heresies were not the staple reading of the big-gunners.[19]

Today it is becoming increasingly clear from a growing body of literature that what one might call 'genetic archaeology' is becoming a sub-field in its own right. It's far from simple – and the complexities are not confined to the organic chemistry. One of the problems its practitioners will have to confront is the linking of genetic maps to archaeological distribution maps, always a process that lends itself to misinterpretation. We saw it with the spread of radiocarbon dates that were linked to the Neolithic 'wave of advance' – and thence mistakenly to the spread of actual people – and I suspect we'll see something similar in this newly emerging field soon. The trouble is, the most misleading papers always look the most convincing at first glance.[20]

One of the reasons I decided to write this and other books for the general reader was that I had acquired personal experience of farming.[21] I had lived through my own Neolithic Revolution. As a sheep farmer of almost twenty years' experience, I am struck again and again by the fact that livestock farming and the husbandry of the herds preyed on by a hunter are two sides of the same coin. I cannot see that there's a big difference between the two. A difference, yes – but not a huge one. This was first brought home to me when I learned how to handle a sheepdog.

My dog is a Border collie bitch named Jess – a short, sharp name, like 'Cap' or 'Dan', that was intended to be shouted across fields and fells. The instructor explained that dogs are descended from domesticated wolves, and that wolves often take their live prey back to the communal lair where it is killed by the top wolf, who takes a few bites of meat before offering some to his current bitch; it is then 'thrown to the wolves' in the time-honoured fashion. Jess was rounding the sheep up for me, the top dog, to kill and eat. It followed that it was essential that she should continue to regard me as the top dog. If ever I fell off that pedestal, she would cease to work for me – or worse, she might even take against me, which could prove scary.

So, what was the domesticated dog found at Star Carr used for? It was smaller than a wolf, and would hardly constitute a direct threat on its own to, say, a stag; but it could well have been used like a sheepdog to drive a flock or herd of animals towards concealed hunters. The flocking instinct often becomes more pronounced when there are younger animals in the flock, and this can be a good time to 'dog' the animals, or put the fear of dog into them. Once 'dogging' has been completed they never forget what they have learned, and immediately form a tight clump when a dog, or dogs, approaches them, making them very much easier to handle. I don't know whether dogs were used in this way in the past, but given what we know about the reduced territories of Mesolithic hunters, it wouldn't surprise me if they, in effect, slightly domesticated their prey in this manner.

Bryan Sykes and his team were probably unaware that many of us archaeologists working in Britain were already unhappy with the idea of large-scale Neolithic migrations from across the Channel, so he may have been surprised that the announcement of his results only stirred up trouble amongst the academic big guns. Far from a hostile reaction, the news of what he had revealed at Gough's Cave caused general rejoicing in the profession as a whole, and not a few mutterings of 'I've been trying to tell them that for ten years now, but nobody bothers to listen . . .'

I make no apologies for having departed from Ursula's story for so long, because the issues raised have a direct bearing on what the discovery of her clan's bloodline was so clearly to demonstrate. After Bryan Sykes and his team completed their analysis of the tooth from Gough's Cave, they decided to turn their attention to living people in the area. They examined mitochondrial DNA obtained from staff and pupils of a local school, and discovered that one teacher, Adrian Targett, provided a very close match for the ancient bones. As if to ram the lesson home, Bryan Sykes has subsequently revealed that two of the teenagers in the teacher's class produced results that were actually identical to the Gough's Cave samples. So all were descendants of Ursula. Very sensibly, Sykes did not reveal their names to the pack of media newshounds who were in full cry when the story broke. I can remember hearing the results in 1999, and let out a howl of pleasure. It really was wonderful to have such conclusive proof that we are the same people we have always been.

We now turn to the second of Sykes's 'clan-mothers', Jasmine, who stands at the head of the youngest of the seven clans. Her origins lie, as some readers might already have guessed, near the river Euphrates in modern Syria, some ten thousand years ago, at the end of the Ice Age. This is the region – 'the Fertile Crescent' – where cereals were first domesticated, and from where they began their long journey into southern Europe and thence the rest of the continent. Jasmine's clan members include just under 17 per cent of native Europeans. They are not spread evenly across Europe, with concentrations in one or two places, as are the other six Daughters of Eve. Her descendants still live along paths that we have already outlined: one leads along the northern Mediterranean, via Spain and Portugal, to the west of Britain; another runs north-west right across the centre of Europe.

This is not to resurrect the 'wave of advance' theory, but is a recognition of the general picture that farming spread from southern Europe, which has never been in any doubt. There are simply too many well-dated early farming sites on the continent that show a clear trend, with the earliest nearest the Balkans and the latest towards the Atlantic. So what was it that spread, if not people? Essentially it was an idea, accompanied, not always at precisely the same time, by new species of animals (pigs, cattle, sheep and goats), and of course plant seeds (wheat and barley). There were other things too, but I shall return to them later.

There are numerous examples from history, and in modern times, of an idea spreading far and wide. But there are conditions that must be met for this to happen successfully: first, the idea must work; then people must want it, and be able to use it without too much social adjustment. A good example is the adoption of the horse by the natives of North America. The horse was introduced by Europeans in the sixteenth and seventeenth centuries, and is not an indigenous animal in the Americas. But it suited their mobile way of life, and was ideal for the open countryside of the Great Plains and prairies. So it was eagerly adopted, and riding spread like wildfire – to the great benefit of the native people, the Wild West and Hollywood.

The origins of farming in Britain were probably a matter of quite gradual change that involved a minimum of actual folk movement. There must however have been a small element of migration, otherwise it's hard to account for the existing representatives of Jasmine's clan;

but essentially it was an idea, a concept, that spread, accompanied by a few breeding animals and seeds. When I first read his elegantly written book, I accepted Colin Renfrew's hypothesis that the Indo-European languages spread across Europe at about the same time as the ideas associated with farming. But now I'm far less convinced. As most Englishmen will tell you, it's difficult and disruptive to learn a foreign language, unless you have a very good reason to do so – and I can't see why the keeping of a few sheep or pigs would necessitate the changing of the way one spoke. I also can't see any evidence for *bona fide* mass migrations after the Neolithic. And Bryan Sykes's data firmly supports that. So the root tongue of what were later to develop into the languages of the Indo-European group must have spread a very long time ago indeed. But these are deep waters, and I am no linguist.

Perhaps I should add here that study of the bones of Neolithic domesticated cattle found in Britain shows that they were introduced from outside. The heavy-boned native wild cattle, or aurochs, was simply too fierce, and does not appear to have contributed to the bloodline of our own farmed breeds. Sheep and goats, whose bones are very hard to tell apart, were introduced species too. So far as we know, the dog was the only domesticated animal to be found in Britain before the arrival of the idea of farming.

One of the reasons why the introduction of farming, and the transition from the mobility of the Mesolithic hunter-gatherer to the more sedentary lifestyle of the Neolithic period, seems so revolutionary is that the two periods are actually separated by about half a millennium of apparent emptiness. There is remarkably little archaeological evidence to account for the second half of the fifth millennium BC (i.e. from about 4500 to 4000 BC). The trouble is that this emptiness is probably nothing of the sort. It's just another of those periods of low archaeological visibility which happen from time to time in various regions. Another example, which also happens to coincide with a transitional period, is that between the Late Bronze Age and the Early Iron Age, in the seventh and eighth centuries BC. But more on that later.

Periods of low archaeological visibility can be accounted for in a number of ways. They may represent years when people adopted a more mobile pattern of life which did not involve the construction of significant home-bases. Imagine, for instance, that somewhere like Morton had been occupied just once. Instead of a huge mound of shells, there would have been perhaps a bucketful, and a few broken flint blades on the main camp site. The great accumulations of material at places like Boxgrove, Star Carr, Morton and Thatcham are the results of repeated visits, possibly extending over centuries. If one tries to narrow the focus to a much shorter time, it is often difficult to find much by way of hard evidence. This is particularly true if, for example, the people one is trying to study have subtly altered their way of life, perhaps introducing a larger proportion of milk and cheese into their diet instead of meat. This would give rise to fewer meat bones in the archaeological record. Less reliance on hunting would lead to the loss of fewer arrowheads, and the manufacture of fewer flint microliths. A change in lifestyle might also lead to new patterns of movement, in which the old haunts were replaced by fewer camps as the community moved about their territory on less traditional routes, driving their flocks and herds to new pastures that they now controlled.

The point I want to emphasise is that the lack of archaeological visibility does not necessarily indicate a lack of people – just a lack of debris in quantities that are archaeologically apparent. The seeming void in the later fifth millennium BC is made to appear even more stark by what happened in the centuries around 4000 BC, when suddenly there is archaeological evidence everywhere. What's more, this later stuff includes items that are entirely new, such as pottery – that maker and breaker of archaeological reputations. No wonder archaeologists prior to about 1970 were happy to accept both that the arrival of farming heralded a real Neolithic 'revolution', and that it was the work of migrants from overseas.

We have seen that although the 'wave of advance' is now largely set to one side, farming did indeed spread across Europe, both overland and via Spain, Portugal and the Atlantic approaches. But what happened when the concept of farming reached the edges of the continent, in places like Britain, Ireland and Scandinavia? The answer seems to be that in these areas the 'classic' model of mixed livestock and cereal agriculture didn't apply, as it seems to have done over large parts of central Europe and most particularly over those areas possessing light, easily tilled loess soils. Instead we find that people at the maritime fringes of Europe were already well adapted to their often rather peculiar or demanding environments. Their societies were stable, and they combined fishing, shell-fishing, gathering and hunting. They were mobile, but within quite closely confined territories. Put another way, they could see no good reason radically to change their way of life, which is why people like those of the Larnian and Obanian cultures of Ireland and Scotland adapted their essentially Mesolithic lifestyle *very* gradually.[22] They acquired Neolithic objects, such as polished stone tools and pottery, but the extent to which they adopted a fully Neolithic lifestyle is still open to debate. I can't really see that their archaeological status matters much: the fact is that they lived and prospered.

It's not always easy to prove absence in archaeology, which is perhaps why it is hard to show conclusively that animal husbandry played the major part in the earliest farming in Britain.[23] As we will see shortly, this also seems to have been the case in Scandinavia – another part of the northern 'fringe' lands of Europe. Certainly the moist maritime climate of the British Isles would have been far better suited to the growing of grass than to the cultivation of cereal plants that had relatively recently been growing on the well-drained hillsides of Syria. Even today, wheat and barley can be defeated by a wet growing season. In the winter of 2000–2001, for example, almost a quarter of the local wheats near where I live failed due to waterlogging.

I've already noted that I can see no vast obstacle that separates the husbanding of wild from domestic animals.[24] But there is also no escaping the fact that the first domesticated animals farmed in Britain and neighbouring parts of the continental mainland *had* to have been introduced from outside. This view of the distinction between the wild and the domestic finds support from an authority on ancient animal husbandry who was an active member of the prestigious British Academy Major Research Project into the Ancient History of Agriculture, which was influential in shaping modern views on the subject – if only in some cases by inspiring vigorous and vehement opposition. One of the contributors to the project, Mike Jarman (who has since had the sense to get out of archaeology and set up a superb restaurant in the picturesque fenland city of Ely), realised that the sharp distinction between hunter and livestock farmer was both false and greatly oversimplified. He was able to define four transitional stages between the two extremes of massive intervention and no intervention at all, which he labelled 'factory farming' and 'random predation' respectively. In between we have 'controlled predation', where the prey was only controlled at certain times of year – during drives, for example; 'herd following', which as its name suggests, involves a human group living alongside a herd of, for example, reindeer; this can develop into 'loose herding', in which more close control is exercised at certain times of year, for example to divide the herds that have grown with the new season's crop of young animals into fresh herds for different groups of people. Finally we have 'close herding', which is the system that most British farmers operate, myself included.[25]

It seems to me that in the final millennia of the Ice Age, and in the Mesolithic period, people were doubtless practising some random predation, but also controlled predation and herd following. During the fifth millennium BC, I suggest we see a gradual switch to loose herding, followed by close herding towards the Later Neolithic and Early Bronze Age. Both would have been made a great deal simpler by the use of herding dogs. The final step to close herding could have been hastened by the introduction of new species, such as sheep and goats, which would certainly have benefited from closer herding. Unlike modern animals, which have to be shorn, primitive sheep don't retain their fleeces, but naturally shed them in the early summer. This means that in June they have to be caught up in order to 'roo' or pluck the old fleece; alternatively they can be penned in a small paddock and the wool collected from bushes, hurdles and fences which the sheep rub against – they seem to find the old fleece a bit ticklish when it's ready to shed. It's also worth noting that sheep can be milked, and that their milk makes excellent yoghurt and cheese. This is an additional incentive towards closer herding.

It's important to emphasise that Mike Jarman's four transitional stages are not hard and fast: they are merely states in a process of continuous change. Although the general trend is undoubtedly in one direction, it's quite possible, especially after a series of bad years, that evolution could have gone in reverse. There are always two sides in farming: the farmers and the farmed. So far I have focused on the latter. However, as the stages of animal domestication became more and more controlled, so the people exercising this control became increasingly sedentary, and with sedentism came a number of important material developments, such as the introduction of pottery and the construction of larger, permanent houses. It also became feasible to store and guard food over the leaner months of winter. Archaeologically, a more settled way of life brings with it (at last!) *visibility*: houses leave evidence for their construction in the ground; pottery survives very well in the soil; old storage pits soon fill with debris from the kitchen floor, and so forth.

But archaeological visibility didn't happen immediately. As one would expect, like the introduction of farming, which it reflected and was a part of, it came into focus gradually. We see this too on the mainland of Europe, in those other 'fringe' areas, where adoption of the new way of life was also a gradual process. In Denmark, for instance, the earliest Neolithic way of life was well adapted to a closely forested landscape, and included the gathering of shellfish, fishing and hunting, but with the addition of so-called slash and burn agriculture and animal husbandry.[26] Slash and burn is a system where clearings are made, and then expanded, but the original plot is abandoned after a few seasons, when the rich forest-bed soil loses its natural plant nutrition. The forest will then spring up again, to form what is known as secondary woodland. Eventually this will revert to forest, providing people don't interfere with the process yet again.

In other regions, such as the tangled maze of small islands, open water and marsh around the flooded lands of the Rhine/Meuse delta, directly across the North Sea from the low-lying coast of East Anglia, Dutch archaeologists have revealed a very complex picture, which is a long way removed from the simple 'wave of advance' juggernaut. Instead we find evidence for some people who are 'fully hunters' – in Mike Jarman's terminology I'd guess this refers to 'random predation', or more probably 'controlled predation' – but the majority, between 50 and 90 per cent, are 'semi-agrarian'.[27] The rest, presumably, are 'fully agrarian'. What we see in this instance is people adapting their lifestyles to a hugely complicated landscape. It's perfectly possible that these different ways of life did not necessarily represent separate communities. I suspect that living in such an unstable environment, people learned quite rapidly that if they did not adapt, they would perish.

Further north, in southern Scandinavia, a particularly successful culture of hunter-gatherers, who lived around the coast and were also heavily reliant on shellfish (oysters!) and fishing, managed to retain their way of life for a full millennium after their neighbours to the south had adopted farming.[28] During this time there is clear evidence that they became increasingly more sedentary and the sizes of their communal territories grew smaller. At the same time they adopted pottery and their flint implements became increasingly sophisticated. This does not seem to have been a static or stagnant culture by any means. So why, eventually, did it change? I don't think it's necessarily always helpful to look for simple or complex *causes*. In fact, I'd go so far as to say that archaeologists can be obsessed with the need to find causes for everything. The important fact is that it happened. In part it may have been a result of a natural decline in the numbers of oysters, but this didn't apply to the entire region. We know there was communication between the two 'cultures', otherwise the idea of pottery would not have found its way north. My own feeling is that as time progressed the people on the coast simply wanted to adopt the new way of life. And why not? Their social system was certainly well up to it. And it did offer a less unpredictable and more stable way of life, with a minimum of disruption. They were sensible people, and they made a sensible decision, but in their own time.

I've spent my professional life working with sites and finds that date to the period after the arrival of farming in Britain, and I do not believe that this process of introduction was ever simple. To read some of the earlier accounts, one gets the impression that large numbers of people arrived in skin boats, bringing with them the complete DIY kit for setting up a self-sufficient smallholding. They got off the boats, maybe shot a few natives with their new style of arrowheads, and built themselves substantial houses in which they then lived the Good Life. The older textbooks stress the newness and complexity of the kit they brought with them. It included pottery, and with it ground or polished stone tools, as well as houses and burial mounds and new varieties of plants and animals. The arrival of the Neolithic really did seem revolutionary.

We have subsequently realised, largely through radiocarbon dating, that the process was in fact very much more prolonged. We have also realised that people adopted different aspects of the new 'culture' at different times and at widely varying paces. They were quite quick, for example, to take over the new implements and pottery containers. This is something that we also see in the next, Bronze, Age, when metal tools were adopted with remarkable rapidity.[29] Bronze axes were extensively used in the construction of the 'Seahenge' timber circle in 2049 BC, just a century or two after the introduction of bronze to Britain.[30] So people weren't slow in grasping the new technology of metal. In the Neolithic we find evidence for pottery and ground stone tools in the archaeological record quite quickly, around 4000 BC. But people seem to have been very much slower in moving over to a fully agricultural (in this instance I include stock raising) way of life, not completing the process in some instances until into the Bronze Age.[31]

I want now to move from the general towards the particular, by way of a man who worked in the Somerset peat industry. I don't suppose Raymond Sweet ever imagined that his name would become internationally famous in archaeological circles. But he made a most astonishing discovery – and he reported it immediately, which is perhaps even more important.

The low-lying marshy lands around Glastonbury are known as the Somerset Levels, and in 1964 John Coles of Cambridge University established the Somerset Levels Project, whose main aims were to examine archaeological discoveries made in the commercial peat-cutting industry, and to place them in their ancient environmental contexts. From the start it was a multidisciplinary project, involving archaeologists, biologists and geologists.[32]

Before the war the Somerset peat-cutting industry had been comparatively small-scale, but the post-war boom in gardening had led to a hugely increased demand, and most of the work was now done mechanically. Mercifully for the archaeological remains, the huge machines are driven by human beings. And human beings have eyes, intelligence and a conscience. Raymond Sweet possessed all three. He worked for the Eclipse Peat Works, near Shapwick, and he had a good record for making important finds. In early spring 1970 he sent John Coles a parcel containing his latest discovery. I'll let John's own words describe the moment:

> The parcel contained a piece of ash plank, clearly split from a large tree; with it was a note that it had been found in a deep ditch on Shapwick Heath. I hastened to the Levels to meet the finder, Raymond Sweet, and a small exploration soon revealed more of the same wood together with pegs still driven into the lower peats, and axed debris. A fine leaf-shaped [flint] arrowhead had already been found by Sweet nearby, as well as a hoard of flint flakes only 100 metres away, lying about 1 metre above the blue-grey clay at the base of the peat. It all looked Neolithic. In the summer of 1970 teams of students arrived and . . . we excavated a small part of the new structure, soon to be called the 'Sweet Track'.[33]

Over the years the Somerset Levels Project revealed numerous prehistoric trackways and platforms amidst the pools, peats and small dry islands of the Levels. The work was masterminded by John and Bryony Coles, neither of whom was averse to getting their hands and knees as wet as their students' (John's from Cambridge, Bryony's from Exeter). Anyone who has dug on a waterlogged site soon learns to cope with cramp pains in knees, thighs, back and neck. It's because you can't spread your bodyweight as on dryland. You can't even place an elbow on the ground. Everywhere is soft, so you have to work from planks or kneelers, and they soon become excruciatingly uncomfortable. The craving to stand up and stretch becomes almost too much to bear. The wood is sometimes softer than the peat surrounding it, so you can't always use the standard tool of archaeology, a small bricklayer's pointing trowel. In Somerset they use lollipop sticks; in the fens, where the ground can be more clayey, we use plastic garden labels, or quite often our bare fingers.

The Sweet Track was essentially a narrow footpath made from split planks raised and supported on timbers driven into the peat. The construction is remarkably sophisticated. A long straight pole, or rail, was laid on the peat surface and pegged firmly into place by pairs or groups of long pegs which were driven into the peat at an angle, in such a way that pegs on either side of the pole formed a cross, and in effect a V-shaped crutch above it. The plank of the walkway was then lodged in the crutch about sixteen inches (four hundred milli-metres) above the rail. It was an ingenious way of raising the walkway, but it meant that it had to be narrow. Two people could just pass each other, provided they were good friends.

The Project spent fifteen years working on the Sweet Track, and has been able to build up a remarkably vivid picture of the Levels in Early Neolithic times. The track ran for some 1800 metres from the drier ground of Shapwick Burtle in the south to the natural dry island of Westhay in the north. The bog it crossed was very wet, and the peat grew rapidly there: an object dropped beside the trackway would be covered by vegetation, and then by peat in two or three years. The dryland around the bogs was thickly wooded with deciduous trees such as oak and ash, whereas the wet areas were far more open. There's also evidence for arable farming on the drier, sandier ground of Edington Burtle, not far away.

Arrows, or rather arrowheads, have featured quite regularly in our story so far, but now I want to say a few words about the bows that propelled them. Recently a group of schoolchildren on a visit to our archaeological park at Flag Fen made themselves bows and arrows – as children do. They took some trouble over the arrowheads, but the bows were just bent sticks and string. If they didn't snap, you could perhaps shoot an arrow five paces, and if it landed right it might kill an ant. When I told them about the Neolithic yew bows found in the Somerset Levels, their eyes grew round as they learned about the lethal and highly efficient killing machines of 3500 BC. The yew bow from Meare Heath in the Levels could shoot an arrow over a hundred metres.[34] It was the same length (1.90 metres) as the classic medieval English longbow which wrought such havoc on the mounted French knights at the Battle of Agincourt in 1415.[35] The distinguished actor and specialist in medieval archery Robert Hardy has worked out that arrows released from a longbow had an initial velocity of fifty-seven yards (fifty-one metres) per second and carried 140 joules of kinetic energy, which was quite enough to pierce plate and chain armour.[36] In certain respects the Neolithic bow was less technically advanced than the medieval longbow, but its firepower would certainly have been comparable. It was also beautifully reinforced and decorated with elaborate criss-cross leather bindings.[37] These were weapons to fear and be proud of.[38]

At first glance it would appear that the people who used the Sweet Track were either very careless or had the bad luck to meet unpleasant people on their journey, because some very interesting things have been found beside the trackway. They include a complete ceramic pot with a wooden spurtle (a type of porridge-stirrer), six flint arrowheads (one still tied to its hazel shaft with fine twine made from nettle fibre), and a number of flint flakes whose microwear traces show they were used to cut wood and reeds. These flakes were good examples of a light, portable, general-purpose Neolithic toolkit. A partially-used prepared flint core was also found, which would suggest that flakes were removed as and when they were needed. There were other finds too, such as a complete polished flint axe, produced by 'factories' near some known flint mines in Sussex.

Then in 1973 came the star find. The volunteer excavator at first thought she'd come across a large shell, protruding from under a piece of split oak. The peat was cleaned back further, the wood lifted, and there, for everyone to see, was a beautiful polished axe made from a stone that resembled jade. There was no handle, which would have been preserved in the wet ground had it been there in the first place. The axehead was in mint condition, and had not been used. Subsequently, experts at the British Museum identified the stone as jadeite, and its source as the foothills of the Alps. There were many other remarkable finds along the track – a pot full of hazelnuts, to mention just one – but that jadeite axe was undoubtedly the main attraction. Its discovery caused an immense stir.

Were the Neolithic inhabitants of Somerset unusually careless, or were these finds near the Sweet Track deliberate offerings of some sort? I think there can be no doubt that most of them were indeed offerings. The very fact that the jadeite axe was in perfect condition and not hafted is peculiar. John Coles has pointed out, on the basis of New Zealand Maori axe-polishing techniques, that the manufacture of the Sweet jadeite axe could have taken a hundred hours.[39] So this was a very special item indeed. The finds from along the Sweet Track seem to mark the beginning of a long tradition of making offerings at trackways across watery landscapes. Very often, as at Sweet, these were of objects that must have been extremely scarce and valuable; very often, too, the trackway would lead to a smaller island just off the mainland. I'll discuss what these offerings could have symbolised in Chapter 10, but here I want briefly to consider the contexts of their origins.

We do not yet know of any British Mesolithic sites where objects were dropped into water or a bog as offerings, although such practices are known in Denmark and Sweden. Having said that, I'm not sure how we'd recognise them if we found them, because arrows and spears do sometimes turn up complete. But a quiver of arrows might give us a clue. As we've seen, it appears that Star Carr could have been a religious site, complete with a wooden platform and antler head-dresses, and its location on the edge of a lake must surely tell us something about the attitude to water of those who used it (a paddle was found in the original excavations). There are Later Mesolithic boat burials in Scandinavia, where the tradition of associating death with the sea continued well into the Bronze Age, and of course later.[40]

Fishermen depend on, and live in fear of, the elements – and if the crew of my Grimsby trawler were anything to go by, they can be extremely superstitious: good and bad luck features prominently in many of their decisions, such as when and when not to sail. To my mind the practice of making offerings to the waters has origins that probably extend back into Mesolithic times. We know of many examples from the Neolithic, Bronze and Iron Ages, and also in Viking times in Scandinavia. And we shouldn't forget the sword Excalibur and the Lady of the Lake. As we will see later, these rites survived because they were deeply embedded within the structure of society. What they symbolised mattered profoundly to people. These are no mere superstitions – the casual tossing of coins into a fountain. That's why they survived for millennia after millennia.

If we take the archaeology of the Sweet Track at face value, there's very little that's Neolithic about it. There are arrowheads and axes, but both of these were common in Mesolithic times. There are dense woodlands, and only small evidence for farming or horticulture. Certainly the quaking peats and thick deciduous woodland would not have been helpful to farmers trying to operate a close herding system. True, the jadeite axe implies social connections over long distances, but as we've seen, there was nothing unusual about this as long ago as the Early Upper Palaeolithic. It would be helpful if we could obtain an accurate date. At this point dendrochronology comes to our rescue.

Dendrochronology, or tree-ring dating, works on the simple principle that trees lay down growth-rings of different widths in good and bad growing seasons: wide in good, narrow in bad.[41] Dendrochronologists have revealed a British 'master curve' sequence of good and bad years back to before 5000 BC; provided a sample is sufficiently long-lived (usually more than fifty years old at felling) it's possible, with the help of a computer, to match its sequence to the relevant parts of the master curve. This gives us a date – providing, that is, the bark is intact. If the bark is missing we have to guess a bit, but even a guessed dendro date is more precise than a radiocarbon date. If the bark is intact, close examination of the last growth-ring will show the actual season when the tree was felled.

John Coles sent wood from the Sweet Track to the dendrochronological laboratory at Sheffield University, and after a prolonged technical struggle they came up with a precise date: the timbers had been felled during the winter of 3807–3806 BC.[42] Laying aside the extraordinary precision of such a date (something that, after many years' involvement with tree-ring studies, I still can't get used to), it showed that the Sweet Track was the oldest-known timber trackway in the world, and that it was built at the very start of the Neolithic period. This would explain why some of the objects – polished stone axes and pottery – were of Neolithic type, but the way of life was still much as before. No sign of a Neolithic Revolution here.

CHAPTER SIX

The Earlier Neolithic
(4200–3000 BC)

Part 1: The Daily Round

FOR MY MONEY the Neolithic is the most exciting period of British prehistory. Laying aside the question of agricultural origins, it's the time when we first encounter the great field monuments, such as barrows and henges, that are all around us even to this day. So much happened in such a relatively short time that this chapter would become hopelessly prolonged if I attempted to cover everything in strict chronological order. Such a treatment would also break up any coherent themes that might begin to emerge. So my intention now is to examine the nature of Earlier Neolithic societies in Britain, and to look more closely at how they lived. In the next chapter, which is also devoted to the Earlier Neolithic (4200–3000 BC), I want to move beyond the domestic realm, towards what Mark Edmonds has called 'the ancestral geographies of the Neolithic'.[1]

Like most archaeologists, I was taught at university to view the Neolithic as an earlier version of the subsequent Bronze and Iron Ages. It was earlier, but essentially the same. We learned that for the last four thousand years of British prehistory society was organised in broadly the same way, except that in Neolithic times people didn't have the use of metal tools. However, as if to compensate for this perceived deficiency, they were seen as efficient farmers who used their wealth to construct a range of ceremonial monuments, some of which were enormous. The style of farming they were thought to practise came pretty well intact from the Near East. It's known as mixed farming, because it balances the cultivation of arable crops with the keeping of livestock. They even managed to build a few fortified sites, with dry-stone walls, deep ditches and steep banks that resemble the much later hill-forts of the Iron Age. It was for these reasons that Neolithic people were considered to be altogether different from their hunter-gatherer forebears.

According to this view, the big split happened with the arrival of large numbers of farmers around and just before 4000 BC. Now, of course, we know that farmers didn't arrive in huge numbers, and that different aspects of farming – maybe stock raising first, cereals later – were taken up piecemeal, region by region, when and if it seemed appropriate to do so. Where does that leave the theories about the nature of Early Neolithic society? Is there any good evidence that it was so radically different from what had gone before, in Mesolithic times? On the whole, I think not.

I mentioned earlier that many field archaeologists weren't at all convinced of the large-scale folk-movements that were meant to accompany the spread of farming to Britain. Many theoretical archaeologists had their reservations too. One of these is Julian Thomas, whose book *Rethinking the Neolithic* (1991) had a profound influence on the way we thought about the period.[2] Julian has reversed our view of the Neolithic by stripping it back to essentials, and regards it rather as Clive Gamble sees the Palaeolithic, from a minimalist perspective. For him the Neolithic was a period that arose directly out of the hunting societies of the Mesolithic; he has tried not to impose a set of explanatory ideas rooted in later times. This deconstructive way of working stems from Julian's philosophical approach to archaeology, which is avowedly post-modern. If that sounds difficult, I can only say that it is; but it's also based on good old-fashioned observation. Perhaps I should make it clear that I don't agree 100 per cent with Julian's minimalist view of the Neolithic, but I also believe that it would be a great mistake to throw his theoretical baby out with some observational bathwater. A couple of examples will show what I mean.

Seamus Caulfield is one of Ireland's most distinguished archaeologists, and like many people on that island his roots are rural. He comes from a farming family in County Mayo, and he well understands animal husbandry. In the early 1970s he made an extraordinary discovery that was to change his life. He noticed that deeply buried below layers of peat in his home county were fields, which were enclosed,

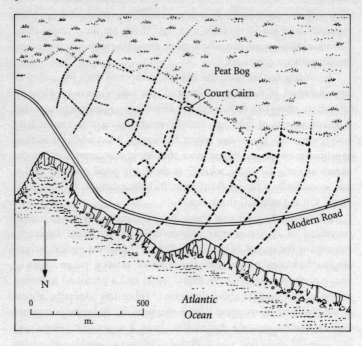

FIG 22   *Plan of Neolithic fields from County Mayo, Ireland (about 3500 BC).*
The fields were enclosed by dry-stone walls, which were discovered beneath
layers of peat that formed after their abandonment. The court cairn, a
Neolithic communal tomb, was in use at the same time as the field system.

like their modern counterparts in the area, with unbonded dry-stone
walls. He named these fields the Céide Fields, and I believe they are
still the earliest known fields in Britain, indeed in north-western
Europe.[3] He considers that they were primarily intended for livestock
rather than for cereal crops. I well remember when he gave the news
of his discoveries at a conference I attended in Bristol in 1976. People
were astonished at the radiocarbon dates, which indicated that the
fields were in use before 2000 BC, and were most probably originally
constructed around 3700–3500 BC. The finds from Seamus's excavations supported these dates, and a court cairn – a type of Neolithic

communal tomb – was shown to have been a part of the field system when it was in use. To my mind there is no doubt that the Céide Fields are indeed fully Neolithic, and I think it highly probable that there are other areas of Ireland where the landscape was also parcelled up into field systems in Neolithic times.[4]

My second case-study is based on my own work at Fengate, on the eastern fringes of Peterborough. I'll have more to say about this extraordinary landscape in Chapters 10 and 11, when I discuss Flag Fen and its setting. But for present purposes I merely want to note that that field system, which flourished on the edge of a marshy, wet area in the Bronze Age, had its roots very firmly in an earlier, Neolithic, landscape. A major part of this Bronze Age field system was a double-ditched droveway, which was tied in closely to some small fields or paddocks which produced radiocarbon dates of about 3000 BC.[5] Although the main part of the field system may have been somewhat later, an important element was already in use at this very early date. Again, like Seamus's Céide Fields, the Fengate fields were laid out to be used for livestock.[6]

There are other reasons, which we'll come to shortly, why I don't fully accept Julian Thomas's minimalist view of the Neolithic period and the development of Neolithic landscapes, but I am quite sure he is correct in essentials: Neolithic landscapes were mainly small-scale. They were also diverse, and had their roots firmly in the Mesolithic. Yet the Neolithic is the period when human communities literally began to make a mark on the landscape of Britain. I also think it would be unwise to discount completely that 17 per cent of our population who are descendants of the daughters of Jasmine. They surely must have introduced many new ideas and practices – and not just about farming. Their immediate ancestors having crossed an entire continent, their social structure must have been resilient, to say the least. I feel sure that, like immigrants of more recent times, they would have enriched the society, or societies, in which they found themselves.

I don't suppose there can be a single county in the British Isles that cannot produce evidence for Neolithic people in the form of communal burial mounds and other earthwork monuments, some of which are truly huge. These were people who seemed intent on leaving their mark. The conventional wisdom would have it that the monuments of Neolithic times are a reflection of the more settled lifestyle that was introduced to Britain with the arrival of farming. As we have seen, that straightforward and rather attractive idea now seems far less probable. I mentioned that Seamus Caulfield and myself had produced evidence for parcelled-up landscapes towards the latter part of the Neolithic, and it's not unreasonable to assume that these had origins earlier in the period. Landscapes take time to clear and develop; they don't just spring up unannounced. When we were doing our original research at Fengate back in the 1970s, everyone confidently expected to find examples of Neolithic fields all over the place. But that hasn't happened. We do know of other Earlier Bronze Age field systems, and these may well have been built in landscapes that were beginning to be parcelled up in Neolithic times, but they're by no means widespread, and tend to be confined to quite specific, mainly lowland, areas. We'll discuss them further in Chapter 9.

The north Mayo Neolithic landscape that Seamus Caulfield worked on was buried under blanketing peat, and the one I excavated near Peterborough, on the other side of Britain, was hidden under a sticky, river-borne flood clay known as alluvium. When rivers are in spate, their waters turn a mustard colour because of the soil that has been washed into them. When they leave their upland channels and flood huge areas of lowland countryside their flow naturally slows down, and the minute suspended particles of soil slowly sink to the bottom, where they form thin bands of clay alluvium. This process often happens each year, leaving behind a thin – maybe just a millimetre thick – sheet of clay wherever there was floodwater. After a millennium, these thin bands would have formed a deposit a metre thick. The process of alluviation gathered momentum from the Later Iron Age (perhaps around 250 BC), when large areas of the countryside began to be ploughed. Before that there was too much woodland and pasture to allow soil erosion to take place on anything more than a very local scale.[7]

In the 1970s we began to realise the archaeological potential of the buried prehistoric landscapes that lay below the vast sheets of alluvium covering the floodplains of British lowland river valleys. Where I work, in the fens, alluvium covers square miles of the landscape. We turned our attention to the alluviated parts of the gravel quarries, road schemes and other places where we were being paid to do so-called 'rescue' work – in my case it was development as part of a New Town. Did we find evidence for large, permanent Neolithic settlements and field systems? We did not.

On the continental mainland, prior to 5000 BC the Earlier Neolithic is characterised by settlements or hamlets comprising up to ten or fifteen long rectangular houses, often arranged in a gridlike pattern.[8] After 5000 BC the evidence for large settlements on neighbouring parts of the continent seems to disappear. We hoped to find rectangular houses under the alluvium, but they weren't there. Having said that, nor was anything else that predated 5000 BC, so it could be argued that the absence of such houses and settlements in Britain simply reflected what was happening at the same time on the mainland – a view for which I have some sympathy.

In all, we know of about twenty very much smaller rectangular buildings in England and Wales, and a few in Scotland, where numbers are currently rising.[9] I say 'buildings', rather than 'houses', because their purpose was not straightforwardly domestic. In at least one instance the building was used to house the dead, not the living. That example was excavated by myself in 1972 at Fengate.[10] It measured about seven by 8.5 metres, and a radiocarbon date indicated it was built between 3310 and 2910 BC. The ground-plan resembled a well-known example from Haldon, in Devon, published before the war by Grahame Clark.[11] Soon stories of our discovery were in all the newspapers. Like many important archaeological finds, it was revealed at a time when the financial future of the project was in some doubt, so I welcomed it with open arms.

Thanks to that discovery, the project prospered, and after another six years of research it became apparent that the Fengate 'house' was nothing of the sort. It was almost certainly a very special building, constructed to accommodate the remains of the dead.[12] There were no grain storage pits or wells near it, and the finds we made were very unusual, and not at all domestic. They included a beautiful, shiny jet pendant, and a large flake which had been struck from off a polished stone axe. This damage wasn't caused by cutting down trees, but was quite deliberate. The axe had been made from a distinctively green-coloured, fine-grained volcanic tuff, not to be confused with jade or jadeite, which occurs at Langdale, in the Lake District, about 175 miles north-west of Peterborough. I shall have more to say about the Langdale 'axe factories' shortly.

Julian Thomas doubts that these rectangular buildings were simple domestic houses, and after my forced re-evaluation of the Fengate example, I agree with him wholeheartedly.[13] Let us take just two examples, the 'houses' at Lismore Fields, in Derbyshire, and the one at Haldon which has just been mentioned. As we have already seen several times in this book, interpretations can begin to wobble precariously if discoveries are taken out of context. It's the context, or setting, of a particular site that provides the clues to what was going on there. My first interpretation of the Fengate 'house' was based entirely on its rectangular ground-plan, but my reinterpretation was the result of rethinking the significance of the finds the site produced. Later I discovered that it formed part of a row of structures that were all about death and the afterlife. Also in the row was a multiple burial of a small Neolithic family: a man, a woman and their two children. The man had been killed by a flint arrowhead that we found lodged between his eighth and ninth ribs. After that, I could be in no doubt: the Fengate building was not about life, but death.

The two main buildings unearthed by Daryl Garton at Lismore Fields in the Peak District of Derbyshire are probably the best-preserved and grandest yet found in Earlier Neolithic Britain.[14] Building I is particularly imposing. It could be viewed as a single building, measuring five by fifteen metres and subdivided into four compartments, two of which contained hearths; or it could have comprised two smaller, Fengate-style buildings of 7.5 by five metres each. It produced fine Earlier Neolithic pottery, including a nearly entire vessel and a complete polished stone axe. Careful sieving revealed surprisingly large quantities of cereal grains. Radiocarbon dates suggest it was built and used between 3800 and 3650 BC.

The site at Lismore Fields is located at a key point in the landscape, on a plateau between two rivers and at a prominent position where routes are likely to have crossed. It was also long-lived. There's evidence for a Late Mesolithic hunter-gatherer settlement that included a slightly flattened circular ring-gully, reminiscent perhaps of the small houses at Mount Sandel. In the Earlier Neolithic period there was a

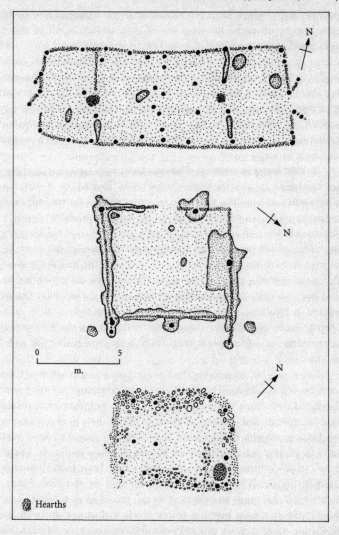

FIG 23   *Ground-plans of Neolithic buildings from Lismore Fields, Derbyshire (top); Fengate, Cambridgeshire (centre); and Haldon, Devon (bottom).*

peculiar alignment of large posts, and the two buildings, I and II, are separated by an unusually long gap of three centuries. All of this is rather odd. If it was a straightforward long-lived settlement, one would expect far more ground disturbance than Daryl encountered. There ought to have been thick accumulations of occupation debris, too. It's also unusual to have such longevity: first a Mesolithic settlement, then two Neolithic buildings centuries apart. The finds, too, are pretty special, and were found in large pieces, which is not what one would expect had they lain around on the kitchen floor for long in a normal domestic house.

Haldon was also unusual. The excavator, with typical archaeological restraint, noted that the 'house' was located in a striking, windswept location: 'the position is very exposed and commands magnificent views'.[15] This is not the sort of place where Neolithic domestic settlements were usually located. There were other odd things going on. Some of the hearths that accompanied the 'house', for example, seemed to have been constructed and used after the building's abandonment. It is now clear that the site at Haldon was a hilltop enclosure, and not a simple, straightforward settlement – if indeed such a thing existed in Neolithic times.[16] This explains its seemingly strange siting atop a windswept hill: like many other enclosures of the time it was intended to be a focal point that would have been visible for miles around.

There can be no denying that these fine, rectangular structures were roofed buildings. There can also be no denying that they were inhabited from time to time by people, both when they were roofed and standing, and subsequently too. And there's accumulating evidence to suggest that in some instances they may also have been used to store grain. But were they houses in the domestic, or 'home-base', sense? I think not. One or two may have been built to accommodate the dead for a part of their physical or spiritual journey to a communal tomb and the next world; others seem to me to have been built as special meeting places positioned at key spots in the landscape – rather as we saw at Paviland Cave. These were places that may well have been important in Mesolithic times, as we saw at Lismore Fields. They were important in people's minds, in the collective historical geography of the shifting communities living and passing through the area. It's possible, of course, that the rectangular shape of these buildings was a short-term 'folk memory' of the much larger and earlier structures built by the so-called 'wave of advance' farmers on the continental mainland up to a millennium earlier (i.e. before 5000 BC). If that sounds improbable – and at face value I admit it does – there are two other strands of evidence that can be used to reinforce it. But before we discuss them I must return to those rectangular houses in the British Isles. But this time we'll examine the situation in Ireland, where their occurrence is anything but rare.

The most recent summary of the evidence for Irish Neolithic houses listed over ninety examples of the type of substantial rectangular structures we have just been discussing.[17] It seems that hardly a month goes by when I don't hear of yet another one. One of the peculiar aspects of the phenomenon is that these substantial buildings were built for what in prehistoric terms is a short period – no more than five hundred years, between 3900 and 3400 BC. Then they simply stop. Normally one would expect them to peter out, or give way to a new but clearly related type of house – but they don't. The houses that follow are very much smaller, and fall more within the later tradition of round buildings.

Many Irish rectangular Neolithic houses have trampled floors that are littered with what can only be described as domestic refuse, and many too have internal hearths that look very much like ordinary fireplaces. So people must have lived in these places. But does that make them 'ordinary' or 'domestic'? The problem, it seems to me, is largely of our own making. We are applying modern, and rather loaded, terms to a situation and a society that is quite unlike anything we might encounter in the Western world. Was there such a thing as 'ordinary domestic life' in the Earlier Neolithic period? I suspect not. 'Ordinary domestic life', as we know it, is just that. With the possible exception of mealtime Grace, said in a few avowedly religious households, it excludes anything that might be seen as religious or ceremonial. Yet only a century ago it was common, for example, in the manor houses of the English countryside, for the squire to lead the household in daily prayers. For centuries the manor house was more than a mere domestic dwelling: it was a court, a place of employment, prayer and celebration; but it was also the place where the squire, his family and servants lived their daily lives.

I'm not suggesting that the Irish rectangular buildings were Neolithic manor houses; but I am suggesting that the concept of 'ordinary domestic life' is not appropriate to British prehistory – of any period. Prehistoric people did not draw a hard and fast distinction between religion and daily life. In their minds the next world, the ancestors and other powerful forces played a direct role in daily life. For example, to unthinkingly cross the line between one settlement and another would be to risk the wrath of the ancestors whose spirits resided in barrows and hidden, solitary graves that were positioned along the boundary. As we will see, these spirits could cause disease and other disasters to afflict the world of the living. The landscape in which people lived was real, but it was also in part a landscape of the mind: hills, trees, rivers and manmade monuments such as barrows had their own tales to tell. Mythology and the supernatural formed more than just a background: they interleaved and intertwined everything, binding the landscape together and forming a reality which had an existence in its own right.

We get a flavour of the additional, or non-utilitarian, roles of the Irish rectangular houses when we look at what they have revealed. I'll take one example: House 1 at Ballygalley in County Antrim, excavated by Professor Derek Simpson.[18] This rectangular house, which gave a radiocarbon date of 3776–3386 BC, was accompanied by a semi-circular post-built yard or annexe. This annexe is most unusual; as is the fact that the house was taken to pieces and demolished, its site levelled and paved with a layer of cobbles. But if the features – the post-holes, gullies and other archaeological components – of the building were out of the ordinary, they were nothing compared to the finds.

For a start, there were so many of them. Morton (Site A, not the shell midden), which might be considered a fairly typical and well-excavated settlement, produced 13,500 pieces of chipped flint and stone. This figure includes both finished implements and the by-products of their manufacture, such as waste flakes. The dig at Ballygalley produced several hundred thousand waste flakes alone, not to mention eight hundred cores, and two thousand artefacts. There were also huge quantities of pottery and more exotic materials, such as

FIG 24   *Reconstruction of the Earlier Neolithic house with a semi-circular plank-built yard or 'annexe' at Ballygalley, County Antrim (3776–3386 BC).*

clear volcanic glass, shiny black pitchstone from across the sea at Arran, and two flakes from polished greenstone axes from the 'factories' at Langdale in the Lake District – which we last encountered at the supposed 'house' in Peterborough, hundreds of miles to the south-east. There was evidence, too, of ordinary domestic settlement, such as corn-grinding stones known as querns; but one of these, found buried in a pit inside the building, had been placed in the ground upside-down. We will see later that this probably wasn't accidental.

Derek Simpson, the excavator, was as confused as anyone else by this extravagant collection of finds. He argued that the 'house' had to be part of a place that was altogether more significant, and there is now evidence that it had been enclosed by an encircling ditch. So what was going on? Did the house lie at the centre of, say, a trading or redistribution centre, and was ritual or religion involved? Derek felt that the finds, and the way that many of them, such as the quern, appeared to have been deliberately placed in the ground, were highly reminiscent of a group of Earlier Neolithic sites known as causewayed enclosures. I'm convinced he's right, and that House 1 was anything but ordinary or domestic.

The accumulating evidence from Ireland – the houses, Céide Fields, not to mention the great passage tombs that we'll come to in the next chapter – is starting to indicate that the Neolithic there was less mobile than that across the Irish Sea. If that's the case, then if my argument for continuity between the Mesolithic and Neolithic is accepted, it would suggest that the earlier period there was also less mobile than was once believed. I think the situation in Ireland was by no means a carbon copy of that in Britain. Indeed, no less a person than Peter Woodman, who gave the world those extraordinary houses at Mount Sandel, has dropped hints that he now inclines towards this view.[19]

Perhaps the commonest and best evidence that Earlier Neolithic communities on the mainland of Britain were mobile is provided by the thousands of so-called 'flint scatters' that are distributed all over the country, but especially along the great lowland river valleys.[20] These scatters are the remains of flint tools and by-products that were used in domestic life. In other words, the sites where they are found are the real settlements, the home-bases where the majority of the people lived their daily lives.

I've dug several of these flint scatters, and without exception I've been sadly disappointed by what I've found below the ground. On the surface, things look very promising. You measure-in a grid of pegs and systematically collect hundreds of flints from the surface. Then you bring in a machine and carefully scrape off a few inches of plough-soil. Below the topsoil you discover a few darker patches, which are filled-in pits and post-holes, if you're in luck. More often you'll find more irregular, amorphous splodges of darker soil which probably represent the scoops and hollows of a naturally undulating prehistoric land surface, planed flat by centuries of ploughing. These post-holes and natural hollows will be filled with flint debris and broken, abraded pieces of pottery, plus a few butchered animal bones. Maybe there's a hearth or two, and a few fire-cracked stones and charcoal. And that's usually it: no complete pots, no polished stone axes from Langdale, no jet pendants – just some scraps of flint, pot and bone; precisely the sort of material one would expect to find around a hearth or on a kitchen floor. It can be discouraging. Real archaeology seldom mimics *Raiders of the Lost Ark*.

If Julian Thomas is right, and the imposing rectangular buildings were special in some way, then what did the houses of ordinary Neolithic people look like? I suspect we have already seen the answer to that at Mount Sandel. While archaeologists, myself included, have been looking for the more imposing and permanent structures that would go with a sedentary lifestyle, the evidence now strongly indicates that throughout the Neolithic most people moved around, in much the same way they had done in postglacial times. The same places were repeatedly visited, and just as in earlier times their flint-tool technology was light, adaptable and, as we saw at the Sweet Track, multi-purpose. Only towards the end of the Neolithic does the size of flint scatters on the ground surface increase. This is most significant. The flint- and stone-working specialist Mark Edmonds puts it clearly: 'The dramatic increase in the size of Later Neolithic scatters adds support to the argument that there was a considerable decrease in the degree of mobility compared with the Earlier Neolithic.'[21] That would suggest that in certain parts of lowland Britain the pattern of seasonal movement only really began to slow down in the centuries after, say, 3000 BC. Elsewhere shifting settlement, within clearly defined and sometimes quite restricted territories, continued much as before.

To return to the houses of the Earlier Neolithic in southern Britain: what did they look like? The short answer is 'not much'. Essentially they were light, easily dismantled structures that may have been repeatedly erected over a low mound or a hollow, depending on the local drainage and ground conditions. The archaeological evidence is likely to consist of a few post-holes, a scattering of flints and maybe the odd piece of pottery. There are many sites answering that description, and I've excavated one myself.[22] They are by no means exciting. But I believe they would repay much closer investigation now that we are beginning to understand their potential significance.

The Neolithic saw a number of innovations to Britain. For archaeologists, one of the main ones was pottery. It's a plastic medium, unlike flint or wood, which are essentially reductive. You start with a small piece of clay, and add more coils, or whatever technique you employ to build the object up (the potter's wheel wasn't introduced until the last century BC). You can also add decoration very readily. Then you dry it thoroughly, fire it in a bonfire and later in a kiln (with several stages of development in between). With flint or wood, you start with a large lump and chip away at it. It's a less flexible way of working, and it allows less freedom for *identifiable* individual expression. So there is less incentive to diverge from an established tradition. One could put it the other way round: there is more incentive to stay within an established tradition.

Whatever you make, your object – be it pot, flint, carved wood or basketry – will symbolise all manner of things, in the same way that even the most everyday items in a modern kitchen tell stories about their owner's age, sex, wealth, lifestyle, religion and ethnic background. My kitchen, for example, boasts a wok, which means on the face of it that Maisie and I like to cook Chinese food. That's certainly true, but that wok also says something about its owners' attitudes to other cultures, and to life in general. We mustn't forget that objects have their own stories to tell. They may be inanimate, but that doesn't mean they remain lifeless in our perception.

While the earliest pots were plain, they were generally well-made, functional and finely finished. Craftsmanship in other media was equally competent, and sometimes showed an extraordinary flair for design. In the past, archaeologists tended to ignore Neolithic woodworking simply because the evidence wasn't there; it didn't survive. But the Somerset Levels Project has done much to set that right, and a highly exciting timber burial mound has been excavated recently in the fens (see next chapter). An example of this bias in archaeological attention is provided by the study of stone axes. To Maisie's knowledge there are only ten Neolithic wooden axe hafts known in Britain and Ireland (we had the great good fortune to discover one of them ourselves, dating to around 3800 BC[23]). As a result, all the attention has been on the axeheads themselves, and it is simply assumed that they were all hafted, which I increasingly think is improbable. Many are so beautiful that they must have been made as fine objects to be admired in their own right.

When I discussed flint-working in earlier chapters, I described how various stages of manufacture had to be completed. First the soft outer, or cortical, material was chipped off, then further flakes were removed, and eventually a finished implement was produced. This was then taken somewhere else to be used, and was ultimately discarded. Imagine for a moment that it was possible to collect every one of those waste flakes of flint, and then reassemble them. At the end one would possess a flint nodule with a hollow centre. If one poured plaster into that central void, then broke the nodule open, one would have a plaster cast of the implement. The process would be difficult, but the idea behind it is simple enough.

Barrows, or burial mounds, are almost always surrounded by a substantial ditch that was dug, among other things, to provide the material that would be used to form the mound. It would appear that this ditch was seen as a special feature, doubtless because it formed a boundary between the area reserved for burial and the world outside. This was probably why special offerings were placed in the ditch. They included not just axes and other complete flint implements, but heaps of flint-knapping debris. As Julian Thomas puts it, 'These collections of flakes frequently refit to form complete nodules without implements having been made and taken away.'[24] In other words, knapping took place in or near the barrow ditch, for no practical purpose whatsoever. It was 'working for its own sake', but in a very special place, and presumably as part of a very special occasion. In this instance, work and religion are very hard to differentiate – and I'm not sure that it would be all that enlightening to distinguish between them. There's a danger of imposing our twenty-first-century values on people who lived in the fifth millennium BC.

We encounter broadly similar problems when we come to consider the mass of prehistoric material dredged from the Thames in the nineteenth and twentieth centuries. Today this huge array of stone and metal artefacts, human skulls and other bones, is to be found on display and in the collections of the British Museum and the Museum of London.[25] Most archaeologists would now agree that much of this material was dropped into the waters of the river deliberately, as offerings, perhaps from boats or quays, or from post-built fords or crossing places such as the one recently discovered near Vauxhall Bridge in central London (see Chapter 10).

The last survey of Neolithic axes from the Thames was published by the British Museum in 1978.[26] This comprehensive catalogue lists and illustrates no fewer than 368 axes, of which just seventeen appear to be broken or severely damaged. In spite of how they were meant to have been used, there is rarely much chipping, bruising or other damage to their cutting edges. By and large they are in remarkably good condition – very much like the beautiful jadeite axe that was found by the side of the Sweet Track in the Somerset Levels. The axes were mainly found in a relatively short reach – roughly thirty miles – of river, between Maidenhead upstream and Richmond on the edge of central London. Here the river is wide but crossable, whether by boat, ford or artificial crossing place (I hesitate to use the term 'bridge'). The prehistoric 'tidal head' was just upstream of Vauxhall Bridge. Below that point the river flow would have reversed when the tide came in. It would have been an altogether different river – and was probably regarded as such in ancient times.

We might expect the Thames axes to have been made from the only locally available suitable stone, namely flint nodules from the river gravels. Some were, but many weren't. In fact they derived from so-called Neolithic 'axe factories' considerable distances away. Twenty came from Cornwall, fifteen from Langdale in the Lake District, and seven from Penmaenmawr in north Wales, not to mention thirty-five from exotic volcanic and other rocks found miles away.

We have seen that axes from Langdale were found as far apart as Peterborough and Ballygalley in Northern Ireland. In a study published in 1974 the authority on the Neolithic stone axe 'trade', Professor Bill Cummins, examined 1840 stone axes from known findspots in England and Wales.[27] He found that far and away the largest proportion (27 per cent) were made from the attractive greenstone volcanic tuff that was mined at Great Langdale.[28] But they were actually found on the other side of the country, in Lincolnshire and the east midlands. This indicates something of the sheer scale of the 'trade' in Neolithic polished stone axes.

I put the word 'trade' in quotation marks because, as we will see in the next chapter, true trade can only take place in the setting of a market economy. In the recent past archaeologists assumed that such an economy existed. Of course there wasn't money, as coinage was only introduced to Britain in the final centuries before the Roman

Conquest, but an exchange system was operated: say half a pig for an axe, depending on the local value of pigs or axes. It was that climate of thought that led to the description of the axe-production centres as 'factories'. Places far away where their products occurred frequently, such as the site at Etton, were sometimes seen as 'redistribution centres', like the ones operated by supermarkets today. Presumably the axes were finally 'retailed' at farms and hamlets in the country. It was a rational enough theory, but it was wrong.

It has been known for some time that the Great Langdale 'axe factory' was located high in a mountainous fell on the Pike O'Stickle, beside a steep drop and overlooking a dramatic valley of outstanding beauty. It was, and still is, something of an ordeal to reach. The Victorians, on the other hand, located their factories with convenience and accessibility in mind. They were close to canals, railways or roads, and had good access to raw materials and fuel. The special fine-grained stone used to make the Langdale axes doesn't only outcrop at that remote spot, but nonetheless, that was the place selected. In simple, practical terms, it doesn't make sense – any more than it makes sense to transport huge bluestone rocks from the Preseli Hills of south-west Wales to Stonehenge; but that's what happened. Strangely, there is a link between the two places: they are both high and remote, with spectacular views; but more than that, the rock itself is sharp, angular, strangely columnar and almost artificial in appearance. It would not take an overactive imagination to see these rocky outcrops as something removed from this world, perhaps assembled or created by a race of altogether more powerful beings than us.

By looking at places like Langdale and Preseli as mere quarries or factories, we are commodifying them: the axes become mere products, with no further significance, and we lose sight of what Richard Bradley has termed the 'archaeology of natural places'. As the cover blurb to his book succinctly puts it: 'natural places have an archaeology because they acquired a significance in the *minds* of people in the past'.[29] We saw something closely allied to this at Goat's Hole Cave at Paviland, and it's reasonable to wonder whether places like Langdale and Preseli were important to people even before the Neolithic. Ten years ago, I'd have said no. Now I'm less certain.

No matter how much you advertise, in a market economy you

can't sell catfood that cats won't eat. By the same token, you can't distribute greenstone axes if they shatter on impact with a tree. Yet many of the finest polished flint axes found in Neolithic ceremonial monuments would undoubtedly have shattered if used. I found one myself in a so-called henge monument in the Welland valley, north of Peterborough. It came out of the ground in perfect condition. It was stunning: highly polished, and marbled like the swirling multicoloured endpapers of an old book. I knew I had to treat it with care. I couldn't even risk dropping it, because the beautiful swirling pattern, deep within the flint, which the polishing had brought out so well, was caused by freezing and thawing in the Ice Age, and is a sign of internal flaws and weakness. Such material would undoubtedly have been rejected by the inhabitants of Boxgrove, who were looking only for tools that worked. Almost half a million years later, their Neolithic cousins were more concerned with appearances.

Although Langdale axes were effective tools, some flint, and perhaps jadeite, ones were not. It's not unusual to find Langdale axes in the east of England that have been worn down through use, but many more – in fact I'd say the majority – are complete and in very good condition. Sometimes they're placed in burials, or in wet spots, presumably as offerings. Clearly these were special items, not just utilitarian trade goods. We've seen that the 'factories' where they were produced were special places, and it seems reasonable to extend that argument to the axes themselves, which are, after all, objects that had been hewn from the living rock.

What was going on? There can be no simple answer, such as trade. Doubtless some axes were indeed exchanged for pigs, but if trade really did form a significant element in the distribution of axes, one would expect a fall-off pattern to develop around the sources of production. To take a modern example: in the days before supermarkets, you could buy strawberries very cheaply in the fens around Wisbech, where they were grown. In the towns around fenland, like Cambridge and Stamford, they were more expensive, but not prohibitively so. At Covent Garden market they were yet more pricey. Then when the tennis began you could buy them at Wimbledon for a king's ransom. So the price was determined mainly by distance, although other complicating factors entered the equation.

If you apply the strawberry model to the distribution map for Langdale axes, you'd be likely to conclude that they were mined and made on the Lincolnshire coast, rather than the Lakeland fells, because the fall-off in the distribution pattern is reversed. In simple economic terms, it doesn't make any sense at all. But it does if you view the situation slightly differently. Langdale axes are found most frequently in Lincolnshire and the east midlands, because that is where they were most appreciated. That, in other words, was where they were most valued and sought after, both for chopping wood and as beautiful objects to be given to other people or offered to the world of the ancestors. We cannot yet say why the people of Lincolnshire liked the Langdale stone so much, but they did; perhaps tales of its origin at a sacred place high on a mountain affected the inhabitants of landscapes that were altogether different.

Flint was the steel of the Stone Age in Britain. It felled trees, killed prey, built houses, butchered meat and fashioned clothes. Without it, almost every daily task would have been harder work. No wonder it was highly prized. By Neolithic times people realised that the very best sources of top-quality flint were below the ground, in seams that had lain undisturbed since they formed on the seabed in Cretaceous times. This flint worked better because it contained far fewer of the internal weaknesses found in gravel flints that had been rolled by rivers, scraped by glaciers and repeatedly frozen by the penetrating cold of the Ice Ages.

Most of the flint mines of the Earlier Neolithic are found on the rolling chalklands of southern England.[30] They have recently been surveyed by the English Royal Commission on Historical Monuments (now part of English Heritage),[31] and like most English Royal Commission volumes, this report manages to combine erudition with accessibility. The heyday of most mines was surprisingly early, from a century or two before 4200 BC until about 3000 BC, with most in use in the half millennium between 4000 and 3500 BC. Perhaps the most famous of all the flint mines, that at Grimes Graves in Norfolk, was significantly later than the rest (say 3000–2000 BC).

The Royal Commission survey debunked a number of false or disputed flint mines, including one at Whipsnade Zoo in Bedfordshire, on which they commented: 'A series of depressions within flamingo, wallaby, bear and cheetah pennings most likely to represent the quarrying of clay' (pp.80–1). That particular case-study must have been stimulating. They deleted no fewer than forty-four false flint mines and relegated ten to the 'possible' category, which left just ten 'definite' mines, all of them in Sussex, Wiltshire or Hampshire, with the single exception of Grimes Graves.

These were not little scoops, like the things at Whipsnade. They were proper mines, with shafts, supporting pillars and galleries deep below the ground. The chalk was levered from the ground with hand-held 'picks' made from red-deer antlers, and the miners worked by the light of small oil lamps, whose five-thousand-year-old carbon stains can still be seen on the walls and roofs of the galleries.

I well remember my first visit to Grimes Graves as a child in the 1950s. People were less health-and-safety obsessed then, and it was possible to descend the open shaft (one of at least 433 that were opened at various times in the Later Neolithic and Bronze Ages). The shaft branched out at the bottom, giving the effect of an immensely tall hall with a light high up in the roof. Like all schoolboys of that era I wore shorts, and I distinctly recall that the air was cool around my legs. The galleries were three to four feet high, and at floor level. One had been lit, rather dimly, by electric light. Of course I took off my coat and scrambled in. As I squirmed my way forward it grew cooler, and when I passed a light my body cast a dark, almost impenetrable shadow before me. It also smelled odd: musty and stale, as if the air hadn't moved since Neolithic times (in fact that particular shaft had been excavated in the nineteenth century by Canon Greenwell).

I began to feel uncomfortable. Suddenly I knew I had to get out. Immediately. Then I made a ghastly discovery: the gallery was now too low for me to turn around in. I tried several times, but only succeeded in grazing my knees and tearing my shirt. Waves of blind panic spread over me, and I had to stifle my cries with my sleeve. Then a momentary calm descended, and I realised I must wriggle my way backwards to a spot about five yards behind me, where a side-gallery gave enough room for me to turn around. For several weeks afterwards the grazes on my stomach where my shirt had ridden up as I forced my way backwards were a vivid red. After that experience

I could understand why miners have always had a healthy respect for the forces they believed existed below the ground.

Many fields of archaeological enquiry have been pushed forward by the keenness of one individual, often an amateur. In the case of the flint mines of Sussex, the field was pioneered by a remarkable man called John Pull, whose team of volunteers excavated at most of the well-known flint mines; together they devised an effective way of doing what was often difficult and dangerous work.[32] When he reached sixty, in 1959, Pull retired from the Civil Service and took a job at the newly opened branch of Lloyd's Bank in Durrington, just outside Worthing. On 10 November 1960 the bank was attacked by an armed raider, who shot and killed him. Pull's murderer was one of the last men to be hanged in England.

Like Langdale, most of the flint mines of southern England overlooked spectacular views. Sites like Harrow Hill, or Cissbury (excavated by Pull's team) in West Sussex, dominate the landscape for miles around. I'm convinced that this was not coincidental. These had long been significant places, and in many cases would continue to be important right through the Iron Age. Grimes Graves, located in flat and altogether unspectacular country, may appear to be an exception. But the black, lustrous flint from the mined seam, known as 'floorstone', is very, very special. I've had the pleasure of working some, and it's like knapping a cross between treacly toffee and black glass: it's hard, sweet and deeply satisfying. It's magical stuff.

The importance of ritual and ceremony in the winning of flint from deep in the ground has been well summarised by the Royal Commission report in a single illustration which superimposes some of the offerings, burials and other non-mining discoveries made in flint mines onto a hypothetical shaft and gallery. After a description of some oddly-placed hearths found deep below ground, the report continues:

> More intriguing are apparently placed deposits of pottery, antler picks, animal bones and human skeletal material. Then there are occurrences of 'graffiti' and unusual axe markings ... all of these could be tied in to the extractive process, but taken together they indicate that the recovery of flint was perceived as more than a simple process of raw material extraction.

It's interesting that the shafts were often deliberately filled in, as if signing off or sealing access to and from a world below the ground. This is a theme I'll return to when I discuss the motives behind the erection of the central tree at 'Seahenge', which was constructed just before 2000 BC, in the Earlier Bronze Age. By this time the ceremonies and rituals that were enacted close to the shores of the North Sea in Norfolk were already very ancient, with roots in Britain that were then even older than Christianity is today.

The story of the British Neolithic is a complex and archaeologically fascinating one. It's a period when we see the appearance of certain

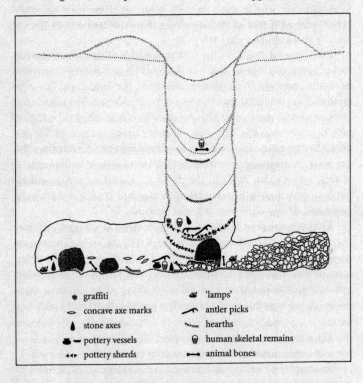

* graffiti   'lamps'
— concave axe marks   antler picks
stone axes   hearths
pottery vessels   human skeletal remains
pottery sherds   animal bones

FIG 25 *An idealised cross-section through the shaft and galleries of a typical Neolithic flint mine in southern England, showing the variety of 'placed' and unusual finds that may be encountered.*

themes that will dominate our story henceforth. It was also a time when people felt a need, in Richard Bradley's memorable phrase, to 'alter the earth',[33] not only by constructing tombs and monuments, but also by smaller works, such as the thousands of small pits and scoops right across the British Isles and most of mainland Europe which were filled with a mixture of daily objects and special things. It may well be the case that this need to alter the earth had roots that went back to Mesolithic times, not just in Britain, but elsewhere in northern Europe. The presence of Mesolithic precedents doesn't explain, however, the ubiquity of the practice, although it might help to account for why it was so readily taken up. New ideas are often better received if they accord with something similar that was already present in a culture.

I have noted that the shape of those large rectangular buildings may have been a folk memory of the type of houses that existed on the continental mainland before 5000 BC. Perhaps more significantly, the continental houses were often wider at one end than the other, giving them a distinctive trapezoid shape. This shape is precisely 'recalled' by the ground-plan of many British long barrows (a form of communal tomb), again nearly a millennium later. Richard Bradley has further suggested that British Neolithic enclosed sites, such as Haldon and the so-called causewayed enclosures that we'll encounter in the next chapter, are also a later folk memory of earlier continental enclosed settlements.[34]

At first glance such links with the continent would appear to suggest strong ties; but do these have to be cultural or physical, in the sense of actual folk movement? It's difficult at this stage to be certain. Ten years ago I would have argued in favour of massive folk movements, but today there is also compelling evidence in the other direction, such as Bryan Sykes's work and detailed field surveys, as we saw in fenland, where there seems to have been continuity between the Mesolithic and Neolithic. I suspect we will soon arrive at some form of consensus which will acknowledge the contribution made by communities on both sides of the Channel. Meanwhile, the origins and development of Neolithic culture will continue to be one of the hottest topics in archaeology. I think that is a lot healthier than our old obsession with the origins of farming alone. One cannot separate out one aspect of life from an ancient culture. If you want to understand farming, you must also look at the way people disposed of their dead.

That brings me back to two other aspects of ancient life that archaeologists are still wont to remove from their cultural contexts. In the earlier discussion of those mainly Irish rectangular houses, I concluded that their uses were both domestic and ritual. The trouble with this is that it assumes there was a distinction between the two in prehistory – an assumption which arises purely and simply out of the way archaeologists live their own lives today. I have long believed that the distinction is invalid, and causes more problems than it solves. Richard Bradley writes about 'the ritualisation of domestic life', and sees no hard and fast distinction between the two.[35] In his and my view it's all a matter of degree. It doesn't really matter whether those houses were built for domestic or for religious purposes, or for both. What *does* matter is that they were built, and were used. Instead of trying to narrow down or define a precise role, defined in modern terms, we would be better off discussing their origins, who used them and why they used them. We could also think about how the buildings would have been regarded – in other words, how they would have fitted into the world view or cosmology of people living at the time. To take a modern example, what does the construction of so many Victorian churches to a medieval ground-plan say about Victorian attitudes to life? What was the nature of that 'folk memory'? That, it seems to me, matters very much more than whether the buildings themselves were used for ritual or domestic purposes.

At various points in this book I've tried to give an impression of the size of the British population at certain times. I need hardly repeat that these are shots in the dark. It's noticeable that good textbooks fight shy of such things. That's understandable, because they are more concerned with historical frameworks: with events, artefacts, sites and chronologies. They don't exist to paint a broad picture of the way human society grew and developed in these islands – and I don't see how one can attempt to chart such a thing if one ignores population. So, for better or worse, I must speculate.

Mercifully for me, from time to time someone else sticks his neck out. In Chapter 4 we saw how in 1992 Christopher Smith estimated that the population range for Britain, excluding Ireland, in about 5000 BC, at the end of the Mesolithic period, was around 2750 to 5500 people. When I read that I was frankly amazed – it had never occurred to me that the population could have been so small. But I can find no obvious flaw in Smith's argument. I suppose my doubts were somewhat irrational, being based on what I thought I knew about the Neolithic; but it seemed to me quite extraordinary that some of the great monuments we'll encounter in the next chapter were constructed by communities that were so recently descended from such a tiny population.

After considering the matter further, however, I became more persuaded by those figures. For a start, the end date of 5000 BC is interesting, because that was shortly after the time when Britain separated from the continent. Could that have affected the growth, or lack of it, of the newly insular population? The short answer is that we don't know, because the period from 5000 BC to about 4200 BC is, as we've seen, archaeologically almost invisible. Is there any objective means of tentatively estimating population – if only to arrive at a very broad, order-of-magnitude figure? I think there just might be, and that the clue possibly lies in those ninety or more rectangular Neolithic 'houses' in Ireland. The point is that they were confined to four or five centuries of the Early Neolithic, and don't appear subsequently. The Irish archaeologist Eoin Grogan estimates that they were large enough to accommodate from seven to twenty-four people. That's possibly true, *if* they were just houses. But if, on the other hand, we see them as something more than that, as perhaps a focus for, say, an extended family, most of whom would have lived in smaller dwellings round about, we might speculate that perhaps thirty to seventy people could have had access to them.

To make the maths simpler, let's assume that a hundred rectangular buildings have survived in Ireland. If we assume a life of fifty years for each building, and that the tradition remained active for five hundred years, then twenty would have been built each century, of which approximately ten would have been in use at any one time. Now we come to a bigger imponderable: what proportion of the total population of Neolithic houses do our ten represent? Clearly not 100 per cent, or there would be no discoveries in the future, which is plainly ridiculous. What about 10 per cent? I think that's still massively too high: even Second World War sites in Britain survive at far lower percentages than that.[36] I would guess it would be closer to 1 per cent, or more probably 0.1 per cent. Working on the basis of thirty to seventy people living in or associated with each of our ten houses, we come up with a population range of thirty to seventy thousand (at 1 per cent survival), or 300,000 to 700,000 (at 0.1 per cent survival).

These figures are so broad as to be almost meaningless, and I apologise for that, but we've got to start somewhere. I think we can safely discount 300,000 as being far too high, although seventy thousand is not altogether impossible. But I would tend to favour the lower range of the 1 per cent survival figures – i.e. in the region of thirty to fifty thousand. If we accept as a working estimate that Ireland had a population of around forty thousand, then Britain probably had twice or four times that – perhaps around 100,000 people.

How can one account for what seems at first glance a rapid rise in population from Mesolithic to Earlier Neolithic times? For a start, we have almost a millennium of archaeological invisibility to play with, and what I'm proposing is by no means an impossibility over such a long period of time, especially if Irish society was somewhat less mobile than has been believed up to now. Second, I believe that in certain regions of Britain and Ireland – like, for example, the Céide Fields of County Mayo – the landscape was well developed very early on, and would have been capable of supporting quite large numbers of people. Field boundaries require patrolling and maintenance if they are to work properly, and it seems improbable that such elaborate and well-laid-out systems were operated by a tiny handful of people. In such instances we must surely be talking about dispersed communities comprising over a hundred people each.

I've ended this chapter with a rather uncomfortable attempt to guess at the population of Earlier Neolithic Britain and Ireland. Next I want to examine what motivated that population, and what made societies tick. Was it something simple, like the ever-present need to feed themselves? Or was it more complex than that? As we've seen when we looked at Great Langdale and the flint mines of southern England, the people of Neolithic Britain led extraordinarily rich and diverse lives. They were not ruled by external imperatives alone, such as the need to stay warm, fed and secure, but had the time and ability to create imaginative and exciting mythologies for themselves. In the next chapter we'll see what they were capable of creating when they really needed to contact the supernatural.

CHAPTER SEVEN

The Earlier Neolithic
(4200–3000 BC)

Part 2: Monuments and Pathways

THE NEOLITHIC IS CHIEFLY KNOWN as the time when communal field monuments, such as great burial mounds, or barrows, appear in Britain for the first time. This happened quite quickly in the centuries after 4000 BC. The monuments come in all sorts of shapes and sizes, and most seem to have something to do with death – but that is an oversimplification, because death is always about life and the living too. Some of the large communal monuments must have been constructed by hundreds of people; which brings me to a long-standing objection some archaeologists have had to a vision of life in the British Neolithic as being essentially small-scale and mobile.

Surely, this argument goes, extraordinary monuments like Stonehenge and Avebury, which have their origins in the Neolithic, could only have been constructed by societies with a sedentary lifestyle and a highly developed farming economy that produced the economic 'profits' ('surplus' is the term used) needed to construct them? At face value this seems hard to dispute. Certainly, if today one were to attempt to construct something like Avebury by hand, the cost would be truly mind-boggling. But the same could be said of the great medieval cathedrals, and they were constructed all over the land – even at little fen towns like Ely. The mistake is to apply modern market economics to history and prehistory. There was a market economy of sorts in medieval times, but there were also forces which mitigated its effects, such as the guilds, and of course the Church itself. They saw to it that the cathedrals were built, to the glory of God – and of themselves.

I remember when I lived in Canada visiting some of the extraordinary ceremonial sites south of the border. I saw the serpent mounds of Ohio, and they were spectacular beyond belief. But much further south, along the Mississippi valley, there are manmade mounds and vast ceremonial enclosures that dwarf anything we have to offer in Britain. The huge enclosure at Poverty Point, Louisiana, for example, was surrounded by no fewer than six earthwork rings that covered a staggering 370 acres (150 hectares).[1] It is the largest of several huge enclosures, and was built by sedentary hunter-gatherers in the Late Archaic period (1800–500 BC). By comparison, the great ditch around that most spectacular and massive monument of the British Neolithic, at Avebury in Wiltshire, encloses an area of 28.5 acres (11.5 hectares). There are many other massive ceremonial sites in the Mississippi valley, also built by societies that did not practise the type of close herding (to use Mike Jarman's term) and mixed farming that was once thought to have been the economic basis of the British Neolithic. What I'm saying is that elaborate and labour-intensive ceremonial monuments are not an economic indicator of any sort. They merely demonstrate that, for whatever reasons, the societies in question had a need to construct such things.

The motives that lay behind the construction of the Neolithic monuments of Britain were both complex and deeply rooted within the different societies that built and used them. The fact that many share common design principles does not mean that the activities that took place within them were necessarily closely related too. Although some similar themes, such as a concern with the sun's orientation, can be detected across the country, these are almost so broad as to be meaningless: tombs, for example, are to do with death and the afterlife – but they're also to do with the social bonds that hold extended families together: I find that funerals are almost the only occasions when I get to meet my more distant cousins. Such things, surely, would have been equally important to people in the Neolithic.

Recent research has thrown new light on the way these structures were built and used. Given the wealth of fresh information, the best I can do is offer some examples of what may have been happening at these still rather mysterious places over five thousand years ago. I'll start with a group of very early sites which at first glance seem entirely senseless. But they are potentially the most important field monuments of British prehistory, because what went on within their boundaries was to formalise, if not actually to create, a pattern of behaviour that would flourish in Britain and Ireland for at least three thousand years.

From the air they resemble a string of sausages laid on the ground in a huge circle. They're known as causewayed enclosures, after the gaps or 'causeways' that separate the individual segments of ditch, and they were in use from about 3800 BC.[2] None appear to have been constructed after 3000 BC. The best way to describe these places is to imagine the events that might have surrounded their construction. The following is based on my own excavations at Etton, a small causewayed enclosure on the edge of the western fens, dated by radiocarbon to around 3800 BC.[3] This is how I imagine the site might have come into being.

Word has spread through all the communities living and moving through a large lowland river valley that there was to be a special gathering at the traditional, ancient place known as the Mist of the Souls, a foggy hollow near a U-shaped bend in one of the courses of the river Welland. It was to happen on the day following the first hard hoarfrost of autumn.

The day dawns, and hundreds of people arrive. Their leaders, who saw how such things are done when they visited a valley ten miles to the south, set the people to work. Relations between the various groups in the region have not been good of late, so everyone agrees that this gathering will celebrate the ties that bind, rather than the forces that separate. So, following a word from their leaders, people start to group themselves into work gangs that include only members of a single family – perhaps the descendants of common great-great-grandparents.

The scene resembles a seething, crowded marketplace as people look around for long-lost relatives. Meanwhile, away from the crowd, the group of elders are marking the bounds. They repeatedly walk in a huge circle, while young men follow behind them at a respectful distance, dragging a wooden plough which scours the stony ground. After numerous circuits they have laid out a circular area about two hundred metres across. Then the elders look to the sky for direction, and divide the enclosure in half with another scoured line. They then walk the outer circuit a final time. By now the crowd has returned. They stand respectfully outside the great circle, as they have been bidden. Mothers keep their children in check; it would be bad if they entered the great circle. That is for adults only.

By now the people have formed themselves into family groups, separated by a space the length of one man lying down. Each family has assembled around its usual sign or token, mounted on a spearshaft held aloft by a senior man of fighting age. Perhaps it's a fox or human skull. As the elders pass each family group, they take the token off the shaft and place it on the ground at the point where the group starts. When they pass the last family member, they drive the shaft into the earth, and so on for the entire circuit. At the end of the first day, the land has been marked out and the circuit arranged into separate family segments. The feasting and celebration continues late into the night.

The next day dawns, and the men of hunting age set to work digging a length of ditch between their family's two markers. They dig for two days and one night without stopping. It's an ordeal, and they may not eat until the task has been completed. They pile the earth and gravel from the subsoil carefully around both sides of the ditch, but they don't dump earth on the short gap that separates their segment from their neighbours' at either end.

At first light on the fourth day the families reassemble around the great circle of ditches. The women arrange themselves on the banks inside the circle, and the men on those outside. The children have been removed to a new campsite, hidden from the enclosure by a stream and a wood. The oldest and most senior family members stand on the flat ground at either end of the family's ditch segment. At the centre of the enclosure a group of drummers are growing tired. Ever since the marking-out three days previously they have been beating out a slow, pulsating rhythm to keep the evil spirits away. The Mist of the Souls has been a special place for as long as the oldest memories run. It is where the dead have been laid to be taken by the floodwaters in winter. It is a place close to the next world, the realm of the ancestors. There are quicksands that have taken the lives of many unwary hunters. It is a place of peace, but a place of pain, evil and danger too.

Suddenly a loud blast blown on a ram's horn signals the start of the ceremonies. The senior members of each family meet at the centre of the circle. Behind them come a group of younger people carrying large pots, wooden boxes and birchbark trays in which are arrays of valuables: honey, salt, fine pottery, polished axes, amber necklaces and strange carvings that come from distant lands. These are exchanged between the elders with much pomp and ceremony, and are then shown to the families for their approval. Soon people are moving between the different family groups to admire the treasures that others have acquired. Now the drumming is growing more insistent. People sense the tension, and movement between the groups slows down, then ceases. They return to their own kin, as if under threat. The drumming reaches a climax, then stops. All are aware that this is a moment of great danger. They stand exposed to the forces of the next world, to the wrath of the ancestors who could strike with flood, fire, death, disease and famine. Their weapons are terrible.

The people stand in silence, heads bowed, deliberately exposing themselves to this danger, as a sign that they acknowledge the power, but also the great mercy, of the ancestors. Then the drumming resumes, and each family group produces its most prized treasure. This once belonged to a long-dead relative of great fame, whose deeds are known to all the family. It is carried along the ditch, under the gaze of the onlookers standing on the banks above, and placed on the bottom, at the spot where the family token was placed on the ground four days previously. Then other mementoes of family history are placed at the bottom of the ditch: the skull of a much-loved grandmother; a beautifully made bowl, painted with the family design; a ceremonial comb made from red-deer antler. These last were taken from the family tomb when it was sealed for ever, in the summer. There are also offerings of meat, but not from hunted animals. This meat is safe: it comes from the sheep and cattle herded by the family.

The men who had excavated the ditch have taken great pains to clean it meticulously. There isn't a scrap of mud, a fibre of root or a blade of grass within it. It was dug and cleansed by men who were themselves fasting, and were therefore cleansed. This state of purity is essential if the family offerings are to reach the ancestors unharmed and uncorrupted. Quickly the offerings are covered with clean gravel that has been kept to one side for the purpose. The ridge of white gravel that conceals the offerings is then covered with a carpet of animal hides, and when this is in place, the head of the family takes a basket of soil and empties it into the ditch. This is a signal for everyone to join in, and in three hours the banks on each side of the ditch have vanished. The ditch has vanished too, its place taken by a mound of soil and gravel some four feet high. This is then carefully trodden down to prevent it being washed away by the rain. By now it is growing dark, and the people return to their camps outside the enclosure.

Three hours later they reassemble within the enclosure. The children and the very elderly are now asleep at the camp. The line scored down the centre of the great circle has been replaced by a fence or screen of closely woven hurdles. The eastern half of the enclosure, where the family ceremonies of the first four days took place, is now a private space in which people can remember the dead, or commune with the souls of the departed. This half of the enclosure has been ritually cleansed many times, and is protected by the spirits of the ancestors. It lies at the threshold of the next world. This is the morning, and yet also the mourning, half of the enclosure, where the sun rises and where the spirits of the departed begin their new lives.

The western side of the enclosure symbolises the here and now. It is the place where people will congregate every autumn when the communities return to the enclosure. It faces the setting sun, the direction of evening and the time when families gather to celebrate the recurrent milestones of the passing year: harvest home, the first lambs, the first cows' milk, the new year and the height of summer. At home these events are greeted with food, feasting and merriment. Within the new enclosure they do the same, but in the company of other families. At the end of each gathering at the enclosure within the Mist of the Souls, sheep and cattle that have been penned there are slaughtered. Then everyone sits down to eat. At the end of the meal the bones are carefully placed in the ditch segments, one beast at a time: first a heap of sheep bones, next cattle, and still more sheep. When the last bone has been placed in the ditch, the heaps are covered by fresh, clean gravel. These bones aren't rubbish: they are being returned to the spirits of the land that fed them. Food, like the lives of men and the seasons of the year, comes in cycles which must never be allowed to cease.

To my mind, causewayed enclosures are among the most remarkable and enigmatic places in prehistory. Having spent seven years of my life totally immersed in the excavation of one – and a small one at that – I feel I have glimpsed something of what was going on there. But it is just a glimpse. The archaeological evidence is so slight, and depends so much on little contextual things, such as whether a piece of pottery was placed in the ground upside-down or rightside-up. It's rather like trying to recreate the magic of Derby Day from a few champagne corks, a page of the *Sporting Life* and a broken horseshoe.

There are layers of symbolic complexity at Etton. If we take just one example, the eastern or private side of the enclosure, I've suggested that here ditch segments were to do with individual families. We also find small filled pits which have been placed near the ditch segments,

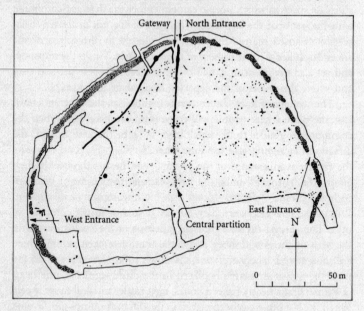

FIG 26   *Ground-plan of the causewayed enclosure at Etton, near Maxey, Cambridgeshire.*

which I believe commemorated departed individuals of the family whose history is recorded in the placed deposits within the nearby ditch. These pits can be seen as the equivalents of Christian grave-stones. But right at the centre of the private side of the enclosure we found a large, complete lower quernstone (corn-grinding stone) which had been placed on edge in a small pit. Directly below it, face-down at the bottom of the pit, was the topstone, which would have been grasped by the hands and used to rub grain against the lower, or bottom stone.

It's the context of these finds that appears to be telling us some-thing here: the topstone below the bottom stone, which was placed on edge – a position that would have rendered it functionally useless. Other quernstones, which had been smashed, were found, sometimes on edge, in segments of the ditch enclosing the eastern half of the enclosure. They were spaced out at regular intervals, as if marking significant points in a family's history – perhaps when grandchildren agreed to set up more autonomous units. In effect, all the quernstones at Etton had been ritually 'killed', just like the inverted quernstone we encountered in that strange 'house' at Ballygalley. But they're also telling us something else. Surely the quern represents mealtimes, and with it domestic life and the family. So the private side of the enclosure seems to be about individuals within families, and about families as distinct entities; but it is also about family as a concept, and perhaps as an emerging social institution. I have said it before: if British prehis-tory is about anything, it is about families.

Causewayed enclosures are known over most of north-western and central Europe, from Scandinavia and Germany to the Low Coun-tries and France.[4] In Britain they are mostly found over southern England, from Leicestershire and the Wash southwards.[5] They've puzzled prehistorians for a long time, because at face value they seem to resemble those hilltop fortified sites of the Iron Age, the hill-forts. But it's only at face value. Recent research has shown that many – most even – were positioned on the flatter land of plains and valley bottoms. And then there's the strange phenomenon of an interrupted ditch. A defensive ditch, by definition, is continuous – or else it wouldn't be defensive. The point of it is to exclude, not to admit. The hill-forts of the Iron Age, as we'll see later, were often packed with houses, but it is rare to find so much as a hut within a causewayed enclosure. They weren't villages, which fits with what we now understand about Earlier Neolithic lifestyles.

So what were they? When excavated they reveal large quantities of pottery, flint implements, waste flakes, polished stone axes and animal bone – not to mention corn-grinding querns, human bones, occasional burials and so on. Sometimes, as at the Trundle in West Sussex, they're positioned close to flint mines.[6] Often they're placed in spectacular or impressive positions – like Hambledon Hill in Dorset, or Windmill Hill near Avebury. It's not unknown for them to be located on the top of a hill that was later turned into an Iron Age hill-fort, as at Maiden Castle, also in Dorset. So these are all rather special places – and it's that which holds the clue to the mystery.

The large number of finds these enclosures produced when excavated led people to believe they were inhabited for some time, which is how they acquired their original name of causewayed 'camps'. Then, in 1965, the great prehistorian Isobel Smith suggested that they were used as meeting places for several communities. This was of crucial importance, and started people wondering what went on at the meetings. Her proposals are still widely accepted, and are admirably succinct:

> Assembly of the scattered families or tribal units takes place at one or more intervals during the year, at the slack periods in the agricultural . . . or stock-tending cycle, and affords opportunities for the transaction of the necessary business of tribal life. In addition to those matters which may come within the political field in its broadest sense, such other matters can be attended to as the holding of initiation ceremonies, matchmaking and weddings, the exchange of stock and seed-corn and perhaps of more durable goods. Rites and ceremonies are performed to ensure the fertility of the flocks and herds and the growing of the corn, and finally to celebrate the harvest.[7]

The site at Etton illustrates many of these things. It is roughly oval when viewed from the air, and is encircled by a single segmented ditch. As we've seen, it was divided into two halves, which I've interpreted as being public (to the west) and private (to the east). The public gatherings which happened at least once a year took place on the west side of the enclosure, and with them went the exchange of animals, seeds and gifts, and feasting – not to mention the politics of life, such as the construction of family alliances through marriage. At the same time, families could assemble on the other, private, side of the fence, to mark the passing of a relative and to send him or her on the last journey to the world of the ancestors. This final journey was the ultimate rite of passage that all humans had to take.

Rites of passage have always been important to human beings. Nowadays we have many: marriage, funerals, even passing a driving test or taking an exam. They become rites of passage when your success or failure is acknowledged by your friends or family and the wider community. Nowadays the formal stages of a rite of passage have become blurred, but let's take as a case-study the sitting of exams. There are three stages that have to be gone through.[8] The first is *separation*. In this the applicant is removed (or removes him or herself) from friends and the community to revise and mentally prepare for the ordeal ahead. Separation is followed by *liminality*, a word derived from the Latin *limen*, meaning a boundary. Liminality here means actually sitting the exam and that ghastly period afterwards, the state of limbo before the results are declared. In this stage one is actually straddling the boundary: one is neither an undergraduate nor a graduate. One can slip back, or move forward. Then comes the last stage, *reincorporation*, in which one is welcomed back into the community, one hopes with rejoicing.

In many tribal societies the stages are more formally marked. The first stage may involve actual incarceration or exclusion from the community. It is not necessarily very pleasant, and often requires sustained fasting, which may be seen as a form of ritual cleansing. The liminal stage is probably best seen as frightening. One is neither one thing nor another; one is also alone and unprotected, very much at risk from hostile outside forces. It's a time when the person undergoing the rite must show his or her strength, resolve and fitness to achieve the final stage. Very often it takes place in a special space that is clearly bounded and is physically removed from the day-to-day domestic world. Causewayed enclosures would be just such places. What happened there was seen as dangerous: in the case of a soul journeying to the next world, the ancestors might choose to send retribution back to earth when the new soul opened the portal and sought admission to their world. Finally, reincorporation is usually, but not always, a rapid process of welcome and celebration.

British causewayed enclosures have provided abundant evidence for the final rite of passage to the next world. Sometimes there are burials, but more often the departed souls are commemorated by small pits, dug and filled as part of the same event, which contain the remains of a pyre or bonfire and perhaps one or two treasured items, such as a fine polished axe. Sometimes these items will have been deliberately smashed. There is also evidence for rites to do with fertility, and perhaps with puberty. Doubtless others took place as well.

There is some evidence to indicate that causewayed enclosures were used regularly – perhaps annually – after their initial laying-out. Most of this 'use' has left little sign that it ever took place, apart from a few commemorative filled pits. But after two or three generations it was apparently felt necessary either to resanctify Etton, or to modify and enhance the family stories that were preserved in the ditch deposits. Life being what it is, the family groupings would doubtless have undergone change, with new ones splitting off from old ones, which then declined or died out, and so on. The segments were redug down to the layer of animal hides, but no further, so as not to disturb what had already been placed in the ground. New offerings, which show a development in symbolic 'language', being continuous (i.e. not separated by gaps or voids), smaller in scale and more intricately structured than the earlier ones, were then placed in the ground, covered, marked and reburied. The entire process was repeated a third and final time a few generations later. This process of multiple redigging, redeposition and refilling has been noted at most excavated causewayed enclosures in Britain.

Etton was placed in marshy ground that flooded most winters. It was separated from dry, habitable land by an old stream course to the north and a large area of tiny islands and rivulets to the south. Its main entranceway gave straight onto the boggy streambed, and was protected by a massive gatehouse constructed from trimmed-up oak trunks. It was clearly meant to impress and deter. Very similar massive gatehouses had been built for causewayed enclosures in Germany a few centuries earlier. One of the entrance causeways at Windmill Hill, near Avebury in Wiltshire, is approached via an extremely steep climb, and there are many other examples of deliberately treacherous or hazardous entranceways to British causewayed enclosures, as if to emphasise the enclosure's special status of physical liminality. Having struggled to get there, everyone would be aware that this was not a place to be taken lightly.

Causewayed enclosures are not standardised or uniform sites. Some are small, and occur in groups: Etton, for example, was one of possibly eight. Others are large, and can occur either alone or in groups. The enclosure on Hambledon Hill in Dorset can be seen from miles around, and covers the hilltop. Very often a causewayed enclosure provides the point of origin from which developed a so-called 'ritual landscape', a concentration of religious and ceremonial sites – of which more later.

The causewayed enclosure at Windmill Hill lies at the heart of the immense ritual landscape that grew up around Avebury and Silbury Hill (the largest manmade mound in ancient Europe) in Wiltshire. Avebury and Windmill Hill were later surrounded by dozens and dozens of smaller sites including barrows, and timber and stone circles. Stonehenge, whose very first phase resembles a causewayed enclosure, was also later surrounded by a vast array of Later Neolithic and Bronze Age ceremonial sites. Even the little enclosure at Etton seems to have given rise to its own ritual landscape which contained many dozens of barrows, henges and other shrine-like places. I have discussed these three ritual landscapes at some length elsewhere,[9] and will return to Stonehenge and Avebury in Chapter 9.

The problems of archaeological visibility in the Later Mesolithic period make it hard to prove conclusively that causewayed enclosures, and the ritual landscapes that developed around them, were necessarily located in places that were significant or sacred to earlier hunter-gatherer people. Having said that, I am in no doubt that they were. The probable causewayed enclosure at Dorstone Hill, Hereford and Worcester, for example, revealed a large number of Mesolithic flints, and it seems likely that the hill was important to hunter-gatherer, and indeed much later prehistoric, communities.[10] The causewayed enclosure at Briar Hill on the outskirts of Northampton produced a number of Mesolithic radiocarbon dates.[11] Other sites are positioned in prominent places in the landscape, but in a way which suggests they weren't meant to dominate the scene. At Etton, for example, the enclosure was placed to one side of a semi-circular meander in the river; the enclosure at Windmill Hill could easily have been placed like a crown, encircling the hilltop, but was instead placed off-centre, slightly to one side. It's as if the landscape feature – the hill or the land within a meander – was already significant in some way. So the enclosure can be seen as a new special area within a place that was already revered by communities living in the vicinity.

Stonehenge itself provides a striking example of such long-term sanctity. As has been noted, the first phase of Stonehenge, which comprised only the ditch and bank which encircles the subsequent Stones, resembles a causewayed enclosure, albeit a late one (2950–2900 BC). Sadly, Stonehenge does not have the happiest history of archaeological investigation, and the two principal archaeologists who worked there, Lieutenant Colonel William Hawley in the 1920s and Professor Richard Atkinson between 1950 and 1964, both appear to have suffered from severe doses of writer's block – although Atkinson did manage to produce a popular paperback.[12] Hawley's field notes survive, but Atkinson's don't. I have to say I find the treatment of Britain's most famous site by my profession a source of huge embarrassment, but recently English Heritage has published a massive volume which goes a long way towards expiating the guilt.[13] It makes it clear that the encircling ditch excavated by Hawley was originally dug in a series of segments that were only poorly linked together. Clean chalk rubble was found at the bottom, suggesting that the ditch was deliberately filled in, as at Etton. There were also heaps of red-deer antler, one heap of which appeared to have been set alight *in situ*, perhaps as a form of burnt offering. To my eye at least, many of the sections showed clear signs that the ditch had been recut and then filled in several times. Again, this recalls Etton, and many other causewayed enclosures both in Britain and on the continent.

On the other side of the A344 from the Stones themselves, in the present-day car park, were four mysterious pits. The first three were found in a row when the car park was first built, in 1966. The fourth, about a hundred metres to the east, was found when new visitor

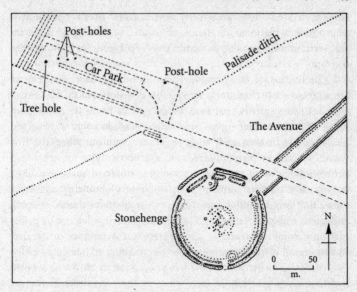

FIG 27 *Plan showing the position of Stonehenge and other ancient features close by. Excavation carried out before construction of the car park began revealed four very large Mesolithic (8500–7650 BC) post-holes (numbered here 1–4) and a supposed tree-throw pit (TP). A palisade trench, set with closely spaced posts, was found in excavations south of the car park closer to the Stones. This palisade was probably constructed in the Late Neolithic, perhaps around 2200 BC.*

facilities were constructed in 1988. The pits had been dug to contain pine posts of about six to eight hundred millimetres in diameter (say two to three feet – the diameter of a very large telegraph pole), and it's difficult to suggest any practical purpose they might have served – they simply *had* to have had a ritual or religious function. What makes these four post-pits remarkable is their range of radiocarbon dates, which spread between 8500 and 7650 BC. So by rights I should have mentioned them two chapters ago, when I discussed Star Carr and the postglacial period. The radiocarbon dates are supported by pollen analyses carried out on samples taken from the pits. These show a 'classic' early postglacial environment of an open mixed pine and hazel woodland. Hence, of course, the choice of wood for the posts: around 8000 BC oak hadn't yet recolonised Britain after the Ice Age.

The finding of the massive Early Mesolithic posts so close to Stonehenge is one of the most remarkable discoveries in British prehistory, because it proves that Stonehenge and its immense ritual landscape of barrows and other sites was positioned within a sacred landscape that was already four thousand years old when the first Neolithic monuments appeared on the scene. The apparent gap between the posts and the earliest Neolithic evidence can be explained in two ways. First, in terms of archaeological visibility: by and large, Mesolithic people didn't construct permanent monuments of earth and stone. I suspect their sacred landscapes were marked out by paintings on natural rocks, and by special trees, ponds, springs or streams. In this regard it's interesting to note the presence of a large so-called tree-throw pit (a natural hollow left when a tree is blown or toppled over) which is precisely aligned with the three post-pits in the car park.[14] Second, people haven't looked. There have been surface surveys nearby, but no digs – and those pits in the car park were found by good old-fashioned excavation. Perhaps we could use geophysics to see whether there are any more massive post-pits on that alignment.[15]

Was the positioning of the tree-throw pit mere coincidence? It's impossible to be certain, but it seems unlikely. For what it's worth, I've excavated dozens of tree-throw pits, and this one is very much deeper, more regularly shaped and steeply-sided than any I've encountered. It's also quite narrow, which doesn't fit with what happens if a tree topples over in a storm, when an upside-down, mushroom-shaped scoop of earth and subsoil is wrenched out of the ground. Pines, unlike oaks for example, aren't particularly deep-rooted either. I wouldn't be at all surprised to learn that the car park tree-throw was yet another post-pit, but perhaps one where the post had been removed, allowing the pit's sides to weather back naturally.

What did these great posts represent? A building, perhaps? No – buildings have more than one wall. Besides, we know more or less what Mesolithic houses looked like from places such as Mount Sandel, and they didn't involve the use of massive posts. I believe it always was what it now is, namely a row of huge posts, and that the clue to what those posts actually *did* was found on the south side of the A344 during excavations that took place in 1967. At the risk of being irritating, I shall leave that hanging in the air, but will return to it in Chapter 9.

We cannot as yet estimate the size of the Mesolithic sacred landscape, if indeed it did have fixed boundaries, but we can get some idea from a detailed survey carried out by the archaeologist-cum-broadcaster Julian Richards. His work at Stonehenge was published in 1990, predating his appearance as presenter of BBC2's highly successful series *Meet the Ancestors*. The survey was known as the Stonehenge Environs Project, and took place when Julian worked for the Trust for Wessex Archaeology.[16]

Perhaps the most remarkable feature excavated during the Stonehenge Environs Project was known as the 'Coneybury Anomaly' (an anomaly is the term usually applied to buried archaeological features revealed by geophysics). It appeared on a geophysical survey of the well-known henge at Coneybury, some 1300 metres south-west of the Stones. On excavation it proved to be a large, round pit, almost two metres across and dug about 1.25 metres into the chalk. Shortly after being dug it had been filled with a mass of material: large and fresh pieces of pottery (including one complete vessel), flints, part of a polished flint axe, and numerous animal bones. In his report Julian remarks how the filling of the pit resembled the carefully arranged offerings that had been placed in the ditch segments at Etton. I agree wholeheartedly – and so does the radiocarbon date, which centres on 4040–3640 BC. This makes it the earliest known Neolithic feature of the Stonehenge ritual landscape, around eight centuries earlier than the Stonehenge ditch, and 1300 years earlier than the Stones themselves.

The bones from the Coneybury Anomaly were fascinating. They were mostly of roe deer and cattle, with some pig, red deer and beaver, and all (except the beaver) showed the clear scratches that are evidence of butchery. The roe deer and pig were eaten on the spot, but the choice cuts of beef and red deer were taken away and consumed somewhere else.

While the animal bones seem to have been the result of a single event – perhaps a feast – the pottery and flint shows slight evidence for having been exposed on the surface for a short time. Many pieces of both can be joined together, and the large number of rimsherds (pieces from the vessels' embellished and decorated rims) suggests that this is selected material, not domestic debris. Julian Thomas proposes that it was selected from an above-ground heap or midden, and was deliberately buried as a means of giving permanent expression to some memorable occasion which had been celebrated by feasting. Towards the eastern side of England a tradition arose of digging and filling much smaller pits than the Coneybury Anomaly. We encountered it at Etton, but it is also known in Kent and Essex, through East Anglia and northwards to Lincolnshire and Yorkshire. These small filled pits may have commemorated a community's seasonal visit to its summer or winter camping grounds, but the pits themselves were probably placed in a significant or special part of that particular tract of landscape. The presence of pits does not necessarily indicate a settlement at that precise spot.

The tradition of digging and filling pits was intended to transform a temporary event or occasion into something enshrined within tribal lore and ideology. It's a process of creating and fixing history, and with it come new, or renewed, social relationships. With this process of transformation come added dimensions of meaning and significance. So a marriage, for instance, becomes more than a simple union of two people. By fixing the event in time and space it acquires a fresh context: one of already complex family ties and obligations, which may be expressed in the future by exchanging livestock, land or prestigious gifts from distant places. In our times the place of such behaviour has largely been taken by written documents, such as the various legal forms which accompany and outlive important, but ephemeral, occasions like marriages and funerals. The point to emphasise is that while the documents define the continuing arrangements on earth, the ceremonies invoke the next world and a higher authority. In the resonant words of the marriage service in the Book of Common Prayer: 'Those whom God hath joined together let no man put asunder.' In Neolithic times all of this was achieved by a group of people coming together, then digging and filling a small pit.

I've mentioned that deliberately filled-in pits are quite commonly found in Earlier Neolithic contexts in southern and eastern Britain, but they are also found in northern England, Scotland and Ireland.[17] Very often these pits, filled with fresh flint, pottery and bone, occur within sacred enclosures such as henges (about which more later). Their occurrence in contexts that were patently religious or ritual used to mystify archaeologists, who were sometimes reduced to suggesting that rubbish formed a part of Neolithic ceremonial. The problem lay, of course, at the archaeologists' door: it was they who had labelled the objects found in these pits as rubbish, which they then had to explain away. 'Rubbish' was not a concept that existed in prehistoric Britain. There was casual settlement debris, but the systematic disposal of unwanted material in large quantities is not a phenomenon we encounter until the urbanised styles of life found in Roman and early medieval Britain.

One site in Northern Ireland clearly illustrates the problems of referring to 'rubbish' in a ritual context. The site at Goodland, County Antrim, is near the coast, and was sealed and protected by layers of peat above it. It dates mainly to the Earlier Neolithic, although it remained in use for somewhat longer. It's a peculiar-looking site, consisting of a very roughly square ditch arranged in eight strangely-shaped segments. The ditch contained a minimum of forty-four 'placed' deposits which the excavator, Humphrey Case, described as being 'incorporated into the soil filling or inserted into it . . . At their most elaborate they consisted of glacial boulders with sherds and struck flints packed conformably around . . . all deposits consisted of sherds and flints, some tightly packed as "sandwiches".'[18] As at Etton, the ditches showed clear evidence of having been filled in deliberately.

The small pits within and just outside the segmented ditch were remarkable. For a start, there were 171 of them, in an area of just thirteen by fifteen metres. None was deeper than four hundred milli-metres. A sample from one pit gave a radiocarbon date of 3650–2900 BC. Case noted that, like the ditch, they had probably been filled in immediately: 'many contained deposits of identical nature: boulders packed with sherds and flints, and so on'. Many of the potsherds from the pits came from the same actual vessels as sherds found in the ditch segments nearby. This would suggest either that the two features were open and in use at precisely the same time, or that a common midden had been used to provide material to be placed in the ground.

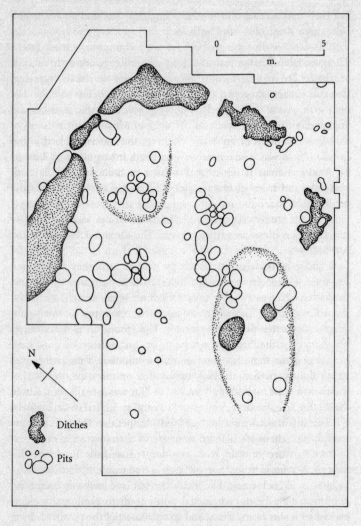

FIG 28   *Plan of the Earlier Neolithic (3650–2900 BC) site at Goodland,*
County Antrim, Ireland.

Evidently very similar things were happening at Goodland as at the Coneybury Anomaly – and elsewhere.

I remember discussing Goodland with Humphrey Case back in the 1970s. He suggested that it seemed as if ordinary domestic rubbish was being given some form of special religious or ritual treatment. He wasn't taken altogether seriously then, but in many ways he was right – this wasn't the only occasion on which he was ahead of his time. I think today we would differ from Humphrey's first thoughts only in his mention of 'rubbish'. Whatever the material placed in the Goodland pits was, and whatever it signified, it was never rubbish in the modern sense. It represented aspects of domestic life that had been removed from their normal sphere, and given some added or strengthened symbolic meaning simply by the process of removal. This can be seen as a part, or an extension, of the process of 'ritualisation' that was discussed earlier, with reference to those Irish rectangular buildings.

In all essential respects Goodland has the attributes of a causewayed enclosure, but in miniature. Unlike the big enclosures, it probably never served as a meeting place for different communities moving about the region. Instead, the similarity – perhaps 'homogeneity' would be a better word – of the 'offerings' found in pits and ditch segments, plus the fact that so many pieces of pottery join together, suggest that the same family group repeatedly visited the site to pay their respects, perhaps every year for two or three centuries. This indicates that the mobile or cyclical style of life was actually remarkably stable and free from friction – that mobility in Ireland, if not in Britain, did not equate with out-and-out competition for new or larger territories. Perhaps it's best to see it simply as restricted mobility.

The mixture of wild and domesticated animals found in the Coneybury Anomaly contrasts with what one would expect to find at a causewayed enclosure, where the emphasis is usually very much on the latter. It's as if the enclosures were meant to symbolise a more controlled realm of avowedly Neolithic domesticity, as distinct from the wilder, more Mesolithic world out there, represented in the Anomaly. It's tempting to suggest that the more controlled pattern of life we see expressed symbolically at the causewayed enclosures was something the people who used them aspired to, but had yet actually to achieve. Indeed, as we will discover in Chapter 9, it would take upwards of two millennia before the landscape would become 'tamed' to a significant degree.

The Stonehenge Environs Project survey revealed almost no Mesolithic flints, although this may have been, as Julian Thomas himself suggests, a 'visibility' problem. But as well as the Coneybury Anomaly there was massive evidence for Neolithic activity in the area prior to the erection of the Stones. This included a full-sized causewayed enclosure at Robin Hood's Ball (about four kilometres north-west of the Stones) and some fifteen long barrows (more about these in the next chapter), not to mention numerous finds of pottery and flint. The pottery and many of the barrows are found on land towards the Wiltshire river Avon, which skirts the Stonehenge area to the south and east.

It is surely not coincidental that water should be found so close to our hypothetical Mesolithic sacred region. As we continue our journey through prehistory, we'll encounter water on many occasions. It was of fundamental practical and ideological significance in ancient Europe, and nowhere more so than in the British Isles. It sustains life, and on a clear, still day it physically reflects life. But it destroys life too. It also separates islands from the mainland. It follows that in symbolic terms water can be seen to separate our world from the next world, or that of the ancestors.

Rivers are frequently found near prehistoric religious or ceremonial sites. I believe this was probably for symbolic reasons, but as we saw at Etton it would be very easy to oversimplify our reading of that complex, layered symbolism that contained within it the shared histories of the people who created, nourished and guarded it. To say, for example, that water symbolised a soul's journey to the next world is banal. It may have done – indeed it probably did – but it also marked boundaries in this world, and provided corridors along which people could move without crossing too many tribal frontiers.[19] Perhaps it was for these reasons that the so-called 'ritual landscapes' that we'll discuss further in following chapters very often grew up in wide river valleys.[20] Perhaps they acted as neutral buffer zones between major tribal or cultural territories, within which different rules applied to those of the regions on either side. In particular the laws, custom and practice of land tenure and inheritance were different. Communal or individual holdings of land, if they existed at all within a ritual landscape, were rarely marked by permanent divisions.[21] I believe these were fluid landscapes that weren't parcelled up to serve the practical needs of farming, whether livestock or arable. I accept that wealth and power played a major part in the ceremonies that took place in a ritual landscape, but I suggest that they were amassed or attained in the wide world outside that landscape.

An example of the fluidity that may have obtained within the bounds of a ritual landscape is provided by the so-called cursus, a class of monument so far known only in Britain and Ireland.[22] Cursuses have been known about since the eighteenth century, but they came to archaeological prominence only between the wars, when aerial photography began to reveal more and more of them. They tend to be concentrated on the flatter ground of lowland river valley floodplains, but not exclusively so. Two, for example, are known near Stonehenge on Salisbury Plain, and the most famous of them all, the Dorset Cursus, rolls across hill and dale regardless.

The dating of cursuses is slightly problematical, but most seem to have been constructed in parallel with, or very slightly later than, the causewayed enclosures – from about 3800 or 3600 BC until just after 3000 BC. They consist of two parallel ditches, the earth of which was usually piled as two banks on the inside, although sometimes as a long mound down the centre. Most often the ends of the cursus were closed off, but sometimes again they were left open. Their length varies a great deal, typically from about 150 metres to over ten kilometres. The presence of cursuses demonstrates that quite large areas of the lowland landscape had been cleared of forest, because in many cases the ditches and banks are quite small and straight. They would have been hard to lay out in woodland, and even harder to appreciate. But seen as two parallel white slashes cut across a flat grassland landscape, they could have been spectacular.

Over the years I've been excavating parts of a long (2.5 kilometres) cursus near Maxey, just north of Peterborough. The Maxey Cursus cuts a diagonal swathe across a low gravel 'island' in the heart of the floodplain of the river Welland. It begins alongside the Etton causewayed enclosure, and near the centre of the island it passes beneath

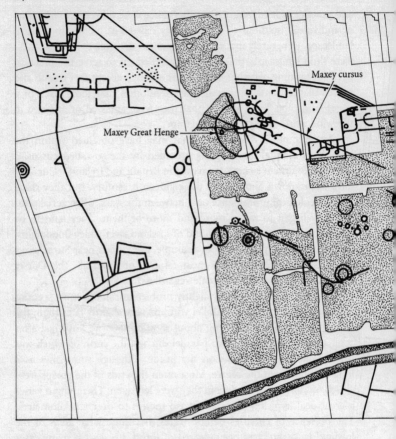

Maxey cursus

Maxey Great Henge

FIG 29 *Cropmarks revealed by air photography near the village of Maxey, Cambridgeshire.*

a huge circular ceremonial site, known as the Maxey Great Henge.[23] In fact it probably isn't a henge in the strict meaning of the word, because it's rather too early in date (about 3500 BC), but we do know that it was constructed when the cursus ditches were still open – and as they're very shallow, they could only have remained open for a handful of years. There's evidence, too, that this particular cursus was

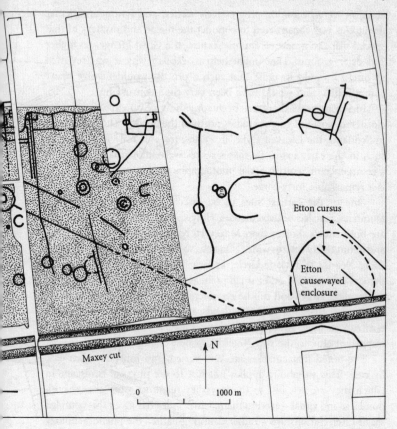

Etton cursus

Etton causewayed enclosure

Maxey cut

N

0   1000 m

constructed in lengths of about two hundred metres, which would suggest that it was repeatedly visited over the years, and that its alignment was significant before any ditch-digging began.

Why was this? It seems to me that cursuses are so variable that we must try to explain each one on a case-by-case basis. At Maxey the alignment of the cursus takes you from one of the lowest spots in the landscape (where we find Etton) to one of the highest (the site of the Great Henge, and near to the church). It ends at another low spot on the north-west 'shore' of the 'island'. We know that conditions at Etton were becoming progressively wetter, and I wonder whether the cursus was constructed to conduct the magic and mystery of that special place to a new ceremonial centre, the Great Henge, on higher and drier ground. That might help to explain why it was revisited so often. I would imagine that such a process would involve many communities, and would have been very time-consuming.

In recent years there has been something of an explosion in the cloistered world of cursus studies north of the border. The first cursus in Scotland, the Cleaven Dyke, in Perthshire, was only recognised as such in the early 1980s. By 1985 six sites were known, and thanks to a resurgence in Scottish aerial photography the latest published score is a remarkable forty-three.[24]

One of the earliest sites to be discovered, at Holywood, near Dumfries, consists of two cursuses, Holywood North and South, which are both much shorter than Maxey (three to four hundred metres), and about thirty metres wide.[25] One has squared and the other rounded ends. Nearby is a stone circle, known as the Twelve Apostles, and there is evidence for other small prehistoric ritual sites in the immediate locality. Holywood can be considered a smaller complex of ritual sites, rather than a larger 'ritual landscape', as we have been using the term up to now. Although relatively small, it contains within it an important clue to the way Neolithic people thought.

I've noted that cursuses are very varied, and must be taken case by case. This variability applies not just to the physical landscape in which they are set, but to the way they relate to other sites – both domestic and ritual – around them. Chris Tilley has given this complex set of interrelationships a rather daunting name, 'the phenomenology of landscape'.[26] Essentially, this approach treats landscape as more than a mere stage for a play. Tilley doesn't use the word 'landscape' as you or I might – as something to be observed and admired. To him, the prehistoric landscape was more of an active phenomenon. It forms part of the play, because it includes beliefs, myths, legends and stories that profoundly affect what is taking place on stage. Sometimes the input of the landscape to the play might be distant, for instance when sunset at the summer solstice coincides with a chink in the hills on the skyline. At other times it may be more local or intimate, such as when an ancestral burial mound is, or is not, visible behind something

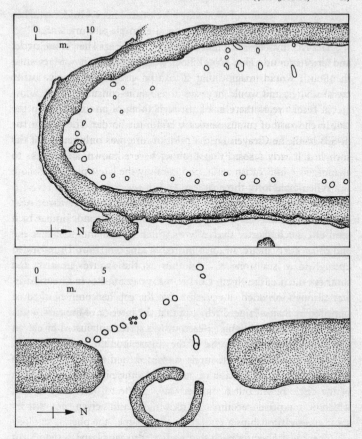

FIG 30 *Plans of the two excavations at the Neolithic Holywood North Cursus, near Dumfries. Trench 1 (top) revealed a long, horseshoe-shaped arrangement of posts, which formed a vertical frame to the cursus's rounded terminal. Trench 2 (below) shows an entranceway through the North Cursus southern ditch, which has been obstructed by a small ring-ditch and obscured by a screen supported by an oblique line of posts.*

as insignificant as a low hillock, or indeed another barrow. Or it can be a mixture of both. Either way, the play, the players and the landscape that once lived in all of their minds are inseparable. Of course, we will never grasp the totality of what may have existed in past landscapes, but the Holywood ritual complex is a good example to work with.

The North Cursus is aligned on the 'Twelve Apostles' stone circle, and terminates on top of a low hillock with extensive views. Meanwhile the South Cursus runs along a natural promontory and, rather unusually, has two entranceways through its ditches, which allow access from the North Cursus through to the stone circle. In other words, the various monuments are laid out with close regard for the details of the landscape and the position of other monuments of the complex. It would seem that nothing here is haphazard, or left to chance.

When excavated, the northern end of the North Cursus revealed a setting of some twenty-seven posts which ran around the inner edge of the cursus, like the raised prow of a ship. This was similar to a semi-circular setting of twelve posts which I remember seeing at the end of another cursus, an uncomfortably long way from Dumfries, at Springfield in south Essex.[27] Another excavation, this time on the southern ditch of the North Cursus, was positioned over an entrance-way through the ditch. It revealed that the gap had been blocked or impeded by a small ring-ditch, and that the interior of the cursus was concealed from those who entered it by a screen supported by eleven posts. The framing of the end of the cursus, and the management of people crossing through it, surely suggest movement: that the end of the cursus was a destination or stage of a journey, as were the stones of the circle beyond. Put another way, this was a theatrical setting, which was experienced through movement and action, not just by static observation.

There was also evidence that earlier features played a significant role in whatever it was the Holywood cursuses stood for and cele-brated. They were part of a long-standing tradition of ritual and ceremony at this special place. We see much the same thing at the longest (ten kilometres) and most spectacular of British cursuses, the Dorset Cursus at Cranborne Chase. Here the cursus is aligned on, and respects, earlier monuments such as long barrows as it traverses the gently undulating chalk downland in a manner which indicates not only that the form of the landscape was significant, but that its history shaped and affected the path of the cursus.

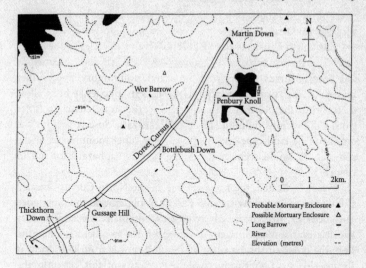

FIG 31   *Plan of the Dorset Cursus and other Neolithic monuments at Cranborne Chase, Dorset.*

Other things may also have affected that alignment, such as the orientation of the midwinter sunset. But the authors of a recent study do not see the cursus as some sort of observatory, concluding instead that 'by relating such an enormous monument to the movements of the heavenly bodies, its builders were making the Cursus appear part of nature itself and freeing its operation from any challenge'.[28] One could see the relationship of people to monuments, astronomical alignments and landscape as being interlinked and reciprocal. What I'm trying to say is that prehistoric monuments were not like modern churches: places to be visited on Sunday and then forgotten about for the rest of the week. They were always there, an ever-present, but nonetheless constantly evolving, core of stability in daily life.

CHAPTER EIGHT

The Archaeology of Death
in the Neolithic

SO FAR I HAVE DISCUSSED Earlier Neolithic religion, ceremony and ideology without directly referring to death. This was deliberate, because death in our society is about pain or loss, and I wanted to keep the emphasis of my story on life. But now I must look death in the face. To me, a typical citizen of the Western world, it's an unforgiving and unhappy face. It speaks of irrecoverable finality: an unfinished symphony, or a young life whose promise will never be fulfilled.[1] Death to us is almost always a tragedy.

But to many non-Western societies, death is as much a beginning as an end. Of course people in prehistory felt grief, pain, loss and emptiness; but there was hope too, and in the longer term there was the prospect of a transformed existence and renewal. Life and death, like the seasons themselves, formed part of a continuum.

Several chapters ago, at Gough's Cave in Cheddar Gorge, we came across some grisly remains which might be evidence for cannibalism. More importantly, whether or not human flesh was actually consumed, the treatment of the bones indicated that early communities of *Homo sapiens* in Somerset were disposing of their dead in a series of pre-ordained stages. This concept, already thousands of years old, is crucial to a proper understanding of what Neolithic 'tombs' are all about. I put the word 'tombs' in quotes because, in common with the term 'grave', it implies permanence, like some long-forgotten dusty lead coffin, lodged deep within a family vault, a final resting place. The reality was altogether different.

The Earlier Neolithic tradition of formal disposal was collective.

The tombs – which one must think of as shrines, temples or churches, rather than just as final resting places for the dead – were among the earliest field monuments of Britain, and they occur in a great variety of shapes and sizes. I'll begin by considering some examples from England which demonstrate the extent to which funerary sites of the Earlier Neolithic varied over quite a small area, and which illustrate and echo many of the points that have been raised so far. They also reveal how the tradition was constantly evolving and reinventing itself. By Later Neolithic and Bronze Age times – say from 3000 to 2000 BC – the regional differences of burial practice, already apparent shortly after 4000 BC, were becoming most pronounced.

The first point to make is that by no means everyone was buried in one of the collective tombs of the Earlier Neolithic. Burials and loose human bones can be found in causewayed enclosures, flint mines, isolated graves in the open, and in settlements, right across the British Isles. We don't know what proportion of society was buried in tombs, and we mustn't leap to the conclusion that those who were necessarily came from the upper echelons. They may have, but we lack the evidence to prove it. One should also bear in mind my earlier remarks when discussing Ian Hodder's ideas about symbolism and intention, and not be fooled into a simplistic interpretation of burial practices. It's worth noting Julian Thomas's words: 'If mortuary ritual is a communication system, it tells us more about those who conducted the ritual than those who were buried.'[2]

The first site I want to examine was one of the most meticulous and technically competent excavations ever carried out in Britain. It's located at Hazleton North in Gloucestershire, about eight miles (thirteen kilometres) east of the beautiful spa town of Cheltenham. The dig director was Alan Saville, and the detailed report he wrote has done the dig ample justice.[3] Alan's own special interest is flint-work, and before Hazleton North he was principally known for his truly astonishing reports on the thousands and thousands of finds from the flint mines at Grimes Graves. He's someone who can handle both detail and quantity simultaneously – an ability that played a key part in the success of Hazleton.

There are two long barrows in Barrow Ground Field, a few hundred metres north-west of the village of Hazleton, in a landscape of rolling limestone hills. In the 1970s an archaeological survey showed that the barrows, Hazleton North and Hazleton South, which were entirely made up of millions of pieces of limestone, wouldn't last long if they were ploughed many more times – as would sadly have been inevitable under the Common Agricultural Policy. This imminent threat led to Alan's dig, which was funded by English Heritage.

The two Hazleton sites are part of a widespread funerary tradition of the Earlier Neolithic known as long barrows, or long cairns (barrows are mounds; cairns are more specifically mounds made from stone). They belong to a well-defined class of barrows, distributed across south Wales and the Cotswolds, known as the Cotswold-Severn group, which includes some of the best-known sites in England, such as Ascott-under-Wychwood, West Kennet, Notgrove and Wayland's Smithy. These are tombs that belong to the megalithic (literally 'big stones') tradition of building that was widespread across northern and Atlantic Europe.

It used to be thought that the builders of megalithic tombs shared a common ancestry and culture, but today we realise that it's not as simple as that.[4] In some instances the contact between different people within the tradition was close; in others the appearance of tombs built from huge stones was coincidental. In many cases we can also trace close connections between communities who built megalithic tombs and those who built tombs from other materials, such as wood.

To return to Hazleton North: I'll start with what Alan terms 'pre-cairn activity' – in other words, the use of the site before it became a barrow. Archaeological finds from below barrow mounds are usually taken as straightforward evidence for what was happening in the landscape before the mound was thrown up. But there's a problem here. If one takes a longer view, one must keep in mind the possibility that the place chosen to erect something as significant as a communal burial ground could well have been important, in its own right, for some considerable time. A good example of this is the criss-crossing plough furrows found beneath the mound at South Street, another Cotswold-Severn long barrow, a few miles south of Windmill Hill and Avebury.[5]

At first sight these furrows appear to be clear evidence that the land was used to grow crops in the years before the mound was

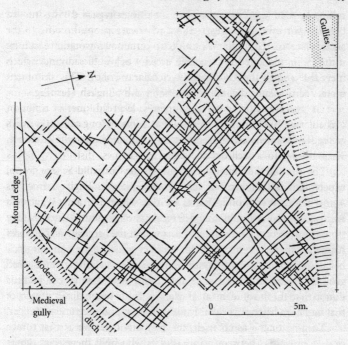

FIG 32 *Plan of Earlier Neolithic plough marks revealed below the mound of a long barrow at South Street, near Avebury in Wiltshire.*

erected.* But is it as simple as that? To my eye the marks are altogether too neat and regularly spaced; they look more like the product of a single episode of criss-cross working. Elsewhere, especially in eastern England, the turf below a mound was first removed, probably as an act of ritual purification.[6] Could something similar have been going on at South Street?

The 'pre-cairn activity' at Hazleton looks at first to be the debris of straightforward settlement. But there's a great deal of it, and some of the many flints are Mesolithic. Were these the remains of a hunting

---

* Incidentally, the 'furrows' aren't furrows at all, because Neolithic ploughs, known as 'ards', acted rather like a hoe, and didn't have a mould-board that turned the soil over to make a true furrow.

camp, as Alan suggests, or are we looking at repeated visits to this precise spot over many years? If so, why were people coming to the same place so regularly? We can't be certain. However, we can be more definite about the Neolithic activity below the mound, which included a dark-stained, roughly circular midden area, about ten metres across, and a group of post-holes and a hearth, forming some sort of structure of five by three metres. Was this part of a house? I'm not sure, but I am fairly certain that a small pit a few metres north of the structure was one of those steep-sided, deliberately filled-in pits we found in such numbers at Etton.

The finds are also most intriguing; they include, as one would expect, flint and pottery, but also the smashed remains of quernstones – another echo of Etton. Thanks to Alan's meticulous excavations it was possible to rejoin smashed fragments of a quartzite quernstone from the pre-cairn land surface, proving that the breakage had actually happened there.[7] Finally, as if this indirect evidence for non-domestic behaviour wasn't enough, loose human bones, including three small groups of skull fragments, were also found. I think there can be little doubt that the long cairn at Hazleton North was erected at a spot that had been 'special', probably for centuries, and maybe even longer.

Turning to the tomb itself, the first point to note is that tombs of the Cotswold-Severn group are very varied within themselves. There are, as we'll see, certain organising principles that are held in common, such as forecourts, where the main ceremonies took place, and evidence for partition or segmentation in the way the mound was constructed. But the range of sizes and shapes is important. It indicates that these monuments were constructed by people who shared a common belief, for example, in the world of the ancestors, and indeed a desire to construct and use long barrows. But it also suggests that the events and ideologies that were celebrated at the tombs had been developed by the communities who used them from their own sources, the origins of which were both diverse and ancient.

First, let's consider the date and time Hazleton North was in use. Radiocarbon dating showed that this was for a relatively short period (between three hundred and 150 years), at some time between 3800 and 3500 BC. This would place it early in the Cotswold-Severn tradition – a fact, as we'll see in a moment, that's borne out by its shape. Like most long barrows, Hazleton North is trapeze- or wedge-shaped, with a carefully marked-out 'forecourt' at the wide end. This was the area where funeral ceremonies took place. The edge of the mound in the forecourt area was a carefully built dry-stone wall with two projections, or 'horns', which helped to frame the forecourt between them.

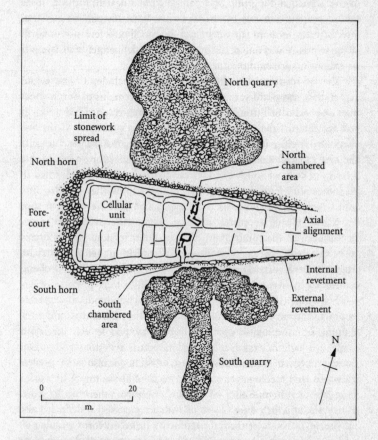

FIG 33 *Ground-plan of the Earlier Neolithic (3780–3640 BC) long cairn at Hazleton North, Gloucestershire, showing how the mound was constructed in a series of cells arranged on either side of a central axis. The two burial chambers are constructed from large stones.*

The tombs themselves, which were placed opposite each other, slightly off-centre on the long sides of the trapeze, consisted of two chambers reached by short passages. Directly outside the entranceways to the tomb passages were two large quarry pits, about six feet (two metres) deep, which provided the stone for the cairn, or mound. We've seen that the tomb was constructed at a special place in the landscape, but when it ceased to be used the megalithic chambers were covered over by the cairn, and the site was then abandoned. In other words, the erection of the barrow mound was a final farewell, or sealing off of the monument.

Viewed from outside, the mounds of long barrows or cairns look remarkably smooth. They are higher at the wider end, by the forecourt, and slope gradually down towards the narrower 'tail'. But if you remove the turf that covers them and look very carefully at the way they were built, you discover that they aren't just a simple dump. In the case of Hazleton the interior of the mound was divided up into a series of cells, of about five metres square. Each cell was formed by an informal style of dry-stone wall, to make in effect a revetted box, into which mound material was tipped. The cells formed two rows on either side of a central, or axial, alignment, which was also a dry-stone wall. Cellular construction is quite frequently encountered in British long barrow mounds – at Skendleby in Lincolnshire, for example, the cell walls were made from wooden fencing, probably reinforced by woven wattlework.[8]

Sometimes this cellular system of construction has been explained in practical terms, as a means of preventing the mound material from slipping or creeping. It has also been attributed to the use, quite simply, of gang labour. Neither explanation is very satisfactory. One doesn't need so many transverse or crossing partitions to prevent outwards slippage, nor are actual physical walls necessary to work a gang-labour system – after all, Britain's railways were built by gangs of navvies, and they didn't leave us with a segmented system. It's also unwise to introduce practical arguments to account for peculiar or odd aspects of religious sites. It's rather like trying to explain the font as a source for the water used in the mortar for the church walls – a suggestion that's just possible, but not very sensible.

So what was going on? Segmentation in one form or another has cropped up quite frequently in our story so far. We saw it in the stop-start ditches that surrounded causewayed enclosures, and in the individual offerings that were made within those ditches. A single segment may represent a family, as I suggested at Etton, or some other social group. The point is that long barrows were communal burial places – and by 'communal' I don't just mean that groups of dead bodies were buried in them. They were communal in that they served the needs of living communities, which in turn were represented, physically and symbolically, in the cells or partitions within the mound. So it was gang labour, but willing gang labour provided by the people of the community involved with the project.

The earlier long barrows of the Cotswold-Severn tradition, such as Hazleton, had burial chambers set into the long sides of the mound. These usually contain loose bones, or one or two articulated bones, such as arms or legs, often minus the hands and feet. Skulls commonly occur in groups, and there is clear evidence for a degree of sorting or rearranging of the body parts. A pioneering study in 1982 showed that the organising principle behind the way that bones were rearranged within the chambers of Neolithic tombs was the human body itself.[9] That may sound strange, but after all, our bodies express any number of symbolic meanings – including our gender, our age, our social position, our religion and so forth. We saw at Gough's Cave that bones were systematically and carefully defleshed, and there is abundant evidence for this happening in the Neolithic as well. Sometimes it occurred at communal graves, other times at different places, such as at causewayed enclosures, where loose human bones are frequently found, often with clear evidence that they had been gnawed by dogs. We found many examples of gnawed human bones at Etton.

When we discussed the bones from Gough's Cave (Chapter 3), we saw that defleshing, or excarnation, represented the departure of the soul. It could also be seen as the departure of the individual person. We are left with the bones. Sometimes they don't matter, and get chewed by dogs. At other times they do, in which case they often find their way into chambered tombs. In these instances bones can be seen as a new, stylised or transformed representation of a human being, rather than an individual as such. A skeleton represents a person, but at the same time it isn't a person. It can also be taken apart and recombined with ease – we often find the bones of, say, heads, arms and legs together in separate parts of the tomb. This recombination expresses the close-knit, unified aspect of a family or a community, the body social, as it were. That sounds fine in theory, but how would it work in ordinary life?

Alan Saville reckons that Hazleton was 'used' for quite a short time – perhaps 150 years – before it was finally sealed off by the mound. This period of use seems to have involved the separation and sorting of bones, perhaps on a regular basis. Evidence from other Cotswold-Severn tombs suggests that bones may quite commonly have been moved between different chambers, or indeed between different sites. They could be seen as a type of symbolic 'currency', which served to seal or endorse a range of new family ties and obligations, ranging from marriage alliances to land or hunting deals, or whatever. In a very real sense, the dead were playing an active part in people's daily lives. So during this period the site at Hazleton would have remained open, essentially two megalithic chambers set slightly to one side of a forecourt, which provided the theatrical setting for ceremonies to do with death and the next world. It would also have been available should people require to remove or reorder bones in either of the two chambers. To describe it as simply a 'tomb' is largely to miss the point.

We see a subtle but significant change in emphasis in the later tombs of the Cotswold-Severn tradition. Side or lateral chambers along the mound are replaced by a single passage which is set into the forecourt at the wide end of the trapezoidal mound. Chambers were arranged off the passage and at its end. These were all megalithic, and were roofed with large, flat capstones. One of the most famous of all single-passage megalithic long barrows is that at West Kennet, just over a mile south of Avebury, in Wiltshire. It was excavated and published by the great archaeologist Stuart Piggott.[10] Today the site is in the care of English Heritage, and it is well worth a visit, even if most of the great stones, much of the dry-walling and roof of the tomb have been restored. The entranceway forecourt stones, that are so striking as you approach the site, were straightened and partially re-erected by Piggott and the men from the Ministry of Works in the mid-fifties. Allow a weekend, and see Avebury, Silbury Hill and the

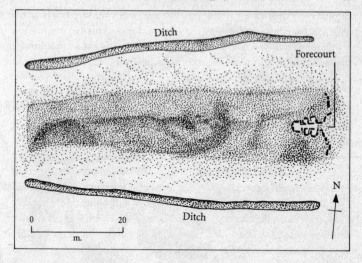

FIG 34   *Ground-plan of the Earlier Neolithic long barrow at West Kennet, near Avebury, Wiltshire.*

other sites of this ancient landscape at the same time (to my mind they far outshine Stonehenge).

The West Kennet long barrow was positioned near the end of a northwards-facing spur in chalk downland. The mound has a core of sarsen boulders (a hard crystalline sandstone that occurs locally), but the main mound material, chalk rubble, was mined from two side ditches which run parallel to the long sides of the trapezoidal mound, which is 330 feet (one hundred metres) long. The wide end is at the east, and here there is a magnificent revetment sixty-five feet (twenty metres) wide, to the higher end of the mound which is made from huge sarsen boulders. It's quite clear that the mound was built in two distinct phases (a fact given spurious emphasis by the remains of a medieval trackway which crosses it), and this fits with the sequence Piggott revealed within the tomb itself. The high sarsen boulders at the wide end, where the modern visitor enters the monument, form a massive screen or theatrical backdrop to the forecourt – which was the scene of the principal ceremonies. In fact, you could argue that the forecourt and the ceremonies that took place there were the main

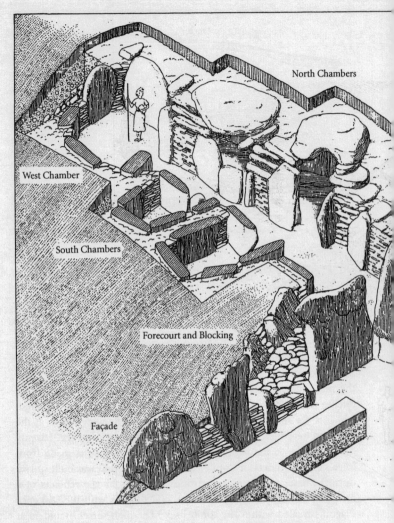

North Chambers

West Chamber

South Chambers

Forecourt and Blocking

Façade

point of the monument, rather than the chambered tomb within the mound.

The forecourt, as at Hazleton, is flanked by two slightly projecting horns of the megalithic revetment. At the centre is a short passage,

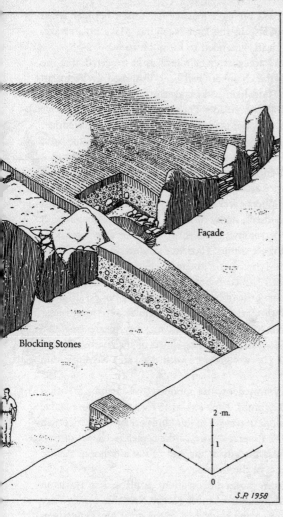

Façade

Blocking Stones

2 ·m.

1

0

S.P. 1958

FIG 35 *A view beneath the mound of the Earlier Neolithic West Kennet long barrow from just outside the forecourt, showing the megalithic façade, blocking stones and tomb chambers. (Artist: Stuart Piggot.)*

formed by two boulders and a capstone, leading to two side chambers; then another short passage followed by two more side chambers; and finally a single, slightly larger, chamber at the western end, again reached by a short passage. The entranceway into the passage from the forecourt was closed off by a massive flat sarsen boulder when the tomb went out of use in the later Neolithic. Make no mistake, this huge stone was clearly intended to mean business.

When Piggott came to excavate he found, as he expected, that the human bones within the chambers had been disturbed by Victorian archaeologists. John Thurnham had excavated there in 1859, the year of Darwin's great publication. Sadly Thurnham was a less meticulous scholar than Darwin, and the plans of his dig are not very accurate. In his account of the work he describes what he saw in the west chamber at the end of the passage: one body was 'apparently in a sitting position' and another with the legs 'flexed against the north wall'.[11] Clearly these are articulated bodies, albeit with skulls or limbs missing. The five chambers excavated by Piggott revealed the remains of about twenty individuals, many of which had been tampered with shortly after burial, by removing skulls or limbs. To give some idea of the population of these tombs, Hazleton produced the remains of twenty-one adults and twelve to nineteen children and teenagers, whereas West Kennet revealed twenty-plus adults and thirteen-plus youngsters. The vast majority of human remains were bones, although two cremations at both Hazleton and West Kennet were found near entrances. It's tempting to suggest that these may have been associated with ceremonies to do with the closing down of the tombs. By and large, cremation is a rite we associate with the Later Neolithic and Early Bronze Age.

So far I've concentrated on the mounds and chambers within these Earlier Neolithic tombs. Now I want to turn to the more active side of their use. In modern terms I'm thinking perhaps of the Scottish or Irish wake, plus the funeral service in the cemetery chapel of ease and the whisky-tea-and-biscuits at the end of the afternoon. All are important components of the funeral.

It's quite clear from modern excavations at places like Hazleton that the barrows and mounds of most Earlier Neolithic tombs were added as a final gesture – the equivalent of the great blocking stones at West Kennet (where the mound seems to be as old as the rest of the site). It's very hard to remove the image of the mound from one's imagination, as that's what dominates the scene at these places today. But in Earlier Neolithic times one would have seen something very

FIG 36   Structures that predate the Earlier Neolithic barrow mound at Street House Farm, Loftus, Cleveland. To the left is the forecourt, which is separated from the low, roofed mortuary structure by the façade palisade and a massive central timber. Beyond the mortuary structure is a low, kerbed enclosure with two paved areas that may have been used as exposure platforms for corpses.

different. For a start, there'd be no mound, and the principal focus of interest probably wouldn't have been the burial area at all. Instead, people would have gathered in and around the forecourt, the ceremonial area located at the wide end of most trapezoidal long barrows. Next to the forecourt, and symbolically separated from it, was a special mortuary structure, to which access would probably have been restricted – to judge from their size. In some instances this was probably a temporary resting place for bodies. Here they would be stored, perhaps defleshed – either naturally, by carrion crows, or by physically removing the flesh, or sometimes even by fire (a process that could also have taken place off-site; charred bones were encountered at both West Kennet and Hazleton).[12]

A particularly fine example of a pre-barrow ceremonial funerary area was excavated between 1979 and 1981 by Blaise Vyner at Street

House Farm on the cliffs overlooking the North Sea near Loftus, midway between Hartlepool and Whitby.[13] Here the forecourt was framed by a close-set palisade of large posts whose arrangement resembled the horns of Cotswold-Severn tombs. Within the forecourt itself were five post-holes arranged in two parallel rows. These may have formed the end of a processional avenue, or part of a lightweight structure erected on the forecourt.

At the centre of the horned palisade was a massive post, and behind that was a small mortuary structure built of stone and wood. Burnt human bones and a partly articulated human skeleton were found within it. At its other end was a smaller, but still very substantial, post. Behind the mortuary structure was a rectangular kerbed structure with two entranceways aligned along the central axis of the site. There were two small, roughly paved areas within the enclosure whose purpose is unclear – but they might just have been used as low platforms on which to expose corpses for defleshing by natural means.

Once picked clean, the bones would have been removed to the mortuary structure, where they were stored. After some time the mortuary structure, and the bones within it, were set alight. The entire complex, excepting the forecourt, was then buried beneath a trapezoidal stone cairn which was built up and enlarged over some time, suggesting that the site was revisited on several occasions after the mortuary structure had been burnt.

Again, all the evidence suggests that the Street House cairn was a site of long-term importance. Its location overlooking the breakers of the North Sea is most striking, and the evidence for repeated use of the site in Neolithic times – say, centred on 3500 BC – is very strong. To cap it all, a Bronze Age barrow was constructed alongside the Neolithic cairn, almost two millennia later. It's hard to prove continuity between two sites separated by such a long span of time, but by the same token it's equally difficult to prove that they are *not* connected in some way. To my mind the connection lies in that spectacular location, and what it may have represented in people's minds.

Before we leave long barrows I must briefly mention one in my own backyard, discovered by an old friend and colleague, David Hall. I remember standing on top of the mound with David on a fresh autumn day in the late seventies discussing whether the spread of gravel at our feet was the remains of two Bronze Age round barrows or a single Neolithic long barrow. Earlier that summer he had discovered over a dozen round barrows which were protruding through the later peats of Haddenham Fen, not far from Ely, and he was keen to find something a bit earlier. He did, and the site has turned out to be most remarkable.[14]

David Hall's Haddenham long barrow was still partially water-logged when excavated, although when it was originally constructed the ground wasn't quite that wet.[15] Blaise Vyner had to recreate his mortuary structure at Street House Farm from slight traces in the soil, but Ian Hodder and Paul Shand, who dug Haddenham, had far more robust remains to work with. It was an extraordinary site to visit. You had to squeeze into a tent rigged up from clear polythene. Once inside, you were confronted by what looked like an enormous oak trunk lying on its side, around which three or four archaeologists and conservators were excavating with enormous care. Their painstaking work revealed an oak mortuary structure whose walls (which were 1.3 metres high and four metres long), floor and sides were built from massive planks split off from a single huge tree. At either end of the structure were large oak posts, just as at Street House. However, the Haddenham mortuary structure didn't join directly onto the forecourt façade, but was distanced from it by a short 'vestibule', also built from timber. This vestibule is best seen as a deliberate attempt to distance what was happening in the mortuary structure from the ceremonies taking place in the forecourt. Incidentally, I was intrigued to discover when I visited the dig that decorated pottery in the style we found at Etton was found in the forecourt, whereas undecorated pottery alone was found in the mortuary structure. Again, this would suggest that the two areas were regarded as being distinct.

As time passed there were gradual, but very important, changes in Neolithic burial practices. We've seen how the chambers of Cotswold-Severn tombs were moved from the sides to the end of the mound, and there is some evidence to indicate that bodies in the later of these tombs were more articulated than dis- or re-arranged.[16] However, some of the changes that took place after about 3500 BC were more obvious, such as the massive extension of the mound to form so-called bank barrows, which frequently occur in Dorset (one of the best-known examples is in the interior of the massive Iron Age hill-fort at Maiden Castle).

The deliberate distancing of mortuary structures and megalithic chambers from the activities that took place in the forecourt was probably part of a process in which the dead began to be seen as inhabitants of their own world, which was physically and emotionally removed from ours. This process is mirrored by the way bones were treated. As we've seen, at the outset of the long barrow tradition, there's much evidence that skulls and limbs were moved around. Earlier I used the word 'currency' to describe their role, which, like coins, was in the here-and-now. But at the same time these bones had lost their individual identity as the remains of specific, named, people. They had been subtly transformed by the process of defleshing and subsequent sorting and storing.

In the thousand years after 3500 BC we find less evidence for the mixing and sorting of bones. Corpses are buried, or cremated, entire. Communal burial occurs less frequently, and most bodies are placed in single graves. Again, this indicates a shift in belief. The dead are now seen to play less of a role in the here-and-now. Instead of being transformed by defleshing or decomposition into a more generalised, representative state of symbolic being, they retain their personal identity on burial, and continue a parallel existence, as individuals, in their own realm, which is that of the ancestors. One can see cremation, which was becoming increasingly popular, as a logical development of this process, in that it made *post mortem* manipulation of body parts impossible. It was very much a one-way journey.

I suspect that these changes in funerary rite went with a shift in the way people regarded themselves and their surroundings. Family history was not something to be studied in retirement; it was a vital and cohesive force. I can imagine that after dark children sitting around the fire would be rehearsed in their family lore by parents and grandparents. Maybe, as in early historic Ireland, the myths, legends and tales would be remembered in ballads and verse. And they would probably have been remarkably accurate, even down to dates and seasons. The oft-repeated achievements of individual ancestors within developing family histories provided people with new, powerful sources of identity at a time when wider allegiances to tribal groups were giving way to smaller-scale social networks, as communities became less mobile and farming families identified themselves more closely with bounded tracts of landscape. Paradoxically, it was also a time when competition for power and prestige was of increasing importance. So at one level people were becoming more inward-looking, but at another their attention was focused far beyond their immediate surroundings.

Many of the processes of change that we've been looking at in this, the previous and indeed the next chapter are actually illustrated on the ground in the form of complex 'ritual landscapes'. I've mentioned that Stonehenge and Avebury sit close to the centre of their own ritual landscapes, which I discussed at some length in *Seahenge*.[17] Mike Pitts has taken a fresh look at these two famous Wessex ritual landscapes in his excellent and accessible book *Hengeworld*.[18]

There are, of course, many ritual landscapes in Britain outside Wessex – I've already mentioned the Etton causewayed enclosure, which was the starting point for the Maxey ritual landscape in Cambridgeshire. I now want to look at a relatively compact one in the Oxfordshire Thames valley, midway between Radley and Abingdon.

The Barrow Hills ritual landscape is particularly striking because of the way it was laid out.[19] As is often the case, there's a causewayed enclosure – in this instance the famous Abingdon enclosure – at the heart of it. Presumably this was placed in a spot that was already important to people in the area. Its position, cutting off a spur of gravel between two converging streams, is significant, if not spectacular. There isn't much evidence for Mesolithic activity, although a number of tree-throw hollows, one of which produced a slightly unreliable radiocarbon date of 7450–6600 BC, indicate a possible phase of forest clearance – but what this was for remains a mystery.

Barrow Hills has been ploughed flat for a very long time, and it probably acquired its name back in Saxon times. It was spotted as cropmarks on air photos taken in the 1920s. Sadly most of it has vanished into gravel pits and the housing estates of rapidly growing Abingdon, but after *some* excavation – which is a minor consolation, I suppose.[20] The small ritual landscape is remarkable because of the way its component parts – mainly Neolithic and Bronze Age barrows

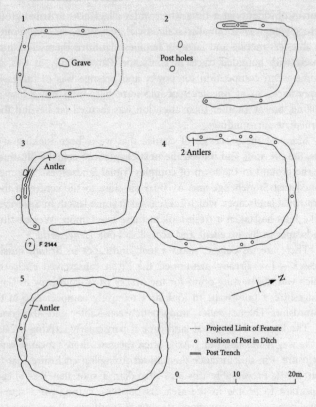

FIG 37 *The phases of development of the Neolithic oval barrow at Barrow Hills, near Radley, Oxfordshire (about 3500–2900 BC).*

– are aligned on or towards the Abingdon causewayed enclosure, whose precise extent isn't known, but is generally thought to respect the courses of the two converging streams.

Apart from the causewayed enclosure, Barrow Hills is famous for one of its two oval barrows, which was excavated by Richard Bradley from Reading University, nearby. This barrow is positioned east of the causewayed enclosure, and it illustrates some of the points I have

Meticulous excavation of the Old Stone Age or Palaeolithic site at Boxgrove, West Sussex (500,000 years ago). In the foreground are two hand-axes still *in situ*.

Caves on the shore at Paviland on the Gower Peninsula, south Wales, viewed from the low-tide mark. The Goat's Hole Cave, which yielded the skeleton of a young man, the so-called 'Red Lady' of Paviland (about 24,000 years ago) is the higher, oval cave-mouth at the centre of the photograph.

The great grass-covered mound of the Later Neolithic passage grave at Knowth, County Meath, Ireland (3200 BC). This tomb formed part of a large group of monuments, mostly constructed during the fourth millennium BC, within a bend of the River Boyne. In the foreground are smaller passage graves which cluster around the great tomb.

A view inside the Newgrange passage grave, County Meath (3200 BC). This great tomb is part of the Bend of the Boyne group, and like Knowth many of its stones feature so-called 'Megalithic Art', such as the triple spiral on the left-hand stone. This view is taken from the back of the burial chamber, looking towards the entrance passage in the background.

ABOVE RIGHT Perhaps the greatest artwork from the British Neolithic, the carved flint ceremonial macehead from the Knowth passage tomb. The source material, a rich brown and white mottled flint, was carefully selected and the carving was largely executed by polishing, using fine abrasive sands.

Timbers of the Later Bronze Age post alignment or causeway at Flag Fen, Peterborough, looking west. This view was taken during an early stage in the excavations and shows horizontal timbers that were positioned towards the latter part of the causeway's construction, around 1000 BC.

Another view of timbers at Flag Fen, but looking east. This view was taken in the later stages of excavations and shows some of the lower timbers that were positioned towards the end of the Middle Bronze Age, around 1200–1300 BC.

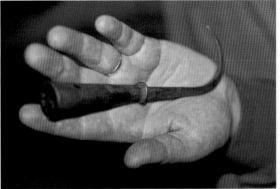

LEFT A bronze 'flesh-hook' found beneath the lowest timbers at Flag Fen and therefore dating to about 1300 BC. There was part of a wooden shaft in the socket (towards camera), but this was in roundwood (a small side branch); it was not a dowel, which suggests that the flesh-hook could only have been used for very gentle work.

RIGHT Bronze shears and their ash 'shoe' box, from Flag Fen, Early Iron Age (possibly 500 or 600 BC). The box has provision for a short, bar-shaped whetstone and is closely similar to Victorian boxes for steel shears. It is questionable whether these shears would necessarily have been used to clip prehistoric sheep, which retain their fleeces less efficiently than modern breeds. Perhaps they should be seen as barbers' implements.

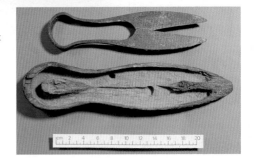

BELOW A group of bronze objects (1100–900 BC) from Flag Fen. To the left are swords and daggers, including a very rare miniature sword (second from bottom) and a dirk, or thrusting weapon (third from bottom); the three upper swords are slashing weapons. Lower right are two short spearheads and a dagger with its antler hilt; in the lower right corner is a chape, or sword scabbard protective tip.

LEFT One third of a Bronze Age tripartite wheel (about 1300 BC), a form that is found widely across western Europe, from Flag Fen. This example uses three species of wood, each carefully chosen for its special properties: the body of the wheel is in alder, the dovetailed cross-ties on each side (only one visible here, to the right) are in oak, and locating dowels or pegs (not visible) are in ash.

BELOW AND RIGHT Two views of the sharpened tips of oak posts from the post alignment causeway at Flag Fen. The central view shows an unusually large post which has been sharpened by a single row of hewing cuts along each corner. This work could only have been carried out when the wood was still 'green'. A bronze axe could not have left such a clean cut had the wood been allowed to season.

FF 531/2

BELOW A complete axe haft for a bronze socketed axe, in oak (about 1000 BC), from Flag Fen. The axe was placed at the tip of the hook-like point, and the nick cut halfway along the hook may have been used to secure a twine tie or lashing to secure the axe-head. The hook was split from out of the trunk and the handle is a side branch, with bark still adhering in places.

The author's long-term collaborator, Dr Charles French, acts as the human scale in this view, taken in 1974, of the traces of the foundations of a Bronze Age roundhouse at Fengate, near Flag Fen (about 1500 BC). The circular eaves-drip gutter empties into a larger droveway drainage ditch via a short S-shaped gully. The two prominent posts of the doorway are towards the bottom of the picture, below the lower of the two red and white scales.

Reconstructing the Fengate Bronze Age house excavated in 1974. The main roof rafters and wall posts are in ash, the smaller-diameter woven wattle of the walls is in hazel.

Four views of the reconstruction of the Fengate Bronze Age house. Note the flat angle of the roof. Had this been steeper, as thatch would require to work efficiently, the turf could not have been retained in place during wet weather. Below the turf is a six-inch layer of reed, lashed into place (above). Two layers of turf are laid on the reed thatch (right). The completed turf roof during the damp months of spring (below). The same a few months later, in high summer (bottom).

A general view of the reconstructed Bronze Age farmstead at Flag Fen within its fields and paddocks. The bank in the background retains the canalised River Nene; beyond it lies open Fenland.

made about the development of funerary rites in the Neolithic. As is always the case on an archaeological site, Richard was faced by all the phases of the barrow's development in one jumble of oval ditches. His job was to disentangle them, which he did with great success.

He showed that the ditches were dug in five distinct episodes, working from the inside outwards. In phases 2 and 4 the oval area was open at the south-west, towards the end of the promontory on which the causewayed enclosure was built – presumably to allow access to and from it. The U-shaped phase 2 ditch was dug very close to the original, phase 1, rectangular ditch, and two posts were placed in the centre of the gap to the south – again slightly angled to the south-west – presumably to frame a portal of some sort. In phase 3 the open side was blocked by a curved ditch, and there was access to the interior by way of two narrow gaps. In phase 4 a new U-shaped ditch was dug around all the previous ditches, and in the final phase, 5, the circuit was completed by digging another short, curved ditch, but leaving the narrowest possible entranceway to the west. The barrow mound began gradually to accumulate after the digging of the first, inner, ditch, and in all phases there is evidence for posts being set in the ditches.

There are echoes of the nearby causewayed enclosure in the various phases of the oval barrow. For example, the ditches of phases 2–5 appear to have been dug in short segments that were then joined together, a technique that recalls the 'gang labour' we encountered in the ditch segments at Etton, and also in the cellular construction of the Hazleton barrow mound. Richard's team found 'offerings' of antler in the ditches; in phases 3 and 4 they were at the ends. Near the antlers, but higher in the ditch filling (i.e. very slightly later), they found fragments of human skull. The ends – or butt-ends, to use the archaeological jargon – of ditches were the places where significant finds such as complete pots, animal or human skulls were made at Etton. It's quite clear that every aspect of the barrow's construction and use was steeped in complex layers of symbolic meaning which intentionally reflected what had been – and maybe still was – celebrated in the causewayed enclosure nearby.

The central grave probably went with the first phase, as it and the two skeletons it contained are aligned identically.[21] The bodies were

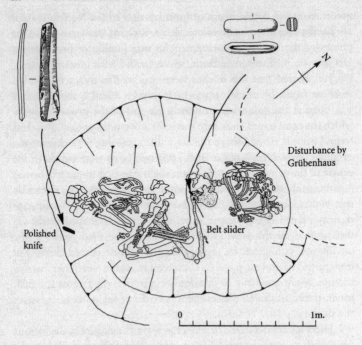

FIG 38   *The central grave of the Barrow Hills oval barrow, near Radley, Oxfordshire. The bodies were both aged thirty to thirty-five at death. The skeleton on the left is female, the one on the right male.*

of a man and a woman, both aged between thirty and thirty-five. He was buried with a polished jet or shale belt slider (a stone version of the leather loops that help keep the two ends of a knotted belt tucked away and tidy), she with a polished flint knife. The man's skull had been disturbed by a Saxon Grübenhaus (a type of house with a sunken area below the floor) in post-Roman times, and a flint arrowhead was found within it. Had it not been moved by the digging of the Saxon 'cellar', the arrowhead would most probably have laid in the ground in the mirror-image position of the polished knife at the other end of the grave. The symmetry and careful arrangement of the bodies was plainly a matter of some importance, and it is hard to believe that there was ever any intention to unearth them in the future. The burial of grave goods was another feature of the funerary rites that developed during the Neolithic – and it continued throughout prehistory and the Roman period, until the arrival of Christianity. Indeed, the people who built the Grübenhaus would probably have buried their own loved ones with a selection of often lavish grave goods.

I mentioned above that the Barrow Hills ritual landscape is important because it shows clear evidence of having been arranged or laid out. The evidence resides in the position of the various components of the landscape – mainly, but not exclusively, barrows – and also in an extensive series of radiocarbon dates which give us another important dimension to work with.[22] We start with the initial causewayed enclosure, and presumably, too, the phase 1 oval barrow ditch, which we can place within 3700–3300 BC. In the next phase (3400–2900 BC) we see the causewayed enclosure massively enlarged. This is also when the remaining four phases of the oval barrow were fashioned. In the next three phases (2900–1500 BC) we witness the development of the barrow cemetery on two slightly diverging alignments that had already been established by 2900 BC.

Barrow Hills, like most large-scale excavations, revealed a number of 'stray', or isolated, Neolithic and Bronze Age features away from the main monuments. But one roughly circular area between the two lines of barrows and the original oval barrow seems deliberately to have been kept open. This open space holds the clue to how this mysterious landscape of barrows developed, and how it may have been used. Radiocarbon dates allow us to distinguish an early period of barrow construction after that of the original oval barrow and causewayed enclosure. It's represented by the three southerly barrows of the north alignment (nos 1–3), and all the barrows of the more spaced-out south alignment (nos 12–15). Together they form two parallel rows, with no divergence. Then, sometime between 2100 and 1500 BC, the north alignment was shifted very slightly at the double barrow, no. 4, to form a diverging avenue or processional way (nos 4–11). Another double barrow, no. 16, at the north-west end of the south alignment, was placed across its axis, in effect forming a restricted portal or entrance into the avenue.

People processing south-westwards along the avenue would come across a small barrow, no. 201, which was probably erected in this last phase. It is positioned in the centre of the avenue, at the precise spot where the open space revealing the oval barrow and causewayed enclosure beyond becomes visible around the flank of the mound of barrow 1. We can't tell whether this little barrow was intended to

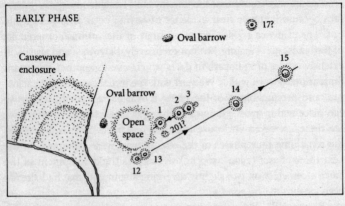

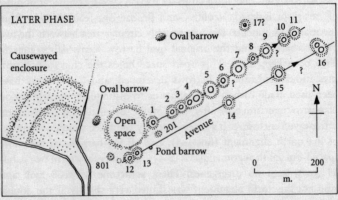

FIG 39   *The development of the Barrow Hills Later Neolithic and Bronze Age ritual landscape (2100–1500 BC). The causewayed enclosure (shaded) probably extended as far as the two streams. It is regarded by the excavators as the 'founder monument' upon which everything else was subsequently aligned.*

constrict and slow down access into the edge of the open space, or to divide the traffic into two streams. But the barrows certainly weren't the prehistoric equivalent of a row of traffic cones, as the foregoing description perhaps makes them sound. Far from it. Each monument was just that: a monument, like the Cenotaph in Whitehall. But instead of a list of engraved names on the surface, deep within them resided the actual physical remains of the heroes of family and tribal history. Everyone would have known the stories, and it must have been a truly awe-inspiring experience to pass so close to such powerful forces. The great bulk of their mounds would have obscured all views of the earlier sacred places until that crucial moment towards the end of the procession when suddenly all was revealed.

We've merely glimpsed the principles behind the subtleties of the layout of the ritual landscape at Barrow Hills, but it should already be clear that there was a great deal of theatrical skill involved. For a start, the heart of the experience, the view across to the ancient sacred places, would have been climactic. That open space deliberately kept the spectators at a distance. It's the principle behind the holy-of-holies: something out there, hidden for much of the time, never to be grasped by mere mortals. You could look, but not walk over, or touch. The theatrical skill was such that at key moments, as on entry to the processional way and later at barrow 201, the tension was deliberately heightened, then sustained, then raised yet again. This was achieved by restricting access – which we also saw in the layout of the oval barrow – but also by hiding a sacred view that people yearned to see, and by making them walk so close to the line of barrows that stood between them and the causewayed enclosure. A pilgrimage to Barrow Hills would have been a very moving, and probably physically exhausting, experience; something to be remembered for a long time.

I want now to turn my attention across the Irish Sea. It may come as a surprise that there are about 1400 megalithic tombs in Ireland, which surely indicates the presence of a reasonably large population merely to build and maintain them. The most remarkable tombs of the Irish megalithic tradition are undoubtedly the passage graves, and the most extraordinary of these are to be found in the lush green valley of the Bend of the Boyne, or Brú na Bóinne in Irish, in County

Meath. Huge sums of money have been spent investigating and restoring Knowth and Newgrange, two of the three great passage graves that dominate the landscape. Only the great mound at Dowth remains uninvestigated in modern times, although it was mutilated by 'diggings' in the first half of the nineteenth century.[23]

Before we dive into the archaeological meat of these extraordinary sites, we should consider the controversy surrounding the near-total excavation of two tombs out of three – leaving just one intact, and a damaged one at that. What are the ethics behind this enormous expenditure of time, money and effort? Will future generations ever be able adequately to reassess what the archaeologists of the twentieth century thought was there? Is restoration driven by the twin needs of research and the encouragement of tourism a valid reason for such a wholesale carving-up of two vitally important monuments? Finally, how accurately do the restorations reflect how these great sites might have appeared to people in the Neolithic and Early Bronze Age?

The knowledge we have gained from the two excavations is undoubtedly *most* remarkable, and a tribute to the archaeologists involved. But is the cost, in terms of archaeological damage and the loss of authenticity, acceptable? With the advantage of hindsight I now very regretfully consider that it isn't. Nobody can run a perfect excavation, not even Alan Saville of Hazleton fame, and without absurdly vast budgets, sites as massive as Knowth and Newgrange can't possibly be examined stone by stone. Even today, with state-of-the-art surveying technology and laser-based digital scanning becoming available, we'd be very pushed to make anything like a comprehensive record of two such complicated sites. We should also remember the warning of the great archaeologist Sir Mortimer Wheeler: excavation is merely methodical destruction.[24] Reconstruction, however carefully it is done, destroys authenticity. With a reconstructed monument, what you see before you isn't what was built in antiquity: it's what somebody in the twentieth century *thought* was built in the remote past. As a result, for me at least, the magic vanishes almost entirely. And that's a very high price to pay.

The matter is made more difficult by the extraordinary reconstruction of the great mound at Newgrange. The excavator, Professor Michael O'Kelly, thought he had found evidence in the rubble of the forecourt for a steep, high revetment, or mound support-cum-edging, made from white quartz and a scattering of granite. This interpretation has been challenged many times, and I well recall the cries of anguish in the academic press when the plans to reconstruct were announced.[25] So, it has always been controversial. But when you actually see it, all doubts vanish: it doesn't *look* like something prehistoric people could have built. It's as simple as that. Today the vast green mound at Newgrange resembles a chirpy pillbox hat with a bright white hatband – something Aer Lingus might one day adapt for its stewardesses.

What makes the entire concoction worse is its height and angle – so steep that it has had to be reinforced by a hidden concrete wall, or it would collapse due to the pressure of the mound it skirts. Frankly, it should be removed or hidden in some way, and soon. We all know how hard it is to erase a striking image, however false, from the public imagination: Boudica's chariot with its revolving knives, the Vikings in their horned helmets and King Arthur in his shining plate armour will be with us for a long time to come. It would be a travesty if one day the Irish Neolithic were to be represented in the popular mind by that grotesque hatband.

The Brú na Bóinne is a ritual landscape in its own right, and although it doesn't possess (so far as we know) a causewayed enclosure as a 'founder monument', the three great passage-grave mounds are placed in very prominent positions in the landscape, and could have served the purpose. Newgrange sits at the very centre of the great Bend of the Boyne, with Knowth and Dowth atop rising ground to the east and west respectively. It would appear that the Bend of the Boyne had been largely cleared of forest cover by 3200, when the great tombs were built, and that people in the area, whose roundhouses have been found, seem to have prospered on a mixture of livestock and arable farming. Taken together with other growing evidence from Neolithic Ireland, it's hard to see these as being very mobile communities.

The Bend of the Boyne ritual landscape has a character of its own, and although there are certain features in common with those of Britain, it is nonetheless very Irish. To give two examples: to date Knowth and Newgrange have revealed over two hundred examples of the strange swirling or geometric designs that were pecked in light relief on the surface of many of their stones. It's a style that has come

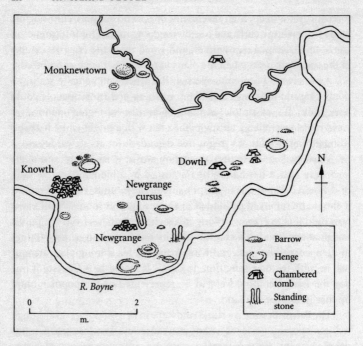

FIG 40   *The main Neolithic and Early Bronze Age sites in the Bend of the Boyne (Brú na Bóinne).*

to be known as Megalithic art, and these two passage graves have revealed more of it than anywhere else in Europe.[26] Another very Irish feature is the way a huge number of smaller, satellite tombs cluster around the great mounds: at Knowth there are no fewer than seventeen smaller passage graves nestling up to the great mound, like chicks around a mother hen.

There are around forty barrows and other circular ritual monuments in the Bend of the Boyne. These include the strange Monknewtown earthen enclosure or 'ritual pond', which measures one hundred feet (thirty metres) across and is surrounded by a raised bank seven feet (over two metres) high.[27] It still holds water! A more recent discovery (1978) is of a classic cursus, with a rounded end, a few metres east of the great Newgrange mound. Its ditches are twenty metres apart and run due north–south for a traceable distance of some hundred metres. This alignment is the same as that of the Newgrange passage grave.

An interesting point worth mentioning here is that we are starting to see water being mentioned in connection with formal ritual or religious monuments. We have seen that Etton, like many other cause-wayed enclosures, was located near a river, while in the case of the Abingdon enclosure at Barrow Hills, two of its sides were bounded by converging streams. But the Monknewtown ritual pond actually incorporates water into the structure, what one might term the 'fabric', of the ritual monument itself. One end of the cursus at Newgrange appears to end in boggy ground which could well have been open water in Neolithic times. Other British and Irish cursuses are known to cross water or to end near boggy land.[28] If cursuses are indeed involved with the movement of people through a ritual landscape, then in these instances their journey was deliberately directed towards wet places. We'll see in Chapter 10 that water was to play a very important role in the way religion and ritual evolved during the subsequent Bronze and Iron Ages.

It's hard to be precise about what was happening in the Bend of the Boyne before Knowth, Dowth and Newgrange, but it is clear that the area was far from deserted, and I see no reason not to suppose that it was already of some significance. As we've seen, the great passage graves acted as a magnet for many other smaller tombs, and during the later Neolithic there was a steady increase in monument-building in the area. By this time the passage-grave tradition had ceased, and new rites and ceremonies required a fresh generation of ceremonial monuments to be erected. Besides the Monknewtown 'ritual pond' there were other circular monuments at Monknewtown and elsewhere in the Bend of the Boyne that recalled the 'henges' then being built on the other side of the Irish Sea (about which more in the next chapter). The British henges very often produced pottery in a distinctive style known as Grooved Ware. It's a type of pottery that often occurs on ceremonial or ritual sites, including Monknewtown. This later phase of monument construction seems to have come to an end around 2200 BC, at the turn of the Bronze Age – at which point, somewhat abruptly, the erection of ritual sites in the area stopped.

I will confine myself here to the initial phases of Newgrange, and will only mention Knowth in passing. I'm acutely conscious that I won't be able to do even one of these extraordinary monuments justice in the space available to me, so I will concentrate on aspects of layout and use that throw light – in one instance quite literally – on the way their builders were thinking when these great monuments were being planned and built. The excavations of Newgrange and Knowth, by Professors Michael O'Kelly and George Eogan respectively, have transformed our understanding of Neolithic religion, art and funerary practice in Ireland.[29]

Like Knowth, Newgrange was laid out and constructed around 3200 BC. Also like Knowth, it was a long-lived tomb, and probably continued to be regularly visited throughout the life of the ritual landscape around it.[30] In its later phases Professor O'Kelly recovered fragments of Grooved Ware, the ceremonial pottery also found at Monknewtown. The huge mound is roughly circular, and conceals a single passage grave which penetrates one third of the way into the barrow. Below the hideous white revetment is a continuous kerb of ninety-seven kerbstones, many of which have been decorated with megalithic art. In front of the passage, in the forecourt, is the entrance stone, which is carved all over with swirling spirals. This is possibly the finest example of large-scale or architectural megalithic art known in Ireland.

Deep within the mound, the end of the passage opens into the burial chamber, a hall-like open space whose roof seems to soar upwards into the darkness. At first glance this tall roof looks arched, like a medieval church, but the principle of the true masonry arch was then unknown, and the soaring effect was achieved by gradually overlapping a series of slabs to form a so-called corbelled vault, in this case twenty feet (six metres) above the floor of the central 'hall'. Three side-chambers open from the main burial chamber, the one on the left-hand side being notably smaller than the other two. A similar lopsided arrangement of chambers and a soaring corbelled vault is found at the end of the eastern passage at Knowth. Each side-chamber contained a large, decorated stone 'basin', which we know played an important role in the funerary rites.

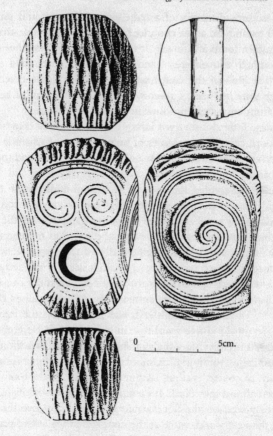

FIG 41 *Four views of the polished flint macehead from the passage grave at Knowth, County Meath (about 3200 BC).*

The passage at Newgrange was sealed by a huge blocking stone in the Later Neolithic period, and it remained closed until 1699. Thereafter it must have been visited by hundreds of people, so that when O'Kelly excavated (between 1962 and 1975), most of the bones and other offerings made during the funeral rites had been removed. We get some idea of the wealth of material that must have vanished from

George Eogan's discovery of a quite extraordinary – and unique – stylised human head at the entrance to one of the three side-chambers in the eastern tomb at Knowth. It's in the form of a macehead made from polished lustrous cream-and-red flint that looks good enough to eat. The skill of the craftsman who made it defies description. Although only fist-sized, I reckon it to be one of the most beautiful objects from any site in pre-Roman Britain, or Ireland.

Because little else survived intact, O'Kelly carefully excavated the earth floors, revealing quantities of human bone, of which less than half had been cremated. It was mainly concentrated around the three stone 'basins' where presumably it had originally been laid to rest. The bones represented the remains of a minimum of five people, although the original (pre-1699) total was probably very much larger. There were a few small and rather insignificant objects with the bones, but nothing remotely comparable with the gorgeous macehead.

One of the most remarkable of O'Kelly's discoveries at Newgrange wasn't megalithic art, nor an object at all. It was a small, rectangular window-like opening, known as the 'roof box', carefully constructed above the lintel of the passage entranceway. O'Kelly realised that the 'roof box', which faced south-east, was lined up on the midwinter sunrise. So on cloud-free mornings (in Ireland!) of 21 December, and a few days on either side, the sun shines directly down the passage and illuminates the burial-chamber floor deep within the mound. Normally, of course, even in daytime the interior of the tomb would have been almost inky black. It's tempting to suggest that light falling on bones placed on the floor would be thought to give them new lives in the next world, while at the same time they would play their part in ensuring the annual rebirth of the seasons in this one. It's worth noting that the alignment and length of the passage, together with the placing of the 'roof box', the arrangement of the roofing slabs, and the gradual rise of the passage floor to coincide with the near-horizontal beam of light, must have taken much time and effort to get precisely right. It involved sophisticated surveying, and probably the use of poles and string lines. I certainly wouldn't fancy attempting the job myself without modern instruments.

I mentioned that the layout of the great mound at Newgrange was 'roughly circular'. In fact it is very much more subtle than that,

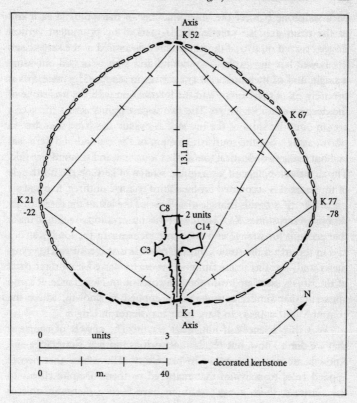

FIG 42 *Plan of the kerbstones around the base of the mound at Newgrange, County Meath (3200 BC). The plan shows how the mound was laid out in units of 13.1 metres. The principal axis is six units long. It runs from kerbstone K1, down the passage grave, through the back wallstone of the burial chamber (C8), and ends at kerbstone K52.*

as a fascinating and convincing study by Andrew Powell has recently demonstrated.[31] Powell has shown that the main axis of the mound, and the passage grave within it, runs from the centre of kerbstone K1, at the entrance, straight back to kerbstone K52 on the back-side of the mound. At precisely one third of its length this axis crosses the back wallstone (C8) of the inner chamber of the tomb. At each end of the main axis the precise line is marked by prominent vertical designs carved on two of the most highly decorated of the kerbstones.

Powell has shown that the mound and kerb were laid out using a single unit of measurement, 13.1 metres in length. The main axis is precisely six of these units, and the intersection with the backstone of the deepest chamber is two. The two widest points across the access are on opposite sides of the mound, at exactly the same spot, but in mirror image. So, the southern element of the mound and kerb was laid out using two identical triangles of four, five and six units per side. The slightly sloping, and less regular, stretch of kerb on the north side of the mound is accounted for by a third triangle of three, five and six units. The apex of this triangle makes use of the last of the three highly decorated kerbstones, K67. There are other observations one could make that account for strange and off-centre elements in the tomb's layout and in the art on the stones, but the point is that measurement, symmetry and – just as importantly – *asymmetry* played important parts in the rituals associated with the construction of Newgrange. It's also apparent that similar considerations applied at Knowth, where the common unit appears to have been 11.1 metres in length.

Was this 'science'? If not, what was it? The answer of course is that we don't know, but regularities such as those at Newgrange and Knowth are not uncommon in prehistory. They show that people applied rules to activities that mattered to them. Despite claims to the contrary, there doesn't seem to have been a common unit of measurement – the so-called 'megalithic yard' – throughout Neolithic Britain.[32] But people did measure, because measuring and method mattered. They were part of the processes that had to be gone through to do things properly. They also allowed people to construct monuments that could provide onlookers with extraordinary experiences, such as the midwinter sunlight down the Newgrange passage. We'll see in the next chapter that the existence of formal layout allowed people to depart from it when they needed to express or contain asymmetry, which might symbolically represent a potential source of tension in some other sphere of life. Perhaps we are witnessing something of the sort in the asymmetrical layout of the three chambers at the end of the passages at Newgrange and Knowth.

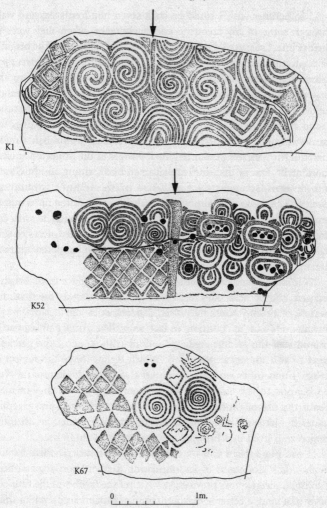

FIG 43   *Three stones decorated with examples of megalithic art from the kerb of the Neolithic passage-grave mound at Newgrange, County Meath (3200 BC). The arrows above kerbstones K1 and K52 indicate the precise position of the central axis of the mound.*

I sometimes wish I could go back seven hundred years and walk through some of my favourite parish churches, when they were in their prime. I suspect I'd be in for a shock. The walls would be brightly painted, and the candle or rushlight illumination would give their interiors a theatrical-cum-fairground feel, quite different from the austere beauty of whitewash and clean stone that I find so appealing today. The same applies to prehistoric tombs, which today are often found neglected to the point of vandalism in an arable setting, the farmer seemingly obsessed by the need to plough within half a millimetre of the concrete posts marking the edges of the protected ancient monument. Failing that, they are clean and tidy, sitting amidst closely mown lawns, scrupulously maintained by the relevant government agency. The latter are almost invariably over-restored in a rather severe, middle-class, civil-servant sort of fashion, complete with the dreaded and completely inappropriate 'Ministry mortar'. I'm not sure which I dislike most: the nearly destroyed or the supposed tourists' dream. Neither does justice to the original.

Neolithic chambered tombs would probably have been brightly painted, and on feast days filled with perfumed smoke, the rhythmic beating of drums, booming horns, dancers, cries and incantations – having quite a lot in common, in fact, with the garishly painted parish churches of the Middle Ages; or indeed with some of the parties I went to as a student in the 1960s. Which brings me to the subject of drugs. I remember writing a piece for the radical underground New York erotic review *Suck* – or was it *Screw*? I forget which – in 1969, about the use of cannabis in prehistory. At the time I was sleeping under the kitchen sink of the editor of both magazines, an eccentric genius who lived in a brownstone apartment in Brooklyn.

I was aware that a note on excavations of a frozen Scythian barrow in the Altai Mountains of Russia, dating to about 500 BC, had been published several years previously.[33] Within the tomb was the tattooed body of a man, a ceramic dish containing cannabis seeds, and a small tent which was placed over the dish to collect the smoke. This fixed the association of drugs, death and ritual in my mind, and I duly shared my thoughts with my readers. These days so-called 'recreational drugs' are usually enjoyed in what one might pompously term a 'social context' – i.e. for fun. But this was the first time I realised they could play a more structured, ritualised or formal role, within a religious or shamanistic context – to be pompous for a second time.

It came as a pleasant surprise to discover that serious scholars of the trance-like or 'entopic' state agreed with me. Medical experts have noted that certain designs and symbols are commonly seen by people in such states, especially when on hallucinogenic drugs, such as magic mushrooms (so far as we know, cannabis was not available in Britain in the Neolithic Age, and anyhow it's not hallucinogenic). These neurally-generated symbols, which include zigzags (or chevrons), meanders, spirals and circles, are all commonly found in the repertoire of megalithic art. A paper by Jeremy Dronfield has analysed this aspect of the art and its location within sites like Knowth, Dowth and Newgrange, and has drawn particular attention to the experience of travelling or floating down a long tunnel or passage.[34] The long passage to the burial chamber is often decorated with swirling designs, and it is not hard to associate it and other parts of the tombs with such experiences, whether directly or metaphorically.

The tunnel sensation and other experiences of the entopic state aren't only imagined by people under the influence of hallucinogenic drugs. 'Near death' experiences and other conditions of extreme stress, fasting and sensory deprivation can also bring them about. And of course they can be heightened by suitably atmospheric surroundings. Imagine that the swirling spirals of the megalithic art of the passage tombs were picked out in paint. Add to that the presence of the dead. And darkness, followed suddenly by bright sunlight. Music and drumming. With or without mind-altering substances, it's not difficult to sense the power such ceremonies would have had over the people taking part. In modern terms one could think of it as a multi-media theatrical experience, but with added dimensions of cold, claustrophobia, terror, death, awe and foreboding. It's no wonder places like Newgrange were in use for such a long time.

We're now approaching the end of the long Ages of Stone, and soon the pace of change will move up another gear. We are entering a fascinating period of transition; but as sometimes happens, the results of a process of change only show themselves towards the end – when the period of flux is beginning to calm down or stabilise. Perhaps this is why the centuries around the transition from the Neolithic to the Early Bronze Age are in archaeological terms strangely homogeneous. Nothing appears to alter much. In fact, some archaeologists have dubbed the period 2500–2000 BC the 'LNEBA' (Late Neolithic/Early Bronze Age). As we will see in the next chapter, it's a time when emerging British and Irish identities become more firmly established than ever before. It's also a time of remarkable technological development, of which the control of fire and heat – i.e. pyrotechnology – was to prove of lasting importance. It may be obvious, but it's worth restating that without the pyrotechnical skills of Bronze Age metal-workers, the Industrial Revolution of the eighteenth and nineteenth centuries would have been an impossibility. It's 2200 BC, and we're standing at the threshold of the modern world.

PART III

The Tyranny of Technology

Shetland Isles

Skara Brae • Orkney Isles

Dun Carloway •
Cnip •

Dun Vulan •

Loch Tay •

Buiston •

Navan •

Driffield •

Corlea •   Brú
                na Bóinne •   Llyn Cerrig   Great
                               Bach •   Orme   Fiskerton •
                                                                        'Seahenge'
                               Brenig •   Holme •   The
                                               Pierrepont   Fens   Fison Way,
                                                                        • Thetford
                               Copa •   Flag Fen •
                               Hill   Barleycroft •
                                                            Farm   Colchester •
                                         Severn   Welsh
                   • Llawhaden Levels   St Albans •
Mount   Avebury
Gabriel   •   • Reading   Dover
                          Somerset   Potterne •   Folkestone •
                          Levels   • Danebury
                  Dartmoor   Stonehenge • Little Butser
                  Reaves

0   50   100   150 km

FIG 44   *Main sites discussed in Part III.*

CHAPTER NINE

The Age of Stonehenge
(the Final Neolithic and Earliest
Bronze Age: 2500–1800 BC)

THAT HORRIBLE STATE of intellectual and emotional paralysis known as 'writer's block' doesn't only afflict poets and novelists. I recall unwittingly helping to free my old friend Richard Bradley from a bad attack when he was writing his superb book, *The Social Foundations of Prehistoric Britain*.[1] He was staying with us, and we talked late into the night about all sorts of things. In the morning he announced that the block had cleared, only to be replaced with a man-sized hangover, which was greatly to be preferred. Anyhow, he dedicated that wonderful book to us – and I still don't know what it was we said to deserve such an honour.

I found myself in a similar position with regard to the present book; but my problem wasn't so much a block, as a blockage. I didn't have a problem finding something to say, instead I desperately needed a way to pare down the wealth of material that needed to be discussed. I required a set of intellectual dyno-rods to drill through the stuff, otherwise I could see this book having to be published in several volumes.

The 'stuff' in question is what makes British prehistory renowned throughout the world: the megalithic constructions that cover so much of the Orkney Islands, not to mention tracts of the Wiltshire countryside at spots like Stonehenge and Avebury.[2] How could I get to the essence of these extraordinary ritual landscapes without having to describe each and every monument, stone by gigantic stone?

The answer was provided by Mike Parker Pearson, of Sheffield University. I'd known about Mike's thoughts on places such as

Stonehenge from a pair of papers he had written for the journal *Antiquity* in 1998.[3] He has been running a long-term research project in Madagascar,[4] where there is a continuing tradition of communal burial, and his co-author in both papers was a Madagascan colleague, Ramilisonina. I'd read their papers when they appeared, and found them very exciting, although their proposition was still not fully worked through, and had only really been applied to the Stonehenge ritual landscape.

Not long afterwards, I experienced a strange series of coincidences. I had been asked to contribute to a film the BBC were making about King Arthur (I have a pet theory that the legend of the sword Excalibur being thrown into the lake by Sir Bedevere had roots that extended back to the Bronze Age). I drove down to the West Country, and found myself standing in a marshy field in the Somerset Levels, with Glastonbury Tor glowering over us in the middle distance, as a backdrop for my interview. It always takes time for a film crew to set up, and while they were working I chatted to the producer, Jean-Claude Bragard. 'J-C' had been an academic before becoming a producer, and I recalled a wonderful film he'd made a few years previously about Stonehenge, with Mike Parker Pearson. It was J-C who had paid for Ramilisonina to come to Britain, and while he was here he wrote his *Antiquity* pieces with Mike.

That chance encounter revived old memories, but then Christmas disrupted normal life, and I thought no more about the problems that faced me until New Year's Day, when I was idly leafing through one of the many presents I'd bought for myself. Then I spotted that name again: Mike Parker Pearson, but this time he was writing about Orkney and Avebury, as well as Stonehenge. I devoured the piece in half an hour. It was superb. He had taken Ramilisonina's original idea and applied it to the other key ritual landscapes of Neolithic and Bronze Age Britain.[5]

I don't want to give the impression that Mike's view of those famous ritual landscapes is the only one, or that it's necessarily correct. I don't think he or Ramilisonina would dream of making such a claim; but they have provided a genuinely fresh way of looking at Britain's most famous ancient sites. It's a view that doesn't present them as dead monuments in a vanished landscape, to be categorised by archaeologists whose experience of life in the past is essentially Western and second-hand, gleaned from books, computers, or university lectures. Ramilisonina's understanding is entirely different. Of course it's academically rigorous, but it's first-hand, and derives from a living tradition of communal burial and ceremonial. It is also analogy – and analogy, however convincing, is often flawed. Despite that, I believe it does give us an interpretation that makes sense of the different sites within their ritual landscapes – something that has never been satisfactorily explained before – and for me at least it works wonderfully well, on several levels.

Like all good ideas, it is based on a simple core belief, which has ancient roots that make symbolic sense. Put briefly, Ramilisonina and Parker Pearson suggested that stone, being dead, is for the dead, and wood is for the living. But it's not a simple symbolic transformation: you don't drop dead, and suddenly be represented by stone. It's a gradual, staged process, rather along the lines we saw at Gough's Cave, which incidentally also conforms to the model. Caves, after all, are formed within stone, and it is likely that the bones found there had been defleshed outside. After a few days or weeks they were transferred from the world of the living to that of the ancestors, within the cave. It was all part of a highly ritualised transformation process.

If we doubt the validity of this idea of gradual transformation, or 'hardening', from being a living being to a more permanent state in the next world, Mike reminds us of modern British funerary customs, where 'the social process of memorialising the dead begins with flowers at the graveside, followed by the erection of a wooden cross, culminating in the erection of a gravestone'.[6]

If materials such as wood and stone can stand as symbols for the living on one hand, and for the dead now resident in the realms of the ancestors on the other, then surely a whole range of manmade and natural items can acquire special significance too. Pottery is a case in point. As we've seen, pottery was a Neolithic introduction, and by the LNEBA (say by 2200 BC) it had already been in use for some two thousand years. That's more than enough time for it to become deeply embedded within the fabric of British society. Put another way, pottery by 2200 BC was far from an innovation. It could be decorated and formed in various ways, which were significant to the people at the time. The different styles of pottery shape, manufacture and decoration carried within them meaning, just as the shape and decoration of a chalice, although variable between one church and another, are loaded with symbolism for modern Christians.

There were two general styles of Late Neolithic pottery which for various reasons Mike has identified with the realms of the living and the dead (or the ancestors). The style he associates with the ancestors belongs to a very broad tradition found throughout north-western and Atlantic Europe. These are vessels decorated with impressions made by pushing a distinctively-shaped object, such as a twisted string, the jointed end of a bird bone (which leaves a pair of smooth, oval impressions), or a grain of wheat or barley, into the clay. In Britain this type of pottery is known as Peterborough Ware, after discoveries by a remarkable local solicitor who would regularly visit the hand-dug gravel pits on the edges of the fens at Fengate (the site where I cut my archaeological teeth) before the Great War.[7] Sometimes, as we still see today with vessels used in church services, the shape of Peterborough pottery is deliberately archaic, with round-bottomed bowls that hark back centuries to ceramic styles found in causewayed enclosures of the Earlier Neolithic.

The style of pottery linked by Mike with the living is unique to Britain and Ireland, and nothing like it is known across the Channel. Instead of a resoundingly British name like Wellington or Britannic Ware, it was first named, somewhat prosaically, Rinyo-Clacton Ware, to mark the fact that it is found throughout the length and breadth of Britain from Rinyo in Orkney to Clacton in Essex. Latterly this name has gone out of fashion, and the pottery is now known as Grooved Ware – because, even more prosaically, it is decorated with grooves.[8]

Prehistoric pottery is never made from pure clay, and there are various reasons why foreign material, known as temper, is added. It's quite difficult to be certain what is temper and what occurred in the clay in its natural state, but I was taught that temper was always added for practical purposes – with the exception of the mica which was sometimes added to the clay of certain Early Bronze Age pots known as Beakers, to give them a glittery appearance. Crushed shell, ground-up pieces of old pots (known as 'grog'), pounded or burnt

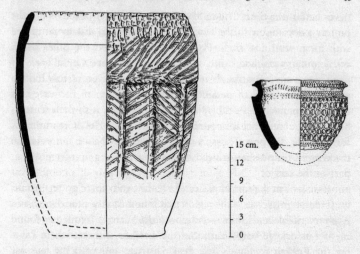

FIG 45 *Two styles of Later Neolithic pottery (about 2500 BC): Grooved Ware (left) and Peterborough Ware (right). The vessels are illustrated in the conventional archaeological way, with the profile and interior shown to the left, and the exterior to the right of the central division. The Grooved Ware jar, whose base is missing, came from excavations at Durrington Walls, a huge timber circle henge site north-east of Stonehenge. The Peterborough jar was found in the north-east chamber of the West Kennet long barrow, Wiltshire; it is decorated with bird-bone impressions on the interior and around the rim, but the main part of the body is covered with rows of neat fingertip impressions bounded by at least one row of bird-bone impressions above the rounded base, which is missing.*

flint, stone, sand or shell – even, on occasions, chopped vegetable matter – was added to the clay and then thoroughly mixed in. The temper allowed the unfired pot to dry without cracking. It made firing both simpler and more effective, and when the firing process was completed it meant that cooking pots could be placed on and off a fire without cracking.

As I have said, I was taught that temper was usually added for practical reasons only. But if the manufacture of pottery was like anything else in prehistoric life, surely symbolism and ritual would never be far away. And I don't believe they were. Grooved Ware, the pottery associated with the world of the living, was usually tempered with grog, sand and shell. Peterborough Ware, on the other hand, often contains crushed stone, sometimes in quite substantial (pea- or peppercorn-size) chunks. Is it coincidence that, even at this hidden and miniature level of detail, stone and the realm of the ancestors might be connected? Possibly, but I don't think so. It's worth remembering here that detail is important in ritual. After Holy Communion, for example, the priest doesn't casually pop the chalice and paten in the verger's dishwasher; instead he does the clearing up reverently, as part of the service.

If we look at the sort of places where the two types of pottery occur, we find that in Wessex – the region that is home to the Stonehenge and Avebury ritual landscapes – Peterborough Ware is frequently found in sites associated with death and the afterlife: with burials in caves (in the English midlands and Peak District) and with the late use of long barrows and megalithic tombs. During the ceremonies that accompanied the rolling of the great blocking stone into place at the West Kennet tomb, the worshippers made offerings of the largest collection of Peterborough Ware in Wessex. Grooved Ware, on the other hand, is not often found in tombs, but frequently occurs at ceremonial timber circles and in the ditches and pits of the great henges, such as Durrington Walls near Stonehenge. Incidentally, the word 'henge' comes from Stonehenge, which literally means 'the hanging stones'. As a student I thought this referred to the way the great lintels seem to hang in the air, but Mike Pitts has convincingly shown that the hanging (which took place a long time after the Late Neolithic) was of a more grisly sort.[9]

I wish we could demonstrate beyond doubt that the correlation between the two types of Late Neolithic pottery and the different aspects of life and the afterlife was consistent. But unfortunately there are problems, not the least being that in many instances the two styles of pottery were not in use at the same time – as we find, for example, at Knowth. There are other difficulties. The newly discovered enclosure in Longstones Field, Avebury, for example, has yielded the 'wrong' pottery, Grooved Ware, from funerary contexts. But – and I think it is a big but – however pottery was used in prehistory, it was unlikely to have been treated as a mere fired clay container. It was very important to people, as we know from the way it was treated (for example as a container for cremated human bone) and decorated with such great care. Whether or not one agrees with Mike Parker Pearson's life/death scheme – and I still find it very attractive – it does point us in directions which are likely to yield exciting new results.

Strictly speaking, a true henge consists of a circular ditch with a bank outside and one or more entrances. Within this defining circular enclosure can be circles of posts, either concentric, as at Woodhenge,[10] or grouped, as at Durrington Walls.[11] Sometimes the posts are eventually replaced by standing stones, as at Stonehenge, or Stanton Drew in Somerset.[12] Sometimes the interior has nothing but a few pits – or just nothing – but this can often be put down to modern plough-damage. By the way, the timber circle off the north Norfolk coast, dubbed by the press 'Seahenge', lacks an exterior ditch or bank, and is consequently not a true henge at all. But the site clearly belongs within the same general tradition of British circular shrines – and anyhow, it's a good, evocative name, which has stuck.

I've mentioned that at numerous henges and timber/stone circle sites in Britain, settings of posts were replaced by standing stones. At Stonehenge this process started around 2500 BC.[13] In Mike Parker Pearson's terminology this represents 'hardening', and as we'll see shortly, it went with a significant change in the way that a particular site was used and perceived.

How does the stone/wood distinction 'work' on the ground, and what can it tell us about the ways in which people used ritual landscapes? Let's go in at the deep end, at Stonehenge itself, where the ritual landscape surrounding the famous Stones is truly vast. In this brief case-study we'll look at an area eight kilometres square, which includes all the major sites and most of the outlying barrows. The Wiltshire river Avon (not Shakespeare's river), which enters the English Channel thirty-five miles away at Christchurch in Dorset, wiggles its way southwards, along the eastern side of our area. It tends to be ignored in most discussions of the Stonehenge landscape, which is possibly a mistake, given what we know about the religious significance of rivers in prehistoric times. For what it's worth, I predict that one day this century there will be a hugely important archaeological discovery made near the banks of the Avon, within ten kilometres of Stonehenge.

The clue to the way the Stonehenge ritual landscape may have been organised lies in the so-called 'envelope of visibility' around the Stones. Mike Parker Pearson and Ramilisonina were intrigued by the fact that when you stand at the Stones, looking away from them, the nearest round barrows are some distance away, towards the horizon. As we know, round barrows are later than long barrows, and generally belong within the Early Bronze Age (i.e. after about 2500 BC).[14] This suggested that the empty land around the Stones, and indeed the Stones themselves, were reserved for 'the disembodied ancestors'. It was their realm, or domain. This was the starting point for a period-by-period analysis of the way the ritual landscape developed.

Mike and Ramilisonina were able to define three distinct periods. The first, from 3500 to 3000 BC (not illustrated here), predates the digging of the partially segmented ditch around the Stones, at about 2950 BC. In this initial landscape the domain of the ancestors was to the west of the site where Stonehenge was eventually to be erected, and communication – or rather gradual transition – between their realm and that of the living was by way of Robin Hood's Ball, the causewayed enclosure to the north-west of the Stones, and the otherwise inexplicable Lesser Cursus.

We see this landscape subtly shifting, and becoming more coherently structured, in the second period, from 3000 to 2500 BC. The construction of the first two phases of Stonehenge itself, from 2950 to 2400 BC, involved the erection of rings of posts and the digging of pits and smaller holes into the chalk. One can think of this as the timber-and-chalk phase of Stonehenge. This new arrival replaced the Lesser Cursus, and provided a timber monument at the very edge of the realm of the ancestors. Placed right at the boundary, it was in every sense of the word liminal. As if to emphasise this liminality, the Palisade Ditch, set with large and closely spaced posts, passed close by the newly dug Stonehenge outer ditch, to the north-west. This wall of posts separated timber-and-chalk Stonehenge from the domain of the ancestors, but at the same time provided restricted access each way, via two entranceways.

This brings me to the cliffhanger I left unresolved in Chapter 7.

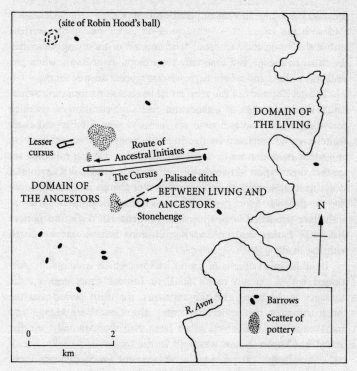

FIG 46   *Layout of the Stonehenge ritual landscape, 3000–2500 BC.*

The Palisade Ditch was excavated in 1967, as part of the work that revealed those large and mysterious Mesolithic post-pits in the car park. It's just a wild thought, but maybe those huge posts served a broadly similar function to the Palisade Ditch – only more than five thousand years previously. If this is true, the implications are extraordinary.

The great Stonehenge Cursus, which runs east–west for 2.7 kilometres, north of Stonehenge, was constructed at this time, and would have provided a special or ceremonial route for the dead to pass through the dangerous no man's land or liminal zone occupied by timber-and-chalk Stonehenge, between the two domains of the ancestors and the living. Spreads of Peterborough pottery – the style associated with the ancestors – were found on either side of the western end of the Stonehenge Cursus.[15] The domain of the living surrounds the ritual landscape, but especially towards the river Avon, where the land was richest and where barrows don't occur so frequently.

The development of the great ritual landscape surrounding Stonehenge reaches a peak of elaboration and sophistication in its third period, between 2500 and 2000 BC. As we've seen, timber-and-chalk Stonehenge was replaced by the Stones around 2500 BC, marking an important reorientation of the ritual landscape. During this time we see the construction of two major timber circle centres at Durrington Walls (a huge henge) and the smaller Woodhenge nearby. Both are close by the river Avon, three kilometres north-east of the Stones, and both have produced large quantities of Grooved Ware, the pottery that Mike Parker Pearson and Ramilisonina believe was associated with the living.

In addition to dozens of round barrows which were mainly positioned within the no man's land, or liminal zone, between the domains of the living and the ancestors, the third period sees the construction of two other new sites, the Coneybury Henge and the Avenue. The henge was much later than the 'Anomaly' we discussed in Chapter 7, and was built in the timber-and-chalk style of early Stonehenge.[16] It provided a replacement for Stonehenge itself, which had undergone the process of 'hardening' and now formed the core of the realm of the ancestors – Mike dubbed it the circle of the ancestors.

The second new monument of the third period of the ritual landscape's development was the Stonehenge Avenue. This consists of two parallel ditches that run north-west from the river Avon, then turn left and left again (the so-called 'Elbow'), to approach the main entranceway through the Stonehenge outer ditch from the north-east, the direction of the midsummer sunrise. The ditches were quarries for two continuous banks that ran between them, thereby constricting the width of the Avenue, which tapered along its length, from about thirty-four metres wide near the river to about twenty-one metres at the point where it joined Stonehenge.

There have been many theories to explain the Avenue. Professor

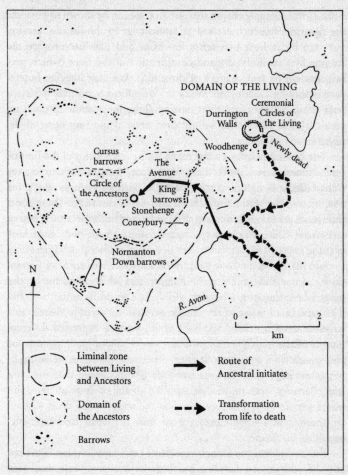

FIG 47   *Layout of the Stonehenge ritual landscape, 2500–2000 BC.*

Richard Atkinson, who dug Stonehenge between 1950 and 1964, believed that it was constructed to ceremonially transport the Bluestones from the river Avon, at the end of their long journey from the Preseli Hills of south-west Wales. It's a nice idea, but was proved wrong for the simple reason that the Avenue can be shown to postdate the Bluestones (which arrived at Stonehenge in the decades around 2550 BC) by at least two centuries. Mike and Ramilisonina see the Avenue as a symbolic dryland continuation of the river (which may help explain its two changes of direction). We may imagine funeral parties leaving Durrington Walls or Woodhenge, possibly taking a boat along the river and then passing along the Avenue through no man's land to the Stones within their circle at the very heart of the realm of the ancestors.

The boundary between the realm of the ancestors and the liminal zone around it was marked by three linear barrow cemeteries: the Cursus Barrows to the north, the King Barrows midway along the Avenue, and the Normanton Down Barrows to the south. These linear cemeteries are very reminiscent of what we saw in the previous chapter at Barrow Hills. Maybe they marked points where one could look over the realm of the ancestors, but not actually enter it. It's interesting to note that the large New King Barrows, which crown King Barrow ridge, immediately south of the Avenue, and which mark the precise point where the Stones become visible, are made from earth. Could it be that in addition to the simple earth/stone division there was a larger, and more subtle, symbolic lexicon which expressed different aspects of the main themes? So, barrows or cairns made from rocks and stones were somehow 'harder' – perhaps closer to the realm of the ancestors – than earthen barrows. It's intriguing that the New King Barrows were positioned so close to the Avenue at the point where people or spirits (possibly just the souls of the dead without any human accompaniment) passed into the open landscape surrounding the Stones.

I've considered the Stonehenge ritual landscape in some detail not only because it's so famous, but because it's so diverse, has been thoroughly studied and fits the Parker Pearson/Ramilisonina model so well. But it's not alone in these respects. Of the others, Avebury and Orkney are possibly the most important.

The ritual landscape around Avebury includes some remarkable tombs and other sites. I've already mentioned Windmill Hill, the causewayed enclosure that can claim to be the 'founder monument', and the West Kennet long barrow. At the centre of it all lies the enormous henge of Avebury and the West Kennet Avenue leading up to it from the Sanctuary. We should also not forget that gigantic earthwork known as Silbury Hill. If all this wasn't enough, there have been some remarkable new discoveries, including a second avenue (the Beckhampton Avenue), another causewayed enclosure and two massive timber enclosures.[17] It's hard to know where to start.

The ritual landscapes surrounding Stonehenge and Avebury were not static, and both show evidence for a major reorientation. Both, too, made use of a river – at Avebury it is the Kennet – to add further structure to the landscape. Evidence for the organisation of the Early Neolithic landscape at Avebury is thin, and amounts to the causewayed enclosure at Windmill Hill, a newly discovered one in Longstones Field and a few long barrows. The central focus must surely have been on the two causewayed enclosures, with the domain of the ancestors more or less where it appears in the next of the two main periods. Shortly after the initial setting-out of the causewayed enclosures, and overlapping with their later use, we come to the first period in which we can discern structure in the Avebury ritual landscape (3500–2500 BC). This period sees the first construction of the great Avebury henge, which at that stage was a timber-and-chalk monument – evidence for the timber element being hints of two concentric post circles recently revealed by geophysics.[18] As at Stonehenge, the early timber-and-chalk monument was at the very edge of the no man's land between the realms of the living (which we presume to have been towards the river, to the south-east) and the ancestors.

The second main period of ritual landscape development at Avebury recalls that at contemporary Stonehenge. Again we see the henge suddenly 'harden', with the construction of the great outer circle of massive stones, spaced around the inside of the henge ditch, and of two (actually three)[19] inner circles of stones. This transformation marks Avebury's change into a new monument. The domain of the living would have been south of the Kennet, and access to the no man's land between it and the realm of the ancestors would have been via the river and the complex of great timber circles and enclosures recently excavated by a team directed by Alasdair Whittle. From this 'reception' area funeral parties would move to the West Kennet Avenue. Turning right, to the south, would bring them to the Sanctuary, which had

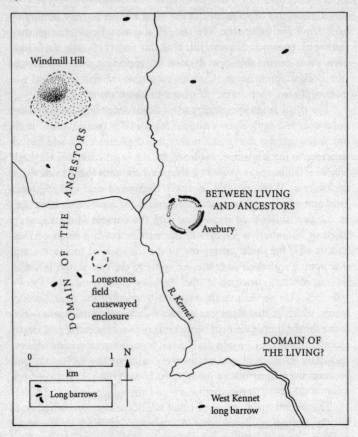

FIG 48   *Layout of the Avebury ritual landscape, 3500–2500 BC.*

also 'hardened' from a timber to a stone circle by this time.[20] There is now some doubt whether the timber phase of the Sanctuary was ever a simple circle, as the standard texts and guidebooks have it. Instead, posts seem to have been erected and taken down in an extraordinary display of 'activity for its own sake'. Most parties visiting the ritual landscape in ancient times would have taken the processional route northwards, leaving the vast bulk of Silbury Hill on the left, a

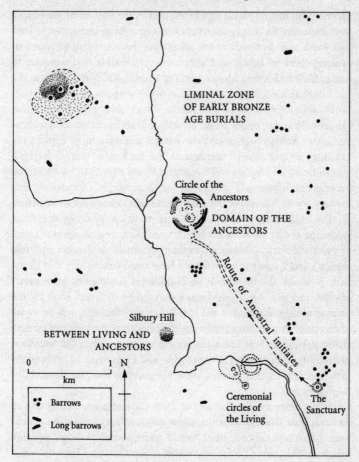

FIG 49   *Layout of the Avebury ritual landscape, 2500–2000 BC.*

silent outpost on the edge of the next world. Eventually they would pass through the enormous portal stones that still guard Avebury's southern entrance into the West Kennet Avenue. They were then within the circle of the ancestors.

If travel, or some form of symbolic progression from one state to another, did indeed play a significant part in the way ritual landscapes were experienced, it may sometimes also have been important to look backwards and forwards at the same time: back towards previous or existing states of being, and ahead towards worlds that were yet to come. Maybe that was why certain key transitional places, such as the Sanctuary or the King Barrow ridge at Stonehenge, were so important. To be able to look both ways can be a humbling experience, but it can also sharpen one's sense of self and appreciation of the here and now. Archaeologists, in their natural enthusiasm to explain the workings of prehistoric minds and the landscapes they inhabited, should be aware that we will never explain *all* aspects of past spiritual experiences. There will always be lost dimensions of meaning and mystery – which is one of the things that make the subject so addictive.

I'm conscious as I write that this partitioning-up of the ritual landscape might sound a bit like a town planner's blueprint: 'realm of light industry', 'shopping precinct', 'domain of leisure and rec-reation', etc. I don't think it would have been viewed like that in the past. Some of the thresholds or boundaries could have been pretty woolly, and may well have been perceived in different ways by the various groups that visited the space. Any archaeologist will be aware of exceptions to the ancestor/living attributions of the different pottery styles; similarly, there are a few round barrows within the 'envelope of visibility' surrounding Stonehenge – and I can think of other prob-lems too. But I am convinced these are quibbles that, fundamentally, don't matter.

What Mike Parker Pearson and Ramilisonina are attempting to do is recreate the way in which these extraordinary landscapes would have been experienced; what would have passed through people's minds as they moved from one realm to another, and how the emo-tions of awe, tension and foreboding would build up as parties approached the great circles along the Avenues. But it isn't an easy matter to enter into the thoughts and emotions of ancient people. Even on the off-chance that we believe in anything supernatural at all, our ancestors and gods are safely tucked away 'up there' some-where. We have also grown used to living in a society where, for practical day-to-day purposes, laws are imposed on us. We don't park on double yellow lines; and, as a farmer, I try to avoid breaking too many absurd food hygiene regulations. As a consequence, it's easy to assume that in prehistory similar hard-and-fast laws applied, and that they were obeyed by everybody. But it wasn't like that. People of different communities had the freedom to make laws for themselves.

I well recall the first time I saw the Orkney Islands. I was on that trawler I wrote about in Chapter 5, and we were steaming north towards the Pentland Firth in a Force 9 gale. Off our port side I could see the headland of John o'Groats, and to starboard the intricate, treeless coastline of the Orkney island of South Ronaldsay was beginning to emerge through the spume. For a moment the storm abated; but it was only a pause, as if to draw a deep breath. As we entered the firth the wind grew stronger and stronger, while at the same time the waves dropped, and the sea hissed and seethed like water boiling in a cauldron. Instead of rising and falling, the ship's bows were caught by conflicting currents, and she juddered and yawed unpredictably from side to side. It was a terrifying experience for a landlubber, and one that I'll never forget.

It could be argued that Orkney is the most exciting prehistoric site in north-western Europe. Everything is there, and what's more, it's superbly preserved. There are many reasons for the fine preservation, but the fact that the sites and monuments are so magnificent in the first place cannot be explained so readily. As I steamed past the islands towards Iceland, I didn't know that Orkney's lack of trees was more than compensated for by the superb local stone, that cleaves, splits and behaves like timber. This is undoubtedly one of the main reasons why the ancient sites of the islands have survived so well for so long. And of course their remoteness has helped protect them from subsequent abuse. Maybe too their location, on the extreme edge of mainland Britain, gave them a very special sort of liminality that had appeal beyond the immediate confines of the islands.

The literature on Orcadian prehistory is vast,[21] but Anna Ritchie has written an excellent overview for the general reader.[22] However, no book can substitute for the real thing: the megalithic tombs of Orkney almost defy description, and that at Maes Howe actually does. It's a passage grave beneath a great mound and with a corbelled burial chamber – not dissimilar in general plan to those of Ireland. But that's where the similarity ends. The masonry at Maes Howe is as near perfect as it's possible to get without the use of mortar. If one did not know that the passage had been constructed five thousand years ago, one could easily imagine it to be the work of Victorian masons working with modern tools and lifting equipment. The burial chamber rivals anything in Neolithic Europe. It has a powerful acoustic that seems somehow to magnify, and not just echo, sound. This has been studied by Aaron Watson, who concluded that 'the precise joining of the dry-stone walling creates a virtually unbroken surface from which sound can reflect. For this reason, sounds within this resonant cavity are heard quite differently, appearing fuller and louder.'[23] Watson is in no doubt that this effect was deliberately achieved, and was intended to enhance the 'magical' (my term) qualities of the tomb as a theatre for shamanistic ceremonies.

The visual effect would have been strikingly enhanced if the interior walls and ceiling had been painted. Exciting new evidence for this has recently been revealed by Richard Bradley and others, who detected clear scratched or incised lines on the walls of Maes Howe and other tombs when lit at a flat angle by spotlights.[24] They believe, I think correctly, that the scratches marked the edges of painted zones of different colours – or of painted and unpainted areas. It's just about possible for us to imagine what the physical experience of shamanistic ceremonies in such extraordinary chambers could have been like: whirling shamans, chanting, drumming, flickering lights, painted walls and ceilings – a heady cocktail. But what we can't recreate is what was passing through people's minds. They were, after all, in the presence of their ancestors, and of the forces which created and controlled their world. Words like 'awe' or 'fear' are simply not up to the task. I leave it to your own imagination.

Skara Brae is one of Orkney's greatest delights. It dates to the Middle and Later Neolithic (say 3100–2500 BC), and was excavated by the famous Marxist prehistorian from Australia, Professor Vere Gordon Childe, and published in 1931.[25] I remember when I saw my first photos of Skara Brae as a student being unable to grasp how anything so perfectly preserved could possibly have survived for so long, but subsequently I have learned that it's by no means unique – there are others, of which the example at Knap of Howar, excavated more recently, is closely comparable, if somewhat smaller and several centuries earlier.

These sites are conventionally explained as houses or villages. They consisted of interconnected, oval-shaped rooms with dry-stone walls and roofs made from timber covered with turf, dry vegetation and so forth. What makes them so remarkable is the stone furniture which survives intact. There are clay-lined basins, box-like beds and, most extraordinary of all, dressers complete with shelves and cubby-holes that would not look out of place in a modern farmhouse. It's a picture of snug domestic bliss: outside the North Sea gales are raging, but inside their houses the residents of Skara Brae sit dozing with their feet stretched towards the hearth, pleasantly replete after a gull's-egg-and-wild-mushroom omelette, washed down with hot mugs of honey-flavoured milk. A dram of whisky would have completed the scene, but unfortunately it had yet to be invented.

Was it really like that? Again, we are faced with a problem ultimately of cognition. Is our idea of domestic bliss consonant with those of prehistory? I'm sure that family life was important, and that men and women loved each other, and formed lifelong attachments. But did they share our ideas of domestic privacy and home life? Was the Neolithic and Bronze Age Orcadian's house his or her castle? I suspect that their attitudes to domesticity were less cosy and complacent than ours. To them domestic life did not exist on its own, within a self-contained bubble, but instead was part of something altogether larger, and less comfortable. Is this mere speculation? Actually, it isn't.

Colin Richards was one of Richard Bradley's brightest students, and on graduation from Reading University he came to join my team digging at Etton. I still remember his excitement as he excavated a small, bucket-sized pit filled with Grooved Ware. He dug it meticulously, and was able to demonstrate beyond doubt that the pit's filling wasn't just rubbish, but had been carefully positioned there, with pottery placed around the sides and other material heaped within the space at the centre. Colin was always looking beyond what lay beneath his trowel. Nothing to him was simple, or to be taken at face value. I admit that this could be irritating at times, but it also led him to propose some wonderfully imaginative ideas, which have moved Neolithic studies forward a very long way.

Possibly Colin's greatest contribution to archaeology to date was the discovery of a Neolithic settlement, complete with Skara Brae-style houses, at Barnhouse,[26] near the Stones of Stenness, that most eerie of stone circles, whose shaped uprights have a futuristic feel that recalls the film *2001*. The houses were organised in much the same way as those of Skara Brae, with stone-slab beds, dressers and covered drains to remove sewage, which could then be rotted down to make manure for the land.

Colin was struck by the way Orcadian houses showed consistent patterns in their layout: a deliberately restricted entranceway led into a small, unlit room or front hall. Visitors then moved to the right of the hearth that provided the only light for the entrance space. This took them past a stone bed. Opposite the doorway, and facing it, was a stone dresser, with another box-bed on the left-hand side, opposite the first bed. There is evidence that the left-hand bed was slept in by women and children, while men slept in the bed to the right of the entranceway. This is important, because it has resonances with a very much later time: we will see that in the wheelhouses (stone-built roundhouses) of the Scottish Iron Age the living space was arranged in a way which separated the domestic sphere, to the left of the main entrance (in this instance represented by the sleeping places of the women and children), from a different, perhaps rather darker, part of the house to the right of the front door.

The ground-plan of the Barnhouse buildings has good ethnographic parallels. For example, the roundhouses, known as *hogans*, of the sedentary Hopi Indians separate males and females on either side of the hearth.[27] This in turn reflects aspects of the way their society was organised. The layout of the *hogan*, like that of the Barnhouse buildings, seems to have had little to do with the simple, practical organisation of space, but was more about other, equally important, aspects of life, such as social organisation, the symbolic representation of the passage of time, and the distinction between day and night, or indeed life and death.

Two houses were notably bigger, and different in layout. One was a doubled-up house with two hearths; the other was a heavily constructed rectangular 'hall', set inside a high outer wall. Strangely, these buildings have many points in common with contemporary

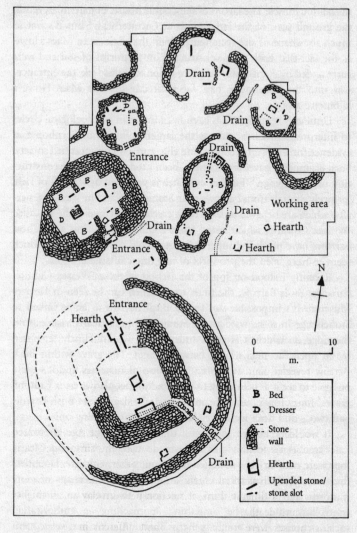

FIG 50 *Plan of the Neolithic 'village' of Barnhouse, Mainland Orkney (about 3100 BC).*

megalithic tombs. The layout of the double house, in particular, recalls the ground-plan of the large tomb at Quanterness;[28] but it's not so much the shape of the rectangular 'hall' that links it to Maes Howe, as the fact that both were constructed on platforms of soil and were surrounded by stone walls.[29] As if to emphasise this link, the entrance-way into the Barnhouse 'hall' faces directly towards Maes Howe a kilometre away.

Until very recently, it has been fashionable in archaeological circles to interpret structures such as the larger buildings at Barnhouse as evidence for a powerful controlling elite and a highly stratified society. Such arguments have, for example, been used to explain the construction of Stonehenge.[30] Further evidence is provided by a series of rich, 'princely' burials from barrows near Stonehenge and in Wessex generally, which are believed to have been erected by people of the so-called 'Wessex Culture', which lasted from about 2000 to 1800 BC.[31] These barrows have produced superbly crafted gold objects, many of which seem to have been the products of just one craftsman.[32]

Recently I stood on top of the richest of these 'Wessex Culture' barrows, Bush Barrow, the finds from which can be seen in Devizes Museum. It's impossible not to see Bush Barrow as being linked to Stonehenge in some way, as the Stones are quite clearly visible from the ridge on which it is sited. Indeed, the two are clearly separated by an open 'no man's land' between them. The grave within Bush Barrow revealed an astonishing collection of material, and it's quite possible to see it as belonging to perhaps two people ('Wessex Culture' graves, for example, usually contain just one dagger, yet Bush Barrow had two – and both were very large).[33] What was going on?

It would be absurd to suggest that Early Bronze Age, or indeed Later Neolithic, societies in Britain were completely egalitarian. Clearly they were not: very few societies anywhere in the world are. Doubtless there were powerful tribal chiefs – the equivalent perhaps of petty warlords. But I do not think it necessary to invoke an all-mighty controlling elite. Maybe something approaching an authoritarian social structure arose briefly in Early Bronze Age Wessex, subsequent to the construction of Stonehenge, and was mimicked elsewhere in Britain – but one has to ask why it vanished so quickly. I'm far from convinced that there ever was anything as coherent as a 'Wessex

Culture'. Instead I see these rich graves as part of a general tendency in Later Neolithic and Bronze Age times for burials to be single, rather than collective, and accompanied by grave goods – as we saw at Barrow Hills. In other words, I believe that burials such as Bush Barrow are saying more about the afterlife, and people's attitudes to it, than about the actual lives of the people who have just died. There's a danger in interpreting these things too literally: rich grave = rich (and therefore powerful) person.

Archaeologists of the 1970s and eighties were deeply involved with concepts such as power and authority, and there was more than a passing tendency to view prehistoric authority figures in terms of our own society.[34] I concede that there may well have been powerful people at the time, but as we've already seen along the Mississippi, you don't necessarily have to have settled communities, with big chiefs and little chieftains, to construct great monuments.

The rich barrow burials near Stonehenge show that gold was also becoming a fashionable material to place in graves. This wasn't happening in Wessex alone: a contemporary burial in a barrow at Little Cressingham in sleepy rural Norfolk contained gold-work that mimicked that of Wessex, although the workmanship was inferior.[35] I know of no sites near Little Cressingham in Norfolk which could remotely be compared with Stonehenge or Avebury; presumably the controlling elites thereabouts were as dozy as their pleasant surroundings. I should add here that gold-work doesn't only occur in rich Wessex graves – or indeed in graves of any sort.

A recent discovery at Lockington, just south of Derby and Nottingham in north-west Leicestershire, caused a great deal of interest. It's not an area particularly noted for rich Bronze Age burials, and when it was proposed to excavate a round barrow threatened by the construction of the A564 Derby Southern Bypass, the archaeological world did not exactly leap to attention. This apathy was rapidly dispelled by what was found within the barrow.

The dig took place in 1994, and has been fully published.[36] The main discovery was a small pit which was found at a probable entrance-way into the area that was later to be covered by a mound. Within the pit were some fragments of Early Bronze Age pottery, two decorated gold armlets (bracelet-like bands worn on the upper arms) and a long copper dagger made in Brittany and still in its scabbard. We can't be absolutely certain when the pit was dug and filled, but it was probably sometime around 2100–1900 BC. The pit was too small ever to have held a body, but the site where it was found was later used as a barrow (around 1870–1520 BC). I can't see how the Lockington find can possibly be linked to something like a 'princely' burial. For a start, the two metal items are not ones I would expect to have found together, and might well have been owned by two separate people. It seems to me that the simplest explanation is that these were objects that had been taken to an already hallowed place, where they were buried in the belief that they could have been used by their one-time owners (or their ancestors) in their new state in the next world.

What are the alternatives to the idea of powerful, controlling elites? I said in Chapter 7 that if British prehistory is about anything, it's about families. This is what Mike Parker Pearson and Ramilisonina believed was the motivation behind the use and construction of Stonehenge: the strength of family tradition and family history. If 'Big Men' did indeed exist, it would be within a family or clan context. In other words, the scope of their power and influence would have been limited by purely local constraints. It's an analogy I shall return to later, but they would have been 'big' in the way that the lord of the manor was 'big' in medieval rural England: essentially a large fish in a small pond.

It is of course entirely possible that places like Stonehenge were actually constructed by specialists, with or without large-scale assistance from members of the community.[37] That community could perfectly well have been egalitarian, with only a limited amount of ranking, and that confined within families. It would come as no surprise, for example, to discover that grandparents and great-grandparents were held in respect and affection by their living descendants, and were given a rich send-off so they could hold their own in the next world. There is no need for higher levels of social control. Power politics, as such, does not have to enter the picture.

Can we see something similar happening in Orkney? The two large buildings at Barnhouse *could* be seen as special houses reserved for powerful people. But there's something very odd about them. The way, for instance, that the entranceway of the large house points towards Maes Howe, and the fact that its construction seems to mimic the great passage-tomb. Could we not be looking at something more akin to the Parker Pearson/Ramilisonina no man's land or in-between buildings – perhaps a residence of the ancestors within the settlement of the living? That double house is odd, too. Why have a *double* house for a Big Man? Would it not make more sense, perhaps, to construct such a double house to commemorate or celebrate the coming together of two established families? Of course we can only guess at these things, but the idea of a simple settlement given over entirely to domestic life received a body blow when Colin Richards realised that the hearths at Barnhouse, which are hefty affairs, made from good, solid stone slabs, were all arranged on the same alignment, despite the fact that the houses themselves faced in various directions. The alignment in question is four ways: to midsummer sunrise and sunset, and to midwinter sunrise and sunset. Colin also realised that the entranceway to the large 'hall', itself marked by a hearth placed at the centre of the way in, lined up on the midsummer sunset.[38]

The uniform layout of the houses, and the alignment of the hearths within them, seem to be a deliberate symbolic expression of unity or family solidarity. I'm not suggesting that this level of integration would rule out feelings of self-contained family contentment, but modern notions of independence and 'domestic bliss' are probably inappropriate. People would have had far stronger feelings of identity of, and involvement in, their wider families, both past (i.e. ancestral) and present.

The passage at Maes Howe faces south-west, and the dying light of the midwinter sun shines along it to illuminate the burial chamber within. What was going on with these solar alignments? There can be absolutely no doubt that they were intentional, but why? The most convincing answer is in some ways the simplest. By lining their sacred places up with the movements of the heavenly bodies, people were making them a part of the natural order of things. The same could also be said of the realm of the ancestors, which was either represented (in stone), or given access to (in wood). This could be seen, perhaps, as a way of giving new places legitimacy within an ancient, timeless landscape controlled by forces far greater than mere mortals. It's illustrated vividly by the final approach to Stonehenge along the Avenue, which swings sharply south-west to approach the Stones from the

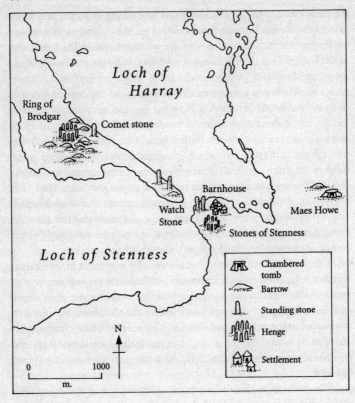

FIG 51   *The central area of Mainland Orkney.*

north-east, the direction of the morning and the midsummer sunrise. The ancestors, on the other hand, could be seen to have come from the south-west, the world of the night and the direction of the mid-winter sunset.

Mike Parker Pearson and Ramilisonina have shown that in stone-less regions of Madagascar other materials can be made to 'stand in' for stone.[39] Perhaps the all-oak construction of Seahenge, which I'll discuss shortly, is an example of a very hard wood 'standing in' for stone in a stoneless area. The Orkney situation is the opposite: here timber is rare, and stone all but ubiquitous. Perhaps the large slabs used in the construction of tombs, which are roofed in stone, were deliberately built to contrast with the smaller stones of the dry-stone walls and the driftwood or timber-and-turf roofs of domestic buildings – the residences of the living.

Mike Parker Pearson sees elements of his realm of the living vs realm of the ancestors contrast in the neighbouring stone circle henges on Mainland Orkney, the Ring of Brodgar (or Brogar)[40] and the Stones of Stenness. The two are at opposite ends of a narrow peninsula which almost (but not quite) divides the Loch of Stenness from the Loch of Harray. Perhaps this narrow strip of land formed some sort of ceremonial way marked by standing stones, some of which (including the so-called Comet and Watch Stones) still stand today. The peninsula is broken by open water, as Mike notes, 'in the same way that the Avon separates the processional route between Durrington and Stonehenge'.

The Stones of Stenness stood for the living: they are associated with quantities of Grooved Ware, and there is a large hearth at their centre.[41] Excavation has also revealed two timber post structures that predate the standing stones. The Ring of Brodgar, on the other hand, is surrounded by a complex of Bronze Age round barrows – the domain of the ancestors if ever there was one. Mike also makes a fairly convincing case for a shift in landscape orientation, as we saw at Stonehenge and Avebury. This is the ritual landscape which Colin Richards has suggested was a three-dimensional expression of the higher or cosmological beliefs of Neolithic and Bronze Age Orkney. Of course most of what they believed is beyond our grasp, but Colin's thoughts on what was happening within the Mainland Orkney ritual formlandscape can also, I am sure, be applied to Stonehenge and Avebury:

> Perhaps the most important point to recognise is that 'landscape' was continually created and transformed over several hundred years through different activities occurring at different times of the year, and as such it will have assumed different qualities according to key points in various cycles of human existence. The dominance of the monuments will always have overshadowed daily tasks and practices, just as they do today, but at particular times each place in this created landscape will assume special significance. This is

why the so-called 'ritual landscapes' of the Late Neolithic are nothing more than a formalisation of the social landscape of daily life.[42]

The ritual landscape of Brú na Bóinne can also be given the Parker Pearson/Ramilisonina treatment.[43] The stone/wood contrast, separated by long distances by Avenues or cursuses in Britain, is more closely juxtaposed in Ireland. At both Newgrange and Knowth the great stone passage-tombs lie immediately next to timber structures which are associated with Grooved Ware – the ware of the living.[44] Impressed wares, fairly similar to Peterborough styles, are found with the passage graves. Sadly, the two styles of pottery are not strictly contemporary. I'm not convinced, however, that this necessarily invalidates the life/death association suggested for the two styles of pottery. We could be looking at changes – perhaps 'hardening' – as time passed. We saw how the Stonehenge and Avebury ritual landscapes became modified through use, and there's no *prima facie* reason why something similar could not have happened in the Brú na Bóinne. Indeed, given the variety and chronological spread of the various tombs and other monuments in the area, I'd expect a great deal of change in the way the landscape was used as time passed.

The Bend of the Boyne ritual landscape would appear to have been less centralised in its layout, with more and smaller ancestral realms. It's tempting to suggest that this contrast with Stonehenge and elsewhere in Britain is a reflection of two rather different patterns of social organisation. If the pattern of Irish Neolithic society was indeed more settled than its British equivalent, and for longer, it might well result in a multi-centred style of ritual landscape which reflected the longer-lived and smaller-scale 'territories' that had been established in the countryside round about. In Britain, on the other hand, a more mobile population required more centralised social 'glue' to hold communities together, and to provide people with regular opportunities to gather, meet potential wives or husbands, exchange livestock and prestige goods such as polished stone axes and, of course, the new metal implements that were just beginning to appear.

I don't want to give the impression that the great ritual landscapes were confined to small areas of Britain and Ireland. As I've already

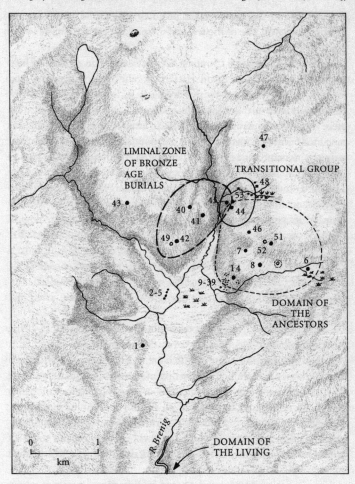

FIG 52 *The upper Brenig valley and reservoir (shaded). The numbered sites are discussed in the text.*

noted, there are large and important examples in eastern England and along the Thames valley. Sadly, I don't have the space to cover more than one further example, and I've decided to go for something a bit different. It's in the Brenig valley of north Wales, and was excavated by Frances Lynch, one of the few Welsh-speaking archaeologists working in the principality.

The river Brenig is a tributary of the river Dee, in an area of high moorland known as Mynydd Hiraethog. The valley is shallow, and today is partially flooded by the Brenig Reservoir. The main barrow cemetery was in use between approximately 2000 and 1550 BC, and there was a later flurry of minor activity around 1200 BC. The dig was called for because it was feared that the flooding of the reservoir would seriously damage many barrows. In the event the water was not as deep as had been anticipated, so none of the barrows have been destroyed. Indeed, far from it: the land around the reservoir is now a park, and many of the cairns and barrows have been restored to their former glory and can be enjoyed from an excellent Archaeological Trail. Frances has resisted the temptation to do something spectacular with reinforced concrete, and although the restored stonework looked a bit garish when first put in place, it has now mellowed considerably. It still makes the point, though, that some of the stone-built cairns – especially the platform and ring cairns – were very striking when first erected.

Up until now I've only really talked about barrows as being mounds, either round, long or oval. But they are also found in a variety of other forms, most of which are basically round, and defined by an outer ring-ditch. Some have tiny mounds surrounded by a large ditch; others have banks and mounds or mounds alone – or banks alone; others have no mounds at all, instead the ground within the encircling ring-ditch is removed to form a pond-shaped hollow – hence their name: ring or pond barrows.[45] In the upland areas of Britain we find a slightly different tradition developing, in which stone replaces soil.

Brenig has traditional soil or turf-built barrows, many of which include multiple concentric rings of posts, and the stone-built cairns. Cairns can be simple heaps of loose rocks, or they can be carefully constructed monuments, of which the so-called ring and platform cairns are the best known. The Brenig platform cairn (no. 51) is a very striking construction, with a hefty kerb of boulders and a low central ring of stones. It was clearly intended to impress.

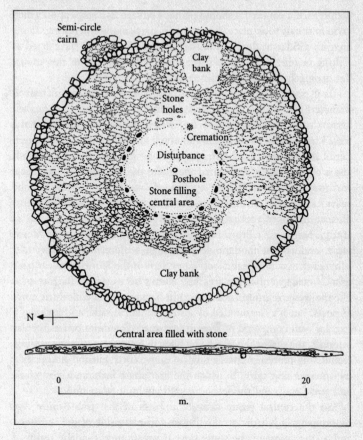

FIG 53 *Brenig platform cairn, site 51, lower level. The higher level was a flat platform of stone.*

Groups of barrows and cairns are usually referred to as barrow cemeteries or cairnfields, and Frances Lynch makes the point in her discussion of the excavations that Brenig never was a cemetery pure and simple. Rather it was a landscape of limited scale, in which people carried out ceremonies which may or may not have included the burial of bodies or cremations. The platform cairn only really makes sense within such a context; it should perhaps be seen as a stage upon which various rituals took place. Barrow 47 is particularly interesting. It sits high on a ridge at the head of the valley, and seems to have acted as a siting or reference point for the three western barrows, nos 40–42. Yet, strangely, it never contained any burials.

Is it possible to apply the Madagascar wood/stone distinction to Brenig? Surprisingly, the analysis seems to show that the earthen barrow/stone cairn distinction that was tentatively suggested for the New King Barrows also appears to apply to north Wales. The eastern cairns and mounds (nos 6, 8, 14, 46 and 51) are essentially stone-built and include the platform cairn, no. 51. On the other side of the valley, barrows 40–42 (which look up towards no. 47 at the head of the valley) are 'classic' earth-and-timber circle barrows. Between these two distinct groups is another, transitional group, comprising nos 44, 45 and 53. No. 53 isn't Bronze Age or a barrow at all. It's mainly Meso-lithic, and is best thought of as a small settlement. But I wonder whether it may not be the local equivalent of the Stonehenge car park posts – evidence that the area had always been special. Barrow 45 is like the western group (nos 40–42) in having several concentric rings of posts, but it's surrounded by a substantial palisade, and includes a circular wall composed of large stones spaced at more or less regular intervals, the spaces between being filled in by rough dry-stone walling. Could this represent 'hardening' of some sort? Finally, no. 44 is a two-phased ring cairn, in which the first phase includes a post circle and stone ring, and the second is entirely built from stone.

So the central group actually consists of just two Bronze Age monuments: a barrow on the timber-and-earth side of the cemetery, and a ring cairn on the stone side. If we suppose that the realm of the living was on lower ground downstream, to the south, mourners would enter the complex from the east. After ceremonies in or around the platform cairn (no. 51) or others of this group, they would then move to the ring cairn (no. 44) of the 'transitional' group. Perhaps a smaller party would then take the body or the cremated bones to a final resting place in one of the western group of barrows. It's possible that this process could have taken place in reverse, which would accord better with wood – the post circles in the barrows – representing the living; but I can't see those barrows as being meeting places. They are

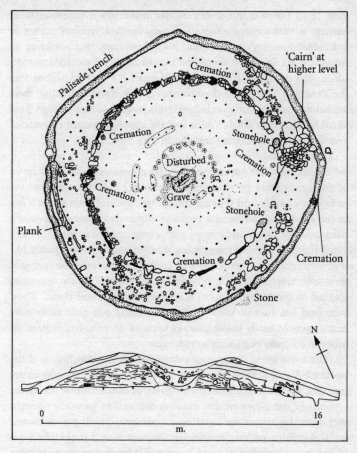

FIG 54   *Plan and section of Brenig site 45. The centre of the mound has been disturbed by twentieth-century diggings.*

quite different in scale and style to sites like Durrington Walls or Woodhenge. Admittedly, funeral parties in the Welsh mountains are likely to have been smaller than in the lowlands of Wessex, but these are nevertheless not meeting places for any number of people.

One could discuss precisely how this landscape was used for a long time, but I doubt if one would make much progress. What matters is that pattern exists. This was never a random scatter of individual funerary monuments. It's a landscape that works as an integrated whole, and it should be treated as one. It's carefully structured, and doubtless it changed with time. It's also interesting that the 'cemetery' was placed close by the river. It seems to me that there are many points in common between this modest and quite short-lived ritual landscape in north Wales and the more celebrated ceremonial centres in Wessex, Orkney and the Brú na Bóinne.

As British and Irish society became more sedentary and the pattern of the countryside grew better defined, with the emergence of the earliest large-scale field systems around 1500 BC, the main *raison d'être* of the great ritual landscapes began to slip away. There was less of a need for huge annual gatherings; with a more settled style of life came a different set of more frequent but smaller-scale routines, rather like the more recent pattern of visits by country families to sales and fairs in market towns, which is now sadly dying out. Greater sedentism also led to the development of a network of roads and tracks. These were laid out to suit local needs, and would not necessarily have helped people reach major centres such as Stonehenge. Britain, in other words, was beginning to close up.

The last stage of Stonehenge's development was the digging of the so-called Z and Y holes (the latter around 1600 BC). These holes are arranged in two concentric circles towards the centre of the circle, around the periphery of the standing stones. It's generally thought they were dug to receive bluestones – whether existing ones moved from elsewhere within Stonehenge, or new ones brought in from Wales, isn't clear. But it never happened. Stonehenge seems to have fizzled out, more with a whimper than a bang. This suggests a general lack of interest. Life had moved on, leaving the Stones in their magnificent stillness, a brooding presence in the changing Wiltshire landscape. Starting in the Middle Bronze Age (by, say, 1300 BC), the area occupied by the once all-enveloping ritual landscape has largely been covered by a net-like arrangement of little square fields.

My inclination at this point is to move on to a discussion of early field systems, but I'll have to leave them to the next chapter, because

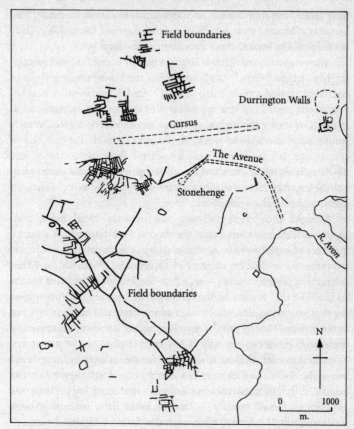

FIG 55   *Plan of Later Bronze Age fields on Salisbury Plain in the area around Stonehenge (dating uncertain but approximately 1300–800 BC).*

I'm very aware that this is the *Bronze* Age, and so far I've said little or nothing about bronze.

On the mainland of continental Europe there is a distinct Copper Age, or Chalcolithic, which precedes the Bronze Age. The most famous discovery of this period is the so-called Iceman whose frozen corpse was found high in the Alps of south Tyrol, and can be dated to around 3500 BC. In Britain the first bronze tools appear at about the same time as the first copper ones, so the distinction cannot be made. This happens at around 2500 BC. The transitional period (or LNEBA – Late Neolithic/Early Bronze Age) lasts from 2500–2000 BC.

The production of metal is largely a matter of creating and sustaining high temperatures.[46] Lead, which has the lowest melting point of commonly found metals, melts at 327°C (620°F), but in order to smelt it from the parent ore you must heat it to about 800°C. Copper melts at 1083°C (1981°F), the highest temperature of the early metals, so early smiths were also able to work silver (960°C), gold (1063°C) and of course lead. It's far from simple to achieve these temperatures, and much archaeological attention has quite rightly been paid to the technology involved. But there is another side to it as well: I refer, yet again, to ritual and symbolism.[47]

Modern and recent societies that produce metal using non-industrial techniques often treat the process as very special. For a start, the craft of metal-worker is nearly always a male one. The furnaces are often pot-bellied to allow gases to circulate efficiently, and thus resemble a pregnant torso – an effect sometimes heightened by the addition of clay breasts to the outside. The pumping of the bellows is a rhythmical business which takes a long time, and one gets very hot in the process. Having done it myself as part of a team of experimental metal-workers, I can see why it has been likened to the act of sex. Then, as if to complete the analogy, the furnace is broached low down, below the 'belly', and the red-hot metal pours forth very much like vaginal birth.[48] In many societies women – and more importantly 'the presence of female fertility'[49] – are excluded from witnessing these processes, just as men are often excluded from childbirth.

The production of an implement from a stone or clay mould can also be seen as a kind of birth process. Swords, for example, could have been named (like King Arthur's Excalibur) or dedicated to a particular individual when they were removed from the mould. This might help to explain why, in Later Bronze Age times, swords which had broken along casting flaws weren't simply melted down on the spot. Instead, as we'll see in the next chapter, they were often taken to special places and offered to the waters. They had acquired an identity, and just as today a stillborn baby is not discarded with the rubbish, Bronze Age swords were given a proper burial.

Our story is now well into the first true age of metal; so what happened to flint, which had provided the raw material for most implements for the previous half-million or so years? Its decline was not as rapid as one might suppose. This has led some to assume that there was initial resistance to the adoption of the new technology. Maybe, it is argued, bronze was so scarce and so valuable that flint and stone continued to be used for, say, making axes. That may indeed have been the case for certain types of artefacts like, for example, daggers. Many graves in Britain dating to the two or three centuries before 2000 BC contain beautifully worked flint daggers that have no stone antecedents, and appear on the scene fully formed, as it were. They are complete in themselves, and don't consist of a separate flint blade to which has been added a handle of, say, bone. They are, in other words, copies of complete daggers, and from their appearance there can be little doubt that they are imitating the very first bronze and copper daggers. Very often the graves in which they are found

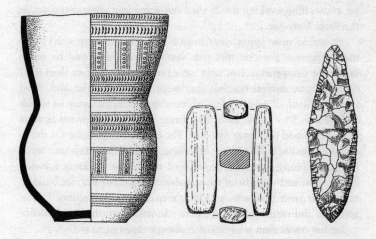

FIG 56   *A group of objects found in a grave beneath an Early Bronze Age round barrow at Amesbury, Wiltshire: a highly decorated Beaker drinking vessel (left), a small whetstone (centre) and a flint dagger (right). The dagger is copying the first metal daggers, which are beginning to appear at about this time (around 2000 BC).*

also contain finely made and highly decorated drinking vessels, known as Beakers. This very distinctive style of pottery is found across most of Europe, and is often associated with the first appearance of metal-working.

The copies of metal daggers are some of the finest flint objects ever made; in Scandinavia in particular they feature superbly regular 'ripple flaking'. But sadly, they were to prove the flint-knappers' swan-song. After about 2000 BC the standards of flint-working begin to change, if not to decline. Metal tools were now used to provide cutting edges and blades, and we find less evidence for controlled flaking. A new class of tool appears, which can best be described as the 'bashed lump'. These odd-looking implements appear to be the result of hope-lessly slapdash workmanship, but actually they were deliberately fashioned in this seemingly careless way to produce a faceted tool with many sharp points that could be used for scoring bone and antler, to remove large splinters. These pieces were then shaved down into pins and needles, which were the everyday fastenings of clothes. So far as we know, flint-working finally died out sometime around 500 BC, in the Early Iron Age.

It would now appear that bronze was adopted very quickly for making axes – the one tool that was radically improved by being fashioned from metal. Not only were bronze axes sharper than their flint or stone equivalents, but they were thinner, heavier and, most importantly of all, less brittle – it's very easy indeed to snap or smash a stone axe. So we find metal axes being used to work wood as soon as we find wood of Bronze Age date. The earliest evidence for the use of metal axes in the British Isles is in Ireland. Here, at Corlea (pronounced Corlay), County Longford, wood used to make a trackway across a bog was worked with metal tools at about 2268–2250 BC. The builders of another Irish trackway, at Annaghbeg in the same county (2140–1980 BC), also made use of metal axes.[50] In Britain, the earliest evidence so far for metal axes is found at Seahenge (2049 BC).

Some readers of my book about Seahenge have told me that they think I overestimated the symbolic importance of timber and woodland. But if anything, recent literature suggests that it is almost impossible to exaggerate the ideological significance of trees.[51] One of the main insights provided by Seahenge was the evidence for the possible existence of a world, or another dimension, that was believed to exist below the ground. We've already seen evidence for this belief in the carefully arranged deposits of pottery, skulls and so forth that were buried in the ditches of causewayed enclosures, and we've also seen how the shafts and galleries of flint mines were littered with offerings of one sort or another.

At Seahenge a small circle of fifty-five posts surrounded the lower trunk and roots of a large oak tree, weighing about 2.5 tonnes. It had been lowered into a pit upside-down, so that the roots protruded above the ground. Richard Bradley has shown how the Saami, an indigenous people of Lapland and north Norway, carried out similar rituals with inverted trees.[52] These rites were connected with their belief in an underworld that existed upside-down beneath our feet. It seems likely that something similar may have existed in the ideologies of Neolithic and Bronze Age Britain.

Maisie Taylor, the expert on prehistoric wood-working who (it may be recalled) also happens to be my wife, has measured every conceivable dimension of the central inverted oak tree, the fifty-five encircling posts and the 412 pieces of wood-working debris that were found when the posts were removed from the ground. She has also measured, drawn and recorded every single place where an axe has 'stopped' or jammed into the wood, leaving a complete profile of its cutting edge. Using this wealth of information, she has been able to calculate that no fewer than fifty-one axes were used to fell and dress the timbers of Seahenge.[53]

That figure is of great importance. It's the first indication from any European prehistoric site that I know of for the actual number of people that may have been involved in the construction of an ancient monument. If we assume that bronze was so valuable in 2050 BC that each person could only afford just one axe, we have an estimate of the absolute minimum number of people it took to erect Seahenge. There would also have been other people digging the trench into which the posts were set, and yet more splitting timbers with wooden wedges. And we mustn't forget the people who towed the logs to the site from the woods, or of course those who fed the workforce. It is quite clear, just from those axe statistics, that the construction of Seahenge – which, don't forget, is a tiny site, a mere six or seven

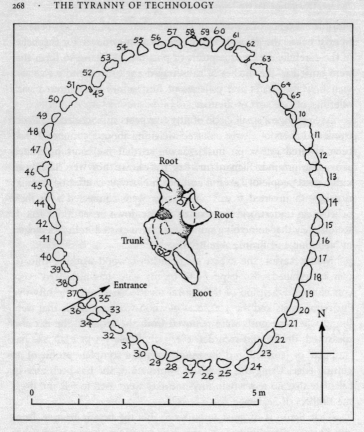

FIG 57   *Plan of Holme timber circle ('Seahenge'). Source: Norfolk Archaeological Unit.*

paces from side to side – was a major communal undertaking. Perhaps, in all, two hundred or more people were involved. There's no evidence to suggest that Seahenge was ever rebuilt or repaired, so it's fair to say that its construction was also its use. It was built to draw people together – a theme we will see repeated, in very different timber structures, much later in the Bronze Age.

*   *   *

Before we close this chapter, I'd like to make a stab at estimating the population of Early Bronze Age Britain, around 2000 BC. In *Seahenge* I arrived at a figure of a quarter of a million.[54] That was for Britain alone. If we add Ireland – say fifty thousand – we come to a total of 300,000. That doesn't sound like many people, if one bears in mind the thousands of barrows, henges and other sites that seem to litter the countryside. But we should also remember that a significant amount of people's time and energy was specifically devoted to communal religious gatherings where the landscape was altered in various ways, many of which have left permanent traces. So they were to some extent 'punching above their weight' in the way they affected their – and our – landscape.

After the Early Bronze Age, starting as early as 2000 BC in some areas, we see evidence for a more sedentary way of life. Fields, roads and trackways come into existence, and permanent settlements become far more common. Society was changing as the population began to grow more rapidly.

CHAPTER TEN

Pathways to Paradise
(the Mid- and Later Bronze Age:
1800–700 BC)

TRADITIONALLY, THE NEOLITHIC has been seen as the great period of change in which Britain and Europe moved from hunting and gathering to farming; but as we've noted, it wasn't quite as simple, or indeed as 'revolutionary', as that. I also believe that there's an element of what anthropologists term 'ethnocentrism' in our perception of the period. Essentially, ethnocentrism amounts to the putting of one's own culture first – as the yardstick against which other communities can be judged. It invariably implies that 'we' are better than 'them', the people we are studying. So farmers, being closer in our perception to us, are somehow better or more advanced than hunters and gatherers. However, there's no real evidence to support such a view. It's true that farmers can feed a greater number of people on a given area of land, but whether they lived happier, better-informed or more 'civilised' lives is another matter entirely. Farming is also a lifestyle that's hard to reverse – you can't return to food-gathering without major economic and social disruption, often accompanied by substantial loss of life. Essentially it's a one-way ticket.

Ethnocentrism is also what lies behind the British misidentification with ancient Rome, instead of with our true prehistoric forebears. The Roman way of life had, it was thought, much in common with that of Victorian and twentieth-century Britain. In those days of empire prehistoric British culture was still poorly understood, and it seemed quite inconceivable that the strange indigenous tribesmen[1] (not to mention subsequent incursions of Saxons and Vikings) who once inhabited the British Isles could have played a significant part in the ancestry of the people who gave the world parliamentary democracy, the Industrial Revolution and the British Empire.

It has only really become apparent in the past two decades that the full effects of the Neolithic happened rather later than was previously thought. As we have seen, the basic way of life in Britain didn't alter very dramatically prior to, say, 2000 BC. But after that, things certainly did begin to change. With one exception (which I'll discuss in the next paragraph), the physical archaeological evidence for these transformations is very much less dramatic and spectacular than sites like Stonehenge, Maes Howe, Silbury Hill or Newgrange – but that doesn't detract from its importance. I believe that the five or six centuries after 2000 BC were of equal significance to the entire Neolithic period in the long-term evolution of British and Irish settlement and culture, and that the 'revolution' of the Neolithic period actually happened several centuries later, in the Earlier Bronze Age.

We're now firmly in the Bronze Age, and bronze is an alloy composed largely (about 90 per cent) of copper. Copper occurs naturally in the British Isles, and it was extensively mined in the Bronze Age. Until the 1970s it was thought that copper mines were quite rare, and were essentially shallow, surface affairs. But recent research has turned that idea on its head, and nowhere has the revolution in our perceptions been more complete than at the Great Orme copper mines in north Wales.[2] It's a most remarkable place (and it's open to the public in the summer).

It is now apparent that Bronze Age prospectors were as systematic in searching out sources of copper ore as any claim-staker of the 1890s Gold Rush. A recent survey by Simon Timberlake has identified five distinct prehistoric prospection areas in mid-Wales,[3] and there is abundant evidence for copper mining elsewhere in western Britain and Ireland – were it not for the breathtaking discoveries at Great Orme, I would probably have devoted this part of the book to the mines at Mount Gabriel in the extreme south-west of Ireland.[4]

What makes this recent research so extraordinary is the sheer scale of the mining operations it has revealed. However, these are mostly mines or surface workings that could have been exploited by communities of farmers during quiet times of the agricultural year. Only at Great Orme – so far – does it seem likely that mining could have been a full-time activity. The sixty radiocarbon dates that have been obtained from prehistoric copper mines in Britain and Ireland suggest that the main period of activity was confined to just four centuries between 1900 and 1500 BC, although at Great Orme it continued for somewhat longer – until around 900 BC, towards the end of the Bronze Age.

I suspect that one reason why the Great Orme mines appeal to the imagination is that they were worked rather like a deep coalmine of the Industrial Revolution, with a series of passages leading off vertical shafts. The workings at Mount Gabriel, on the other hand, sloped downwards as they followed the seams of ore into the ground. Great Orme also resembles its nineteenth-century counterparts in one other, rather chilling, respect: several of the tunnels discovered below ground are tiny, and could only have been worked by children.

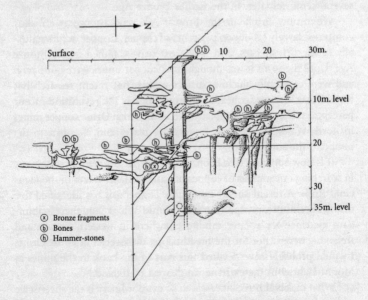

FIG 58   *Three-dimensional plan of the upper-level shafts and galleries of the Bronze Age copper mines at Great Orme, Llandudno. The large vertical shaft at the centre was sunk in the eighteenth and nineteenth centuries, and led to the discovery of the prehistoric workings cut through by it.*

Later Bronze Age wattle-lined well at Fengate, Peterborough (1430–1010 BC). These shallow wells were dug down to the ground water-table, or 'sock'; sock wells are still known in the area.

Another example of a Bronze Age sock well at Fengate. The narrow plank could have served both as a step and as a reinforcement for the woven alder wattle-work which retained the loose gravel sides of the well.

TOP A small flock of Soay sheep grazing in one of the paddocks of the reconstructed Bronze Age farmstead at Flag Fen. These animals belong to the dark strain of the Soay breed and would have been found widely throughout Neolithic and Bronze Age Britain.

ABOVE LEFT A Soay ewe of about three years old. Soay rams have far heavier horns which grow in a typical spiral, ram's-horn fashion.

ABOVE RIGHT A newly born Soay lamb keeping up with its mother. Unlike modern breeds of sheep, Soay lambs are able to move about very quickly after birth.

Exmoor pony. This animal is typical of British prehistoric horses, with a characteristic loose coat and pale muzzle.

BELOW A so-called 'Iron Age pig' at Flag Fen. Native European pigs have long snouts; the short-snouted modern pig results from cross-breeding with Asian breeds. This particular animal is a sow, about three years old, and is the result of crossing a Tamworth with a domesticated wild boar. She was very docile and friendly.

The Great Orme copper mines, Llandudno, north Wales (about 1900–900 BC). The extensive galleries extend deep into the hill behind the cliff-like face. They are entered today by way of the three openings at the foot of the stairs.

An Iron Age logboat from a course of the River Trent, found in a gravel quarry near Shardlow, in Derbyshire. The boat is being studied by the leading authority on the archaeology of the Trent gravels, Dr Chris Salisbury. The boat had been packed full – to the point of instability – with massive stone blocks which are clearly visible, lower left.

Posts of a Middle Bronze Age timber causeway on the south bank of the Thames near Vauxhall Bridge (the wheel of the London Eye is just visible through the central arch). The figures to the right are members of the *Time Team* crew that investigated the site.

A close-up of the only Bronze Age timber of the causeway to be excavated and removed by the *Time Team* archaeologists at Vauxhall Bridge.

Large areas of the pre-Roman British countryside were laid out in a series of carefully arranged fields and droveways (tracks used to drive livestock). This view is of the Fengate, Peterborough, field system with a major double-ditched droveway running up through the centre of the picture. Two fields beyond it joined up with the great timber causeway across Flag Fen. The system was in use between 2500 and 500 BC.

Aerial view of the Iron Age hill-fort defences (fifth–second centuries BC) at Maiden Castle, Dorset, showing the maze-like complexity of the western entranceway in the foreground. At about two-thirds of the distance along the enclosed area, at a point where the outer ramparts kink, a less pronounced bank and ditch crosses the interior. This is part of the first Iron Age fort, which follows the line of a far earlier, Neolithic, causewayed enclosure of the fourth millennium BC.

An aerial view of the cairn surface of Site B at Navan Fort, County Armagh, Northern Ireland. The stone blocks used in the careful spoke, or wheel-like, construction of the mound may well have been taken from an earlier prehistoric cairn nearby. It was constructed on top of a massive timber structure that tree-ring evidence shows was built in the year 95 BC.

The actual process of digging and extraction at Great Orme was carried out using bone, antler and possibly bronze tools. Stone hammers made from beach cobbles, possibly hafted tomahawk-fashion in wooden handles (but more probably grasped firmly in both hands and used as pounders), were employed to remove rock and to crush ore. With such seemingly simple tools the miners were able to sink their shafts and galleries to a depth of *at least* seventy metres. The mine is known to include a staggering five kilometres of passages, which cover an area of over twenty-four thousand square metres. But it isn't just a matter of shafts and passages. There are also at least two huge, hall-like caverns. One was discovered accidentally in the nineteenth century, and was thought at the time to be Roman. It is now destroyed, but artefacts found in it suggest it was dug in prehistory. The other was found more recently. It's positioned at a point where three veins of ore come together, and its huge size indicates that thousands of tons of ore must have been removed.

There is also good evidence that fire was used to split and break the rock, which means that the mine must have had a sophisticated ventilation system to remove the smoke. Like their modern counterparts, prehistoric mines suffered from flooding. Water was removed using a series of *launders*, or wooden gutter-shaped pipes, some of which have been found intact at Copa Hill, another Bronze Age deep mine in Wales.[5]

There's always a danger of archaeologists treating prehistoric metal-working and mining as mere industrial processes, and examining the process by itself, in a contextual vacuum. But there was also a social setting in which these activities took place, and we ignore it at our peril. We've seen how taboos of various sorts may have surrounded metal-working: just twenty years ago these would not have been thought important considerations, even though they could have affected not only the way the implements being fashioned were used, but also how many of them were made – and of course their distribution. The prehistoric world was never a free market, and the way objects 'behaved' was entirely dictated by society's beliefs and conventions. One way of putting it is that in prehistory objects had a social life of their own.

We cannot escape ritual and ideology even down a mine. In fact,

I'm inclined to say 'especially down a mine', given what we know from sites like Seahenge about prehistoric views on the underworld. I think it highly unlikely that people ever entered a mine – even a relatively shallow surface mine – lightly. I imagine that the spiritual dangers that were thought to lie below the ground were vastly more frightening than the prospect of a roof collapse. More likely, the two would have been considered interrelated. At Great Orme and else-where, mines have produced evidence for special offerings of one sort or another. Even the shallow surface working at Great Orme produced large quantities of animal bones, not all of which could have been used as tools, as well as caches of bone implements.

It is perhaps inevitable that modern work on prehistoric mining should concentrate on technology, if only because most of the people doing the research have metallurgical or industrial backgrounds. But I'm convinced that the ideological side of ancient mining has been overlooked for too long. There's a megalithic tomb within sight of the Great Orme surface workings. Is that coincidence? It could be, but I doubt it. At Mount Gabriel in Ireland there seems to be a close relationship between wedge-shaped megalithic tombs and copper mines.[6] Were these the tombs of the miners, or of the families that controlled the mines? We will probably never know, but the occurrence of the two so near to each other demonstrates that the realms of ideology and work were closely knit together.

Industrial activity on this scale would appear to suggest a truly immense amount of metal. Mines and surface workings give us a reliable indication of the quantity of metal smelted in prehistory. You can't replicate that type of statistic with flint, huge quantities of which can simply be picked up on the surface. Calculations carried out by Simon Timberlake and others, suggest that the mines of mid-Wales (including his own project at Copa Hill) produced between six and ten tons of copper metal throughout the Early Bronze Age (i.e. between 1800 and 1500 BC). The Irish mines at Mount Gabriel produced perhaps three to four tons over two centuries. Great Orme is thought to have yielded a rather extraordinary 175 to 238 tons.

These are huge figures, but the span of time is long, and there is increasing evidence that Bronze Age communities were remarkably profligate in the way they 'used' metal. I believe it is probable that the majority of the many thousands of Bronze Age metal implements in our museums were never intended to be 'used' at all. Some were – as is shown by the patterns of micro-wear of their cutting edges – but were then disposed of long before the end of their use-lives. It's remarkably unusual to find worn-out Bronze Age metal tools, or to find metal tools of any sort at Bronze Age settlements or domestic sites. All of which suggests that most of the Bronze Age implements that have survived were disposed of deliberately. This brings us back to the realms of ritual and ideology, because it simply doesn't make sense to throw away sound and valuable tools or weapons when there is still plenty of life in them (especially as they can be melted down and recycled).

I'll discuss my own excavations at Flag Fen, Peterborough, in more detail shortly, but so far we have revealed nearly three hundred prehistoric metal objects – and we've only excavated a small fraction of the known site. I wouldn't be surprised if eventually Flag Fen were to reveal three to five thousand artefacts, most of which would have been placed in the waters as offerings between 1300 and 700 BC. But Flag Fen is quite a lowly player in the league of British Bronze Age metal-work finds. Also on the very edge of the fens, but much further south, near the borders of Suffolk and Cambridgeshire, the largest so-called 'hoard', or cache, of Bronze Age metal-work was found close by the village of Isleham.[7] This extraordinary find included some 6500 pieces, and weighed no less than ninety-five kilograms. In terms of mined metal, this one find would account for about five years' production from the prolific Irish mines at Mount Gabriel.

Why were hoards buried in the ground? Many hundreds, possibly even thousands, are known, the length and breadth of the British Isles.[8] In addition to swords, axes, knives and other objects, the Isleham hoard included 2600 pieces of melted-down metal which had been allowed to solidify in slabs that could readily have been remelted to make new implements. Was the Isleham hoard the stock of, say, itinerant smiths? Perhaps, but I think not. Why, for example, had many of the Bronze Age metal implements dredged from the river Thames, where they had almost certainly been placed as votive offerings, been partially melted down? I remember how odd I found this strange phenomenon when I first came across it in the late 1970s.[9]

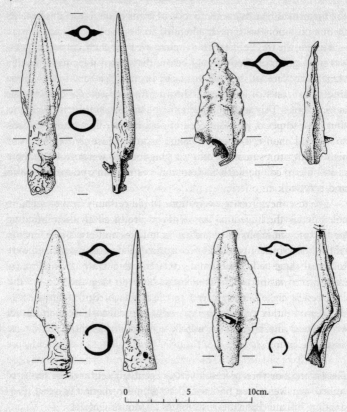

FIG 59   *Four Late Bronze Age socketed spearheads dredged from the river Thames near Reading, in the collections of the Royal Ontario Museum, Toronto. They had been partially melted down before being placed in the river as votive offerings.*

But now I think I'm beginning to understand what might have been in people's minds as they partially melted down their spearheads, then dropped them into the river – doubtless with a spectacular hissing explosion of steam. It would be hard to imagine a stronger symbolic statement.

To dismiss hoards as mere accumulations of scrap metal is to treat them as components in a simple industrial economic process. But as we've seen, life wasn't like that in prehistory. Production of metal-work was envisaged more in terms of birth, and its removal from circulation often took place in special wet places, such as Isleham or Flag Fen. Indeed, at least two hoards are known from the wet marshland close by Seahenge. This is liminal territory, that recalls in essentials the ritual landscapes of previous generations, and hardly the sort of place one would choose if one was planning to produce and control the high temperatures necessary for working metal – water and fire don't make natural companions. So were these extraordinary accumulations of metal-work an offering to the ancestors?

I believe they probably were. That would certainly help to account not only for the huge amounts of metal produced at the mines, but for the large numbers of swords, daggers, axes and other implements that fill our museums. Of course, other explanations are possible. It has been suggested, for example, that this deliberate destruction of metal-work was part of an unconscious plan to keep the value of the commodity high. I'm not sure I agree with such reasoning, which is based on a rather crudely Marxist view of prehistoric economics. As we've seen, much ancient 'trade' was based on far more than such simple economics.[10]

The last two or three decades of the twentieth century and the first years of the twenty-first have witnessed a transformation in our understanding of Later Bronze Age prehistory, from roughly 1500 to 700 BC. Much of the groundbreaking work that brought this about took place in England and Wales south of Yorkshire. Significant work was done elsewhere in the British Isles, but that in the south really was rather special, and it also forms a coherent narrative.

I have briefly mentioned my own work at Flag Fen, and I'd like now to return to it, because it illustrates very clearly how beliefs and ritual behaviour changed after the age of Stonehenge and the great ceremonial monuments of the Neolithic and Earlier Bronze Age. It is a most extraordinary site, which I came across during an archaeological survey of fenland drainage dykes in November 1982,[11] and which continues to reveal surprises – the latest being the remains of what is still,

I believe, the earliest wheel found in Britain. More on that later.

For the rest of this chapter I will attempt to convey what it might have been like to have lived in southern Britain at this important time in prehistory. I shall use Flag Fen to tie the story together, and to provide a thread of continuity[12] – not that this is to suggest that life in the whole of Later Bronze Age Britain was necessarily similar to that small part of northern East Anglia where I have spent thirty somewhat hermit-like, but wonderfully satisfying, years.

Flag Fen is a small area or 'bay' of wetland on the western edges of the fens, those low-lying and flat regions that form a marshy and wet inland extension of the Wash. Until their drainage, first in medieval times and then in the seventeenth century, they were Britain's largest wetland, covering about a million acres. This is now a very rich agricultural area, but even before their drainage the fens had abundant resources: huge expanses of summer grazing, reeds for thatch, vast stands of timber, plus fish, eels, and a wealth of wildfowl. It was also an environment favoured by religious communities, and there are many monastic sites, of which Ely and Peterborough are the most famous. People tended to settle on the drier islands and around the edges of the wetlands, where their houses were free from flooding, but they were able to take advantage of the area's various resources. You could say that the people living close by the fen had the best of both worlds, wet and dry. This is one reason why so many rich medieval towns appeared along the fen margins: King's Lynn, Cambridge, Huntingdon, Peterborough, Lincoln and Boston.

Flag Fen lies on the south-eastern side of Peterborough, and the magnificent cathedral church of St Peter is clearly visible from it. I sometimes tease my friends at the cathedral that they are the religious

FIG 60   *Map of the Flag Fen basin, Peterborough, in the Later Bronze Age (1300–900 BC). A post-built causeway crosses a kilometre-wide stretch of fen or wet ground from Fengate on the mainland to a large 'island' at Northey, to the east. An artificial island-like timber platform was constructed close to the Northey shore. Offerings of metal objects were placed around the posts of the causeway and along its southern side. Air photos and excavation have revealed a complex system of ditched fields and paddocks on the dry, gravel-based soils on either side of the wet fen.*

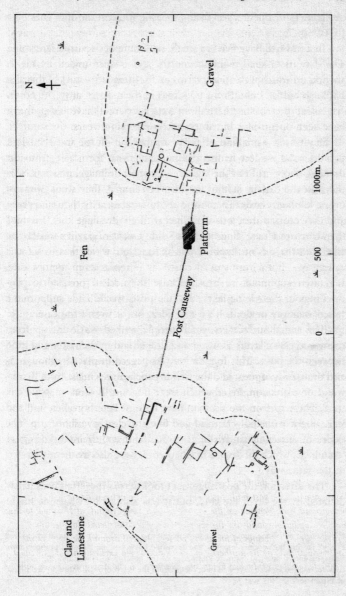

newcomers to the area, as their monastic foundation only goes back to AD 655.[13]

In a nutshell, Flag Fen is a small, self-contained fenland landscape. The 'bay' is entered from the north, and is surrounded by higher ground on which were fields, farms and settlements – part of this area has been hidden beneath the buildings of the modern city. The northern entrance is in effect a 'strait' of wetter ground that would probably have been open water in winter, and somewhat drier in the summer. At about 1300 BC a line of posts arranged in four, and then five, parallel rows was set in the ground, traversing the 'strait' from the dryland 'shore' at Peterborough to a large fen 'island' known as Northey, on the eastern side of the Flag Fen 'bay'.* The 'strait' was just over a kilometre wide. There were approximately sixty thousand posts, and they crossed it in a straight line, with a very slight kink. I named this structure a 'post alignment', as I didn't want to give it a misleading label, but there is no doubt about its function, which was to act as a causeway – but a very special causeway – about seven metres wide. It's often supposed, perhaps because they recall prehistoric pile-dwellings in the Alpine lakes, that the posts would have supported a raised walkway or deck. It's a nice idea, but it wasn't the case.

The actual surface on which people walked was built up from many successive layers of wood and timber laid in the water and mud between the posts. This foundation was pegged in place by thousands and thousands of pegs, and the walking surface was made from brushwood or planks, many of which were huge, split from massive oak trees. These surfaces would soon have become slippery when wet, and were liberally dusted with sand and fine gravel to give more grip. The floors of ancient lake-dwellings in Scotland and Ireland, known as 'crannogs', which I'll discuss in Chapter 12, were also frequently treated in the same way.

The direction the post alignment took across the 'strait' was partly dictated by the lie of the land, but it was also set by what one might

---

* I apologise for all the quotation marks here, but in a sense the Flag Fen basin was indeed a 'bay'. During the summer months, and in years of low rainfall, it would probably have been possible, if one had intimate knowledge of the network of creeks and channels that criss-crossed the area, to have walked dry-shod from the Peterborough 'shore' to the 'island' of Whittlesey.

call the 'grain' of the human landscape. When we had excavated about a hundred metres of posts at the Peterborough end of the alignment, we found the faint traces of a shallow field boundary ditch running below the timbers – and therefore earlier than them, possibly Late Neolithic or Early Bronze Age in date. Its existence (and a wealth of other evidence) shows that by 2500 BC the landscape around Flag Fen had begun to be parcelled up into fields. These were laid out at right angles to the fen, and were separated into individual holdings (to use the current terminology) by droveways, special tracks for the driving of flocks and herds of animals. Droves or droveways need to have robust boundaries on each side; at Flag Fen these were made by deep ditches with parallel banks, on which were grown stockproof thorn hedges. So the Flag Fen post alignment was constructed in a fully developed landscape. It was by no means a causeway through a barren wilderness.

The post alignment is indeed a causeway, but it's far more than that. The main evidence for this is provided by the nearly three hundred finds of prehistoric metal-work made to date. They were found within the area of the posts and also along their southern side, but not along the northern side, which faced out from the 'strait' into the wide-open fen. It's tempting to view this in symbolic terms: the open fen to the north was seen as being hostile or untamed. It was on this side of the posts that we found the remains of dogs, and the only complete human skeleton. They were in extremely poor condition after lying for thousands of years in acid peat, and we can only guess at the person's sex, but he or she was large enough to have been adult. How did he/she die? Again, we don't know, but I reckon the death occurred in the Iron Age – a period when Flag Fen was still in use as an important ceremonial centre. Given what we know about the so-called 'bog bodies' of Britain and Scandinavia in the Iron Age, I wouldn't be at all surprised to learn that the Flag Fen individual had been killed before being thrown into the waters.[14] Similarly, there's some evidence to suggest that at least one of the dogs could have been deliberately sacrificed.

The southern side of the posts was protected from the hostile world to the north by an outer barrier of posts that leaned towards the north, and were not arranged in a neat row. This porcupine-like palisade may well have projected two or three metres above the water level, and would have looked spectacular from a distance. The southern, 'safe', side of the posts was surrounded by the fields and farms of the communities who made use of the rich summer grazing offered by the 'bay' of wetter ground.

It's significant that the post alignment was constructed at a time when ground conditions across the fens were becoming very much wetter. It can thus be seen partly as a means of crossing the 'strait', but also as a way of signalling to the outside world to keep away. The lower-lying fens to the north and east were getting dangerously damp at this time (1300 BC), and many communities would probably have been looking towards higher ground to graze their flocks and herds. One could also see the barrier as a symbolic defence against the rising waters: a visible sign of communal opposition to the inevitable. It's no wonder that the open fen was viewed as an unwelcoming no man's land. Some of the offerings of valuable metal-work placed up against the posts on the southern side may well have been intended to summon up spiritual or ancestral support for this important boundary. Once again, this highlights the importance of Ian Hodder's thoughts on the significance of boundaries in times of tension, which were mentioned in Chapter 2.

The posts at Flag Fen ran roughly west–east from the 'mainland', as represented by the Peterborough fen margins, to a 'peninsula' of the large 'island' of Whittlesey. The 'landfall' at the Peterborough end is at Fengate; that at the eastern end is at Northey. It's interesting that this route should run from a mainland to an offshore island. As if to emphasise the point, the builders of the Flag Fen post alignment also constructed a small artificial wooden island towards the Northey 'shore'. At present we don't know what this was used for, although we can prove that people didn't live on it, and that large numbers of offerings were made there.

We find islands, and particularly offshore islands, at other ceremonial or special crossing places. Recently I worked with Channel 4's *Time Team* on a Middle Bronze Age (I'd guess 1400–1200 BC) post-built causeway on the southern banks of the Thames near Vauxhall Bridge in London. This site revealed a pair of bronze spearheads, and its massive posts ran up to a small offshore island. A similar site, but a century or two later, was found at Shinewater Park just outside Eastbourne. Here the posts ran for about five hundred metres across a strait not unlike that at Flag Fen, and broke their journey at least once at small islands. At Fordey, near Little Thetford in the southern fens, posts ran from the 'mainland' to an offshore 'island'.[15]

There are other examples, but none better than that at Fiskerton, in the Witham valley just outside Lincoln. This site is Iron Age, but it very much follows an earlier tradition, and there is evidence to suggest that there was at least one Bronze Age precursor nearby.[16] The post alignment at Fiskerton is undoubtedly a causeway, or perhaps a long pier, and is constructed around an arrangement of paired posts. The ground is extremely soft, and the posts are remarkable for their great length. One that was removed intact, by gently pulling it from the ground with a hydraulic digger, was no less than five metres long.

Like the posts at Flag Fen, those at Fiskerton have long, pencil-like points, and it has to be asked how they were driven into the ground. Another television crew, this time from the BBC's *Meet the Ancestors*, carried out some experiments. One method involved the erection of a huge tripod from which was suspended a large oak log weighing about a quarter of a ton. A team of some twenty to thirty people raised and dropped this weight onto the pile. The second method involved the clamping of a platform onto the pile and two burly volunteers, myself and Mike Parker Pearson, jumping up and down rhythmically on it. As the post sank the platform was repositioned, and we climbed on it again. The final method was the simplest. A pile was festooned with sandbags weighing perhaps a quarter of a ton. It began to sink of its own weight, but when two intrepid volunteers clambered onto it and began to jiggle about, the effect was spectacular. It sank into the ground like a rock through custard.

So which method would have been used? The tripod method was the hardest work and the most cumbersome, and it would have been extremely difficult and dangerous to have driven in piles any longer than five metres. It also required highly flexible, strong and very long ropes, and I have slight doubts about whether material of this quality and length would have been available – but I'd be delighted if someone one day proves me wrong. The second method was the most fun, although Mike and I had a few scary moments when the platform clamps began to slip. Most people I've asked have said they would have chosen the efficient deadweight method over the other two. But I'm not sure.

What has always worried me about experimental efforts to replicate ancient engineering techniques is that the experimenters, who are often civil engineers or archaeologists with a keen interest in such things, are looking for the most efficient and effective method – but judged in *their* terms. The experiment becomes rather like a design competition for a bridge, say: various schemes are put forward, and the one that combines strength, elegance and value for money wins. Is that what happened in prehistory? I think not. Again, as with economics, we're in danger of imposing our methods of judgement on the past. If an Iron Age community was just building a utilitarian structure, and the work was carried out by a group of specialists, then I'd expect it to be done safely and efficiently. But did such rules apply?

We have already seen that in many prehistoric engineering projects, for example the erection of great megalithic monuments, the heavy and difficult work itself played an important part in the ceremonies of construction. The transport of the Preseli bluestones to Stonehenge is a classic example, and we must beware of judging such projects in modern terms.

If the construction of these massive wooden causeways was indeed something of a social event – and I certainly believe it was at Flag Fen – then the method of pile-driving selected would have been appropriate to such an occasion. For that reason I tend to prefer the second of the three methods tried out above, where Mike and I jumped up and down on a platform perilously clamped to the post. It was spectacular, and not particularly quick – a five-metre post would have taken at least a couple of hours, even using relays of jumpers. Doubtless they would have been aided by drums and singing. Most likely, too, other posts would be being driven in by groups from various communities in the area at the same time. It could have been a joyful occasion for everyone, with feasting and socialising in the evenings.

We have one piece of unexpected evidence that the construction and repair of these sites was a major social occasion. As we saw at the Sweet Track, tree-ring dating can be remarkably precise. That precision was put to good use at Fiskerton, where it was possible to identify a series of tree-felling episodes which marked years when the posts were renewed. The first of these took place in the winter of 457/456 BC. A year previously there had been a total lunar eclipse, which would have been visible at Fiskerton on 12 January 457 BC: at 1.35 a.m. the eclipse would have been 56° above the horizon.* The next rebuilding took place ten years later, in the winter/spring of 447 BC. That year the eclipse took place on 10 December at 9.29 p.m., when the moon was 48° above the horizon. Several subsequent episodes of reconstruction also coincided with total lunar eclipses.

It could be argued that these phases of rebuilding simply reflected the fact that an eclipse happened, whereupon it was decided to repair the causeway. Maybe the appearance of the eclipse was a token, a sign, that had been eagerly awaited. The trouble with this idea is that two other episodes of rebuilding coincided with total lunar eclipses that took place just below the horizon, where they would not have been visible in eastern England. In other words, it seems that the people at Fiskerton had worked out how to predict total eclipses. This is not a simple business, as they follow a cycle, known as a 'saros', of eighteen years, ten days.

A total lunar eclipse on a cloudless night is an extraordinary event, even more remarkable when viewed across the huge, shimmering expanses of the river Witham's usual winter floodwaters. The cycle of repairs and lunar eclipses – which incidentally did not happen at Flag Fen – would have united the Fiskerton causeway with the natural world, giving it a sort of permanence and legitimacy within the landscape. The long duration of the eclipse cycle would help link the causeway to those who had gone before.

Fiskerton appears to have been like Flag Fen in its construction: posts with an informal packing of planks and brushwood to provide a dry surface to walk on. The offerings, too, recall Flag Fen, with some broken objects and many swords and spearheads. The causeway led from what one might refer to as 'mainland England' towards the part of Lincolnshire known as Lindsey. In effect Lindsey is a large island, bounded by the Humber and the Trent to the north and west, and

---

* These figures were worked out by Mike Parker Pearson's colleague at Sheffield University, Dr Andrew Chamberlain, using data provided by NASA.

by the Witham and the fens to the south. It's tempting to see such 'islands' as special places, perhaps akin in certain respects to the realms of the ancestors we encountered previously.

The rich offerings in the waters and the lunar cycles certainly suggest religion and ceremonial at Fiskerton, but there's also another element. That particular stretch of the river Witham is home to one of the densest concentrations of monastic communities in Britain; and there is a hint beginning to emerge that the occurrence of these post-Roman religious houses may coincide with later prehistoric causeways, such as that at Fiskerton. Of course, there may be another explanation. Mike Parker Pearson has suggested that the Lindsey or Whittlesey 'islands' could have been separate and independent tribal territories, and the crossing places to them would provide a natural spot for displays to do with political and social competition, doubtless involving much conspicuous consumption and public destruction of valuables. This is a plausible suggestion, but there are others.

I was struck when excavating the metal objects at Flag Fen that many of them were essentially small-scale and intimate offerings. I recall one bronze dagger. It wasn't a highly decorated or flashy piece; its antler hilt or handle had been pulled off, probably with some force, then both blade and hilt were placed in the shallow water, possibly within a scoop in the mud. Another find was a complete Bronze Age pottery jar that had been placed on its side beneath a log which had been carefully pegged into place above it. At Fiskerton two Iron Age jars were found, complete and intact, below the causeway.[17] None of these seems to be the kind of showy offering one would make as part of a display at the boundary of the next tribe's territory. To me they have far more in common with the more intimate type of offering found, for example, at Etton. Perhaps they were offerings to the ancestors, made at a special place to accompany a departed soul's journey to the next world.

Many of the fundamental themes or elements of the religious rituals of the Neolithic and Early Bronze Age are repeated in the Later Bronze and Iron Ages. But they have been transformed into a new range of settings. The idea of monumentality has become less important, and the large numbers of objects found suggest that ordinary people played a more direct role in what was going on. It's rather as if the altar was moved from the east end of the nave into the main body of the church – a sign that the ordinary people of the time played a significant role in the organisation and government of their societies. There may well have been powerful individuals, but I don't think they were *that* powerful. We will see shortly that there is little sign of the existence of a powerful controlling elite in the most basic evidence of all: the layout of settlements.

I remember some twenty years ago, after finding the first sword at Flag Fen, being asked by a reporter what it would have been worth in modern terms. I replied that it could be seen as the equivalent of an anti-aircraft missile – so perhaps £100,000. Since then there have been innumerable finds of Bronze Age weapons, and I now reckon that most tribal warriors could have possessed a bronze sword and spear. So bronze would have been considered valuable, but again, not *that* valuable – and certainly not the equivalent of £100,000. Maybe only one of the spears owned by an individual warrior would have been tipped in metal; those thrown (i.e. javelins) would have had bone spearheads, of which no fewer than sixty-four were found at Fiskerton.

If most warriors would have possessed one or more bronze weapons, which could have been seen as symbols of rank or power, does that mean that these were things *only* to be held up and admired? Were they ever actually used? There are examples of Bronze Age skeletons with cuts, both healed over and fatal, but they aren't common, and we know of no *bona fide* battlefield cemeteries.[18] I incline to the view that much Bronze Age warfare in Britain amounted more to boundary disputes, skirmishing and rustling, than full-scale pitched battles.[19]

Boundaries are an important theme running through our story and they recur again in the Later Bronze Age. By now barrows are no longer being constructed afresh, but people are visiting old burial mounds, and occasionally placing cremations under the surface of the turf. This suggests that many significant prehistoric boundaries were very long-lived. Other means were also employed for marking out key points in the landscape, of which hoards were one. I mentioned that the vast Isleham hoard was found close to the edge of the fen, which would have been an important place in the landscape. Out in the fen pasture would probably have been open, without personal or family

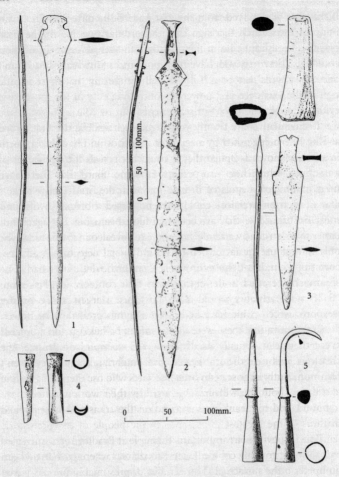

FIG 61   *A selection of Later Bronze Age (1300–900 BC) metal-work from Flag Fen, Peterborough. 1: Rapier (a thrusting weapon). 2: Leaf-shaped sword (a slashing weapon). 3: Dagger with its antler hilt removed (shown above the blade). 4: Carpenter's gouge (a tapered handle would have been driven into the socket hole at the top). 5: Flesh-hook, socketed in the same way as the gouge (a special implement, probably used to remove pieces of meat from cauldrons during feasts).*

holdings. On dry land it might well have been different. So it was important to mark the division between the two in a significant fashion. We should bear in mind that the fen/dryland distinction could also have had ideological significance, with the wetter land and the 'islands' within it being thought important to the ancestors, especially in wintertime.[20]

Recent excavations have been carried out by Mark Knight of the Cambridge University team less than a mile from Flag Fen, along the south-eastern edge of the embayment at a spot on the approaches to Whittlesey known as Bradley Fen.[21] They have revealed some extraordinary finds, which help to explain why some hoards of Bronze Age metal-work were deposited in the ground in the first place. This has always been an archaeological problem, largely because in the past most hoards – like that at Isleham – have been found by accident, either when struck by a farmer's plough, or revealed in the foundations of a new house or factory. Increasingly, metal-detectorists are discovering them, but this too causes problems: the detectorists are usually more interested in the objects than their contexts. In addition to all this, it's nearly always impossible to organise a large-scale excavation at short notice – which is why Bradley Fen has proved so exciting.

The excavation is an excellent example of what developer-funded archaeology can achieve when the project is funded by a sympathetic client (in this case the Hanson Brick Company), and is carried out on a sufficiently large scale by archaeologists who use their imagination and think about the wider issues raised by their work.

Mark and his team have shown that the transition from wet to dry was of the greatest importance to the people of the prehistoric fen. The first evidence for prehistoric people at Bradley Fen is provided by a series of roughly cobbled or metalled areas where gravel had been dumped on the surface of the wet ground, presumably to consolidate it. These more or less followed the line of the modern Ordnance Survey one-metre (above sea level) contour. This would have been the margin of the regularly flooded land, and the 'surveying' would have been done simply by observing the water's edge. Animal bones, flint tools and a pick made from antler lay on these surfaces, which suggests that they were laid down in the Later Neolithic period (I would guess around or just before 2500 BC). A line of watering holes

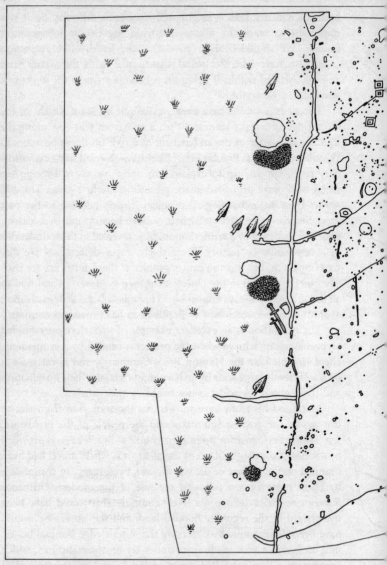

FIG 62   *Plan of Later Bronze Age (1200–800 BC) features at Bradley Fen, Whittlesey, Cambridgeshire (by courtesy of the Cambridge University Archaeological Unit).*

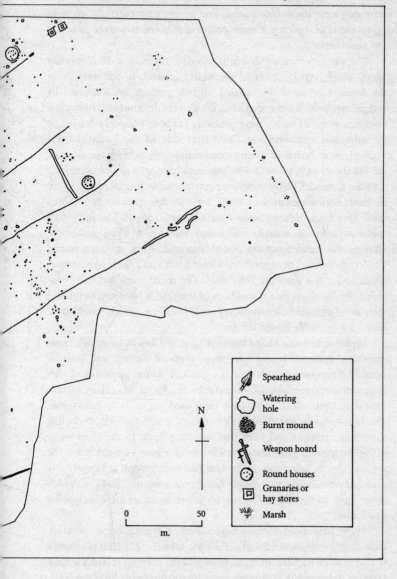

	Spearhead
	Watering hole
	Burnt mound
	Weapon hoard
	Round houses
	Granaries or hay stores
	Marsh

N

0   50

m.

were dug near the cobbled areas, and in one case cobbling led right up to the hole, making it seem probable that the two were in use at the same time.

The site was then divided into two clear zones by a ditch running north–south which separated the wetter ground, to the west, from the drier. A series of five angled ditches, perhaps accompanied by hedge-lines (which have been lost), divided the dry land into individual holdings, some of which were probably yards or paddocks belonging to individual roundhouses. The wetter side of the boundary was marked by a hoard of twenty-six bronze objects and six separate bronze spearheads, some of which seem to have been driven point-first into the ground. Clearly these were ceremonial or formal marking-out or demarcation gestures of some sort, as the spearheads – which must have been of some value – were never removed. The individual spearheads found outside the hoard were in pristine condition, whereas the items from the hoard were old, worn or fragmentary. Objects from the hoard included sword blades and hilts, more spearheads and a few scabbard fragments. The metal-work has been provisionally dated by Stuart Needham of the British Museum to around 1200 BC – precisely contemporary with Flag Fen, which would have been clearly visible across the fen.

Evidence was also found for three so-called 'burnt mounds'. These enigmatic features, found over large areas of Britain and Ireland, consist of mounds of burnt and fire-cracked stones, often mixed with large amounts of charcoal. Sometimes the burnt material covers a steep-sided pit, which could have been used originally to hold water. The burnt mounds at Bradley Fen covered a series of pits, including steep-sided troughs and wells that were dug down to the clean water of the permanent groundwater table, about a man's height below the surface. On the other side of the Flag Fen embayment, at Fengate, my own excavations have revealed two burnt mounds, both of which occur close to the edge of the wetter ground; one of these included a lined tank.[22]

There have been various suggestions to explain burnt mounds, including the splendid idea of prehistoric saunas.[23] My own preference is also that of Richard Bradley, who believes they represent the final remains of boundary ceremonies which most probably involved feasting.[24] Stones heated in a fire and then dropped into water soon bring it to the boil, which accounts for the numerous so-called 'pot-boilers' found in these mounds.[25] Experiments have shown that the most effective pot-boilers are rounded, cobble-size stones, which often split in half when dropped into cold water. Meat bones are often found nearby. Presumably the pits were used to hold water, and also played a role in the rituals.

This discussion of wet landscapes brings us to the question of prehistoric boats, which are found with surprising frequency in the British Isles. It used to be thought that all boats, paddles and bits of boats discovered by archaeologists were abandoned or wrecked, but we are becoming aware that it wasn't necessarily so straightforward. Mariners risk their lives in boats and ships, and all over the world they are treated with special respect, not just as cherished artefacts, but as symbols of a far greater power that can transport our bodies or souls from this world to the life everlasting.

Boats are frequently found to be closely associated with ritually important causeways and post alignments. At Fiskerton, excavations during the summer of 2001 revealed two dugout boats, one of which the excavator, Jim Rylatt, is convinced had been pegged permanently in place as part of the structure (as is Maisie, who's working on the technology of the boat). What makes this boat remarkable is its underside. It's covered with delicate, fluted axe-marks, whose edges are sharp and well defined. To my eye this looks like a boat that had never been grounded or pulled out of the water – at least not roughly or across an abrasive surface, such as a gravel bank. It had been used, but only very lightly. It's hard to avoid the conclusion that it was made to be 'offered' to the structure.

The vast majority of prehistoric boats in the museums of Britain and northern Europe are simple dugout craft, nearly always fashioned from the trunks of massive oak trees. When I call them 'simple' I mean simple in constructional principles, because it takes a great deal of skill to fashion a stable, watertight dugout boat. The standard account of British dugouts is by the archaeologist and master mariner Dr Sean McGrail.[26] He doesn't like the word 'dugout', and I agree, because it sounds rather horticultural and crude; he prefers 'logboat'.

Perhaps unwisely, Sean has also tried to make us go one step further and talk about *monoxylous* boats (a woody equivalent of 'megalithic', derived from the Greek words for 'one tree'). But archaeologists, not normally averse to new jargon, would have none of it. 'Logboats', however, are fine – and the term has stuck.

Sean lists 172 logboats from England and Wales, and although some may be post-Roman, most are probably prehistoric. Since his report appeared in 1978 there have been numerous additional finds; although I'm not a specialist in this field, I've been present at the excavation of at least four. So they are by no means a rare phenomenon. This is partly no doubt an accident of preservation: logboats can become waterlogged, and when they sink into stagnant mud or peat they can last for thousands of years if left undisturbed. But sometimes there is something distinctly 'fishy' about the circumstances surrounding their final resting places.

We've seen how one of the boats from Fiskerton came to an untimely end. Another discovery a couple of years previously in a quarry near Shardlow, in Derbyshire, was very peculiar. Within this boat, seemingly occupying every cubic inch of available space, were some large rocks that had been taken from a known source nearby. Was this an accidental sinking of an overladen boat? I think not. The 'cargo', if that's what it was, was positively stuffed into that craft, in such a way as surely to render it unstable. Would it not make far more sense to transport something as heavy and unwieldy as quarry products on a raft, perhaps even a raft made from two logboats strapped together with outriggers? It seems to me that the Shardlow boat had been deliberately weighted down and sunk.

Logboats are fine as far as they go, which is essentially along lakes and inland waterways. But it must also have been logboats, or very frail coracle-like craft, which around 6–5000 BC kept Britain in some sort of touch with the gradually separating mainland of Europe, and which made the risky crossing to Ireland. It was the mariners, rather than the boats, that were remarkable – logboats don't exactly set the pulse racing: they are more pram than performance car. Did *real* boats that could have been capable of going to sea exist in the Bronze Age?

Britain is alone in northern and Atlantic Europe in having produced several examples of Earlier Bronze Age plank-built boats.[27] It's tempting to suggest that this reflects the fact that Britain was emerging as the most substantial maritime region in the area, but it wouldn't be correct. I believe the survival of these plank-built boats may reflect the fact that they were 'interred' for posterity. Several finds have been made in the marshes around the Humber estuary and elsewhere,[28] but I will concentrate here on what is undoubtedly the most important find of a prehistoric boat anywhere in northern Europe.

It was found in September 1992 during archaeological work associated with the construction of the A20 around Dover.[29] That work had already produced some spectacular results, including new stretches of the town's medieval defences and Roman harbour timbers, but the Dover boat, as it has come to be known, eclipsed them all. I will never forget my first sight of it, shortly after its removal from its resting place some six metres below the modern ground surface. I had seen the remains of Viking ships in Denmark, and at first glance what lay before me looked for all the world like one of them, but if anything its frame appeared more substantial.* It also lacked the characteristic clinker-built plank construction which is only possible with nails – by then we knew that the Dover boat was Bronze Age in date,[30] a time when metal nails simply didn't exist. So how did those ancient shipwrights join timbers without metal fixings of any sort? How did they give their vessel the strength and flexibility to cope with conditions at sea? It was an extraordinary achievement.

A part of the boat, probably from the stern, is still buried in the ground, but it is estimated that over half was removed. The piece we have is almost 9.5 metres long, and 2.3 metres wide at its broadest point. It is made from shaped planks split from a large oak tree. Four planks survive: two along the bottom, and two so-called 'ile' planks which are curved to form the union between the bottom and the sides. These planks were stitched together using twisted, flexible branches of yew passed through holes that were rendered watertight with a probable mixture of wax and resin. We know there was at least one extra plank on the sides, above the ile planks, because the holes for the stitching and some of the yew stitches, which had been severed, remain.

* The Dover boat is a huge find, not just in importance, but in size. I strongly recommend a visit to view it in Dover Museum, where it is beautifully displayed (details on p.444).

The joins between the planks were caulked with moss held in place by thin laths of wood. In the absence of any metal fittings, the two bottom planks were held together by a clever arrangement of angled wedges that passed through loops or cleats carved in the bottom planks. A large board, known as a transom board, would have filled the V-shaped space in the bow, but like the upper side boards, it had been deliberately removed. There's no evidence for a mast or sail, but that doesn't mean there wasn't one. It's not necessary for a boat to have a mast like an ocean-going racing yacht to provide perfectly adequate propulsion.

The question is, was she capable of sailing at sea? The answer is an unqualified yes. Various experts in marine architecture and boat performance have examined her construction closely, and all are agreed that she would probably have foundered in a heavy sea, but could have taken moderate winds if she'd been built with just one side plank; with two she would have performed very much better – but unlike the Viking ships of later times, she would never have survived a gale.

Given a brave skipper with a good eye for the weather, she could well have crossed the Channel, which was the same width in the Bronze Age as today. But most authorities prefer to see her as a vessel that plied the coastal trade, moving from one small haven to another, never so far from the shore that she couldn't duck into shelter should the need arise. There's plenty of evidence for such trade. One example comes from Flag Fen, where a group of four new quernstones was placed beneath the lowest timbers. One of these was made from a particularly distinctive stone which probably came from a quarry near Folkestone, in Kent. Nobody in their right mind would consider transporting such a heavy object overland, with the Thames estuary, among other obstacles, to contend with. It makes far more sense to see such things moving along the coast in vessels like the Dover boat, then heading up the network of rivers and creeks that criss-crossed the fens.

There is, however, abundant evidence for cross-Channel 'trade' and contact in the Middle Bronze Age.[31] The clearest possible clue was provided by the discovery in 1974 by amateur divers of 352 bronze implements, made to distinctive French patterns, on the seabed of

Langdon Bay, just off Dover.[32] These included 178 swords and thrusting weapons, such as dirks and rapiers, plus a range of other items, including 110 axes of various types. Most of the bronzes have a strange, rounded look to them, caused by their years on the bottom. I found this curiously moving when I first saw them – it was as if they hadn't been allowed to rest in peace, and were trying to return home. Most of the finds were made within an area measuring fifty by fifty metres, and I think there can be no doubt that this was the site of a prehistoric wreck. Although no remains of a boat were found, that is hardly surprising given the turbulent conditions in the area.

The Dover boat was found not on the beach, but a short distance upstream, on the side of the river Dour, which drains into the sea at Dover. There's something distinctly unusual about this. For a start, the boat was found close by an apparent settlement, with animal bone and other signs of eating and life. It has been suggested that the upper side planks and the end or transom board were removed to be re-used in other boats. But this dismantling was carried out oddly: more damage has been done, especially to the bottom planks, than was necessary. And the transom board would require being cut up before removal, thereby destroying the point of the exercise. We know that the work was done on the spot, because the mud around the boat yielded pieces of chopped yew ties and moss caulking. We also know that seasoned oak is almost too hard to work with bronze axes. So why remove items that will have to be reshaped – unless, of course all Bronze Age boats were built to an identical pattern, which is an absurd idea. No: when all practical explanations have been exhausted, we must invoke ritual once again.

I would suggest that the Dover boat was ritually 'killed' when there was still some life left in her. Some of the settlement debris around her may well be the remains of food and feasting. The removal of the most complex single piece of carpentry, the very carefully fashioned transom board, was surely symbolic. One reason I say this is that an Iron Age logboat from Hasholme in East Yorkshire had an intact transom board with an intricate carving – perhaps representing the boat's name, or that of its owner.[33] It would be something one would want to remove, and to cherish.

The transom board was the product of a master craftsman, and

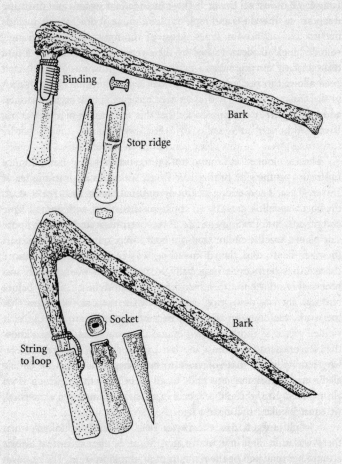

FIG 63   *Two axes from the seabed wreck site at Langdon Bay, Dover. These objects were made in northern France, between about 1300 and 1150 BC. The illustration shows the most important types of Later Bronze Age axe and how they were hafted. The palstave (above) was a solid axe whose haft was bound on and abutted a sharp stop-ridge, which prevented the wood from splitting. The haft of the socketed axe (below) was wedged into an internal socket. A short binding of twine passed through an external loop, and seems mainly to have been intended to prevent the axe from being lost when the hafting failed.*

without it the vessel could never hope to float again. Of course we don't know whether the other plank-built boats found in Britain were deliberately sacrificed in this way, but it would not surprise me if they were. A single plank from a boat was found at a Late Bronze Age post alignment in the grounds of Caldicote Castle in south Wales.[34] That site has also revealed evidence for ritual deposition (dog bones, metalwork etc.) that can be closely paralleled at Flag Fen. Is it mere coincidence that part of a plank-built boat was found there? Possibly, but I wonder.

So far we've looked at large, post-built causeways, but these are not the only examples of Bronze and Iron Age roads or tracks to have survived. Smaller wooden tracks, sometimes made with brushwood or woven hurdles, are known from most of the boggy areas of the British Isles, and the Somerset Levels are positively covered with them. The Sweet Track was the first of many to be found.[35] More recently the equivalent marshy areas on the north side of the Bristol Channel, the Welsh Severn Levels, have also revealed many new tracks.[36] A most remarkable stone and timber roadway forded a channel of the Thames at Yarnton in Oxfordshire.[37] There are many others. What do these trackways that have fortuitously survived, because of their deeply buried or wet circumstances, tell us about the transport 'infrastructure' of Bronze Age Britain?

First, they tell us that the surviving fragments represent a tiny fraction of the original network; second, they show that people needed to move about the countryside; and third, they imply quite strongly that the population was large enough to require something as formal as a system of roads. Since I've raised the subject, I would guess that the population of Britain and Ireland towards the end of the Bronze Age, say around 1000 BC, was about half a million – slightly less than double that of the Early Bronze Age (in over half a millennium).

Aerial photographs, on-the-ground survey and excavation have revealed field systems and entire Bronze Age landscapes. These are, I believe, the most important developments in the archaeology of the period over the past thirty years. In amongst the fields and settlements, tying them together and linking them with other districts, are numerous droves, roads and trackways. When excavated, these trackways sometimes reveal isolated roadside burials, or small pits filled with offerings. Often these routes line up on barrows, the burial places of previous generations, still venerated as the spiritual homes of the ancestors. The river crossing at Yarnton, for example, had offerings of Middle Bronze Age metal-work concealed below its stone surfacing. These finds show that despite the passage of many centuries, ritual and ideology still pervaded every aspect of prehistoric life. The traveller would have been well aware that the country through which he passed had a history that was as old as time itself. So he would respect the road, just as he would acknowledge the people of the region who built and maintained it.

I imagine that most of the traffic that passed along these roads was on foot, although riding was becoming more common by the Late Bronze Age, to judge from the number of horse harness-fittings that begin to be found at the start of the first millennium BC.[38] Many of the feet would have been cloven hooves, because large numbers of sheep and cattle were routinely driven from one community to another. We know from continental finds that wheels would have been available from Later Neolithic times,[39] but the earliest yet found in Britain was one from Flag Fen, which dates to about 1300 BC, in the Later Bronze Age. It was found deep within the horizontal timbers that made up the causeway within the line of posts. A few paces away we found half an axle that had been reshaped to form a crude peg to hold a plank in place. The axle, to our surprise, probably fitted another wheel. Maybe these were coincidental finds – just pieces of wood that were the right shape, and which happened to be lying around. But on the whole I think this unlikely.

We tend to imagine that early vehicles were crude, cart-like affairs; but the sophistication of their wheels' manufacture argues against this. Different woods are used, each with their own properties. The body of the Flag Fen wheel, for example, is in alder, which doesn't split easily and resists rot; the main dovetail braces that hold the three parts of the body together are in oak, which is both strong and flexible; and the locating pegs or dowels are in ash – a wood often used for similar purposes today. Evidence that most vehicles were light is provided by wheel ruts. At Welland Bank Quarry, a few miles north of Flag Fen, I found traces of Bronze or early Iron Age ruts from a

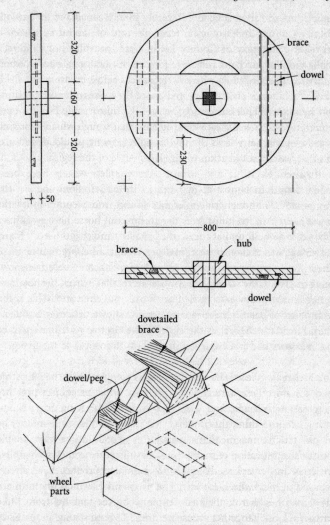

FIG 64   *An idealised reconstruction of the Flag Fen Bronze Age tripartite wheel (about 1300 BC). Three woods were used in its construction: alder for the three planks that formed the body of the wheel; oak for the two dovetail braces; and ash for the two dowels/pegs.*

vehicle just 1.10 metres wide.[40] Recently John Newman of the Suffolk County Council archaeological team has told me about ruts from a prehistoric trackway at County Farm, near the village of Chilton.[41] While the Welland Bank ruts were formed during a single event, when someone unwisely took a narrow-wheeled vehicle across a wet field, those at Chilton represent repeated use of the same trackway, presumably by many vehicles. Even so, the ruts at Chilton were also just over a metre wide. Such widths would suggest that we're probably looking at vehicles that were used to move people, rather than goods in bulk. In other words, a light trap or carriage.

Isolated Neolithic and Bronze Age wooden wheels have been widely found in bogs and marshes in Britain, Ireland and on the continent.[42] They are also sometimes found near wooden footpaths in wet areas.[43] In most instances the ground was far too boggy to have allowed a vehicle to pass, and the wheels must have been carried individually to their places of final deposition. I believe that in these cases wheels are being used to express more than merely transport. Being offered to the waters, the symbolism recalls Charon, the boatman in Greek mythology who ferried souls over the river Styx. This is the symbolism of death's great journey, and it shows that over a millennium after Stonehenge, at the close of the Bronze Age, the realm of the ancestors had not loosened its grip on the world of the living.

The archaeology of fields and farming is a topic which has kept me busy for thirty years. I can't say precisely why the subject fires my imagination, but when we lamb our flock in March there are times, sitting late into the night by a ewe that's either a first-time mother or an old girl having problems, when I'm acutely aware that people four or five thousand years ago must have experienced closely similar anxieties and emotions. Animals are animals, and they have always behaved in much the same way. The problems I face on my farm are the same ones that confronted people when they moved from Mike Jarman's 'loose herding' to 'close herding'. That happened in the Early Bronze Age, when the first field systems began to appear. By about 1500 BC the process was really gaining momentum.

If it's hard to free one's imagination from the icy analytical grasp of modern thought when considering topics as seemingly down-to-earth and practical as mining and transport, it's equally hard to come to terms with the way prehistoric farmers viewed their landscape. There's a tendency – I confess I've been guilty of it myself – to regard the layout of their farms and fields, undoubtedly their greatest archaeological legacy to us, as a problem- or puzzle-solving exercise. So, one asks, why did they lay out their fields in that particular way? Using my practical farming experience, I can come up with fairly convincing explanations, at least where smaller, day-to-day elements of the livestock farmer's operation are concerned. But such simple, essentially practical explanations of cause and effect are not wholly convincing when it comes to the layout and orientation of entire field systems or landscapes. In these instances it's often possible to distinguish a number of elements that might have influenced the way people structured the arrangement of the farming landscape. Some of these were entirely non-practical, and had to do with the location of barrows, major natural features, solar alignments and other factors, long since lost to us, such as the presence of sacred trees, groves, ponds and so forth.[44]

The field systems surrounding Flag Fen are laid out at right angles to the wet areas of the basin, in such a way that each holding of land gets more or less equal portions of very wet ground, wet ground, lightly flooded and flood-free land.[45] This is an essentially pragmatic pattern of landscape partition that has often been observed in, for example, medieval parishes fringing fens or marshes. But there are also non-practical aspects to such an arrangement. What, for instance, determines the size of individual holdings, or the precise orientation of the fields, which only have to be *roughly* at right angles to the flooded land to give each holding a share of land that is wet and dry?

At Flag Fen the fields were formed by ditches and banks on which were planted thorn hedges. It was a simple and practical way of dividing up and draining the land, and it's a system that was widely in use until the recent introduction of barbed wire. The fields were entered at the corners, like livestock markets in medieval times. This allowed two sides of the field to act as a funnel, which made it very much easier to drive animals out of one field and into the next. Even with a dog it's not always a straightforward business to take a large flock or herd through a gate positioned in the side of a field, because the animals tend to bunch and wander.

On the dryland of the Flag Fen basin, sets or holdings of fields were kept separate by double-ditched droveways which ran at right angles to the fen and were spaced at intervals of about two hundred metres. We now have good evidence to suggest that this spacing wasn't only determined by some pragmatic consideration to do with flock or herd sizes in the Bronze Age, but by the position and spacing of earlier barrows and henges. In other words, it was the structure of previous landscapes which helped to determine the shape of the earliest field systems. The same phenomenon is seen in many landscapes both locally and farther afield – in upland and lowland Britain.[46]

The question we have to ask is, were these barrows and other monuments used in the laying-out of the new field systems simply because they were convenient landmarks, or because they were still revered in some way? I think there can be little doubt that they were still recognised as monuments to the ancestors. I say that because some of them were remarkably small and insubstantial. One henge at Fengate, which lay on the alignment of a partitioning droveway running towards the wet ground at Flag Fen, was no more than a small circular ditch and a low bank. By the Bronze Age it would have amounted to a few inconsequential humps and bumps. Yet its presence was scrupulously respected by the alignment of the later droveway. The henge simply *has* to have been thought of as a special place.

Until very recently, what one might term the ritual or symbolic component within the emerging field systems and landscapes of the Later Bronze Age consisted of monuments, such as henges and barrows, from previous generations. Sites like Flag Fen were indeed within the landscape, but they probably followed pre-existing routes, and can be considered in some way an elaboration of something that was already there: people had a need to cross certain wet areas, and had doubtless been doing so for many generations before the first posts were sunk in the ground. Evidence for altogether new religious sites was lacking – until Chris Evans and his team from Cambridge University began their work at Barleycroft Farm, in the valley of the river Great Ouse in Cambridgeshire.

I've known Chris since the mid-1970s, when he joined our team digging at Fengate, in the Flag Fen basin. He now leads one of the best archaeological units in Britain, who have made a speciality of excavating large gravel quarries, using a series of highly original techniques. They have produced some spectacular results, but none in my mind can match what they have discovered at Barleycroft, which forms part of a massive gravel extraction project on a bend of the Great Ouse at Needingworth Quarries.[47] In the Neolithic and Early Bronze Age periods this was perhaps a ritual landscape, with many barrows and a 'founder monument' in the form of the Haddenham causewayed enclosure, which was far more grand than Etton, and possessed an imposing palisaded façade. At Etton and Maxey the glory days of the great ritual landscape were not followed up by the development of field systems or large settlements. On the contrary, when Later Bronze Age communities grew in size they developed the landscape downstream, closer to the edges of the fen, as if deliberately staying clear of the old religious areas.[48] At Barleycroft something very different happened.

Two groups of barrows were erected to the east and west of the river. That to the west was grouped around a natural knoll, known as Butcher's Rise. Sometime after 1500 BC, a series of ditched fields, similar in certain respects to those at Flag Fen, were laid out at right angles to the river (to the west) and radiating around Butcher's Rise (to the east). The field ditches were still in use, but had ceased to be regularly maintained, when a most extraordinary series of post rows was constructed. Large, telegraph-pole-sized posts were set in the ground in two phases. In the first phase, the lines tended to run east–west, as if framing the barrows on top of Butcher's Rise. In the second phase they ran north–south, and could only have been intended to screen Butcher's Rise from the group of barrows on the other side of the river. We saw something similar at Barrow Hills, Radley.

What makes these post rows so extraordinary is the scale of the construction, and the fact that many of them have carefully fashioned T-shaped terminals, as if to emphasise the fact that the row had stopped. So the gaps must have been as important as the timber screens themselves. Chris Evans is in no doubt that these extraordinary constructions served no practical purpose, and having seen the site myself, I can only agree. They make no sense whatsoever in farming

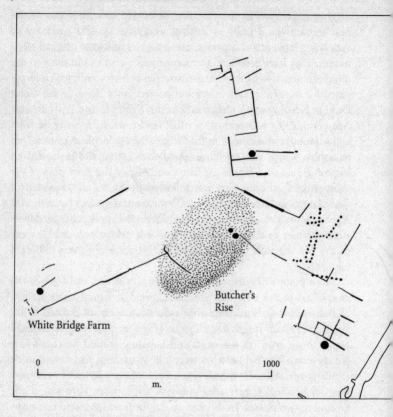

FIG 65   *The Barleycroft Farm Bronze Age landscape (1500–1200 BC). Barrows and other religious sites are shown as black dots. Field boundary ditches are shown by continuous lines. Post rows are shown by dotted lines.*

terms – a view that is confirmed by the very few finds, apart from loose human bones, from the post-holes. Unlike barrows, which can be erected by a group of perhaps a couple of dozen people, these rows look like major engineering events: Chris has estimated that the 950 timbers used in them would have involved the clearance of up to four hectares (ten acres) of woodland – not a task lightly undertaken. And then, of course, there was the transport of the timber. It seems

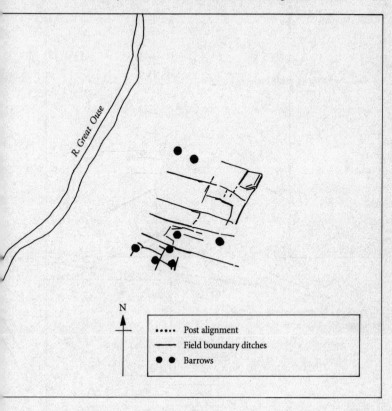

R. Great Ouse

N

····· Post alignment
——— Field boundary ditches
● ● Barrows

inconceivable that the rows could have been constructed by a small group; instead we must suppose a series of major communal gatherings. It's salutary to reflect that all of this happened within the context of a 'working' or farmed landscape – proving beyond much doubt that the hard-and-fast distinction we maintain today between the sacred and the profane did not apply in prehistory. These vast screens also provide proof positive that views and sightlines were an important element in the way that people conducted themselves through such landscapes. It's hard to avoid using the word 'theatrical' when one tries to imagine how these places were experienced.

Pollen analysis and other palaeo-environmental techniques can

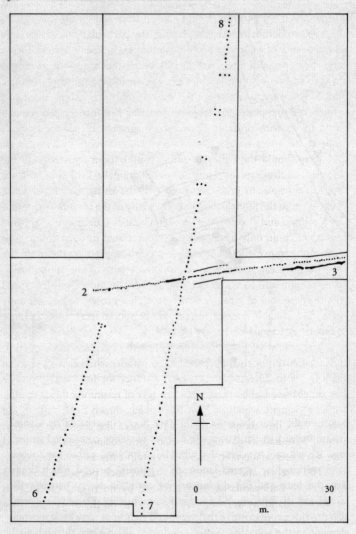

FIG 66   *A close-up of the main excavated area of post rows at Barleycroft Farm (about 1200 BC). Rows 2 and 3 belong to the first phase of construction; here the posts are closer-set and are sometimes bedded within a continuous*

throw much light on the extent to which trees and forests dominated, or failed to dominate, the landscape at any particular time. Invariably the clearance of woodland by human groups is linked by archaeologists and their specialist advisers – usually in a rather simplistic fashion – to the creation of open land for grazing, or for the growing of crops. But as we've seen throughout this book, prehistoric people spent vast efforts creating places like Avebury and Flag Fen for reasons that had little to do with ordinary domestic or agrarian life as we know it today.

Why should the felling of forests simply be associated with the creation of clearings for farms or hunted animals? Why should it not be, for example, to get a better view of the rising sun, or of those huge posts in the Stonehenge car park? Many of the monuments found in Neolithic and Bronze Age ritual landscapes (cursuses are a prime example) could only have been fully appreciated in open country, so why not remove the woods the better to appreciate them? If the moving of great stones was an important part of the monuments' construction and use, why not also include the moving, and perhaps the burning too, of great forest trees? Such a process would certainly provide a suitable context for the use of special axes, such as those quarried at Langdale.

I wonder what proportion of the British landscape was cleared of its forest cover for such purposes. I also wonder whether it's a sensible idea to try to differentiate between clearance for food and clearance for other reasons, because there's a danger of rerunning the domestic/ritual argument, which Richard Bradley has shown to be wide of the mark. Let's just accept that forest clearance, like any other activity, would have had its place within prehistoric cosmologies, and would not have been undertaken merely to obtain extra land for farming.

The ditched and hedged fields or livestock paddocks found at places like Barleycroft and Flag Fen are by no means confined to eastern England, as we'll see very shortly. But on the other hand they

trench. Rows 6–8 belong to the second phase. The posts are larger and more regularly spaced, and the rows end with clearly defined T-shaped terminals. The gap between rows 7 and 8 is subdivided by two structures of two and four posts

don't seem to occur on the continental mainland. This distinction is primarily a result of different patterns of social organisation and farming practice on each side of the Channel. The development of these distinctive livestock landscapes in the Bronze Age would have been made easier by a moist insular climate which, then as now, was particularly favourable to the growing of grass.

I've mentioned that recent changes in planning law have led to an explosion in the number of archaeological projects being carried out before a development can start. Sadly, many of these take place blindfolded, in a contextual vacuum; and budgetary constraints mean it can be impossible to draw results together into a coherent story. Sometimes, however, somebody has the vision and patience to sift through the mass of 'grey literature', as these developers' reports are now known. Among them is one of Richard Bradley's graduate students, David Yates.

Dave has been working his way methodically through the thousands of 'grey' reports that have been produced in his study area, a box of thirty by seventy kilometres extending from the mid-Thames to north Kent. The clues he is looking for are long, straight ditches, or fragments of them, that seem to be 'ignored' by the mass of Iron Age and Roman archaeological features that occur all along the Thames valley. In reports they are often dismissed in a couple of sentences to the effect that they are undated linear ditches, of possible Bronze Age date. But when Dave fitted the jigsaw puzzle together, coherent patterns began to emerge.[49]

What Dave's work reveals is that large areas of the middle and lower Thames valley were parcelled up into field systems interspersed with settlements, droves and tracks. It was, in other words, a fully organised and developed landscape. He also found that the areas where fields occurred coincided with major enclosures, which could be seen as places where regular communal gatherings took place. Earlier, I noted how the river Thames had produced large numbers of stone axes which had been placed in its waters as votive offerings; but they were nothing compared with the vast numbers of Bronze and Iron Age weapons and implements deposited there. The metal-work finds from the river tended to turn up in quite specific places. Alongside them were areas which were largely free of such finds. Dave noted

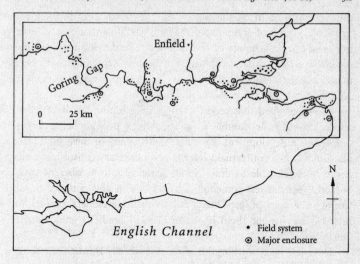

FIG 67   *Recent research by David Yates of Reading University has shown that large areas of the Thames valley and north Kent have revealed sites (shown here by dots) where there is clear evidence for ditched Bronze Age fields. These sites tend to occur in clusters which are separated by tracts of open pasture.*

that these areas without much metal-work tended to coincide with tracts of open or unenclosed landscape between the field systems. Of course, it could be argued that these 'open' landscapes were only apparently open, but the intensity of recent archaeological activity is such that in many cases, such as at Yarnton, we can show that the Bronze Age landscape was largely cleared of trees, but fields were never actually constructed. It's tempting to see these places as having been open, unfenced grazing, similar perhaps to the hilltop moors of the uplands.

One site close to the centre of Dave's research area has produced a wealth of information. It was excavated on a large scale, and the team from the Oxford Archaeological Unit were able to place it firmly within its setting. It's a very important piece of work indeed. The site in question has the somewhat unlovely name of Reading Business Park, and it is now a landscaped hi-tech office complex

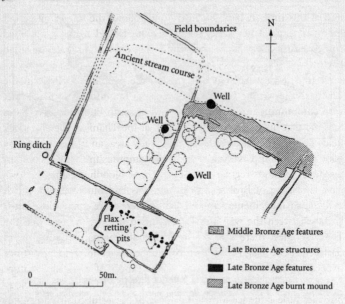

FIG 68   *Ditches of a Middle Bronze Age field system (pre-1000 BC) lying below roundhouses and other features of a Late Bronze Age settlement at Reading Business Park, Berkshire.*

south of Reading and immediately north of the M4.[50] Millions of people must pass it every day, but I wonder how many of them are aware that they are driving across one of the earliest field systems in Europe.

The site is essentially two-phased. The first is Middle Bronze Age (i.e. pre-1000 BC), and consists of ditched fields with corner entranceways. There is evidence from air photos for many droveways nearby. The Late Bronze Age settlement of post-built roundhouses respects the earlier features, and it seems reasonable to suggest that certain of the hedges that would have been planted along the field ditches were still maintained as stockproof barriers. The later settlement included flax-retting pits,* which are also commonly found in the southern

* Retting, or rotting, is the first stage in the production of linen fibres from flax.

fens at this time. A large burnt mound follows the line of an earlier boundary, and a key junction of two fields and a much-modified corner entranceway is marked by a ring-ditch – probably a small barrow.

I find it very hard to believe that the people who lived in the Thames valley in the Bronze Age were not in almost routine contact with communities around the fens and in south England. Dave Yates tells me that his current work shows that the Thames valley livestock fields do extend well outside his core study area, and I know of many good examples in East Anglia and Northamptonshire. The keeping of livestock demands regular infusions of new bloodlines, and the lowland landscape of Bronze Age Britain was laid out in a way which made such movements simpler. While there were many close similarities between the way life was organised in, say, the fens and the Thames valley, there was also a degree of regional variation, as at Barleycroft and Flag Fen. This mix of coherence and regional distinctiveness strikes me as what one might expect of a socially mature and generally prosperous society, at ease with itself. Also, archaeology provides little evidence for the existence of powerful controlling elites or for Big Men. There are no extra-large houses, or buildings set to one side within a special stockade, nor are there many fabulously rich burials (and we've seen how burials can be misinterpreted). I'm not suggesting that there was no class system at this time, but taken as a whole, Bronze Age society in Britain seems remarkably egalitarian and generally peaceful.

Chris Evans reckoned that although Barleycroft and Flag Fen shared field systems in common, the farming regime at Barleycroft was much less intense than at Flag Fen, with far fewer animals (mainly sheep) being kept. And there are those tracts of 'open' but cleared landscape, as at Yarnton and also over most of the hilly areas of southern Britain. But places like Flag Fen are by no means unique. Flag Fen produced evidence for stockyards in which large herds and flocks, of perhaps hundreds of animals, could have been handled in batches – just as on a modern farm or cattle market – and Dave Yates has found several close parallels for these in the Thames valley.[51] Is there evidence for such intensification outside these two areas? There is, and it came to light in the strangest manner imaginable.

The little Wiltshire village of Potterne is just three kilometres south of Devizes, in the gentle rolling countryside of the Vale of Pewsey, within sight of Salisbury Plain. On 23 June 1982 the sexton discovered a Late Bronze Age gold bracelet while digging a grave in the village cemetery. This was the first evidence of a Late Bronze Age site quite unlike anything that had ever been found in Britain before.

In essence, the site at Potterne consists of a truly vast mound or midden of what archaeologists have termed 'dark earth'. This mound covers 3.5 hectares (8.6 acres), and is up to two metres thick. 'Dark earth' is essentially material that was once rich in organic matter, such as manure. I have a huge muckheap on the edge of my yard. Today it's about ten feet high, but in fifty years' time it will be a band of 'dark earth' perhaps a few inches thick. Within this thin layer will be all those bits and pieces that won't rot down: baler twine, bits of polythene, and my favourite penknife.

But at Potterne they didn't find a few unheeded scraps of debris. Far from it. The limited excavations, of just 1 per cent of the mound, yielded a staggering quantity of pottery: about 100,000 sherds, weighing approximately a tonne. Pottery wasn't all that was found. Animal bones (around 135,000) were everywhere, and the dig also produced 187 metal objects, including a fragment of gold sheet. There was also evidence from within the many layers of the Deposit (as the make-up of the mound became known) for structures, most of which were probably to do with the shelter and management of cattle. The mound accumulated throughout the Late Bronze Age and just into the start of the Iron Age, from about 1200 to 600 BC. Other Potterne-like sites have since been unearthed in the area, but so far none has proved to be as vast as the original.

What was going on there? It would be mad simply to describe the Deposit as a muck heap or midden, because there was structure to it. Besides, the sheer quantity of finds shows that humans played a very important role in its formation. Andy Lawson, Director of Wessex Archaeology and author of the dig's report, sees the site as far more than just a long-lived cattle farm.[52] I'm convinced he's right, and that it has to have been a regional centre, where people and cattle in large numbers convened regularly for the sort of rural activities I've alluded to already: socialising, feasting, exchanging livestock for new bloodlines and so forth. The point is that regular meetings of this kind are essential if a pastoral way of life is to be maintained successfully.

So far this account of Bronze Age livestock farming may seem utilitarian, albeit not (as Potterne seems to demonstrate) exactly run-of-the-mill. But is this a true reflection of the actual farming scene three to four thousand years ago? I'm not sure it is. I believe there was another level of meaning which in effect removed certain aspects of the pastoral economy beyond the food chain, pure and simple. We tend nowadays to regard food as just a means of keeping the body together. Fifty years ago, however, I might have said that food kept body *and soul* fit and healthy. In other words, there was an added dimension to food and feeding which we seem to have lost sight of, in our quest for good-looking, but cheap and taste-free, supermarket fare.

Was it just feasting that went on at places like Potterne, or was it something altogether more important? I think the evidence now suggests that the consumption specifically of *meat* during feasts was particularly important in the Later Bronze Age. One of the first people to recognise this was Stuart Needham of the British Museum. The site of Stuart's excavations now lies below and beside the M25 at the point where it crosses the Thames at Runnymede Bridge, on the southern, or Surrey, side of the river, just upstream of London.[53] Stuart was convinced from the large numbers of animal bones he discovered that the conspicuous consumption of meat, probably beef in this particular case, was an important part of Later Bronze Age life along the Thames floodplain. This would fit with what David Yates is finding elsewhere in the Thames valley.

At Flag Fen, which is broadly contemporary with Runnymede Bridge, we had the good fortune to excavate a so-called flesh-hook. It's made from bronze, and is a very beautifully fashioned implement resembling a fisherman's gaff, except that it's not sufficiently hooked or pointed: a fish would soon struggle free. Another example was found at Feltwell Fen in Norfolk, and this one gives the clue as to how they were used, because it formed part of a hoard buried within a bronze cauldron.[54] Flesh-hooks were probably employed for the fishing out of pieces of meat from bubbling stews during feasts. They were special implements for particular occasions. To discover flesh-hooks at Flag Fen, and in a nearby hoard concealed in a fen, is surely not just coincidence, and it strongly suggests that the feasts were about far more than mere gluttony. Perhaps the participants were celebrating the achievements of their forebears, while at the same time demonstrating their generosity to their friends, relatives and neighbours – who would then feel obliged to reciprocate on some future occasion. The sheer scale of such feasting also suggests that these occasions were about more than just consumption.

If you glance at any road map of southern Britain, it's impossible not to notice that a huge swathe of central Wiltshire, north and west of Salisbury and Andover (just across the county line in Hampshire), is largely devoid of roads, towns and villages. This is the Salisbury Plain Training Area (SPTA), acquisition of which was begun by the army in the late nineteenth century as a suitable open landscape for the training of cavalry. The training needs of soldiers during two world wars had also to be met, and as a result the SPTA now covers an area the size of the Isle of Wight – an incredible thirty-seven thousand hectares (ninety-one thousand acres).

One might imagine that churning tank tracks, exploding bombs and live shells would have reduced the landscape to something resembling a Great War battlefield, but actually direct damage to archaeological sites has generally been superficial. Far more importantly, the presence of the army has kept the truly destructive forces of modern intensive farming at bay. It's a sobering thought that a regiment of tanks weighing fifty tons each, and training for a year, would do far less archaeological damage than a single farm tractor pulling a rig of power harrows or ploughs for just one day. As a result of the army's stewardship, the SPTA preserves the fragile surface traces of ancient chalkland fields and settlements, which elsewhere in southern Britain have been largely obliterated by agriculture.

A recent English Heritage survey has revealed the SPTA as an archaeological resource of international importance, not just for its state of preservation, but because it lies so close to places like Stonehenge and Avebury.[55] In effect, it's their ancient landscape, and in my opinion it should be accorded the status of a World Heritage Site without delay. Certainly something needs to be done, otherwise the post-Cold War 'peace dividend' could turn out to be an archaeological catastrophe. I can imagine how farmers and developers would nibble into it, a field at a time, and in ten or twenty years the region would be archaeologically depleted beyond recognition. We must act *now*, before the nibblers sharpen their teeth.

The English Heritage survey investigated a few sites of particular interest within the SPTA. One of them, at East Chisenbury, is a huge midden, not dissimilar to Potterne. The mound is about three metres high, roughly circular (diameter about two hundred metres), and covering an area of 2.5 hectares (six acres). It has been dated to the two centuries of the Bronze/Iron Age transition (800–600 BC). Small-scale excavations revealed a truly staggering quantity of sheep bones, including large numbers of very young lambs which were presumably removed from their mothers to allow all their milk to be used by humans. Large numbers of spindle whorls – bun-shaped pieces of clay with a central hole that gave 'spin' to a wooden spindle used to spin wool before the invention of the spinning wheel – were also found. The authors of the survey concluded that the evidence suggests that the scale of prehistoric sheep-farming in the East Chisenbury area would have rivalled even that of the post-medieval period. It's an astonishing thought, but one only made possible by the survival of the great midden, which would have been ploughed to oblivion had the army not stepped in over a century ago.

I can't finish this chapter without saying something about what is perhaps the most complete Bronze Age field system known in Britain – and possibly Europe. The fields are known as reaves, and they occur across large tracts of Dartmoor, over areas that are now largely open moorland. Today woolly-hatted ramblers tramp across heather-clad heath that was once productive grazing land. The Dartmoor reaves have been known about since the nineteenth century, when they were thought to have been constructed in medieval times. Their prominence in modern British prehistory is almost entirely due to one man, Andrew Fleming, who during the 1970s took parties of students from Sheffield University down to Dartmoor to dig and survey the system. He has published the story of the Dartmoor Reaves Project in a wonderfully anecdotal and readable book.[56]

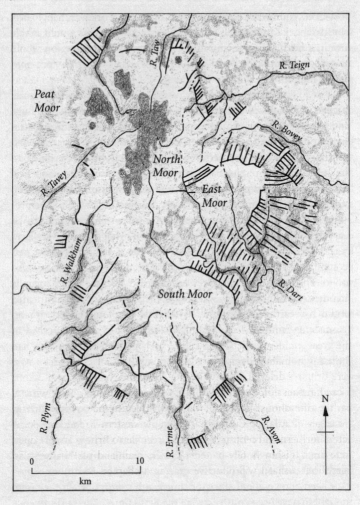

FIG 69   *Map of the Bronze Age (2000–1200 BC) fields or reaves on*
Dartmoor, Devon. The field boundaries are made from banks of stone or earth,
and were probably capped with a hedge. They were mainly used for livestock,
but were also sometimes ploughed, probably to grow cereals.

When Andrew was doing the reaves, I was working on my own reave-like fields near Flag Fen, and we kept in close touch. Both systems started life in the Early Bronze Age, in the centuries around 2000 BC, and both clearly take into account – or 'respect' in archaeological parlance – earlier monuments, which on Dartmoor include stone rows, henges and barrows. It's hard not to become proprietorial about an archaeological project, and 'my' field system lasted slightly longer than Andrew's, which seems to have gone out of use at about the time that Potterne got under way, around 1200 BC. Perhaps by then the fertility that was held for so long in the soil by the roots of long-since-felled forest trees was being washed away. And doubtless there were social factors too. But whatever the causes, the fields and settlements were abandoned to the growing moor.

At their height the reaves formed a coherent pattern that shows every sign of organisation and co-ordination. That is not to say that there was a single controlling authority, but I do believe that the people in question must have kept in close and regular contact. As we've seen, that shouldn't cause much surprise. The reaves were plainly intended for the use of livestock, but there is also evidence, in the form of low earth banks known as lynchets,[57] for ploughing or perhaps for spade agriculture.

If the large, mainly livestock-based field systems of the Bronze Age were Britain's delayed response to the call of the Neolithic revolutionaries, the other ubiquitous and entirely individual insular development was the roundhouse. It was a type of architecture that is found along the edges of Atlantic Europe and into the western Mediterranean,[58] but in northern and central Europe it is peculiar to Britain and Ireland; there are vanishingly few of them on the mainland of Europe. It is roundhouses that I will discuss in the next chapter.

CHAPTER ELEVEN

Men of Iron
(the Early Iron Age: 700–150 BC)

IT HAD BEEN the wettest year on record, with almost double the normal rainfall, accompanied by fierce gales. The man sitting next to me looked tired and drawn. Like me he was a part-time farmer, but unlike me he didn't have a concrete yard in which to escape from the ubiquitous mud. We were sitting by a log fire in his pride and joy, a magnificent Iron Age roundhouse. Behind us a curtain shielded the front doorway, because the large porch had been half ripped apart by a hurricane-force gale a couple of months ago. As ever, it was raining and blowy outside. I glanced up at the roof, expecting to see signs of seepage, but it was dry – absolutely bone dry. Peter followed my gaze, and the smile which was never far from his lips broke out. He whacked me across the back, almost winding me.

'You old bugger!' he guffawed. 'You were looking for drips. This isn't some tatty old fenman's house, this is the real thing, you know.' He went on to rubbish my own efforts at reconstruction in a thoroughly good-humoured fashion.

You couldn't help liking Peter. Maisie had worked for him twenty-five years ago and had been gored by a frisky Dexter heifer, but even so she still had a soft spot for him. Then, about eighteen months after I had sat by his fire, I heard he had died.[1] With the death of Peter Reynolds archaeology lost one of its biggest characters. True, his all-encompassing confidence could sometimes be infuriating, but more often than not, in the long run he was proved right.

Peter was Britain's greatest experimental archaeologist, and his work transformed the way we picture life in the past. He took a holistic approach to his research. In other words, he didn't just work with a single aspect of ancient life – metal-working or archery, for example.

Instead he tried to reassemble a more comprehensive picture. After all, he reasoned, it makes no sense to conduct experiments with prehistoric ploughs if you're pulling them with modern beasts, or to use ancient breeds if they've been fed on high-protein cattle cake or concentrated feed. The only way to do a proper job was to recreate the totality of prehistoric farming, and to record the results over many years in exhaustive detail. For Peter it was a lifetime's work.

He conducted experiments on all manner of things to do with prehistoric farming at his Iron Age farm at Little Butser, near Petersfield in Hampshire.[2] The site he chose had actually been farmed in Bronze and Iron Age times, and that feeling of continuity meant a great deal to him. I remember many years ago, leaning on a woven wattle fence as we looked down the chalk hill into the valley far below. 'Can't you just *see* them down there,' he suddenly exclaimed, 'fighting to plough that bloody slope. It must have been murder to haul your way back to the top at the end of the day.'

You could see in his face that he was back there, in 300 BC. In his mind's eye he was unhitching the plough, fighting off the horseflies and the cramps in his shoulders, arms and legs after a hot autumn day's work. Children from the houses on the top of the hill had climbed the fence and were running down towards him. Soon they'd surround him, grubby arms outstretched, begging for rides on the shoulders of the tired and now docile oxen.

Peter's identification with his Iron Age forebears gave him great respect for them. He hated it when people described their houses as 'huts' – huts were for buckets and hoes; houses were for people, and reflected their occupants' and builders' view of themselves, just as houses do today.

Before Peter burst onto the scene, archaeologists put ancient people into all sorts of strange structures, such as 'pit dwellings' – holes in the ground roofed over with hides and so forth. The trouble with ideas like this is that holes are generally cold, wet places, and people in the past weren't stupid. In very well-drained areas, such as the chalk downs, pit dwellings might work, but on the gravel terraces of lowland river valleys they would soon become pit puddles. Besides, anyone capable of erecting a roof over a large hole was probably able to build a more conventional structure.

Peter's great contribution was to demonstrate that roundhouses, which were then well known in the Iron Age, and were just being identified in the Bronze Age, were proper, substantial and weathertight buildings. It was a big imaginative leap from a ground-plan on a piece of paper to a building capable of housing a family and withstanding the storms and gales of the British Isles, but Peter discovered for himself the basic rules of building a roundhouse. Rule 1: don't leave an opening in the centre of the roof for the smoke (it will act like a blast furnace, and draw the fire up into the thatch). Rule 2: you don't need a supporting post at the centre of the roof (it's the strongest part of the structure).

Smoke stayed high in the roof space, and found its own way out through the thatch. It also helped if you burnt wood that had been cut at least a year before, and was bone dry. Larger houses needed a ring of roof-support posts, but the absence of a central post gave the inhabitants a large area of free space. I remember being amazed when I first walked into Peter's best-known house, his reconstruction of the building found on Pimperne Down, in Dorset.[3] It was vast. The smoke-stained thatch seemed to vanish upwards, rather like the dark, soaring spaces of Westminster Cathedral. The floor area was huge – easily large enough to accommodate two or three coachloads of tourists. Even the more modest, workaday buildings of the time could have comfortably held family gatherings of two or three dozen adults, plus their children, dogs, bags, baskets and other trappings of Iron Age life. As I said before, these were proper houses, not huts.

The Pimperne Down house caused a great stir when it was discovered in the early 1960s. It was just under fifteen metres in diameter, and was perhaps the largest of a small group of very large roundhouses.[4] Since the sixties there has been the great explosion of developer-funded archaeological work, and we now have a far better idea of what the average roundhouse would have looked like. As one might expect, there was a good deal of regional variation: houses tended to be smaller in the uplands; those built on gravel soils rarely exceed ten or eleven metres in diameter. Most of those I've excavated were between seven and nine metres across. Even so, when rebuilt these are still very substantial dwellings, and at Flag Fen our reconstructions comfortably accommodate parties of twenty to thirty people.

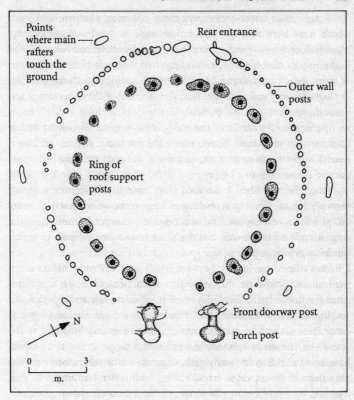

Points
where main —
rafters
touch the
ground

Rear entrance

Outer wall
posts

Ring of
roof support
posts

N

0   3
|_____|
m.

Front doorway post

Porch post

FIG 70   *Simplified ground-plan of the Pimperne Down Iron Age roundhouse,
used by Peter Reynolds for his reconstruction at Little Butser, Hampshire.*

It would be a mistake to think that the design of roundhouses
remained static from the Bronze to the Iron Age. Development wasn't
fast by modern standards, but it did happen, and it varied from place
to place. In my own area, around Flag Fen, Bronze Age houses were
somewhat smaller than their Iron Age equivalents. I have a theory
that they were roofed with turves, laid on top of a thick layer of reeds.
This was a very heavy roof, especially when wet, and needed to be
supported by a ring of stout roof-support posts. By Late Bronze and

Iron Age times cereal crops were more commonly grown, and straw could have been used for thatch, although in the fens I suspect that reed (which is vastly superior) would normally have been chosen. The lighter roofs of the Iron Age buildings had a steeper pitch and formed a more structurally sound cone, thereby dispensing with the need for a ring of posts, and meaning that the interior of these buildings was entirely open.

As has been noted, roundhouses are not generally found on the continent in prehistoric times, where the dominant form is rectangular. It might be thought that something as fundamentally important as the shape and size of people's living-space must reflect in some measure the way they lived their lives and/or the way their society was organised. Thus in recent times large rectangular longhouses are known to have been used to accommodate extended families, so at a very simple level the shape and size of house can be seen to reflect social organisation.

But there are problems with such assumptions. Subdivisions within the longhouse, for example, could become more significant than the house itself. Similarly, while small roundhouses such as occur in Britain *might* indicate that smaller family units were of prime importance, they are often grouped within a stoutly enclosed settlement – in which case it would seem that a larger unit was also considered essential to the way people organised themselves. The best way to work out how people actually lived within their houses is to look beyond the simple size and shape of the buildings. If we are to do this successfully we need an extra intellectual tool – the concept of *agency*.[5]

In archaeology and anthropology, 'agency' is a term that describes the fact that 'human beings think about the intentional actions they perform and the resources they need to achieve their ends'.[6] To give a modern example: life in the Western world today is dominated by a new force – the god of work. In the 1970s it was fashionable to decry the so-called 'Protestant work ethic', but the fact remains that it's still there, affecting almost every aspect of our lives. It also influences, both directly and indirectly, the places in which we live: directly in the sense that many people work at home, and have studies or offices in which to do so.

Its indirect effects are harder to spot, but are just as important. When I cook breakfast, for example, I don't even contemplate plucking a chicken or roasting a rib of beef, because within our society the pressures to start work bright and early dictate that the first meal of the day must be prepared quickly, and from a limited number of ingredients. That's why many modern homes have breakfast counters, where a light meal can be grabbed with a minimum of fuss. These are usually part of, or close to, the kitchen, and are quite distinct from the more formal dining area where food is eaten in the evening, when one is supposed to be able to relax. Without the concept of agency to help him, an archaeologist in the future might interpret this arrangement of eating spaces as evidence for a two-tier society, in which the lower, serving classes eat at the breakfast counter, while the ruling elite use the dining room. Because we know of the way modern people think about the actions they perform – i.e. we understand the role of human agency in this instance – we can see the error of such an interpretation.

I have described throughout this book how formal ritualised behaviour has shaped the religious shrines and monuments of prehistoric Britain. Can the same set of ideas and beliefs provide the context or structure we require to understand behavioural agency within the prehistoric domestic setting? In other words, can we use what we know about the ancient British 'mind-set' to throw light on the sort of things that might have motivated the people who lived in roundhouses? To do so we need to go back in time, to the origins of British roundhouses.

It may one day be possible to demonstrate that one of the origins of roundhouses was in the Mesolithic hunter/gatherer communities who built dwellings like those at Thatcham and Mount Sandel. The trouble is that we know of no *bona fide* roundhouses in the intervening period of more than three millennia. The earliest roundish-houses that I know of are Later Neolithic, and were found by George Eogan beneath the mound of his great passage-grave at Knowth.[7] Here we might have a clue to the actual origin of these buildings. Richard Bradley has suggested that the concept of roundness, which became so important to the life of people in the Bronze Age, may ultimately have derived from the shape of the mounds and the spiral designs that adorned the great stones of passage graves such as Knowth. So it was sometime in the centuries before 3000 BC that our insular concern – some might say obsession – with rings and circles seems to have begun.

One could argue long and hard about the date of the initial appearance of roundhouses in Britain, but they are known in increasing numbers after about 2000 BC, at the onset of the Early Bronze Age. They aren't exactly common in the Middle Bronze Age, but I've dug a few myself. It's in the Later Bronze Age and Iron Age that they really come into their own. I've excavated something in the region of eighty roundhouses, most of which dated to the final millennium BC. And I know of colleagues who have done even better than that.

The earliest British roundhouses do not conform to the almost standardised regional patterns that developed over most of Britain from the Later Bronze Age. A good example, dating to the Early Bronze Age, was found at Blackdyke Farm, Hockwold, on the edge of the fens in Norfolk.[8]

The Hockwold house showed up on the surface as a dark area of earth with many flints. The soil around there is sandy, and colours show up well on the surface, especially after ploughing. The topsoil was removed to reveal a circle of dark sand roughly twenty-two feet (seven metres) in diameter and some eight inches (two hundred millimetres) thick at the centre. The post-holes contained the sharpened points of quite narrow (one-to-two-inch diameter) stakes, which were thought to be of birch, to judge from the bark. In my experience ancient birch often looks rather different, and I would suggest the stakes were made from alder wood, which looks like birch when waterlogged for a long time, but resists rot much better. It would have been growing plentifully in the fens nearby.

One very interesting feature was a gently sloping shallow gully which had been filled with brushwood and ran beneath the floor from the centre of the house to an unknown point outside. Presumably it was dug as a drain to keep the house dry when the groundwater table rose too high.[9] The excavator did not believe that the house had been occupied more than once; it was very lightly constructed, and could not have stayed up for more than two or three years at best. If the stakes really were of birch, I'd give it a year at the outside. But even

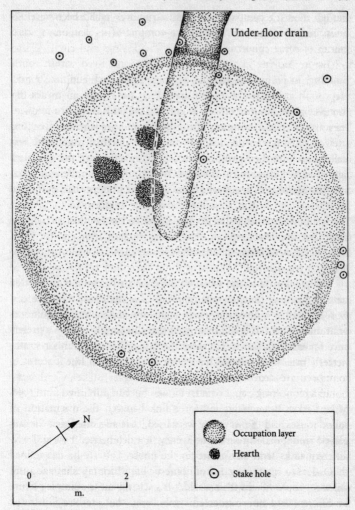

Under-floor drain

	Occupation layer
	Hearth
	Stake hole

N

0   2
m.

FIG 71   *A Later Neolithic stake-built roundhouse at Hockwold, on the south-eastern edge of the fens in Norfolk (after about 2000 BC). The darker earth of the floor contained quantities of charcoal from the three hearths, together with flint and many small, trampled sherds of pottery.*

though it was a comparatively light structure, it had been carefully built, and the drain shows that the comfort of its occupants was a matter of some concern.

Before looking at the way in which people lived within round buildings in prehistoric Britain, we must stand back and take a sideways look at the problem. We have seen how circular shrines like Stonehenge and Seahenge were aligned on the midsummer or midwinter solstices. The Avenue and the entrance into Stonehenge face along such an alignment, and clearly it played an essential role in the way the Stones were used and understood. We've also seen how the much later Iron Age causeway at Fiskerton was rebuilt to coincide with lunar eclipses. So solstices and the movements of the heavenly bodies formed an integral part of the Bronze and Iron Age 'mind-set'.

It follows from this that it's reasonable to assume that such beliefs played an important role in determining human agency at the time. So what happens when we examine the way in which Iron Age roundhouses were oriented? Almost without exception they were entered via a single doorway, and when all the excavated examples are plotted out, we discover that the vast majority have doorways that face east or south-east – a direction which aligns on sunrise at the equinoxes or at midwinter.[10] It could be argued that this simply reflects a preference for warmth, but if that were the case a due southerly or south-westerly orientation would have been chosen; but in fact it seems to have been avoided.

In a pioneering paper written in 1990 but not published until 1996, Mike Parker Pearson argued for a link between the orientation of roundhouses and the way they were used.[11] He suggested that the sun played an important role in the agency that determined how and why different tasks were performed in the house. Latterly he has refined these ideas to create a picture of domestic life which takes into account the way people viewed their world.[12] It's actually quite a simple picture of different and interconnected symbolisms, that are best illustrated by a diagram. The unifying element is the daily movement of the sun, which first shines through the doorway, then moves around the house clockwise. This comes to symbolise time at various levels: daily time, seasonal time, lifetime and seniority. These symbolic time-frames are mirrored by the way the house space was organised.

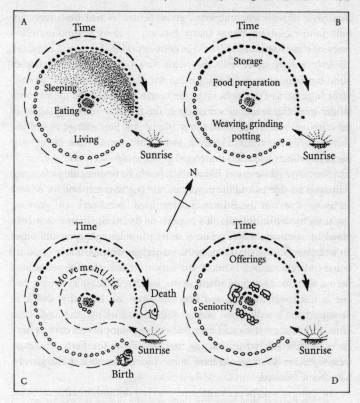

FIG 72 *Four ways of interpreting the layout of Iron Age roundhouses. Most have doorways facing east and south-east, the direction of sunrise. The clockwise movement of the sun provides an actual and symbolic indication of time. A horseshoe-shaped stone hearth faces the doorway. The various schemes are as follows: A. daily time; B. seasonal time; C. lifetime; and D. ancestral time, combined with seniority.*

If we imagine a horseshoe-shaped hearth at the centre of the building (these are not uncommon in Scotland), we find living and sleeping coinciding with the day- and night-time halves of the house. Seasonal time reflects, as any gardener knows, various specific activities to do with crafts, food preparation and storage, and Mike's scheme accords well with what we know about Scottish stone-built Iron Age wheelhouses. Taking things a stage further, it's not uncommon to find baby or child burials near Iron Age doorways (I found one at Fengate), thereby linking birth with the rising sun – hinting at yet another time-based metaphor. Again, we can use the passage of time to construct a pattern of seating around the hearth which reflects the seniority of the inhabitants and accommodates the fact that offerings (again in Scottish wheelhouses) were often placed on the wall opposite the doorway. Perhaps this direction, away from (or directly facing) the sunrise, reflects the ancestral world of the dead.

Scottish highland and island sites, being stone-built and often not damaged by deep ploughing, provide the best illustrations for Mike's ideas on the way roundhouses were used, but there are growing grounds for believing that this pattern of domestic life was not confined to northern Britain. For a start, most Iron Age roundhouses right across Britain share this south-easterly orientation; and there are other indications that it may have been a 'mind-set' that was shared across Britain. There are many examples that fit Mike's pattern, but the best-known was excavated in the 1950s by Nora Chadwick at Longbridge Deverill Cow Down, Wiltshire. This large roundhouse (fifty feet in diameter) had burnt down, and does not appear to have been modified or rebuilt during its brief life in the Early Iron Age. Although the site had suffered some plough-damage subsequently, Chadwick's description fits Mike's theory very well:

> ... on the left side from the door was the emplacement for an upright loom, and in the topsoil above it were the broken fragments of chalk loom-weights. All the domestic refuse was confined to this side of the house, suggesting that this was the living area, with the sleeping quarters on the other, unlittered side.[13]

Although most roundhouses face east and south-east, some face the opposite direction; Mike has argued that these may have been more prestigious dwellings. If the direction of the sunrise is the 'powerful' or important direction, then anyone entering a house that faces north-east will pass through the doorway to find its occupier facing him or her from that 'powerful' direction. In other words, the occupier of the house will have assumed the position of the rising sun. Given a sun/solstice-based cosmology, where solar orientations were significant, such a theatrical arrangement would have been highly effective.

Experimental archaeology can provide some unexpected insights into the past. We reconstructed an Iron Age roundhouse at Flag Fen, based on the ground-plan of one I had dug locally in 1976. That house was part of a small village which we named after the Cat's Water, a stream which skirted the fen along Peterborough's eastern fringes. The rebuilt Cat's Water house did not have a porch, but after it had stood up through eight winters in the open, treeless agri-desert that the fens have been reduced to today, we were forced to add one, as it was uninhabitable without it. So presumably the Cat's Water village in Iron Age times was far more sheltered and pleasant than the same place 2300 years later.

How long did these houses last? The answer depends on the local ground conditions and the care with which each family maintained its own home. Peter Reynolds told me that his houses could last forty years or longer, provided they were kept in good order. But whether people actually *wanted* their houses to remain in precisely the same spot for that length of time is another question.

It is unusual to find much evidence for repair and renewal in Iron Age roundhouses. Sometimes, as at Pimperne, the pattern of post-holes clearly shows that the frame was completely rebuilt. This fits well with what experimenters, myself included, have found: it's easier to patch up and prop an ageing building than actually to replace rotten posts, but sooner or later such makeshift repairs cease to be worth the effort and inconvenience. When that stage is reached, it becomes far simpler just to rebuild the whole thing. I would estimate that the various houses I have excavated probably had life spans of ten to twenty years at the most – enough time to raise a family and see the children on their way in the world. But it's hard to prove the matter positively one way or another.

Peter has described the Pimperne Down house as a 'manor' house. This is an excellent description, because it avoids overblown anthropological language to do with Big Men, or powerful controlling elites. A manor is about control and authority, but on a very limited, parochial scale. The Pimperne Down 'manor' sat within a very substantial ditched enclosure of 4.7 hectares (11.6 acres), and was clearly the dwelling of a person of substance. I've found a slightly larger building, set apart from the main village by an enclosing ditch and bank, at Fengate, in the Flag Fen basin. Again, this was probably for an important person or family, but this person, or people, were still part of a larger community – which is why I like Peter's 'manor' idea (although historians of the medieval period doubtless wouldn't).

As we're now in the Iron Age, I ought to say something about the metal which in the Industrial Revolution was to bring Britain such vast wealth. The smelting of iron from ore was discovered by the Hittites, in what is now Turkey and Syria, in the mid-second millennium BC. They kept the secret to themselves for several centuries, and it wasn't until the sudden collapse of their empire around 1200 BC that the technology reached the world outside. Thereafter it spread across Europe, and we know that iron tools were being made in Britain by about 750 BC.[14]

The change from bronze to iron took several centuries to complete, despite the obvious superiority of the new harder, tougher and sharper metal, and it did not become widely adopted in Britain until the third to fourth centuries BC.[15] Some of the first iron objects actually mimic forms that are more suitably made in bronze. The casting of iron is a recent invention; in the remote past it was beaten into shape by smiths. Thus axes were beaten, not cast like their Bronze Age equivalents. One of the distinctive forms of cast Bronze Age axe is the socketed axe. This is not a form that is readily made from beaten metal, yet make it they sometimes did. We found an iron socketed axe at Flag Fen, although the best-known example comes from a very early Iron Age hoard, of mainly bronze objects, at Lynn Fawr in Glamorgan, on the opposite side of Britain.[16] True Iron Age axes resemble their modern equivalents, and are extraordinarily good tools, vastly more efficient than their Bronze Age predecessors. In terms of sheer effectiveness I would rate the jump from bronze to iron as at least equivalent to the change from stone to metal (bronze).

Books on archaeology tend to dwell on the fabulous and the beautiful, but something well-made and practical can be just as moving, for the simple reason that one can imagine using it. A superb collection of metal- and wood-workers' tools was found at Fiskerton,

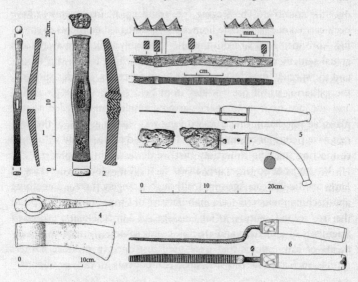

FIG 73   *A selection of iron tools from Fiskerton, Lincolnshire (200–300 BC). Metal-working tools: 1. light hammer head; 2. heavy hammer head; 3. file. Wood-working tools: 4. axe head; 5. pruning pull-saw with decorated blade; 6. push-file or carpenter's float, with decorated antler handle.*

where they had been placed in the waters as votive offerings. Most of these tools probably date to the third century (200–300) BC, and they include items like hammers and files that would look perfectly at home on a modern blacksmith's, or carpenter's, bench. A small pull-saw (a saw whose teeth are reversed so that it cuts on the pull) closely resembles one I use every winter to prune larger stems, such as blackcurrants, that are too thick for secateurs. The iron metal-working files had closer ridges than the wood files, and still had traces of non-ferrous metal adhering to their surfaces.

Iron and its ore occurs widely in Britain, both in the form of metallic 'bog iron' in wet, peaty bogs and as a variety of ores. The ores occur naturally on the surface over large areas of southern Britain, and new evidence for iron-working is appearing on a regular basis all over the country.[17] The forging (i.e. smithing) of iron seems to have been carried out within the homestead, although the process of smelting – producing metal from the ore – probably took place away from actual settlements. This may well have something to do with taboos and the special, 'magical', nature of these processes. Having said that, the gathering-up of ore nodules from field surfaces after ploughing and the use of iron to make farming implements has led to the plausible suggestion that iron-working was viewed as part of the process of agricultural regeneration.[18] This would fit quite well with ideas connecting smelting to fertility that we discussed in Chapter 9.

We know of no large, specialised 'factory' sites for iron-working in Early or Middle Iron Age times, although strangely there is something approaching industrial-scale manufacture of bronze objects.[19] A pit of the late second century BC at Gussage All Saints, Dorset, produced fragments of a furnace and crucibles, plus some eight thousand fragments of clay moulds that were used just once to produce harness fittings, such as bridle bits, and small components for carts or wagons.[20]

The Iron Age was the shortest period of British and Irish prehistory,[21] but in many respects it was the most remarkable. At the beginning of the period, in the Early Iron Age (the two centuries from say 700 to 500 BC), the way of life was essentially that of the Later Bronze Age. There is little archaeological evidence for population growth or social change. Settlements of this early period are often located close by or on top of Later Bronze Age communities, and earlier field systems sometimes continue in use. The big changes appear to start shortly after 500 BC, in the Middle Iron Age. Ask any archaeologist about the Iron Age in his or her region, and you'll usually find there is 'some' evidence for Early settlement, but that Middle Iron Age pottery is 'everywhere'. Is this just another question of archaeological 'visibility'? To an extent, perhaps, because Middle Iron Age pottery was thicker and much better fired than Bronze and Early Iron Age ceramics. Having said that, however, the earlier material *does* survive perfectly well (as the excavators of Potterne showed so graphically), so I don't think one can just plead 'visibility': there is a sudden and quite dramatic increase not just in pottery, but in the gross number of sites.

In the last three decades of the twentieth century there was a hidden and untrumpeted revolution in the way archaeology in Britain is 'done'. If you wanted to excavate a site or survey a given region in the 1960s and early seventies, and needed to discover what was already known about the area, you consulted various libraries, and nosed your way through the dusty archives housed in museum basements. Today the process has become vastly more straightforward, with the creation of local and national Sites and Monuments Records, known in the trade as SMRs. Usually SMRs are housed in county or city council offices, and their maintenance, now voluntary, will shortly become a statutory obligation on local authorities – and not before time. They invariably involve computers, and are becoming both increasingly sophisticated and user-friendly. Consult any SMR and you will immediately be struck by the sudden increase not just in finds, but in sites of all types dating to the Middle and Later Iron Age. It's a process that has been termed the 'filling-out' of the landscape.[22]

I have tended to play down the role of powerful controlling elites in British prehistory so far, but the seven centuries or so of the Iron Age witnessed some very important social changes. That should hardly surprise us: the population was growing – probably quite fast after about 300 BC – and although Britain was an island, it was in touch with the European mainland, where we know that societies were also changing. As time passed, contacts across the Channel became more frequent and the pace of change accelerated. The general trend was towards more hierarchical social systems. Warrior leaders, both male and female, were becoming of increasing importance; by the end of the Iron Age some of these leaders became rather more than warlords or tribal chiefs. They ruled over what were often impermanent confederations of tribal groupings that minted their own coinage and can best be described as early kingdoms, many of whose names we know from Roman authors.

The British Iron Age has, however, produced one uncontested Big Man. His name is Barry Cunliffe, Professor of European Archaeology at Oxford University. Most archaeologists would regard his greatest contribution to Iron Age studies as his work of synthesis, *Iron Age Communities in Britain*.[23] The book was written in 1971, published in 1974, and was followed by a greatly enlarged second edition in 1978.

The current, third, edition, even more massively enlarged, appeared in 1991, and rumour has it that an even longer fourth edition will appear before long. The progressive enlargement of the book graphically illustrates the extraordinary growth of the basic data that has emerged from the ground since 1971. In the five years between the first two editions, no fewer than three hundred books and papers on the topic appeared in print. Between the second and third editions the figure was seven hundred. These numbers remind me of Barry's opening to the Introduction of the first edition: 'When, in 1969, I mentioned to my colleague Leo Rivet that I was thinking of writing a book on the British Iron Age, he said that it could not be done. Now that I have finished the work, I am inclined to agree with him.'[24]

He goes on to say that the task is impossible, not simply because of the constantly increasing database – that he can cope with – but because the subject itself is in a state of flux: 'Thought on the subject is changing rapidly; established dictums which have found worldwide support for decades are being overthrown; and new ways are developing for looking at familiar material.' If that was true in 1971, it is even more so today, when British Iron Age studies are going through an extraordinarily creative period.[25]

Barry has discerned five distinct regional traditions. These aren't 'cultures' as we've seen them defined hitherto: as tissue-thin disguises for distribution maps of different styles of pottery. They were determined using a broad range of criteria, and they haven't been seriously weakened even by some important recent discoveries.

Water and wet places played a very important part in Iron Age religion not just in Britain but right across Europe, and there can be little doubt that the roots of these water-based rituals lay in the Bronze Age, or even earlier.[26] This reflects the fact that many of the themes we have already encountered continued in their fundamentals much as before. Concepts such as the importance of the ancestors to the world of the living continued to be significant, although the rites that attended these ceremonies became distinctively modified from one region to another. In other words, communal identities were becoming more marked as time progressed and as populations grew, but certain core rituals continued despite this. We see this happening at, for example, Fiskerton and Flag Fen. Fiskerton was entirely Iron Age, and

Flag Fen was both Bronze and Iron Age, but both were places where essentially Bronze Age rites were celebrated, but using Iron Age artefacts. Surely this represents the deliberate conservation of ancient rituals to provide people with a core of continuity and stability – something to hang on to in times when society was changing.

Cunliffe was able to reveal patterns within Iron Age culture that did not always coincide with his five main zones of Iron Age Britain. The regional economies of Iron Age Britain are a good example. As before, it's important not to analyse ancient economic systems outside their social context, but even taking this into account, it was possible to distinguish certain general trends. The smaller homestead-style settlements of Scotland and north-western England were largely self-sufficient. This was termed a 'sufficer economy'. They either could not, or were unwilling to, produce an economic surplus that could be traded or exchanged. Central and southern England produced such a surplus, and this area was labelled a 'redistribution economy'. Cunliffe considered that eastern England also possibly belonged within this group; I believe it almost certainly fitted there. South-western Britain showed signs of what Cunliffe termed a 'clientage economy', where there was a clear distinction between producing agricultural settlements and consuming communities of higher status – the former being the clients of the latter.

The types of settlement where Iron Age people lived their daily lives also form coherent patterns. If we take the situation at the close of the Middle Iron Age, around 150 BC, we find that over a large area of south-eastern and central England settlements were open, undefended and sometimes quite large (twenty plus houses). To the south and east of this region we come to the hill-fort-dominated zone; but hill-forts were not the only form that settlement took here. On the lower-lying land, along river valleys, for example, it is not unusual to find open settlements. To the west of this zone, along what one might term the southern Atlantic fringe of Britain, we find smaller communities living in strongly defended settlements. A similar style of settlement is found along Scotland's Atlantic-facing shore, but as we will shortly see, the actual form the defended settlements took was very different to that of south-western England and Wales. There were two zones where hill-forts played a prominent role in lowland Scotland, and in

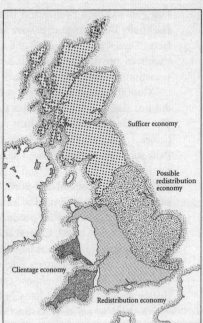

northern England we find enclosed (i.e. lightly defended) settlements, with a fair scattering of hill-forts as well.

This description may seem a little bald, but it demonstrates the diversity of Iron Age life in Britain. Despite modern myths, the 'Ancient Britons' was not a homogeneous culture, with a common religion and shared rules of behaviour. For most of the Iron Age we are looking at societies who probably spoke with distinctive regional dialects. I would be surprised if a man from Kent could understand what a man from Yorkshire was saying with any ease (something that still applies today).

I'll start my necessarily brief tour of Iron Age Britain and Ireland with Cunliffe's eastern zone, with which I am most familiar. It was characterised by open, undefended, village-like settlements, often accompanied by large field systems. The Cat's Water community which

FIG 74   *Three maps, taken from Barry Cunliffe's* Iron Age Communities in Britain, *showing (left) the zones of Iron Age Britain; (centre) the economic systems; and (right) the dominant settlement types at the end of the Middle Iron Age, around 150 BC.*

I excavated in the 1970s is fairly typical of these. It consisted of about fifty-five round buildings, of which ten would have been in use at any one time; of these about half were probably used as byres for farm animals. Many similar open settlements are known to the west, through Northamptonshire into Oxfordshire, and across Lincolnshire and East Anglia.

With a single exception, all the roundhouses of the Cat's Water settlement faced east and south-east, in the manner demanded by Mike Parker Pearson's hypothesis. The exception was known as Structure 7, and its doorway faced in the opposite direction. We know that doorways of roundhouses were given special treatment and were plainly important to people in the Iron Age: for example, Chris Evans of the Cambridge University Unit found that the door-posts of a house in the southern fens at Haddenham were marked by the carcasses of

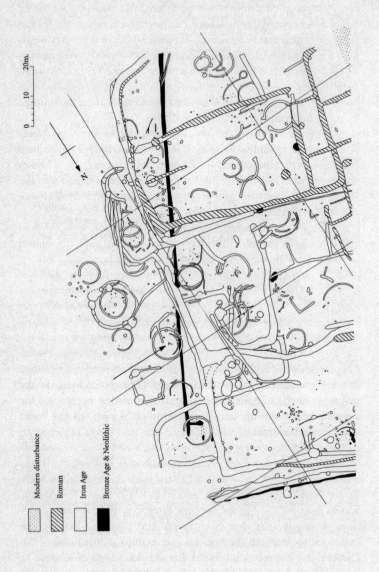

complete sheep. Structure 7 may have faced the 'wrong' way, but its doorway was placed directly above a major boundary ditch of a Bronze Age field system that had gone out of use hundreds of years previously. Was this coincidental? Or was it perhaps a way of symbolically linking this more important building with a largely vanished ancestral world. I say 'largely' vanished because elements of the earlier landscape survived into Iron Age times, possibly in the form of overgrown hedge lines or seasonally flooded drainage ditches.

What one might call the 'style' of hierarchy seen at Cat's Water and elsewhere in south-eastern England in the Early and Middle Iron Age suggests that the important folk were 'of the people'. Their houses may have faced in a different direction from those of the bulk of the populace, but they were part of the community, and did not choose to distance themselves from it physically.

Hill-forts are undoubtedly the best-known type of Iron Age field monuments in Britain. They are very characteristic of the central southern zone to the west, but are surprisingly rare in the eastern zone. It's too simplistic to say that this merely reflects the rarity of significant hills in eastern England – there are well-known examples in Yorkshire, Norfolk and Northamptonshire.[27] They even occur in the Home Counties, at sites like Ravensburgh Castle in Hertfordshire. Incidentally, Ravensburgh belongs to a chain of forts that run along the Chiltern Hills. Midway between each is a linear earthwork – essentially a straight ditch and bank. About ten years before such ideas became academically fashionable, James Dyer (who directed the dig at Ravensburgh) suggested that these straight earthworks marked the boundaries between the territories controlled by each hill-fort,[28] and I'm sure he was right.

One characteristic type of defended site, found along the east side

FIG 75   *A plan of the small Iron Age village at Fengate, in the Flag Fen basin, Peterborough. Beneath the foundations of roundhouses and the drainage ditches of the yards that surround them are the straight ditches of the Bronze Age livestock field system that went out of use in the early centuries of the first millennium BC. The subsequent Iron Age settlement began life sometime around 500 BC and flourished in the Middle and Late Iron Age, from about 350 BC into the first century AD.*

of the country from Kent northwards, is a circular defended enclosure known as a ring-fort. These were often located on low-lying ground. Our team investigated one in Borough Fen just north of Peterborough in 1982.[29] It's a substantial site (diameter about 220 metres), at least as large as many upland hill-forts, although in flatter, lower-lying countryside (it lies at between two and three metres above sea level), with a large inner bank and another smaller one outside it. In those days its deep defensive ditch was still waterlogged, and was doubtless full of all sorts of organic treasures. But sadly it's a Scheduled Ancient Monument, protected by Act of Parliament, so we were very limited in what we could do. This legal 'protection' will ensure that its water-logged ditches will dry out unseen, as the Ancient Monuments Act cannot force drainage authorities to raise water levels in the area. That's the responsibility of another branch of government.

There was wealth in some abundance in Iron Age southern Britain, as is witnessed by the discovery of massive gold torcs, or neck-rings, from votive deposits in small pits at various sites, including Snettisham on the north Norfolk coast and Ipswich further south. It's interesting that the practice of placing votive offerings in small pits continues well into the Iron Age, and it was undoubtedly a very strong tradition in East Anglia. The strikingly beautiful torcs were decorated in a style known as Early Celtic art (see next chapter).

Barry Cunliffe sees the first signs of an emerging elite as early as the eighth century BC, and the ring-forts of eastern England show clear evidence for it. They contain only a few houses, and these are positioned with great care, as if to enhance their prestige.[30] I don't think that elites emerged evenly right across the country, or indeed any given region. In the east of England and the east midlands, for example, I believe the old, Bronze Age pattern of broadly egalitarian societies continued rather longer, until the start of the Middle Iron Age in, say, the mid-fifth century BC. Thereafter things did indeed begin to change.

If offerings placed in pits harked back to earlier practices, the placing of valuable metal objects in the Thames continued unabated.[31] The river has produced some of the finest objects from Iron Age Britain: ceremonial shields, a horned helmet and numerous weapons, including a distinctive series of sheathed daggers that belong at the

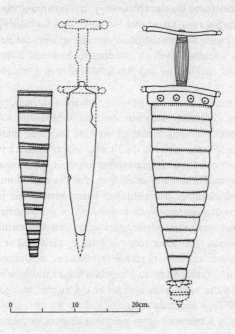

FIG 76   *Two sheathed daggers of Early Iron Age type (500–600 BC), dredged from the Thames at Battersea (left) and Mortlake (right). The dagger from Mortlake was most probably imported to Britain from the continent.*

very start of the Iron Age.[32] Some have seen these as providing evidence for the rise of an elite. I'm not convinced. I can see no real difference between the Early Iron Age daggers and the swords and spearheads of the Bronze Age, which were probably offered to the river during rites of passage, or as gestures towards the world of the ancestors.

One way of acquiring an elite is to import one, which is what happened as a result of the Roman and Norman Conquests. This brings us to the case for Iron Age invasions. We've already seen that the archaeological record can provide no convincing evidence for mass migrations into Britain prior to the Roman Conquest. Simon James has debunked the Celts, and Professor Roy Hodson

effectively destroyed the numerous Iron Age 'invasions' from the continent that the likes of Christopher Hawkes, Barry Cunliffe's predecessor
at Oxford, put forward to explain changes in regional pottery styles.
I've always imagined that an invading force would have comprised
warriors, but to Hawkes and his followers they seem to have been
potters.

There are, however, two possible, but limited, Iron Age invasions
into Britain. I'll discuss one in the next chapter, because it is supposed
to have happened very late in the Iron Age. The other is controversial,
but nonetheless plausible. It didn't take place, as one might expect,
on the south coast, but much further north, in the Yorkshire wolds,
around the small market town of Driffield. The evidence is a concentration of distinctive square ditched barrows surrounding a central
grave, often of a warrior with a sheathed sword, who is sometimes
accompanied by a vehicle. The latter were labelled 'chariot burials' in
Victorian times, but in the 1960s to nineties they were renamed 'cart
burials'. Now it seems we must refer to them as 'carriage burials'. The
culture which produced them is named after a local barrow cemetery,
excavated in the nineteenth century at the rather confusingly named
Yorkshire village of Arras.[33] Closely similar barrows to those of the
Arras Culture are known from northern France, in the broad Marne
valley of the Champagne district – the presumed origin of the
'invasion'.[34]

Modern research into the Arras Culture has mainly been carried
out by two Yorkshiremen, John Dent and Ian Stead. It was Ian, incidentally, who unearthed the fabulous golden torcs at Snettisham for
the British Museum. The Arras Culture came into being in the fourth,
and lasted into the first, century BC. The cemeteries of square barrows
are closely confined to the area around Driffield, but Iron Age square
barrows are sometimes found elsewhere in eastern England – I dug a
couple at Maxey, just north of Peterborough.

Ian Stead, who excavated 250 Arras barrows between 1967 and
1978, is now firmly of the opinion that they *don't* represent an invasion
or movement of people, because only the square barrows and carriage
burials have clear parallels on the continent, while other essential
aspects of Arras funerary rites, such as crouched burials and the grave-
goods buried with them, are British.[35] Similarly, local settlements of

the period have recently been excavated, and these are typically British. The cemetery at Wetwang Slack, for example, was near an open settlement of roundhouses that could have been found anywhere in the eastern zone. But we do know that there was regular contact between Britain and the continent throughout the Iron Age, and it is perfectly possible that a group of more influential people in the Driffield area did indeed establish a distinctive local funerary tradition, based on what they had seen abroad. That tradition was exotic (which may help to explain its appeal to an emerging elite), but not wholly unusual, as it did not differ very radically from what was happening elsewhere in the region. And for a time it flourished.

The square barrow cemeteries of east Yorkshire are also important, because strangely enough, although the population of Iron Age Britain was growing, there is remarkably little evidence for the way bodies were treated after death.[36] This is in marked contrast to the Bronze Age, where barrows and cremation cemeteries are almost ubiquitous. A recent study which analysed the bodies, grave-goods and layout of the Yorkshire cemeteries was able to demonstrate that the distinctively linear arrangement of cemeteries at places like Wetwang Slack was far from haphazard, and concealed evidence not just for social stratification, but also for a concern with some of the cosmological patterns that played such an important role in the way roundhouses were used.[37] It was possible to 'read' other messages in the way people were buried: these included subtle distinctions between men and women. The different joints of meat buried with the dead – usually pork or mutton – reflected social differences, and it is possible to see cattle as symbolising life itself.

The Arras burials, many of which thankfully are still untouched, are one of the most important archaeological resources in Iron Age Britain. They were sometimes accompanied by fabulous grave-goods, but more often than not they contained just a bronze safety-pin-style brooch, or perhaps a pot or a sword.[38] Ian Stead and John Dent worked on geophysical means of detecting carriage burials which used the iron band, or tyre, around the outside of the wheels as a 'target' which could be detected below the ground.

The carriage wheels were quite extraordinary. They were spoked, and very much resembled recent farm wagon wheels. The best one of

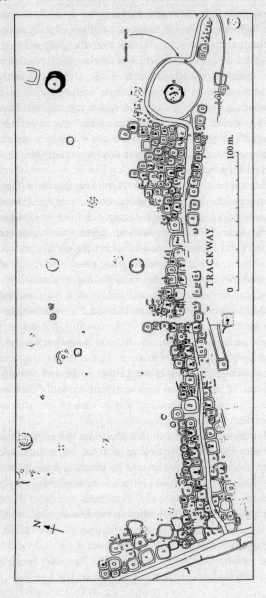

FIG 77 Plan of the Iron Age cemetery of some 446 burials and two hundred square barrows belonging to the Arras Culture at Wetwang Slack, near Driffield in the Yorkshire wolds (350–50 BC). The cemetery developed along a trackway in two phases separated by a central ditch. To the north can be seen the ring-gully foundations of Iron Age roundhouses belonging to an open, unenclosed settlement.

all was not found in an Arras burial, but in a gravel pit in the Trent valley at Holme Pierrepont, five miles east of Nottingham.[39] This find dated to the second century BC (I need hardly note that it would have been perfectly at home a thousand years earlier), and it positively reeked of ritual. Sadly, the discovery was made in the days when archaeologists were called in *after* something was found during quarrying operations, and the conditions in which they had to work were atrocious. The wheel lay directly underneath no fewer than three logboats in a waterlogged but abandoned meander of the river Trent. It had been removed from its axle, but was otherwise complete.

I mentioned that the technology of the Flag Fen Bronze Age wheel was sophisticated, and involved the use of several species of tree. This also applies to the Holme Pierrepont wheel, which could only have been made by a skilled wheelwright. The outer ring of wood, known as the felloe, was made of ash and was in six parts, joined together by oak dowels. Each part of the felloe was socketed to hold two oak spokes, which all located in a single-piece hub, made of birch. The whole construction was held firmly in compression by a stout iron band or tyre, which was shrunk into position by first being heated and then quenched with water. It's a technique used by wheelwrights to this day.

I was talking about the Holme Pierrepont wheel to Maisie recently. 'Was it *really* that sophisticated?' I asked.

'Oh, yes,' she replied. 'But the odd thing is that normal, day-to-day Iron Age woodworking wasn't a patch on what they did in the Bronze Age.'

'Despite their axes being light years more advanced?'

'Yes. In fact, I think that's why. With a good iron axe anyone can chop and botch something into shape. It may not be brilliant to look at, but it worked. And of course, the wood they had then was much worse.'

'Why was that?'

'A lot of the good stuff had been felled in the Bronze Age. But it was more than that: people didn't seem to be so fussy. If it would do, they'd use it – nobody seemed to care much about knots and twists. Some of it's really grotty.'

'Presumably with better tools you needed less skill?'

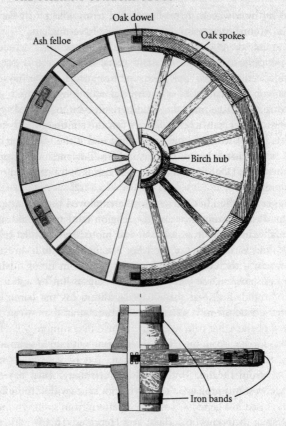

Oak dowel

Ash felloe

Oak spokes

Birch hub

Iron bands

FIG 78   *A spoked Iron Age wheel from an old course of the river Trent at Holme Pierrepont, Nottinghamshire (second century BC). Note the different types of wood used by the wheelwright. The iron bands which held the wheel together were applied hot and then quenched with water to shrink them into position.*

'Yes, like today – electric drills mean anyone can be a DIY expert. But we still need specialists, and they appeared first in the Iron Age. The Flag Fen wheel was made there, on the farm, probably by the chaps who drove the cart it was attached to. Holme Pierrepont was assembled by a wheelwright who moved from village to village. It's superb. No ordinary person could possibly have made it.'[40]

Certainly there were specialists in earlier times – one immediately thinks of shipwrights, mariners and metal-workers – but they were probably seen as people apart, removed from much of normal society. It's the Iron Age that sees the widespread adoption of many specialist trades, from carriage-builder to wheelwright, even to furniture-maker, armourer, potter, salt-maker, vintner (on the continent), blacksmith, jeweller, etc.[41] I would not be at all surprised if the wealthier households of the Later Iron Age in southern England even employed specialist chefs. Doubtless too, there were bands of travelling musicians and players.

Larger communities may well have employed priests, although I find the idea of a universal Druidic religion hard to accept until the very final years of the Iron Age.[42] It is far more likely that the religious beliefs of the various zones of Iron Age Britain had certain core aspects in common – they were, after all, developed from earlier ideologies which we know shared important basic beliefs. But the rites in the regions would, I suspect, have been as diverse as the communities which practised them. We do know, however, that there were certain themes or beliefs that Iron Age societies held in common. Mike Parker Pearson, for example, notes that the concern with lunar eclipses seen at Fiskerton seems to be pan-European, and he can cite Iron Age examples from Ireland, Switzerland and Germany. Also, as we have seen, it now seems probable that the interior space within roundhouses was organised in a generally consistent pattern from southern England as far north as Orkney and the Outer Hebrides. This would suggest that although societies possessed regional distinctiveness, they communicated with each other frequently, and quite possibly over long distances. Almost by definition this would require an efficient infrastructure of roads and navigation, and of course language and dialects that must have been mutually comprehensible.

It used to be thought that Iron Age vehicles were like my 1963 tractor, entirely devoid of any form of suspension, but a very recent discovery (spring 2001) has turned that on its head. This time the Arras burial was from Wetwang, but not from one of John Dent's large excavations; instead, as so often happens nowadays, it was revealed during the building of a new housing estate.[43] It was the burial of a mature woman, accompanied by an iron mirror which lay across her legs. The carriage had been dismantled before being placed in the grave pit, and all the harness fittings were arranged along the north side of the grave. These included two horse-bits, strap unions (flexible metal joints) and terrets (loops through which the reins passed). The terrets were decorated with red enamel or coral inlay, which in one instance had been replaced. This, and other evidence, suggests that the carriage was a real vehicle that had seen much use before it was dismantled. It was not something just made to be buried.

The burial wasn't waterlogged, so preservation was nowhere near as good as at Holme Pierrepont. In fact, all Adrian Havercroft and his team had to go by were voids left in the ground when the wood rotted. These take *very* careful digging: one false step and everything collapses. The wheels were spoked, and like Holme Pierrepont were held together by three iron bands: a large outer 'tyre' and two smaller nave bands, inside and outside the wheel, at the centre. One major discovery was that Iron Age axles weren't simple and barlike. They were complex, tapered constructions, with swellings that acted as stop-ridges inboard of the wheels. Incidentally, the fragmentary Bronze Age axle from Flag Fen has such a stop-ridge.[44]

Experimental reconstructions for television have featured in our story before, and the Wetwang carriage was given the full treatment in a special for the BBC series *Meet the Ancestors*. The programme-makers commissioned a Somerset wheelwright, Robert Hurford, to construct a replica chariot (see p.352). Mr Hurford already had views on how these vehicles could have been built, and he devised a suspension system which used two sets of flexible ash arches from which hung rawhide thongs.[45] This arrangement suspended a riding platform which was attached to the chassis below it by flexible leather straps. It was a method of suspension that quite literally suspends, and that fits with what we know about ancient vehicles from carvings. Most importantly, it worked, and the carriage, drawn by two small horses, positively whizzed across the lawns of the British Museum, where it now resides. I wish the makers of my old tractor had known of Mr Hurford's secret.

The central southern zone of Iron Age Britain differs from its eastern neighbour in a number of respects, but I believe that if Barry

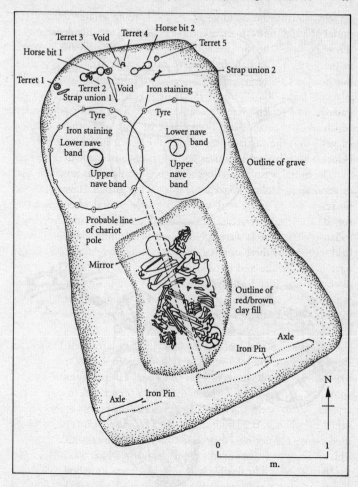

FIG 79   *Plan of the Arras Culture carriage burial at Wetwang, east Yorkshire (fourth or third century BC). The skeleton at the south end of the grave pit was of a mature woman, buried with an iron mirror. Around her were the dismantled components of a wooden two-wheeled carriage, originally drawn by two horses, whose harness fittings were arranged along the north side of the grave pit.*

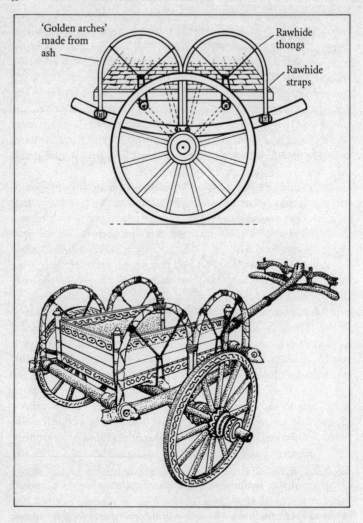

'Golden arches' made from ash

Rawhide thongs

Rawhide straps

FIG 80   *A reconstruction (below) of the Wetwang carriage by Robert Hurford, showing details of how the suspension system was constructed (above). The diameter of the wheels was approximately ninety-five centimetres (three feet 1½ inches).*

Cunliffe produces a fourth edition of *Iron Age Communities*, he will have somehow to blur the boundary between the two, especially as regards the Thames and Nene valleys, which were essentially broad corridors that joined them together. The central southern zone was dominated by hill-forts, usually positioned atop prominent or commanding hilltops and often visible for miles around.[46] Even today the larger examples, such as Maiden Castle in Dorset, dominate the landscape. They were fortified by one or more ditches, which were accompanied by a bank on the uphill, or inside. This bank (or more normally nowadays both the ditch and bank together) is known as a rampart.

Today the ramparts that crown many of the prominent hills of Hampshire and Dorset look smooth and sinuous, and although steep they wouldn't present much of an obstacle to a fit young warrior. But this is the result of millennia of natural weathering. The original fortifications would have been built up with massive, box-like timber revetments, stockades, walls and all manner of obstacles. They were intended to impress and to deter, and in this they were generally successful, as there is very little evidence to suggest that they were ever the sites of large-scale pitched battles. So-called 'war cemeteries' (a misleading and loaded term) are known from near the entranceways of at least two hill-forts in southern Britain. These contain slain and mutilated bodies, so there undoubtedly was tribal conflict. Hill-forts were certainly not built *just* to impress, but to judge by the size of the known 'war cemeteries', the battles were more akin to raids than to wars involving the coming together of two armies. It's possible, too, that such places could also have been the scene of more theatrical styles of warfare, reminiscent perhaps of the confrontation between single representative warriors such as David and Goliath. But medieval-style prolonged sieges, followed by wholesale slaughter of the vanquished population, seem unlikely on present evidence.

It has been traditional to look to hill-forts when seeking evidence for prehistoric warfare. They are after all forts, which are places that hostile forces are likely to attack. But was Bronze and Iron Age fighting 'warfare' in the sense we know it today? Certainly towards the close of the Iron Age there were set-piece battles. Caesar, for example, talks of the British opposing him with no fewer than four thousand chariots (which is probably something of an exaggeration).[47] But before that, fighting was essentially a matter of tribal feuding, combined perhaps with cattle or sheep rustling. So are we actually looking in the right places? We'd probably have better luck if we searched more closely around some of the large areas of settlement that we know existed in the valleys overlooked by the great hill-forts. That's where most of the people would have lived (and died).

Hill-forts spread over large areas of the central southern zone quite rapidly in the late sixth and fifth centuries BC. Barry Cunliffe sees this as a significant social change, probably brought about by population growth and competition between various communities for resources. At first there were many hill-forts, each of which was surrounded by its own territory of fields or more open pasture. As time passed there was a process of consolidation, in which many of the smaller hill-forts were incorporated within the enlarged landscapes that were now controlled by an emerging group of much bigger ones. Danebury, in Hampshire, is an example of such a large, successful hill-fort. It was excavated by a team under Barry Cunliffe, and is the subject of a large-scale and detailed landscape survey, a remarkable achievement published in no less than fifteen volumes, not including popular summaries.[48] As a result of this detailed research we probably know more about Danebury and its hinterland than anywhere else in Iron Age Europe. The site itself now has a fine interpretive trail provided by Hampshire County Council – a huge improvement on the tangle of fallen trees and undergrowth that I encountered in the 1970s when visiting the dig.

Danebury was first occupied after about 550 BC and almost came to an abrupt end around 100 BC, when the main fortified gate was burnt to the ground. This is generally seen as a hostile act perpetrated by an attacking force. It may well have been, but very often in prehistory, simple explanations don't turn out to be right. I'm put in mind of the 'war cemetery' excavated by the great archaeologist and ex-soldier Sir Mortimer Wheeler at Maiden Castle.[49] When re-examined in the mid-1980s by Niall Sharples and his team from English Heritage, it turned out to be a civilian cemetery belonging to a recognised local tradition.[50] So Wheeler's vision of a valiant last stand by the heroic

FIG 81 *Constructional details of the Danebury Iron Age hill-fort, Hampshire, around 400 BC. The timber-faced rampart was replaced by a more massive earthwork.*

Britons against the invading Roman legions is probably a myth – which is a shame, because it was an excellent story.

As for Danebury, I wonder whether deliberate destruction, a tradition that extends back into the mists of British prehistory, may not have been a cause of that hill-fort's apparent demise. I say 'apparent' because after such a send-off, whatever it was that Danebury stood for would have continued in legend and folklore for many generations. The suggestion that the destruction was not necessarily an offensive act is supported by the fact that occupation of the forts didn't cease after the burning of the main gate, which could have been, as Barry Cunliffe has put it, 'symbolic – an act marking a significant change of function'.[51]

As at all the larger hill-forts of the central southern zone, the defences of Danebury were massively elaborated every few generations, and most particular attention was paid to the entranceways. This was almost carried to extremes at Maiden Castle, where the latest entranceway defences resemble a vast three-dimensional maze. Clearly the intention was to impress as much as to secure. At Danebury the western entranceway was the main way into the fort, until it was blocked around 400 BC. Thereafter Danebury was served by the eastern entrance alone, which was promptly elaborated by the addition of extra ramparts.

Having entered by the eastern gateway, the visitor to Danebury

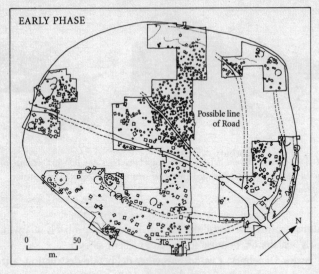

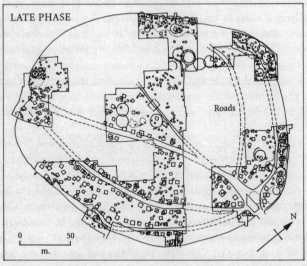

FIG 82   *The interior of the Iron Age hill-fort at Danebury, Hampshire, in its early phase, 550–300 BC (top), and late phase, 300–100 BC (bottom).*

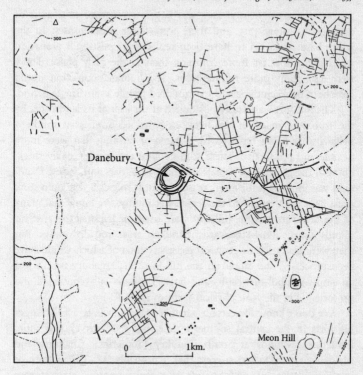

FIG 83   *Danebury hill-fort, Hampshire, and the surrounding field systems (550–100 BC). The presence of long and round barrows shows that the landscape was already long-established by the Early Iron Age, when the first fortifications on top of Danebury hill were constructed.*

would find himself standing on a chalk road which ran in a gentle curve across the interior to the western entrance. This was Road 1. To the left were Roads 2 and 3, which were lined on both sides by a 'ribbon development' of post-built square granaries. At the centre of the enclosure was a temple or shrine which was reached via Road 4. Two roads (5 and 6) serviced the main body of roundhouses which extended along the northern part of the interior. Cunliffe and his team were able to distinguish gradual changes in the way the interior was organised over time. In the early phase, which ended around

300 BC, the north-central area was largely given over to a mass of deep grain-storage pits, and there were fewer roundhouses. In the later phase pits seem to have been replaced by post-built granaries, which were now far more common than in the early phase. There were also many more roundhouses. The human population would have been between three and five hundred people at any single period.

The hill-fort was clearly positioned at the hub of its landscape. By the Iron Age many of the livestock-based economies of southern Britain were being replaced by systems of farming that were more flexible and productive. These still involved the keeping of livestock, but also the growing of cereals such as wheat, oats and barley. Danebury was important for many reasons, but its role as a vast grain store must have been crucial to the region's economy. We know that many of the fields around the hill-fort were used for livestock because air photos clearly show stockyards, handling areas and droveways. But they were also used to grow crops, many tons of which would have been processed and stored in the hill-fort. So Danebury wasn't just an empty symbol of wealth (and power) – it actually contained and protected it in the real, physical form of grain.

We don't know for certain whether Danebury is typical of larger hill-forts in the central southern zone, but field survey and more limited excavations at South Cadbury (Somerset), Chalbury and Maiden Castle (Dorset) suggest that it probably is.[52] This pattern of intensive settlement, with roundhouses and numerous grain-storage pits, seems to be a feature of larger hill-forts in the central southern region. Elsewhere in Britain, in Wales, northern England and Scotland, the interiors of Iron Age hill-forts included very large open spaces; they never begin to resemble small towns, as Danebury does in its later phases of life.

This and the previous chapter have focused on southern, central and eastern Britain not only because research has been active in this area, but also because it was something of an 'engine of change'. It was a dynamic region, with a rapidly expanding population, that was increasingly being stimulated by contact with the continental mainland. Elsewhere, even though populations were growing, life was rather more conservative, and developments happened more gently. Although there were doubtless feuds and local disputes, society does seem to have maintained its equilibrium. The south-western zone, consisting essentially of Devon, Cornwall and west Wales, is a case in point: as we have seen, Barry Cunliffe characterised this region as a 'clientage' economy. It's an ugly-sounding word, but it does seem more or less to explain the pattern of settlement there – although, as always in archaeology, other explanations are possible.

The settlement pattern in the south-western zone may have been diverse, but its various elements had one thing in common: a delight in walls, enclosure and defence. It's worth noting here that defences should not always be taken at face value: many manor sites of medieval England, for example, were given moats almost as a fashion statement – a kind of 'keeping up with the Joneses' – rather than as protection against serious attack. Large Danebury-like hill-forts are absent from the south-western zone, where the basic unit of settlement was the defended homestead, whose numbers, incidentally, increased through-out the Middle and Late Iron Age, in common with the pattern in the central south and eastern zones.

The types of defended settlements vary a great deal, from minor farms or homesteads through various intermediary stages right up to large hilltop enclosures and true hill-forts. Archaeologists often consider that this pattern of evidence forms a hierarchy, and that it provides a good reason for believing in a society that was also hierarchical. Barry Cunliffe's 'clientage economy' model uses this idea. He sees the higher-status sites as being the abodes of an elite whose economy was based on pastoralism and the keeping of livestock. These people essentially exploited the folk at the bottom of the pile, many of whom appropri-ately dwelt at the foot of the hills. These were the farmers living in the small defended homesteads, whose way of life depended on 'man-aging the land' – a phrase which I assume implies static mixed farming of crops and animals. This explanation of the overall settlement pattern seems both logical and coherent. But is it actually right?

My archaeological antennae twitch when I see complexity reduced to general principles. Is there not a danger of being too clever and too analytical? As archaeologists we need sometimes to slow down, to stop endlessly poring over maps and databases trying to wrest hidden meaning from them. In this instance I believe we should simplify our interpretations, and allow the field data to speak for itself. The alternative approach is a regional one, based on careful field survey, excavation and observation. It cuts across the period divisions which can so bedevil archaeology, and which make little practical sense in places such as south-west Wales. It was carried out by George Williams of the Dyfed Archaeological Trust, towards the south-westernmost tip of the Dyfed Peninsula, and was published by him in 1988.[53]

The region in which the study took place can be divided into three smaller areas: a lower-lying 'coastal south-west area', a more hilly or undulating 'inland south-west area', and an area that in Britain we'd recognise as hill, mountain and moorland, the 'upland north and east area'. This is marginal land, today, as it was in the Iron Age, the realm of sheep. During the Bronze Age, in the second millennium BC, much of the higher land, like other areas of upland Britain, was actually divided up by fields. Then the climate grew colder; while this only had a small effect in lowland Britain, it seems to have disrupted patterns of life in the uplands, and many Bronze Age field systems were abandoned at about this time.

The lower-lying, flatter, coastal south-west area had field systems in the Iron Age. These fields were for arable and mixed farming. It's the inland south-west area between the coastal plain and the hills that is the subject of George Williams's study. Perhaps surprisingly, this region does not seem to have had field systems in prehistoric times, but there is abundant evidence for human occupation there, and indeed in the two areas on either side of it. The main form this evidence takes is a dense scattering of small fortified settlements, known as 'ringworks'. These should not be confused with the much larger ring-forts of eastern England, such as the one at Borough Fen, whose diameter was 220 metres. The Dyfed ringworks were very much smaller: two examples we'll look at shortly, at Woodside and Dan-y-Coed, were just over sixty metres (say two hundred feet) across.

Larger fortified sites – in other words, true upland hill-forts – are found on higher land in the coastal south-west area and across most of the upland north and east area. With a sole exception, they do not occur in the area between these two. Both Williams and Cunliffe have taken this distribution of large and small sites to indicate that there was a complex social system. Cunliffe opts for 'clientage', while Williams prefers to see something more straightforwardly hierarchical,

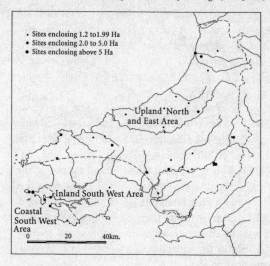

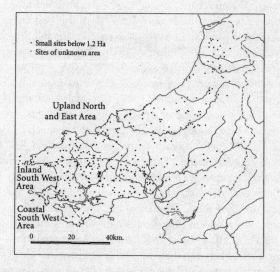

FIG 84 *The distribution of smaller (top) and larger (bottom) defended enclosures in Dyfed.*

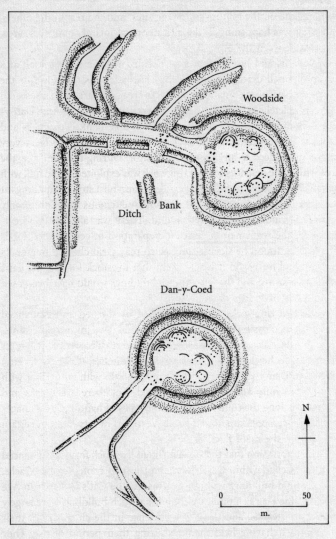

FIG 85   *Two Iron Age ringworks of the Llawhaden group of small defended enclosures, Dyfed. The excavated gullies and post-holes of roundhouses and storage buildings are shown within the two ringwork enclosures.*

with an elite on the hilltops in the big sites, and the rest in the others. But what was happening in the all-important inland south-west area, the area between the other two?

Williams and his collaborators decided to take a close look at a group of small defended sites in the Llawhaden district, towards the northern part of the inland south-west area. As part of this research they completely excavated two ringworks at Woodside and Dan-y-Coed. Both are strongly fortified, with double-banked defences and protected entranceways. Although small, they must have been very impressive indeed to any prehistoric visitor. During the Iron Age, the area within the defences of each ringwork was exploited to the full, with no fewer than seven roundhouses and six four-post storage buildings at the time of their greatest extent. Despite meticulous excavation, only two corn-grinding querns were found. There was also no good evidence for the regular or large-scale preparation of cereal-based foods (this can be found by sieving soil, which may yield charred fragments of grain and husk). So it would seem that livestock formed the basis of the two farms, and that the storage buildings would have been used to hold hay or fodder of some sort.

The two ringworks were approached by ditched and embanked funnel-shaped earthworks, which again would have impressed visitors, although they also put me strongly in mind of the sort of structures one needs to herd animals. The outworks (ditches, walls, banks etc.) leading to Dan-y-Coed are surely as much to do with animals as with people: not only are they funnel-shaped, but there are breaks and diversions along the route. These are the types of handling or management arrangements you need if you have to sort or separate-out certain beasts from the main flock or herd.

The impression that these are fortified livestock farms is enhanced by the presence within the defences not just of roofed storage racks, but of round buildings without hearths. At the Cat's Water Iron Age village in the Flag Fen basin we found that such buildings were largely devoid of artefacts, and there was evidence in the chemistry of their soil for their having held manure during their period of use. They were probably animal byres, yet to judge from their ground-plans they were indistinguishable from houses. I can't imagine why hay or fodder stores would be held centrally unless there were animals nearby. I would suggest that the byres within the ringworks only held key or vulnerable livestock: perhaps next season's replacement ewes, or the best breeding rams.

George Williams's study was published in 1984, at a time when the archaeological world was gladly adopting concepts such as social and settlement hierarchies. As we saw earlier, when we discussed the so-called Wessex Culture, Big Men, elites, power and competition were becoming the rage in academic circles.[54] This received a huge push from an exhibition of beautiful Bronze Age objects, entitled Symbols of Power at the Time of Stonehenge, held at the National Museum of Antiquities in Edinburgh in 1985.

Power, control and elites affected all archaeological thought, and Williams's study was no exception; but like all first-rate work it provided enough objective information to allow alternative explanations. Williams considered all the excavated ringworks of the inland south-west area, such as Woodside and Dan-y-Coed, to be high-status sites. That of itself is odd. It smacks of too many chiefs and not enough Indians. I also find it strange to have two supposedly high-status sites next door to each other. Lower-status sites (which have to exist for others to be 'high') had not yet been found when the report was being written, but it was suggested that they were probably like the open or less heavily defended sites found in the coastal south-west area, and indeed further along the north side of the Severn estuary.[55] Today, however, we would see these sites as far from lowly. In terms of artefacts alone they are 'richer' than their counterparts further inland. I regard them as not so much richer, as different.

So were the ringworks of high status? I don't believe they were. True, they were impressively fortified, which does suggest a certain amount of rustling and local conflict across an open, unfenced landscape. But I see no problems in that – it was the local pattern. Similarly, one doesn't need to explain the presence of larger sites in the regions on either side of the central zone in terms of social status. Although society undoubtedly became more highly structured as the Iron Age progressed, there's no overwhelming evidence for an all-powerful controlling elite, even at massive sites such as Danebury. And we have shown that most claims for such an elite in Later Neolithic and Bronze Age times don't stand up to close scrutiny either.

EARLY BRONZE AGE

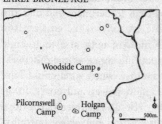

6TH AND 5TH CENTURIES BC

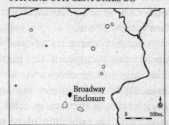

4TH AND 3RD CENTURIES BC

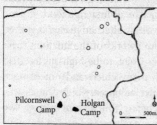

2ND CENTURY BC – 1ST CENTURY AD

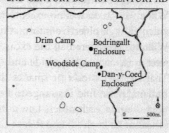

ROMANO-BRITISH OCCUPATION

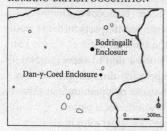

LATE ROMAN AND
POST-ROMAN OCCUPATION

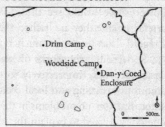

FIG 86   *The sequence of occupation of sites within the Llawhaden group of small defended enclosures, Dyfed, from the Early Bronze Age to post-Roman times.*

If the presence of large enclosed sites doesn't automatically mean that there were princes or other powerful leaders to build and run them, then who did it? 'Nobody and everybody' is the answer: Iron Age societies were perfectly capable of motivating themselves to build and operate such places – it's slightly patronising to believe otherwise. The large hilltop enclosures of the south-western zone could have been places where local communities gathered for seasonal fairs or during times of stress and conflict. They also played a significant ritual role. So, in spirit and in many of the principles behind their operation they can be seen as the Iron Age equivalents of the much earlier tradition of causewayed enclosures.

One advantage of a regional survey that also includes excavation is that the various sites encountered can be accurately dated. This in turn allows a picture of the evolving landscape to be pieced together. That at Llawhaden had its origins in the Early Bronze Age; then there was a gap or hiatus – a phenomenon quite widely encountered in Wales – attributable perhaps to the climatic deterioration mentioned earlier. In the Iron Age we see a number of ringworks appear on the scene. Some continue, some don't. During the Roman period two continue to be used, and that at Dan-y-Coed acquires one of the new, fashionable Roman-style rectangular buildings. It was only after the collapse of the Romano-British way of life, during the so-called Dark Ages, that these small sites fell into disuse.

So, after this excursion into Dyfed, do I still believe that there was a split or 'clientage' economy in the south-western zone? On the whole I don't – but this is largely due to the passage of time. Eleven years have elapsed since Barry Cunliffe published the latest edition of his great work, and archaeology – especially Iron Age archaeology – has moved on from such broad-brush, overarching patterns of interpretation.

We're now approaching the final stages of our story. We've come a very long way, and have witnessed Ages of Ice, sea waters creeping towards the Channel, the first farmers, and the complexities – nay confusion – of Later Iron Age Britain. But is the tale about to end? I think not. For a start, the Roman occupation was just that: an occupation. It was a temporary presence, albeit an influential one. Personally

I like Barry Cunliffe's term, 'the Roman Interlude', which puts the entire episode in proper perspective.

It has long been recognised that the Roman presence in Britain was not a replacement of one culture by another. Indeed, as we'll shortly discover, in certain parts of the country that presence went largely unacknowledged. So archaeologists always use the slightly long-winded term 'Romano-British' (universally abbreviated to 'R-B') when referring to the *culture* of Britain between AD 43 and AD 410 – the date usually taken as the end of the Roman Interlude. By 'culture' I mean everything: society, towns, roads, pottery, burials, temples – the lot. The time period itself, those 367 years, is the Roman period, and not the 'Romano-British period'.

The Post-Roman Iron Age of Britain, otherwise known (in England at least) as the Saxon period, had much in common with what had gone before. We saw this clearly in George Williams's study of continuity and change in south-west Wales, where Romano-British influence was slight. But nowhere is this sense of continuity with an earlier age more apparent than across the Irish Sea. So that's where I'll begin the next chapter: towards the capital of the ancient kingdom of Ulster.

CHAPTER TWELVE

Glimpses of Vanished Ways
(the Later Iron Age:
200 BC–AD 43, and After)

THE CAMERA TILTED, rocked and swooped as it followed the French navy destroyer forcing her way through the massive seas of the south Pacific. Up on deck, sailors leaning over the rails shook their heads and pointed in disbelief as three tiny inflatable dinghies whizzed about the great warship, like so many gadflies around a bull's tail.

I was working in Canada in the early 1970s when Greenpeace began their first campaigns. To many people in the older generation, including some of the academics who worked with me at the museum and at the University in Toronto, these 'stunts' seemed laughable and unnecessarily dangerous. But they worked. The warships, and the politicians who controlled them, were hopelessly outgunned, and people were forced to think about the environment and how we were abusing it.

Time passed, and slowly attitudes changed. My personal introduction into the politics of the real world happened around 1985. The President of the Prehistoric Society was Geoff Wainwright, Chief Archaeologist at English Heritage, and I was on the society's governing council. One evening in the pub after a meeting I suggested to him that the society ought somehow to become more involved with the big conservation issues of the day. It was just a casual thought, no more. The next morning he phoned me to say that I'd got the job. 'What job?' I asked. The newly created job of Conservation

Coordinator for the Prehistoric Society. I should have kept my mouth shut.

In those days scholarly societies such as ours were loath to get openly involved with politics. We saw our role more as expert witnesses or objective, disinterested observers; but if the truth be told, we were well-versed in the art of discreetly pulling strings behind the scenes. By the mid-eighties, however, it was time to come clean and declare that we weren't *just* a learned society: we cared deeply about the prehistoric sites we studied, and we would fight to protect them.

The Prehistoric Society became involved in all manner of issues, from small planning disputes to the really big ones. The biggest by far concerned Navan Fort, the ancient capital of the Kingdom of Ulster. I remember the phone call from Jim Mallory of Queen's University, Belfast: the site was going to be destroyed by a deep stone quarry, and we *must* do something to help. At the time I was excavating at Etton, which was also about to be destroyed by a gravel quarry, so I had a certain amount of sympathy for him – but then, nobody was particularly concerned about the destruction of our six-thousand-year-old religious centre, so why should I get upset about something half its age? I was also beginning to get cynical about the world's lack of interest in archaeology and the physical remains of the prehistoric past. But Jim's powerful feelings of anger, frustration and his sheer pig-headed refusal to give in finally had their effect, and I was won over. I like to think we did our bit to support him and his colleagues Tom McNeill and Richard Warner in their fight, but it was them, and the group they put together, the Friends of Navan, who deserve the credit for the eventual victory.

The operators of the quarry next to the site wanted to expand, and ultimately to engulf it. A planning inquiry was convened in 1986. The Friends of Navan put a strong case, and we supported Barry Cunliffe, whose evidence left the inquiry in no doubt of the site's international importance. Despite this, the commissioner conducting the inquiry ruled that the quarry could not be halted. Then, the following year, 1987, the Secretary of State for Northern Ireland overruled the commissioner at the last minute, and the quarry, which now survives as a pool eighty feet deep, was stopped.

What was it about Navan that made it so very special? The archaeology was undoubtedly most remarkable, but it was more than that. The site was the focus of people's sense of place and identity. It was something to be proud of, and in the depths of their troubles, the people of Ulster needed positive things to show the world. It's worth bearing in mind that time heals. Archaeology isn't a tool of political propagandists alone. It can repair, revive and restore, and in the process soothe wounds and draw communities together.

To judge from its name, and its location on a hill, you'd be forgiven for supposing that Navan Fort was a hill-fort. You'd be wrong. All archaeological sites, like all human settlements, are as unique in their own special ways as the people who made and used them; but Navan seems to break all the accepted archaeological rules and practices. It's a remarkable one-off, and what makes it even more extraordinary is its history. It's as if we knew the name and family of the man who constructed Danebury two and a half millennia ago. Not only that, it's becoming increasingly apparent why the site was built in its unique form. This is one of those rare instances where it's possible to construct plausible links between the physical remains of something buried deep in the ground and the fragments of history, myth and legend that survive in the written record.* The later prehistory of Ireland is perhaps better described as proto-, or 'almost', prehistory, because it doesn't depend on archaeology alone: there are good written accounts of long-lived oral traditions that apply to the period. The earliest actual manuscripts to survive date to the eleventh century AD, but the words themselves were generally put on paper a long time after the events they describe, probably in the seventh century or later. By this time Christianity was well established, and had become both a powerful influence and a source of censorship. So the written records have to be read with some care. Even so, two distinct pre-Christian traditions can be discerned.

The latest, and best-known, was centred on the kingdom of Connacht (Connaught) in the west and centre of Ireland. In the fourth century AD the most famous king of Connacht, Niall of the Nine

---

* At the time of writing (May 2002) the site, and its excellent visitor centre, is not open to the public. It's the old story of easy capital funding and no revenue support afterwards. The operators are desperately keen to reopen, but the finances aren't yet in place.

Hostages, made himself High King of all Ireland, establishing a dynasty which reigned until the eleventh century. The point from which Niall ruled, the Mound of the Hostages, twenty miles north-west of Dublin, has been excavated, and has been shown to be a Neolithic passage grave, broadly similar to, if a little later than, those of the Brú na Bóinne. It forms part of a multi-period complex of earthworks five kilometres east of the river Boyne, and actually lies within a later hill-fort, Ráth na Ri, whose ramparts alter course to respect it.[2] One site immediately outside the hill-fort, the Rath of the Synods, revealed timber buildings dating to the first to third centuries AD, and these may well have had something to do with Niall or his precursors.

It's worth reflecting that the events summarised above took place during the Roman occupation of mainland Britain.[3] It is, however, possible to take Irish proto-history back even further, using the written-down oral tradition. During this earlier stage Ulster, rather than Connacht and Tara, was the dominant power, and the finest literary sources of information are the heroic poems of the Ulster Cycle, of which the best-known is *The Cattle Raid of Cooley*.[4] The poem describes how the mythical hero Cú Chulainn helps Conchobar, king of Ulster, who was based at his capital Emain Macha (pronounced Owain Maha), exact retribution for a cattle raid carried out by warriors from the rival power of Connacht, to the south. Scholars are agreed that *The Cattle Raid of Cooley* refers to events in pre-Christian Ireland.[5] There can also be no doubt that Emain Macha was the capital of the Ulster kings. And it just so happens that it is also the Irish name for Navan Fort.

It's impossible to escape a strong sense of *déjà vu* when discussing the archaeology of Navan. Although the site is Iron Age, it's rather like Stonehenge, or the tombs of the Brú na Bóinne, in that everything is deeply steeped in layer after layer of symbolism, ritual and ideology. As a prehistorian, albeit a non-Celtic prehistorian, I feel oddly at home there, because there are so many recurrent themes. It's a world I'm familiar with, even if I don't altogether understand it.

Navan is a complex site, which was superbly excavated between 1961 and 1971 by Dudley Waterman, in one of the classic digs of the later twentieth century.[6] Sadly Waterman died in 1979, but the full report, which is as fine as the dig it represents, was prepared for publication by Chris Lynn and appeared in print in 1997.[7] Like Tara,

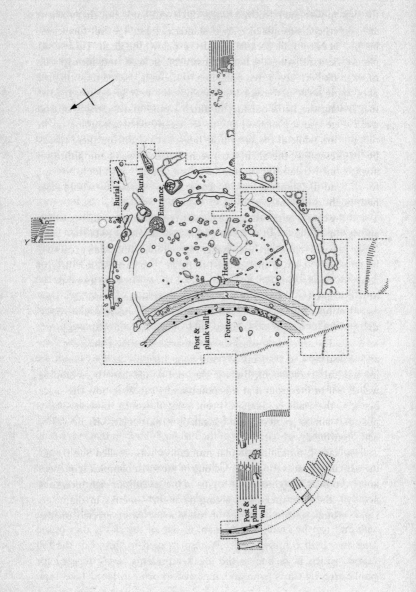

the hilltop was encircled by a single ditch and bank, but that's where any superficial resemblance to a standard Iron Age hill-fort ends, because at Navan the bank is outside, or below, the ditch. This would plainly be a ridiculous way to construct defences, and instead one must think back some two millennia to the great henge monuments, like Avebury, which were enclosed in this fashion. It has been suggested that having the bank outside the ditch would allow crowds on the inner edge and top of the bank to see clearly what was going on in the interior, while at the same time being excluded from these rituals by the presence of the ditch in between. It was a type of amphitheatre: a ceremonial theatre in the round where people could look but not touch. And the audience – or the congregation perhaps – would have had much to look at.

At the centre of the enclosure were two circular monuments which appear for all the world to be 'bog standard' Bronze Age barrows, the larger one with a mound, the smaller one without. But when excavated by Dudley Waterman they proved to be neither barrows nor Bronze Age. The smaller ring-ditch, known as Site A, enclosed the foundations of two round buildings. The first looked exactly like an ordinary Iron Age farmhouse, except that it had been rebuilt no less than three times; we saw in the last chapter that such frequent rebuilding was unusual. The second house was erected some time later than the first, and unusually had two sets of outer concentric walls. This seems an impractical arrangement, because the roof would have been sloping well down to the ground at this point, and I can't see how the space between the walls could have been used. It would, however, have provided almost perfect sound insulation, particularly if the cavity had been filled with straw.

The larger, mounded circular monument was labelled Site B, and its meticulous excavation revealed one of the most complex sequences known to British prehistory. It begins in the seventh or eighth century BC, with the construction of a ring-ditch forty metres in diameter. Later, around 200 BC, a series of roundhouses were erected on the

FIG 87   Navan Fort, County Armagh. Plan of the foundations of two roundhouses found within the smaller ring-ditch, known as Site A. Probably Late Iron Age.

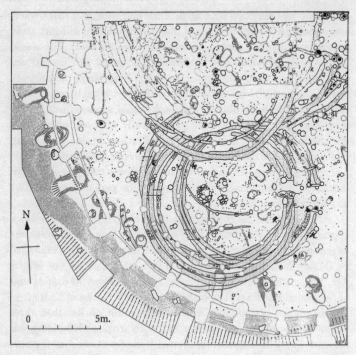

FIG 88   *Navan Fort, County Armagh. Plan of Iron Age features found below the cairn and mound of Site B. The 'nests' of small ring-gullies comprise the remains of eight episodes of rebuilding a 'royal' roundhouse.*

same spot, all (like those of Site A) with front doors which face eastwards – the most common orientation of Iron Age roundhouses. This multiple rebuilding happened no fewer than eight times, and on each occasion the position of the structure was slightly altered. Presumably this was deliberate, and would have marked each rebuild from those that preceded it. Like the roundhouses of Site A, those of Site B superficially resemble contemporary farmhouses, but their repeated rebuilding is most unusual – as was the discovery of the skull of a Barbary ape in one of the wall trenches. Presumably the poor monkey was an exotic mascot of some sort. It has been suggested that these frequently renewed buildings were in effect the royal palace.

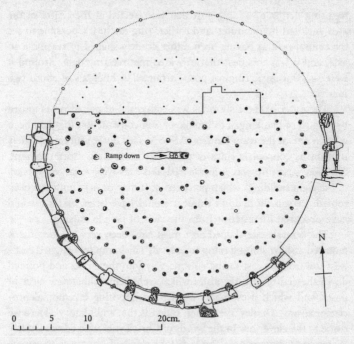

Ramp down

N

0   5   10   20cm.

FIG 89   *In 94 BC the roundhouses at Navan Fort Site B were suddenly replaced by a large timber structure comprising an outer wall of paired posts joined by planks, and five concentric rings of posts centred on a big post, which was erected using a ramp. This ramp is aligned on the entrance, which is reached via three parallel rows of posts, an arrangement called by the excavator, Dudley Waterman, an 'ambulatory'.*

The next phase marks a ritualised and formalised transition, or hardening, from wood to stone. The site abruptly ceases to be a dwelling, more probably the formal or ceremonial dwelling of a king, and becomes translated into something more permanent, just as we saw at Stonehenge, Avebury and elsewhere. I hesitate to use the term 'the realm of the ancestors' once again, but it's hard to think of another phrase that sums up what could have been happening. The abrupt beginning of the new phase has been dated to the year 94 BC by tree-ring dating of a large post that was erected at the centre of the area enclosed by the outer, and earlier, ring-ditch. It's possible to see the central post as having been rather crudely shaped to resemble an axle, and it was this post that provided the tree-ring date. Around it were six concentric rings of posts, arranged at intervals of about two metres.

The outer of these six rings was composed of paired posts joined by lengths of planking, a technique of wall construction that had been used in one of the roundhouses of Site A. This outer wall immediately transforms concentric rings of posts into something more coherent. The new structure was a formalised and massively enlarged version of the eight buildings which preceded it. It may or may not have been roofed. Personally, I don't think it would have been, as that would have obscured the interior from the view of people outside.

The central, axle-shaped post must have been very tall, because it required a short sloping ramp to erect it. This ramp was aligned east–west towards the east-facing entranceway into the circle, and pointed down the centre of three aisles which were kept deliberately clear of posts, and which presumably formed an imposing ceremonial processional way. Dudley Waterman called it the 'ambulatory'. Here we come to the clever bit. In the words of Chris Lynn, who edited Dudley Waterman's excavation: 'The structure was laid out so as to equate the spaces between the rings with the spaces between the posts of the outer wall, and the width of each of the three aisles [of the ambulatory].'[8] That was no mean intellectual achievement, and again it harks back to the far earlier concerns for precision in alignment and layout that we saw, for example, at Newgrange. I don't believe that this concern for measurement was important in its own right, but it served to link the construction to the order of things in the natural world. It was a way of giving the structure a legitimacy that passed beyond the hand of living man.

Shortly after their erection, the timbers were buried beneath a stone cairn which was constructed like slices of brie cheese, in wedges or segments that radiated out from the central post. This has to be seen as deliberate, and the wheel symbolism, which we've already encountered, is obvious. The transition from wood to stone was given additional emphasis by the burning down of the posts after the cairn had been finished. We know this was done because the posts survive as pipe-like voids that run up through the loose stonework. Then, as a final gesture which can be matched precisely in dozens, perhaps hundreds, of Neolithic and Bronze Age ceremonial and burial monuments right across the British Isles, the whole thing was buried under a thick mound, or barrow, of earth.[9] That latest deposit still survived two metres thick when Waterman began his excavations. This final act consigns and then seals the site firmly within the ground below men's feet. It is now an integral part of the world of the ancestors, which by the Iron Age was becoming a heroic world, peopled by legendary warriors. *The Cattle Raid of Cooley* gives us a glimpse of this world. They are extraordinary words from a vanished age:

> Sualtaim went to Emain, and cried out to the men of Ulster: 'Men have been murdered, women stolen, cattle plundered!' He gave his first cry from the slope of the enclosure, his second beside the fort, and the third cry from the Mound of the Hostages inside Emain itself.

I think it is significant that the various round buildings at Navan use the commonest, eastward-facing alignment for their entrances. This suggests that these were never actual dwellings of a rich, powerful person or family. Instead they were intended to symbolise the houses of ordinary people, but transferred by their scale and location into quite another, transcending dimension. These, then, were structures that people could have identified with as they performed their various rituals and ceremonies. It must have been an extraordinary, awe-inspiring and mysterious place.

Normally speaking, prehistorians can only work with evidence produced from the soil. Certainly we may flesh this data out with information provided by anthropology, but it's almost impossible to give identity and human expression to the rituals and practices we can only observe from traces in the ground. Mike Parker Pearson and Ramilisonina came as close as anyone to achieving this, but even they couldn't provide that lost, but all-important historical fuse that links us to the past and explosively fires the imagination. That passage from *The Cattle Raid of Cooley* does it for me, but I would also like to know how contemporary Iron Age society might have interpreted the structure at Navan. Plainly it would be absurd then to take those views and apply them wholesale to Avebury or Stonehenge over two thousand years earlier, but they would provide us with examples of how people *might* have explained their religious and ceremonial constructions. The stories from the world of the Irish Iron Age help us imagine how prehistoric people might have thought.

Chris Lynn has made a special study of the symbolism and imagery surrounding Navan. He considers that the huge, post-built structure that was erected in 94 BC was a bruidne, or magic hostelry; these have been likened to an Iron Age Valhalla. According to the Irish epics the heroes were lavishly feasted in the bruidne, then at the end of the meal it was burnt down around them, and they were immolated where they sat.

The problem with the magic bruidne hypothesis is that no human bones were recovered during Dudley Waterman's excavations. But myths and legends do not have to be observed literally to retain their symbolic meaning – the non-alcoholic wine served by some Christian denominations at Holy Communion is a good example of this. It's also surely natural for people to seek alternatives to the sacrifice of their own kith and kin, and this is what Chris Lynn suggested happened at Tara. He observed that much of the stone used in the construction of the cairn laid around the posts was weathered, and could have been re-used or taken from another, older monument. The excavators suggested that it might have come from the demolition of nearby field walls.

Chris Lynn had a far better idea. He suggested that it came from the demolition of a Neolithic chambered tomb. We know that Iron Age people in Ireland respected and revered these earlier monuments. Indeed, as we've seen, the focus of the later High King of all Ireland, Niall's, domain was the Neolithic Mound of the Hostages at Tara. If their own traditions didn't extend back that far (which I consider most improbable), then they would surely have been familiar with the interior of these monuments, and would have known what they stood for simply by observing the bones within them. Chris Lynn suggests that an earlier, probably much revered, cairn was substituted for living people. Of course it's hard to prove a negative, such as demolition, archaeologically, but I find his suggestion convincing. It fits with a richly imaginative pattern of thought that sees symbols on the skyline and vitality in trees.

However one regards the idea of substitution, the interpretation of the post-built structure as a bruidne, or some other form of ceremonial centre, is perhaps less controversial. I mentioned the care with which the circles of posts and the ambulatory were laid out, but it seems that there was more to it even than that. If one includes, as one surely must, the central post and the outer post-and-plank walls, the structure then consists of seven circular zones or partitions, separated by posts. Chris Lynn points out that where bruidne are described, as in Maeve's palace at Cruachain, Bricriu's hostel or Conchobor's house of the Craebruad in Emain Macha, they have seven – the magic number – compartments. Normally I tend to steer clear of archaeological number games, which generally prove nothing of any real significance, but in this instance I find the simplicity very persuasive.

There can be little doubt that the post-built structure was intended for ritual, and the symbolic imagery of a wheel is attractive. Chris Lynn has examined the archaeological evidence closely, and it was he who pointed out the similarity of the round central post to an axle. It possesses an axed L-shaped socket, which could have been used to secure ropes to drag the timber into place. But it also resembles the socket required by a lynchpin, which prevents the hub of a wheel from coming off the end of the axle.

Other details of the structure give clues as to how it may have been used. The clay that was dug from out of the post-holes was roughly spread on the ground. It wasn't heaped, so although some attempt had been made to even it out, it hadn't been trampled or beaten down to form a proper floor. In fact there was no good evidence for a floor as such. The ground had been left uneven, and there were no signs of a central hearth. So I think we can safely rule out any suggestion that it had once been a massive, palace-sized domestic building with a vast roof. All the evidence points to temporary or short-term use as an open-air ceremonial structure. Again, this is consistent with the bruidne idea.

How would this ceremonial feast in a magic hostelry fit with the ideas of Mike Parker Pearson and Ramilisonina? In my view, very well. For a start, we have a transition from wood to stone, or from the living to the dead, and thence to the realm of the ancestors. We also have a clear consciousness, if not memory, of past rituals and the monuments that commemorate them. All are ideas fundamental to the workings of a ritual landscape. I simply cannot believe that these concepts arose, fully formed and afresh. We now know, moreover, that there was no such thing as a Celtic 'invasion' of Britain or Ireland, so the ideology lying behind these myths must in all essentials be home-grown.

It seems to me entirely reasonable to suggest that legends such as the bruidne and the magic final feast could have been used as the basis for ceremonies in places as far apart as Mainland Orkney, Woodhenge, Durrington Walls, or even Stonehenge during its earlier, pre-stone phases. Perhaps completely different stories were celebrated, but I would be surprised if they did not have certain key themes in common, such as the wood–stone metamorphosis, death and transfiguration, and so forth. This is why I believe that Navan Fort, or Emain Macha, was the latest of a very long line of circular religious sites that had been, even in the Iron Age, peculiar to the British Isles for some three millennia.

Having dwelt at length on Navan, I cannot conclude without observing that the nearby city of Armagh is today the seat of both the Catholic and the Anglican Primates of All Ireland. Can this importance be attributed only to the one-time presence there of St Patrick? Maybe – but one must then ask why that remarkable person himself chose to base his work of conversion at Armagh? Certain places have roots that go back a very long way, but the ideas, stories, myths and legends that make these places so special have origins that can ultimately be traced through the Neolithic period, and possibly even earlier. If archaeology teaches us anything, it is that thoughts and ideas can outlive the most permanent of monuments.

Sometime in the late 1980s or early nineties, I received a phone call from Barry Raftery. Barry is one of Europe's leading archaeologists, and among other things he has made a speciality of wetland archaeology. A few years previously his team had discovered a magnificent prehistoric timber trackway, made from large split oak planks, at Corlea, in the bogs of the Irish midlands. To cut a long story short,

Barry wanted me to come to County Galway and split a huge tree in half with wooden wedges for a video film they were making, which was to be shown in the new visitor centre being built at Corlea.

People don't offer me a free trip to Ireland very often, so I leapt at the chance. But would that tree split? Would it hell! Fast-grown Irish oak normally splits more readily than oak from eastern England, but the local woodyard didn't possess any timber of prehistoric quality. In fact, there isn't much knotless, straight-grained wood of that size anywhere now. In prehistoric times, the selection of trees to be used for making large split planks was itself a matter of considerable experience and skill. I won't say precisely what we did off-camera to induce some movement in the gnarled old trunk, but it was crude and effective, and I gather from those who've seen it that the film works well.

In Britain, most of the peat that is dug from the ground is used as the basic ingredient for garden compost. It's an industry that has caused, and is causing, great harm both to the environment and to the many archaeological sites that lie in its path. But in Ireland, where the heavy rainfall feeds huge areas of blanket bog that cover great tracts of the midlands, there are two threats. Traditionally, peat (or turf, as it's called in Ireland) was dug by hand, stacked and dried, then burnt in the hearth. In County Carlow, where my own family come from, there is a tradition of domestic belt-driven wheeled bellows which fan the normally slow-lighting peat into a white-hot glowing lump.

Domestic-scale exploitation is one thing, but commercial extraction for gardens, or far worse, to fuel power stations, is quite another, and the great bogs of the Irish midlands have been planed down by as much as three metres by huge machines which devour and mill to a fluffy texture everything in their paths – including anything and everything archaeological. In the past there was no way of evaluating the extent of the destruction, because little was known about the concentration or distribution of ancient sites buried within the bogs. Complete ignorance is a wonderful way of stifling research. 'Why do you need the money?' the bureaucrat demands. 'Because we think something is out there,' the archaeologist replies. 'But can you *prove* it?' 'Well, er . . . no.' So nothing happens. Somehow the vicious circle has to be broken, and that's what happened in 1984, when timbers of a wooden roadway or togher, as they are called in Ireland, were found in Corlea bog, County Longford. This togher had been known about by local people for generations, and was simply referred to as the 'Danes Road'. Then a timber from the 1984 exposure of the road was sent to a radiocarbon laboratory, where it was firmly dated to the Iron Age.

An archaeological project was immediately set up. Under Barry Raftery's direction, it started work in 1985, and finished in 1991. A huge and beautifully illustrated report appeared in 1996.[10] The report gives details of fifty-nine toghers from just one bog of about three hundred acres (125 hectares). Since 1991, further work in the area has raised the score to 108, and the neighbouring bog of Derryoghil has revealed another seventy-six. These figures should be set against the fact that there are fifty-four thousand acres (twenty-two thousand hectares) of bog in County Longford, of which just over half (29,600 acres) are being milled for peat. In his report, Barry wonders whether the official response to the archaeological emergency has been too little and too late, and I share his fears to an extent. But at least something *has* been done – and done very well, too.

The toghers investigated in the campaign of 1985–91 date from most periods, although there are few later medieval or more recent examples, as these levels had been milled away by 1985. But with the exception of a small length of the great Iron Age trackway preserved near the visitor centre (which is famed for its superb video film), all fifty-nine of the trackways revealed in the six-year campaign have been obliterated.

These figures illustrate all too clearly the extent of archaeological destruction that has been happening recently. I can understand why people get upset about the destruction of plants and furry creatures, but at least these can be replanted, moved, or encouraged to breed elsewhere. Each archaeological site is unique, and in ninety-nine out of a hundred cases they cannot be moved. Yet only now, at 'five minutes to midnight', as Barry puts it, is officialdom showing a belated interest, and even that is underfunded.

Most of the toghers of Corlea bog consist of woven, hurdle-like plates, laid end to end and secured into position, usually on a foundation of brushwood. Often the surface on which people walked was

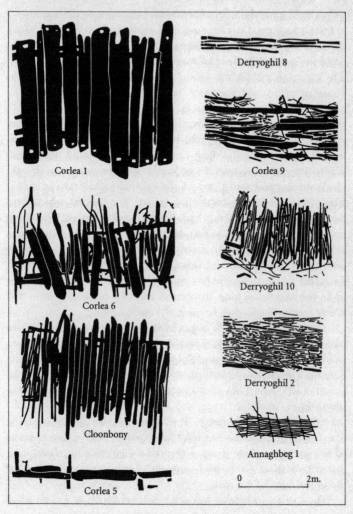

FIG 90   *The main varieties of paths and trackways found in the Mountdillon bogs of County Longford.*

simply built up on bundles of brushwood arranged on the bog surface to form a pathway. Only four so-called 'corduroy' trackways, in which planks or logs are laid railway-sleeper-fashion on rail-like foundations, occur in Corlea bog; the most magnificent is the great Iron Age roadway known to archaeology internationally as Corlea 1. It's an exceptional structure, and the story behind its building and ephemeral period of use is most remarkable.

Tree-ring dating shows it was built in the year 148 BC, which takes it into that time known as proto-history where, as we saw at Navan, the observations of archaeology can be given individuality and a fresh life by the written record. It's of 'corduroy' construction, with oak-plank sleepers laid across two parallel rails, about 1.10 to 1.30 metres apart, which lie directly on the bog surface. The sleepers, which form the surface of the roadway, either have notches or mortice holes cut in the ends, through or against which pegs are driven to secure them in place. Most sleepers were about six to eight inches (fifteen to twenty centimetres) thick, and the roadway was about ten feet to eleven feet six inches (three to 3.5 metres) wide. Corlea 1 is so far known to be up to two kilometres long. Its size and careful construction show that it was clearly intended to be used by wheeled traffic.

This is a major feat of engineering. Split oak planks of this size take a great deal of lifting, especially in boggy conditions. Two men would be needed to lift a single plank, and if it had to be carried any distance I would like to have at least three men with me. The planks are all of oak, which has always been regarded as the finest constructional timber available. It was also a wood that had potent symbolic power, as we saw at Seahenge. The timber used at Corlea had to be of excellent quality, or it wouldn't have split so readily, and in terms of raw materials alone it was a stupendous undertaking. Barry estimated that about a thousand cartloads of oak were needed just for the upper layer of the road.

The Corlea 1 roadway was unique. It was built at a time when

FIG 91 *A typical stretch of the great Iron Age (148 BC) road in Corlea bog, County Longford, showing the road's 'corduroy' surface, built of split oak-plank sleepers (above) and two parallel rail-like runners (below). The gap (1.80 metres wide) where five sleepers are missing, is original.*

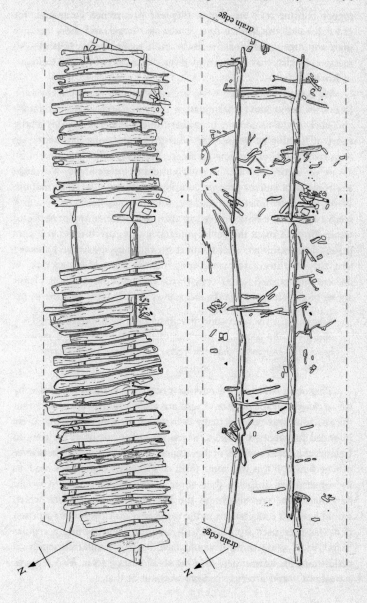

togher construction was not a frequent occurrence compared, for example, with the Bronze Age. It was also larger and more massive than any other prehistoric roadway built in Britain or Ireland – so massive, in fact, that Barry entitled his discussion of it 'The Colossus of Roads'.[11]

We saw at Navan that when archaeology and literature combine forces, the results can be illuminating. But when archaeology, literature and study of the ancient environment come together, the result is little short of floodlight. Despite the widespread and long-term drainage required by the peat-milling machines, Corlea is still a bog, and bogs, as we've seen, are rich in environmental information. Normally environmental studies provide additional, but expected, information. Wells and water holes, for example, often contain seeds or pollen of reeds or aquatic plants – which in turn demonstrate the presence of water. But at Corlea the environmental studies produced a real surprise. Close examination of the peat surrounding the timbers showed that almost immediately after construction, the underlying rails or bearers were pushed into the bog by the weight of the great oak planks above them. Then the planks themselves rapidly sank into the mire.

> All in all, the track may only have been used for a limited period and given the good ... condition of the oak timbers, this may have been not more than ten years, *but perhaps much shorter.*[12] [Italics added.]

This observation by the environmental specialists is supported by the archaeological evidence. There are good grounds to believe that the roadway was never actually completed. Further, although surely intended for wheeled vehicles, which we know existed at the time in Ireland, the upper surfaces of the sleepers show no evidence whatsoever of wheel-ruts. If this was some form of special or high-status road, as its construction suggests, then some of the vehicles using it would have had iron tyres similar to the Holme Pierrepont wheel, which would have left indentations in the wood very quickly. I'd be surprised if it was ever used by vehicles on anything approaching a regular basis. And I don't think it would have been particularly friendly to pedestrians for long either. As a means of getting from A to B it was a washout – and a very expensive washout at that.

Clearly, all is not straightforward with the Corlea colossus. Are we looking here at one of those seemingly pointless activities that was carried out 'for its own sake' – something Mike Pitts observed at the Sanctuary within the Avebury ritual landscape – constructed as a means of bringing people together? As at Navan Fort, it's hard to avoid distinct sensations of *déjà vu*. Could it have been that an individual was simply showing off the extent to which he or she could coerce others into carrying out expensive, pointless tasks? Was it, in other words, a major public work intended to glorify one person – rather like the Sun King's palace at Versailles – that went badly wrong? Or did it go 'wrong'? Fortunately the year in question, 148 BC, is just within the earliest of proto-historic times, and there are literary sources that might help us solve these mysteries.

The study of early Irish literature relevant to Corlea was carried out by Dáithí Ó hÓgáin. One might expect such a report to be brief – it deals, after all, with a very remote period – but it isn't. Our glimpse into the Iron Age is provided by an eighth- or ninth-century AD source, which is based on a much earlier story. The account, known as *The Wooing of Étaíne*, is part of the Ulster Cycle, and tells of the heroic tasks imposed on the mythical personage Midhir by the Tara king Eochaidh Aireamh. These great works included planting forests, covering a plain with rushes, and the building of a causeway over a marsh called Móin Lámhraighe. The causeway is the only one of the tasks whose construction is described in any detail. Dáithí Ó hÓgáin quotes the key passage. Midhir has assembled a huge crowd of men in the marsh:

> They all made one mound of their clothes, and Midhir went onto that mound. A forest with its trunks and roots – they placed that at the bottom of the causeway. Midhir was standing up and encouraging the multitude on every side. You would think that below him all the men of the world were raising a tumult. After that, clay and gravel and stones are placed on the marsh.[13]

Later we read that the road was never satisfactorily completed because Midhir resented having his works checked over by the king's steward. This lack of use fits what we know about Corlea 1. But was the togher across the marsh named Móin Lámhraighe the same road, or merely one like it? The main problem lies in the name, which doesn't occur anywhere in the marshland of County Longford; but Dáithí Ó hÓgáin believes that the two are possibly the same road. Barry Raftery, who has also examined the literature, seems rather more convinced.

What lay behind the construction of this magnificent but strangely enigmatic structure? Barry places it within an Irish context. The Iron Age in Ireland is still poorly understood, and there is a surprising dearth of evidence until the last two centuries or so before Christ, when we see a resurgence of activity. Navan was a case in point, but there are others: the Dorsey, for example, a series of huge linear earthworks in south Armagh, Leitrim and Monaghan, plus others in Cork and Lough Kinale, just forty kilometres north of Corlea. These were all major communal undertakings. Are we seeing here the emergence of more powerful tribal leaders – the elite we have already encountered across the Irish Sea? Quite possibly, but we should always bear in mind that people are capable of motivating themselves, and that stories such as *The Wooing of Étaíne* do not have to be taken at face value: one can write about heroes, kings, mythical champions and so forth without actually living in such a heroic society oneself. They can be about aspiration and motivation as much as anything.

Barry also considers there's a possibility that the sudden appearance of a large, sophisticated 'corduroy' road could owe something to influence from Germany, where roads closely similar to Corlea 1 are known at about this time. As we saw in the so-called Arras Culture, this presents few problems. Barry certainly doesn't suggest any invasions, and the idea of building something foreign and exotic adds to the impression that this engineering project was the result of somebody powerful exerting strong personal influence. But was it?

By now it must be apparent that I'm not happy with the 'controlling elite' theory as the universal explanation for the stranger events of British and Irish prehistory. It's too simple – just as in earlier decades a hypothetical invasion was believed to account for all inexplicable phenomena. As I noted previously, controlling elites had undoubtedly emerged by 148 BC in both Britain and Ireland, but could they have masterminded this great work? Or indeed, would they have wanted to? I have my doubts. I also doubt whether any community in a boggy area with a long history of constructing toghers successfully would have made so many basic errors. Surely they would have known that such flimsy foundations would never have spread the heavy load of the great logs? I can't accept that they were so stupid.

It seems to me far more likely that they knew perfectly well what they were doing. The road was built in the certain knowledge that it would vanish into the bogs. In short, it was an enormous, a gigantic, votive offering – and who knows, maybe the work was coordinated by a great leader. We've seen how trackways had strong symbolic significance in Bronze and Iron Age times. So, of course, did wheels. Perhaps Corlea is a physical expression of that mythical journey. The texts tell us of its construction within a mythical context. What they don't tell us, because they couldn't have known it, is that the stories they were recounting had roots which extend well back into prehistory.

Is there any evidence to support such an interpretation? One of the aspects of Corlea 1 that struck me as odd was the absence of any valuable objects or items that could be seen as votive offerings. There were several fragments of wooden tubs or buckets, a wood trough, a mallet and a wooden plough (or ard) head. I concede that the plough head is peculiar (in both senses of the word), but the other items could all have been debris left behind by the workforce. Then suddenly it struck me: you don't *need* to place votive offerings around something that is itself an enormous offering. But there was one exception which may, I think, prove the rule.

It was found in Cutting 2, towards the centre of the main area of excavation, and it consisted of several carefully fashioned, well-finished and finely jointed pieces of oak, with some ash. They were lying directly below the sleepers, and Barry Raftery has suggested that they form part of a light cart, or trap. I think he is right, and I also think that the deposition of a vehicle beneath and within the roadway is not just coincidental. It's like the wheel and axle fragments at Flag Fen – just one of the many ingredients of a rich symbolic mixture.

In several instances sleepers had been removed from the trackway and there was evidence for fires close by. In one area in Cutting 4, at a spot where the route crossed a pond-like wet depression, there were at least four layers of timber. A jumble of sleepers and other large timbers lay along the trackway, which was plainly unfinished. Not

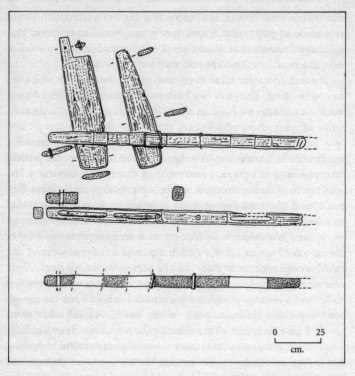

0   25

cm.

FIG 92   *Part of a possible Iron Age (148 BC) cart found in the foundations of the great timber trackway at Corlea, County Longford.*

even four-wheel-drive carts could have got through. If Corlea 1 was indeed intended to be used by wheeled vehicles, then the removal of just a single sleeper would effectively block it. Yet this was done repeatedly. It's almost as if the people who constructed this vast road-way wanted to ensure that no human traffic was ever to use it.

So, was this colossal undertaking unfinished or somehow unsuc-cessful? I don't think it was – at least, not to the people who built it. The work of construction was the rationale behind Corlea 1. True, it was a road between two higher and drier areas of ground, but it was never intended to take traffic in the normal sense. It was a huge communal project not for the glory of a Big Man, but for the good of the community and the ancestors who watched over them. You could say that self-interest motivated the workforce, but it was not the self-interest of a single person, male or female, nor of an elite. The work was done to superlatively high standards because the workforce wanted to do it that way. Anything less, and the shades of their forebears would not have approved.

One should try not to let one's own personal interests dominate a book of this sort, but I've been interested in wet sites and matters watery for a good reason. These are the places where survival of the evidence is so outstanding that it's possible to recreate an extraordinarily vivid impression of life in the distant past. Most of the wet sites we have visited so far have been roads, causeways or trackways of one sort or another. None have been places where people actually lived. I want now to turn to the British equivalents of the famous lake dwellings of Switzerland. These mainly occur in Scotland and Ireland, and are known as 'crannogs'. For some reason there were very few crannogs built in Iron Age Ireland, and none have been extensively excavated.[14] So we must go back across the North Channel, that narrow but very ancient stretch of sea which divides Ireland from Britain.

Barry Cunliffe considered south-western Scotland to be characterised by 'strongly defended homesteads' in the Iron Age. That was the way the majority of us thought about the area in 1991, but now this certainty is beginning to wobble. Crannogs were just one example of such fortified dwellings; another was the dryland defended homesteads, which include some of the most extraordinary stone structures in prehistoric northern Europe. They occur in a variety of forms, with names such as duns, brochs, forts, island duns, galleried duns and wheelhouses.

The best-known type of defended homestead was the broch, examples of which are found throughout the Western Isles, Orkney and Shetland and on neighbouring parts of the mainland. They were massively built, windowless, circular stone towers, and the best-preserved of them, the Broch of Mousa in the Shetlands, still stands an astonishing 13.3 metres high. Their main characteristic was a hugely strong hollow dry-stone wall, through which ran stairs. The interior

FIG 93   *Cutaway view of Dun Carloway broch, Isle of Lewis, in the Late Iron Age (about 100 BC). The stairway (not shown) ran up the wide cavity between the inner and outer walls. Note the 'guard chamber' to the right of the single entrance, the small storage 'cells' within the walls on the ground floor, and the galleries within the walls. (Drawing by Alan Braby.)*

of the tower was most probably roofed, and the wooden supports for an upper floor, or floors, were lodged on an internal ledge known as a scarcement. Each floor was reached by a narrow entranceway through the inner 'skin' of the wall. The cavity within the wall contained small cell-like compartments and galleries at each floor level, and there was always a substantial 'guard chamber' at ground level close to the front door. This was the sole entrance, and it led into a corridor which passed straight through the wall into the interior.

It used to be thought that brochs were places of refuge, but there is now sufficient information from carefully excavated sites to suggest that they were places of permanent domestic habitation. The excavators of Dun Vulan, on South Uist in the Western Isles, Mike Parker Pearson and Niall Sharples, are in no doubt that brochs were never built to deter serious or sustained attack, and see them as monumental houses rather than small forts. Their defences were simply too weak and ill-thought-out: the rough walls could readily be climbed by determined attackers; the roof was unprotected from such assault; the entranceway arrangement lacked any form of outer protection, so the door could easily have been rammed; and it was impossible to get access to the top of the wall. Perhaps worst of all, there were no windows or slots through which to observe what was going on outside.

Radiocarbon dates suggest that the first true brochs were built from 400 to 200 BC, and they continued to be occupied throughout the Scottish Late Iron Age (AD 300–900). It was once believed that brochs were introduced to Scotland by people from outside, but this is no longer generally accepted.[15] Instead they are thought to have developed from an existing tradition of thick-walled round buildings which were being constructed in the region from at least 800 BC.

Another type of homestead was in use at the same time as the tower broch. These buildings, known as wheelhouses, were also circular, but there their resemblance to brochs ends. For a start, they were completely undefended, and had just a single storey. They were often partly set into the ground, and the roof was carried on a series of radiating stone piers which divided the periphery of the building into a series of spoke-like 'cells'. But in common with brochs, they do seem to have been permanently occupied farmsteads.

The report on the broch at Dun Vulan discusses the relationship between brochs and wheelhouses.[16] The authors are not convinced that brochs were necessarily built and inhabited by a powerful controlling elite, while the wheelhouses were for those of lesser status, in part because the difference in numbers seems relatively slight. On South

FIG 94 *A view of life inside the Late Iron Age wheelhouse at Cnip on the Isle of Lewis (about 300 BC). The building was single-storey, and gets its name from the radiating spoke-like piers which supported the roof. The 'cells' between the piers were used for a variety of purposes: for sleeping, storage and for small household shrines. (Drawing by Alan Braby.)*

Uist there are seventeen brochs and twenty-eight wheelhouse settlements (comprising one to three wheelhouses each). So, if it was an elite, it was hardly an elite elite.[17] The wheelhouse settlements tended to be situated on better-quality arable land, while brochs were placed on more marginal sites, which often coincided with medieval and later boundaries, and were better suited to grazing.

Was this a class-based society, akin to Barry Cunliffe's 'clientage economy' of the south-western zone? Quite possibly. But we should also bear in mind that the people who lived in the brochs probably performed a purely local function, more in keeping perhaps with the manorial system of medieval England – or something even more parish pump. Their role was to control disputes over land and grazing, both within the community and outside it. So the brochs probably do represent the emergence of ranking, but within an otherwise classless society. They certainly didn't constitute anything approaching a hierarchical or centralised authority.

It should be borne in mind that tower-like fortified houses were often constructed in regions, such as the bleak borderlands of late-medieval Northumberland, where raiding and rustling were endemic. Very often the raids are part of a social structure which allows for vendettas and long-lived family feuds. It's quite possible, indeed probable, that the brochs were constructed in such circumstances. In a raid, a broch would look imposing to any attackers, and would provide a perfectly adequate short-term defence.

The occurrence of brochs along later boundaries, and the fact that they were occupied and in use until well into the first millennium AD, demonstrates clearly that the heritage of prehistory played a very important role in the development of society in north and western Scotland. Of course it wasn't a simple, straightforward role – the Vikings and the English saw to that – but it was a major component, probably *the* major component, in what was to become modern Scotland. Much the same could probably be said for Ireland as well.

Brochs and duns (a towerless equivalent) were quite frequently placed on islands within lakes. This was presumably done for defence, but also because these situations looked very imposing – which brings us back to crannogs.

If I were to be banished to some desert crannog, and was able to take only five archaeological books with me, I'd choose the latest edition of Barry Cunliffe's *Iron Age Communities in Britain*, then something by Richard Bradley, probably his *Archaeology of Natural Places*. Then I'd take three books that were written a long time ago:

W.G. Wood-Martin's *The Lake Dwellings of Ireland* (1886), Robert Munro's *Ancient Scottish Lake Dwellings or Crannogs* (1882), and Arthur Bulleid and H. St George Gray's two-volume excavation report *The Glastonbury Lake Villages* (1911 and 1917). The illustrations in all three

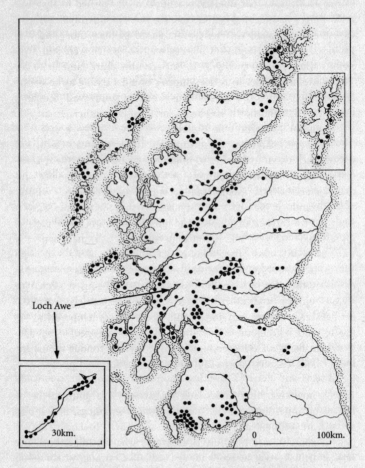

FIG 95   *The distribution of crannogs in Scotland, as known from the archaeological literature. The inset shows how a survey campaign of controlled diving can reveal a large number of new sites in just one location.*

of these older books are wonderful, and their authors knew how to write. They bring the past to life.

Scotland has been blessed by having produced such a remarkable man as Robert Munro. Like his near-contemporary compatriot Arthur Conan Doyle, he was a medical practitioner who turned his hand to other things – and with equal success. His book is superbly illustrated, with maps and plans that were years ahead of their time, and it is peppered with illustrations of objects, many of which were still mysterious when Munro was writing, but are now more familiar to us. This allows the reader to revise Munro's original dating as he or she goes along. Munro did most of his work in south-west Scotland, while the Highland north was being surveyed by another remarkable Victorian, the Reverend Odo Blundell.[18]

There are many crannogs throughout the large area of Scotland where lakes occur naturally. It might be thought that these landscapes would be safe from most of the ill-effects of drainage and modern agricultural intensification; but a recent research project which examined the effects of drainage on sixteen crannogs known from the researches of Munro and others in south-west Scotland found that fourteen had effectively vanished. All that remained were potsherds and other solid objects. The remaining two were still there, but only just. Even more alarmingly, it was found that crannogs that were still within lakes were also being subjected to serious erosion and other damage. This is desperately worrying, because crannogs are very important. Like their contemporaries, the brochs and wheelhouses, they were places where people actually lived, but being waterlogged, much of the organic residue of ancient life – wood, basketry, fabrics and so forth – has survived pretty much intact.

It's now clear that underwater archaeology[19] is going to be of increasing importance in the investigation of crannogs, and major surveys are taking place in Lochs Awe and Tay.[20] In Loch Tay, Dr Nick Dixon and a team of divers excavated what is still, I think, the earliest artificial islet in Scotland, at Oakbank Crannog, where a pile was radiocarbon-dated to 835–655 BC. Radiocarbon dates indicate that most of the Scottish crannogs were rather later than their Irish equivalents, which start just before 2000 BC. The Scottish ones begin, like

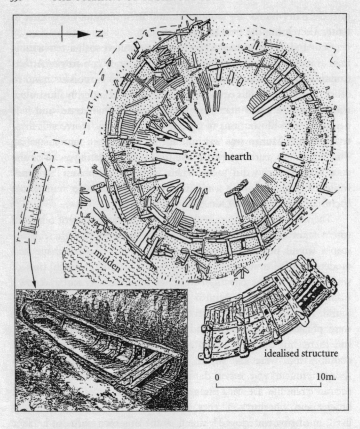

hearth

midden

idealised structure

0   10m.

FIG 96   *A composite plan of Robert Munro's nineteenth-century excavations at Buiston crannog. Munro did not realise that Buiston was a complex multi-phased site which started life in AD 10–120. The plan shown by him includes the foundations of a roundhouse, and probably belongs to the fourth and final phase of occupation (AD 605–665).*

the heavily walled roundhouses of the north, around 800 BC, and continue in use until as late as AD 1200.

There's no such thing as a 'typical' Scottish crannog, but they were generally placed near the edges of lochs, and were built up from a mixture of rocks and wooden piles which were usually driven in to fence and reinforce the edges. In many instances they were reached by a stone or wooden walkway, and often too they would have a landing stage of some sort for boats – usually logboats, which are sometimes found on excavated sites. Many crannogs have complex histories which modern excavation has been able to reveal. At Buiston, in south-west Scotland near Kilmarnock, for instance, Munro, who actually dug the higher layers, believed the site to be of just one phase. However, recent re-excavation has shown it was built up in four distinct phases, starting with a primary 'core' mound made up of alternative layers of turves and brushwood in AD 10–120.[21] There are then two phases of round-house construction and occupation (AD 310–450) before the site was abandoned, only to be reoccupied again around AD 605–665.

I have always been fascinated by the extent to which prehistory affects more recent times, and the crannogs newly revealed by the diving survey in Loch Tay are a case in point. If we combine the position of the crannogs off the lakeshore with the distribution of sheilings (shelters used by herdsmen) and upland ring forts, we see a pattern in which all appear to be evenly spaced along the valley sides, with crannogs at the bottom, sheilings on the higher ground and ring forts on the lower land to the north. If next we add the position of farm boundaries prior to the agricultural Improvements of the eighteenth century, we see that the landscape is parcelled up at right-angles to the loch, much as we saw in the Bronze Age fens, and presumably for the same reasons. The ring forts mark the edges of this self-contained landscape to the north. Then each farm has an area of open upland grazing, of its own upland grazing, and of its own corn land. It's a simple arrangement, but judging by its extraordinary longevity (Oak-bank Crannog dates to the late Bronze Age), it worked well.

In late 1893 the now-famous Dr Robert Munro wrote a letter to a young medical student who was nearing qualification as a doctor. The student was Arthur Bulleid, and in March of the previous year he had come across the Iron Age 'lake village' at Glastonbury, one of the greatest discoveries of British archaeology. Naturally he wanted to tell the world about it. This is what the experienced Scottish scholar, who was then President Elect of the British Association, advised the younger man:

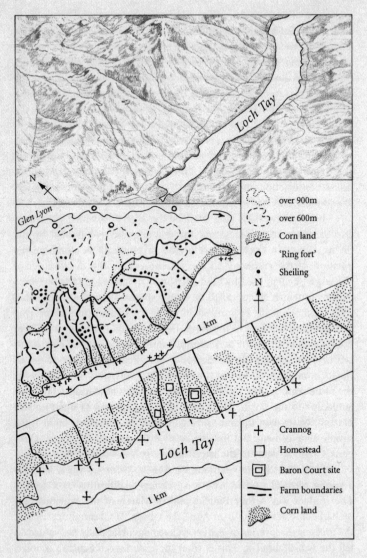

Legend (top):
- over 900m
- over 600m
- Corn land
- ○ 'Ring fort'
- ● Sheiling

Legend (bottom):
- + Crannog
- □ Homestead
- ⊡ Baron Court site
- – – Farm boundaries
- Corn land

FIG 97   *Three maps showing the way in which the hinterland behind each lakeside crannog may have been organised. The landscape is bounded by Loch*

The dangerous rock is to attempt to explain everything. The words late Celtic, pre and post-Roman Gauls or Britons or Saxons should not appear in your paper. Describe exactly what you found, where found and in what circumstances, and you will start [on] a firm basis.[22]

Sound advice.

In 1895 Bulleid discovered the other two 'lake villages' of the Somerset Levels, at Meare. He excavated them between 1909 and 1932, combining archaeology with being the general practitioner of the north Somerset mining village of Midsomer Norton – despite its pretty name, a dull and rather unattractive place at the turn of the last century. Bulleid was something of a workaholic. He often arrived on site at 5 a.m., and wouldn't leave until eight in the evening. When not digging he worried about his personal finances and his wife Annie's apparently extravagant ways. But he was much liked, and he was a very good archaeologist.

Many of his digs, and the subsequent reports, were undertaken in collaboration with a pioneer full-time professional archaeologist, Harold St George Gray. Gray had been assistant to the man who is generally regarded as the father of modern archaeology in Britain, Lieutenant General Pitt Rivers, who in 1880 inherited the estate of Cranborne Chase, in Dorset. On succession to the property, he added 'Pitt Rivers' to his existing name which was already pretty imposing: Augustus Henry Lane Fox. His surveys and excavations at Cranborne Chase were the first scientific attempts to understand an important archaeological landscape.[23] It undoubtedly helped that he had the time and money to carry out this work properly.

As well as the two volumes of the Glastonbury Lake Village Report by Bulleid and Gray with me on my desert crannog, I'd probably try to sneak in a copy of John Coles and Stephen Minnitt's reworking of their data.[24] There were many aspects of Glastonbury which simply

Tay to the south and ring forts in Glen Lyon to the north. Sheilings are herdsmen's shelters. The farm boundaries are based on a pre-Improvement survey by Farquharson in 1769.

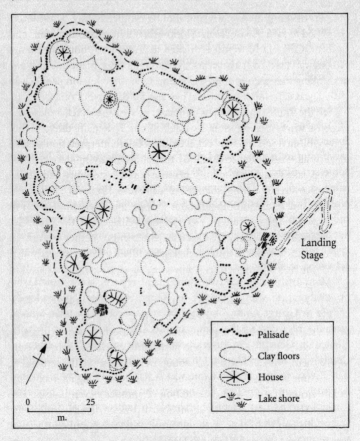

Landing
Stage

Palisade
Clay floors
House
Lake shore

N

0   25
    m.

FIG 98   *Ground plan of Glastonbury 'lake village' at its largest development in its late phase, about 125 BC. Roundhouses and one oval house are shown by the probable pattern of their roof rafters. The hook-shaped wooden structure to the east is a landing stage for boats.*

didn't make sense in the light of what we know now, and an in-depth review was urgently needed. This they did, layer by clay layer.

Bulleid spotted the site by a series of mounds which covered a farmer's field. When he excavated them he found they were composed of layers of clay mined on dryland about a kilometre away. These layers were used to form house floors, working areas, hearth foundations and so forth. Coles and Minnitt estimated that at least a thousand tonnes of clay was used over the years. Bulleid and Gray made the mistake of thinking that each mound was a house, so their version of the 'lake village' was extremely crowded. They also failed to work out the phasing of the site's development properly. It's easy to pick holes in a piece of work so long after its publication. The main thing is that they published in sufficient detail to allow the reinterpretation to take place at all. Sadly, one couldn't say that about many modern reports.

The 'lake village' name stuck because both Glastonbury and Meare were discovered at a time when the recently revealed Swiss lake villages were causing a sensation throughout Europe, and everyone wanted to find one for themselves. In fact the 'lake villages' of the Somerset Levels are better described as 'marsh settlements', as they weren't in lakes at all, but on slightly higher ground in a watery, reed-filled environment, with numerous willows and alder trees growing around the fringes.

The reworking of Bulleid and Gray's data has shown that the 'lake village' had a life of about two hundred years, with small beginnings of five to six houses and a population of around fifty people living in an area cleared of trees. Soon the population grew, and more people joined them. Further houses were built. By about 150 BC the settlement had become a village, but it continued growing, reaching its maximum extent around 125 BC with the addition of another eleven houses. The original settlement had held about four extended family groups. By 125 BC this had risen to fourteen or fifteen, and the population to two hundred – just under half that of Danebury. Then, after 100 BC, things began to go downhill. Flooding became a problem, and the site was abandoned by 50 BC.

The site was surrounded by a low stockade or fence, and there was a landing stage for boats. Perhaps the most important aspect of the new research is that it shows how large areas within prehistoric settlements were left unfenced and open, perhaps being used to stock animals at certain times of the year. Shortly we'll see how this also applied to the earliest places that can be thought of as towns (we must be careful not to impose modern ideas of what constitutes a town or

FIG 99   *A bird's-eye view of Glastonbury 'lake village' at its maximum, around 125 BC (drawing by Jane Brayne).*

village onto the past, where available space was not necessarily a constraint).

Both Glastonbury and the two lake villages at Meare lay close by the river Brue, which John Coles has suggested may have been a boundary between two known Iron Age tribes, the Durotriges, whose territory covered south-east Somerset and Dorset, and the Dobunni of north-east Somerset and Gloucestershire. There is slight, but only slight, evidence for an elite, but by this time society had become

FIG 100   *A selection of Iron Age pottery vessels from the Glastonbury lake village decorated with distinctive swirling designs (250–50 BC).*

markedly more hierarchical than in the Early Iron Age, so I would be surprised if powerful people were not present, at least latterly. Certainly the slow growth and humble origins of the Glastonbury lake village don't suggest anything other than settlement by a small group of people going about their own business.

How did these places operate? I think we can rule out a pattern like that of the crannogs, which were closely integrated into a complex and relatively small-scale system of lakeside arable and upland pasture. The trouble is that most of the evidence we seek is probably hidden beneath the peats of the Levels. If the 'lake villages' were indeed boundary settlements, then defence was clearly not an important consideration. Instead we should think more in terms of meetings and informal assembly at agreed neutral spots on the border. This fits better with the wealth of craft activities found at all three sites, and also with the evidence for trade and exchange. So commerce, rather than confrontation, would explain their roles satisfactorily. John Coles's suggestion that they could have served as border market villages seems very sensible to me.

The wealth of finds from Glastonbury included objects that represented every craft, from fragments of wooden looms to metal-working, wood-working, cooking, farming and even parlour games (bone dice and a dice box). Smashed pottery lay everywhere: Coles and Minnitt reckon that around fifty thousand vessels were used at Glastonbury. Most were plain, but some of the finer wares (sometimes made from clays brought in from as far away as Cornwall) were decorated. These pots were superb. The designs are restless: they seem to swirl and move, and have an Art Nouveau feel to them. They are examples of what has come to be known as Early Celtic art, a form which many consider reached its peak in the British Isles in the two centuries before the Roman Conquest, although it continued to develop and flourish in Ireland and Scotland much later.

I don't want to revisit the problem of the Celts and who they were, because I honestly don't think it matters much. But Celtic art is something else. It rises above time and knowledge, and speaks directly to our emotions. So let's keep the name, which has acquired a resonance of its own, just as we let the 'lake villages' remain in Somerset. But we should always be aware that Celtic art is in fact Iron Age art – and none the worse for that. We should also remember that only durable objects have survived, and most of them in burials and dredged from rivers and other wet places. It's the same story: the old rites were still surviving. We must assume that most of the fine objects that grace our museums were either votive offerings or were buried to accompany their owners into the next world.

Celtic art has generally been studied as an archaeological topic – in effect, as an artefact.[25] It has been classified and sub-classified into different styles which have been given dates of greater or lesser reliability. I don't have the space to discuss each of the main styles and how they developed – instead I refer the reader to the British Museum, which has the finest collections of Celtic art in the world.

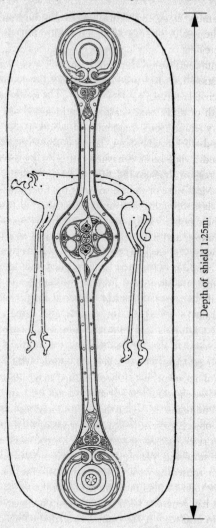

Depth of shield 1.25m.

FIG 101 *Ceremonial Iron Age shield dredged from the river Witham near Lincoln. Second century* BC.

It has produced a variety of publications on the subject, of which the clearest and best is by the excavator of the Arras burials of east Yorkshire, Dr Ian Stead.[26]

For present purposes I shall focus on just two objects: a shield and a mirror. Both are in bronze, and date to the second century BC and the early first century AD respectively. The workmanship of the artist/craftsmen who produced these two masterpieces simply takes one's breath away. So do the designs, which never appear slapdash, but which are seldom balanced in the conventional sense of the word. It's this off-centredness, this eccentricity (to use the word in its literal sense) which helps to give the art its heart-stopping impact and fluidity.

The Witham shield was found in the river Witham, just outside Lincoln, and may even have come from the Fiskerton causeway, with which it is broadly contemporary. What survives is a bronze facing for a wood- or leather-backed ceremonial shield 1.25 metres long. The centre of the shield is dominated by an applied and decorated central 'spine' with a grotesque animal head at the centre and two roundels at each end. What gives the shield a special magic has in fact disappeared: all that's left is a faint outline and some rivet-holes. It consists of a superbly stylised boar with long legs, a curly tail and very piggy snout. There is also no doubt about the animal's gender.

I could stare at the intricacy, balance and deliberate imbalance of the design on the back of the Holcombe mirror for hours. The mirror is a most extraordinary object, found in an Iron Age pit below a Romano-British villa near Uplyme, Devon, in 1970. A few years after its discovery the compass-work required to execute the complex design was worked out by a group including P.R. Lowery, a silversmith.[27] It's most impressive, and illustrates well the art that conceals art. There's one very odd thing about this mirror. If you turn this book upside down and look at the picture, not only does the design make better sense, it seems to have more movement, and the cascading motifs on each side start to resemble tresses of hair.[28] Now look at the elaborate moulding at the base of the handle. There can be no mistake: it's a grotesque face, whose eyes are formed by two studs of red glass. Apart from the inverted face, there's also other evidence to suggest that the mirror was meant to be hung upside down from the large loop at the

Mirror width 26cm.

FIG 102 *Back of a Late Iron Age bronze mirror found in a pit beneath a Romano-British villa at Holcombe, Devon. Early first century AD.*

end of the handle, and there can be no doubt that the decoration was executed with this in mind.

As I've said before, British and Irish prehistory is essentially a story of people, their families, their ancestors and their rural surroundings. Doubtless it wasn't always a tranquil tale: from earliest times there were raids, tribal feuds and so forth, but these have left a remarkably slight trace in the archaeological record. True, there is abundant evidence for elaborate fortification, but when these defensive places are

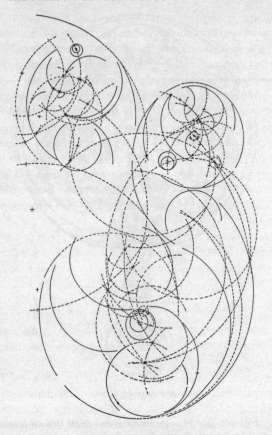

FIG 103   *Compass-work needed to execute the design on the right-hand side of the Holcombe mirror.*

examined closely, as we saw at Danebury, Maiden Castle and in Scotland, it becomes apparent that they are about more than just attack and defence. Instead we find a deep concern for display and for boundaries of all kinds, at the family, community and tribal levels of society.

Over large parts of lowland Britain there is very little evidence for even this style of defensive work. The landscape here is open, it possesses a good network of roads and tracks, and by the final centuries before the Roman Conquest it already had a history of peaceful development that extended back over three millennia. The population was rising during the Iron Age. In lowland Britain, with its good communications, prosperous agriculture and generally peaceful society, communities were getting larger. I believe that along with this growth in population there was also a tendency towards the development of a hierarchical class system, a process which I would see as gathering momentum after about 400 BC. By the last two centuries BC there is overwhelming evidence for the existence of elite classes – note that I don't say 'an elite class' – in central south and south-eastern Britain. A particularly good example was excavated by Tony Gregory at Fison Way, Thetford.[29]

Thetford is in the heart of Norfolk, in a landscape of gently rolling hills and fertile valleys. During most of the Iron Age it was characterised by the type of open, undefended settlements and field systems we saw, for example, at Cat's Water in the Flag Fen basin. I well remember being struck on my visit to the excavations by the way that the hill on which the site was located dominated the landscape, despite the ugly modern tin-clad factories nearby. What Tony discovered on the top of a hill on the outskirts of the modern town was quite extraordinary.

As we have seen so many times before, the site was a special place in the Bronze Age, when a small group of cremations was placed there. Then, between the fourth and first centuries BC, we see the appearance of a series of enclosures from which develops, probably in the first century BC, a single enclosure surrounding a roundhouse. In the first half of the first century AD this is replaced by something far more elaborate: a multiple ditched and embanked enclosure with a palisaded entranceway. The single house within it could possibly have had two storeys, constructed around a large, post-built, tower-like arrangement. Finally, in very early Roman times, around AD 60–70, the enclosure is massively enlarged and surrounded by no fewer than eight lines of hedging – something that to my knowledge is still unique in Britain.

Within this huge enclosure were three roundhouses, facing

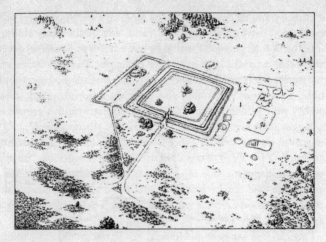

FIG 104   Bird's eye view of the 'royal' enclosure at Fison Way, Thetford, in the Roman Conquest period, about AD 40–60. (Drawing by Sue White.)

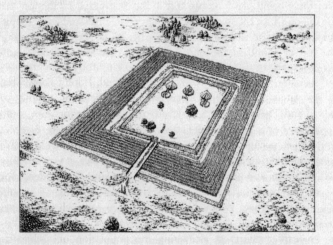

FIG 105   The 'royal' enclosure at Fison Way, Thetford, during its most developed phase (AD 60–80). Note the arrangement of eight lines of hedging between the inner and outer ditches. (Drawing by Sue White.)

FIG 106   *A suggested, and possibly unique, two-storeyed roundhouse at Fison Way, Thetford (AD 40–80). The central 'tower' is constructed around an inner circle of exceptionally large posts. (Drawing by Piers Millington-Wallace.)*

towards the entrance into the enclosure. The central house probably had two storeys. If this isn't a 'royal' compound, I don't know what is. The date coincides with Queen Boudica of the Iceni's revolt (AD 60/61), and Thetford lies at the heart of Icenian territory. So, could Fison Way be her palace? Quite possibly, but the final structures didn't reveal much occupation debris, so if she did live there she must have been neat and tidy. Even if it wasn't Boudica's palace, it was certainly a tribal centre, and provides us with almost unequivocal evidence for a rich and powerful ruling class by the latest Iron Age. I should add here that there is equally good evidence for such an elite at Camulodunum, or Colchester as it is known today.

My earlier efforts at estimating the population of prehistoric Britain may have been hit-and-miss, but I justify them on the grounds that it's impossible to form a sensible picture of the scale of prehistoric societies without having at least a vague notion of the numbers involved. But now, surely, there's such a wealth of extra evidence that I must be able to offer something better than a guess. Sadly not. There may be a welter of data, but it's mostly in the same places, and there are still huge gaps on the map. There is, though, a qualitative difference in the data. We know, for example, that the British tribesmen could offer stiff resistance to Julius Caesar on his two visits, and to the main Roman invasion of AD 43. We know too that the country was linked by roadways, and from pollen evidence and air photos that most parts of Britain were now inhabited, and the forest cover had been much reduced.

Would it be reasonable to suggest that the Late Iron Age population was comparable to that revealed in the Domesday Book of 1086? That survey showed a population in England of 1.5 million, and followed a period of steady growth.[30] By the time of the Black Death (1348) it had grown to about four million (incidentally, such a sharp increase would probably have been impossible in prehistoric times). Where does that leave us? I think Domesday provides us with an upper figure, and I would guess the Iron Age population of England to be around a million, and the population of the entire British Isles perhaps 1–1.5 million. It's a steep increase on the Bronze Age figure, but there were far more than a couple of centuries in which to achieve it.

The large tribal kingdoms of Britain had named leaders – something we also saw at Navan – but those chieftains ruled (if that's the right word) societies that had a long history of thinking for themselves, and I suspect that in most significant matters communities made their own decisions, much as they would like to do today. It would be tempting to suggest that the British love of democracy and instinctive distrust of all politicians is rooted in prehistory, but I shall try to resist it.

These processes of social evolution led naturally to the development of larger settlements, and eventually to the appearance of centres, at places such as Colchester and St Albans, that can be called towns. But it would be a great mistake to regard the pre-Roman towns – I'm tempted to style them 'towns' – of Britain as wattle-and-daub equivalents of their Roman counterparts. They were nothing of the sort.[31] Roman towns were fundamentally different: tightly packed buildings, gridiron layout, massive defences, town halls, squares, etc. etc.

Outside their walls, most Roman towns had large, sprawling informal settlements or *vici*, resembling perhaps a *favela* in Brazil or the townships of South Africa.[32] They were not, however, disorganised. Many contained thriving industries: the huge Nene valley Romano-British potteries, for example, whose products were traded across much of southern Britain, were mainly located outside the walls of the prosperous small town of Durobrivae (modern Water Newton), a few miles west of Peterborough on Ermine Street, or the A1 as it is today.[33] These extra-mural, informal settlements were the true continuation of what had gone before, and the 'main' or walled town was the Roman way of stamping their authority on the recalcitrant natives.

Roman cities were built on the sites of important centres of later Iron Age settlement, so if we look at the way these places developed it should give us an impression of what a Late Iron Age town might have looked like. I'll take as a case-study Verlamion, the British name for the Roman town of Verulamium, or St Albans, in Hertfordshire.

There has been a tendency in the past to view the Iron Age settlement through Roman eyes. Thus, excavation of the Roman remains provides evidence for Iron Age antecedents. Similarly, investigation of great earthwork defences proves them to be of Iron Age date, and immediately (and quite naturally) parallels are drawn with the walls of the later Roman city.[34] I suspect that this way of seeing British culture of the latest Iron Age as a poor cousin of the more civilised Romans says rather more about modern British attitudes to the past than it does about the Iron Age Britons. It would be a mistake to view Verlamion as an earlier, less organised, barbarian and perhaps somewhat shabbier version of a great Roman city. The Iron Age settlements at St Albans were large, sprawling affairs, in many ways closer in spirit to the continuous semi-urban sprawl that covers tracts of Hertfordshire and the Chiltern hills today. By treating Verlamion as Verulamium we are treating chalk as cheese.

Let's approach this as an archaeological problem, forgetting for a moment that there are historical accounts, and that we are nearing the time when prehistory becomes proto-history. The first thing we find is that Verlamion was positioned at the edge of the light, readily ploughed loam terrains of south-eastern England. This change in soil marks a natural boundary between regions, and it's at such neutral, boundary areas that centres of exchange and trade spring up, as we saw in the cases of Glastonbury and the two 'lake villages' at Meare. Verlamion was located in an area where there had been little or no Middle Iron Age settlement previously. We know that the Later Iron Age saw a further expansion of population, and many areas once considered marginal were taken into agriculture. Verlamion was founded in such newly-won farmland.

There has been a lot of archaeological activity along the Chiltern hills, and when this is combined with more recent aerial photographic surveys, it is very clear that Verlamion did not sit on its own, but was part of a huge spread of Later Iron Age settlement with a number of major concentrations. If we look at these main concentrations closely, we find they consist of many earthworks bounding smaller individual territories. There's also evidence for housing, much industry, various shrines, many cemeteries (often with high-status graves), an elite or upper class of richer people, and agriculture. It's the latter which is

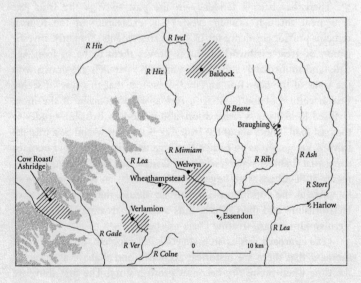

FIG 107   *Major Late Iron Age settlements in Hertfordshire and the north Chiltern hills.*

Three crouched Iron Age burials from Fengate, Peterborough, showing the variation encountered. The centre burial lies on its side in a natural position. The bones of the top burial are semi-articulated, suggesting that burial took place after a degree of decomposition. The lower burial has been referred to as a 'bag' or 'sack' burial, in which largely disarticulated bones were interred. It is possible that such burials represent the reburial of a long-dead ancestor.

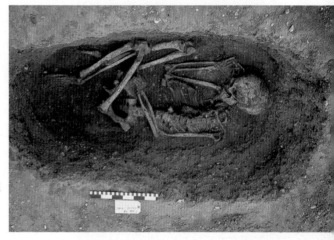

Two views of the reconstruction of a thatched Iron Age-style roundhouse at Fengate. The left-hand view shows the wooden structure of the house. The view above was taken some ten years later, when the thatch was replaced and a porch added to baffle the increasingly strong Fenland gales. Compare the steep angle of the thatched roof of this building with the flatter outline of the Fengate Bronze Age turfed structure.

A general view of the excavation of three Bronze Age roundhouses at Cladh Hallan, South Uist, by a team from Sheffield University under the direction of Dr Mike Parker Pearson. These buildings were constructed in a coastal dune landscape, known as 'machir'.

A close-up of one of the roundhouses at Cladh Hallan. The houses are remarkable for the inclusion of mummy-like burials that were already many generations old when reburied. This practice shows that the Bronze Age inhabitants of Cladh Hallan had a high regard for their ancestors and their influence on daily life.

ABOVE The late Peter Reynolds leads a team of two Dexter cows which have been trained to the plough by Jack Langley, who follows the team. The training took just two years, and the chalky ground being ploughed here is at the famous experimental Iron Age farm founded by Peter at Little Butser, Hampshire.

RIGHT The underside of an Iron Age log-boat from the River Witham at Fiskerton, Lincolnshire. The tool marks of hewing are still remarkably fresh, which suggests that the boat could only have been lightly used, if at all, before being abandoned, perhaps as an offering, alongside the post-built Fiskerton causeway.

An aerial view of the low stone walls that are so characteristic of the Bronze Age fields on Dartmoor, known as reaves. The Dartmoor Reaves are probably the best-preserved and most complete Bronze Age field system anywhere in Europe.

An aerial view of the Cat's Water Iron Age village or hamlet at Fengate, Peterborough. The darker marks are ditches of a Romano-British farm which followed the earlier settlement in the first and second centuries AD. The circular foundation trenches of Later Iron Age round-houses (350 BC–AD 40) can clearly be seen.

Excavation of the Fiskerton Iron Age causeway near Lincoln. The modern river flows behind the high bank to the left. The posts protruding above the surface penetrate a long way below the ground: an example excavated in 1981 was some five metres in length.

Reconstruction of the prehistoric Oakbank crannog at Loch Tay, Scotland. The crannog on which this superb reconstruction is based was excavated by a team of divers under the direction of Dr Nick Dixon.

The Iron Age Broch of Mousa, Shetland. This extraordinary building is the tallest surviving pre-Roman structure in Britain. Brochs are a feature of the Later Iron Age of both mainland and offshore north-western Scotland. They were built using mortarless drystone walling and feature double outside walls, which gave access to the higher floors.

surprising. Farms and fields stood alongside houses and industry in these sprawling settlements. With so many people around, it is not surprising that earlier traditions of building great earthworks to mark the bounds of one's estate were rekindled. And as time passed, doubtless too there was much competition for social status.

If the earthworks of Verlamion are plotted out, it immediately becomes apparent how much larger was the Iron Age *oppidum* than the Roman town.* What was life like within an *oppidum*? If they really were little more than concentrations of unusually intensive rural settlements plus a fair sprinkling of earthworks and industry, was social life within them still organised on the now-ancient rural pattern of family and kinship? This was a social pattern that tied together a rural economy which did not have a strong central, or established hierarchical, authority. A fascinating recent study suggests that, shortly before the arrival of the Roman army, some profound changes were just beginning to happen.[35] There is some evidence that in certain places society was beginning to reorganise itself in a way that was better suited to the new, more crowded, surroundings of the developing *oppida*.

It would be unfortunate if the reader gained the impression that the *oppida* were chaotic. They weren't. They were organised in an organic, rather than a planned fashion, and have been described as 'polyfocal settlements'. Modern London is a polyfocal settlement, with finance and commerce in the City, entertainment in the West End, government in Whitehall and religion around Westminster and Lambeth. There are also distinct residential areas and swallowed-up villages, such as Chelsea. This applied to Verlamion, where some areas were given over to farms, settlements and fields, while others were reserved for communal activities such as burial, religion and metalworking.

Excavations at the Iron Age and Roman King Harry Lane cemetery of Verulamium showed a decline through the Iron Age in the number of grave-goods buried with each body. This went hand in hand with a shift from graves that were placed within clearly bounded family

* The term *oppidum* (Latin for 'town') is generally used to describe the large, town-like settlements of Iron Age date in Britain and on the continent.

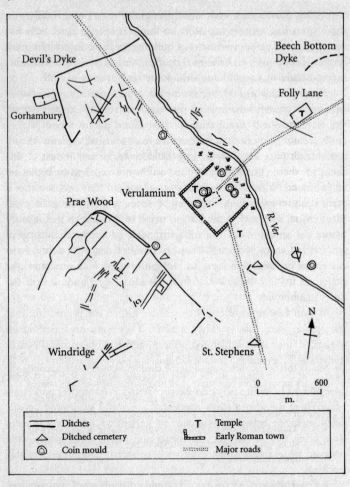

FIG 108 *Plan showing the location of the Roman town of Verulamium (St Albans, Hertfordshire), surrounded by the earthworks and other features of the Late Iron Age settlement of Verlamion.*

enclosures, to burials outside enclosures of any sort. Colin Haselgrove and Martin Millett have argued from this that the old rural network of strong social relationships was beginning to be replaced by a new pattern. People who moved into the *oppidum* could escape from the strong bonds of country life into something freer and with fewer obligations. Their social networks had become smaller, more flexible and more cosmopolitan. With these changes came greater social mobility, and the beginnings of an altogether different way of life.

I will not dwell for too long on the final years of the Iron Age in southern Britain. For a start, this would be unfair to the rest of the country, where the Iron Age continued to thrive, despite events in England and Wales; but I must also admit that it's not a story I particularly enjoy telling. It could be seen as an exciting time of lasting social upheaval, during which many of the benefits of Classical civilisation spread from the Mediterranean to northern Europe, a process that was to have enduring results for European culture. One can accept or reject that view, but any gain is always accompanied by pain, and in this instance the pain was closer to agony. I shall let Barry Cunliffe describe the background to the events that led up to the Roman Conquest of AD 43:

> Until the end of the second century BC it can fairly be said that Britain lay beyond the periphery of the Mediterranean world . . . But all this was to be changed in the closing decades of the second century BC when the Romans began to colonise the southern shores of Gaul [France]. The period, roughly 120–60 BC, saw the establishment of a stable Roman system in the south. During this time the rest of Gaul and southern Britain beyond became a periphery to that system and Britain began to experience the bow-wave effect of Romanisation.[36]

When I worked in Toronto, I would sometimes accompany my colleagues on their excavations in Ontario. I remember working on a native American cemetery of the so-called 'contact period', when imported trade goods would sometimes be buried as grave-goods. It was odd to see English words ('Made in Sheffield') stamped on iron axe-heads that had been placed in the ground to accompany their owner into the next world. In this instance the new, high-status object was being treated like any other valuable item. In other words, the existing social system was still able to adapt to the new situation as it developed. This applied in southern Britain too, but there was an added complicating factor, which we have just seen in the King Harry Lane cemetery. British society was also changing, and it's not always a straightforward matter to determine whether the changes we are witnessing during the British/Roman contact period were autogenic (i.e. self-generated and happening already), or were caused by outside influence.

A case in point concerns the hill-forts of central southern England, most of which, as we saw at Danebury, went out of regular use in Barry Cunliffe's more chronologically defined contact period (120– 60 BC). Why was this? Barry argues, quite reasonably, that this was a time of rapidly increasing trade and exchange with the continent, by way of ports on the Dorset coast at Poole Harbour and Hengistbury. The general trade routes were probably long-established, but the quantities and range of goods were greatly enlarged after the fall of southern Gaul. Exports from Britain included raw materials (metals, grain, hides) and slaves, while imports were mainly luxury goods: large quantities of wine (in amphorae), jewellery and other fine and pretty things. The close similarities with the economic exploitation of the British Empire are hard to avoid.

Was the abandonment of the hill-forts a result of the new trade? In other words, did local chieftains now obtain their fine display items and wine to be used in 'conspicuous consumption' at feasts by way of this new trade, and in the process abandon the old exchange networks which largely relied on hill-forts as centres of redistribution? Or did the hill-forts go out of use as part of a general drift towards larger settlements on the lower land of the river valleys, as we saw, for example, at Verlamion? My own feeling is that it takes more than wine and jewellery to cause such a profound change. I'm also suspicious about the real influence exerted by the tribal elites of Late Iron Age Britain. It seems to me that they were 'ruling' societies that had a long history of self-determination, which may explain why the final decades of the Iron Age, during Barry Cunliffe's 'Caesarean episode' (60–50 BC) and 'impact period' (50 BC–AD 43), were so very unstable. But it was a fickle instability, if such a thing is possible, confined to leaders and warriors rather than the bulk of the population, who got on with life much as before.

It's the bulk of the population that forms the concern of most archaeologists, because it's the remains of their houses, their farms, their bodies and their debris that we have to deal with. Most 'native' settlements of the early Roman period in southern Britain continue unchecked after AD 43. There's no evidence whatsoever for wholesale abandonment or 'scorched earth' retreat. Yet the Romans subsequently maintained a huge garrison, and Queen Boudica's revolt nearly threw them out. That speaks to me of resistance – instinctive resistance perhaps – at the 'bulk of the population' level.

No discussion of the final years of southern Britain as an independent territory can pass over two historical events. Julius Caesar explicitly mentions that people from Belgic Gaul (essentially Belgium and north-west France) raided the south coast of England and eventually settled there. In the past archaeologists have tried, predictably perhaps, to link these incomers with the appearance of new styles of pottery and issues of coinage. But there are problems, as there always will be when one tries to identify historical events in the archaeological record. Barry Cunliffe, who knows the archaeology of the region better than anyone from his excavations at Hengistbury, and most famously at Fishbourne, regards the Latin name for Winchester, Venta Belgarum ('the market of the Belgae'), as being most significant. He finds other evidence to support the idea that this 'invasion', which was on a limited scale, probably took place from the Solent.

It's not generally realised, but the Romans did not introduce coinage to Britain. The first British coins were minted in Kent around 100 BC. Thereafter there were many issues of coins by the various tribal kingdoms of southern Britain. They were based on originals from the Classical world and have the two sides – obverse and reverse – that are still familiar on today's coins. Their value is a debatable point in a pre-market economy where the entire population was illiterate, but gold and silver coins would always have been worth more than those struck in base metals. The actual role of these early coins is still a matter for speculation, although latterly social changes were happening so fast that the emergence of some sort of market economy seems probable. The designs on the coins are wild and wonderfully

FIG 109   *So-called 'Celtic' coins were minted in Britain after 100 BC. 1: Silver coin issued by the Corieltauvi, the tribe that occupied most of Lincolnshire; 2 and 3: Bronze and gold coins issued by Cunobelin ('CUN'), King of the Catuvellauni, from his tribal capital at Camulodunum ('CAM'), present-day Colchester.*

anarchic; far more interesting than their starchy Classical originals.

In the days when Latin was commonly taught, every schoolboy used to know that Julius Caesar made two visits to England in 55 and 54 BC. These two expeditions were essentially to gather intelligence, and should be seen as a part of his campaigns in Gaul. These began in 59 BC, and the attacks on Brittany in 57 BC effectively finished off the flourishing trade that then existed between Britain and the continent.

Caesar's first expedition to Britain in 55 BC involved ninety-eight transport ships carrying two legions (each of some ten thousand men), plus cavalry and many accompanying warships. The landing was resisted, and there were numerous subsequent skirmishes with the British. Eventually Caesar retreated back to Gaul, taking many hostages with him. It's fair to say his (substantial) nose had been bloodied.

The following year he did things on a much larger scale. This time there were eight hundred ships, transporting five legions and two thousand cavalry. This huge force met stiff resistance under the leadership of Cassivellaunus, leader of the Catuvellauni, a tribe centred on

Verlamion and parts of what is today called 'Mid-Anglia' (Hertford-shire and areas around). Caesar had a hard fight through Kent. He crossed the Thames into the Catuvellaunian heartland, and eventually British morale broke down and Cassivellaunus sued for peace. Caesar returned victorious, again with many hostages, but he had met fierce opposition, and was probably relieved to leave Britain with honour intact.

The political history of relations between Britain and Roman Gaul after the second visit of Caesar is complicated in the extreme. There were numerous issues of coinage, which provide us with very useful sources of information; and of course we are now fully within proto-history, verging indeed on history. Contacts with the continent grew stronger as Roman rule provided much-needed stability to Gaul. The Roman army was busy tackling Germany, and Britain, after Caesar's two bloody expeditions, was left alone. The result was prosperity and a measure of stability. Starting very early in the first years AD, a remarkable man called Cunobelin arose as High King of the Catuvel-launi, ruling his kingdom from a new capital he had conquered at Camulodunum (Colchester). His domain consisted of a confederation of tribes comprising most of East Anglia south of Norfolk (home of Boudica's Iceni), plus Kent and parts of southern England. His reign lasted over thirty years, which was no mean achievement – and very much longer than any of his contemporaries. He died sometime around AD 40, and instability returned. Doubtless this political uncer-tainty in southern Britain was a significant factor behind the Roman decision to invade three years later.

So far I may have given the impression that 'trade' between Britain and the continent in the final decades of the Iron Age tended to be exploitative – rather like trade in the time of the British Empire, when Britain sold expensive finished goods to the colonies, who provided low-cost raw materials in return. Certainly Britain did provide raw materials and slaves in exchange for wine and other high-status com-modities, but it wasn't quite as simple as that. In his excellent book on the Celts, Simon James describes how the contacts between Britain and mainland Europe were complex, and we in Britain provided ideas and political inspiration for our cousins across the Channel.[37]

The Druids are a case in point. By Late Iron Age times and into the first years AD, Roman authors record that the Druidic religion flourished in Britain, and had an important influence on the continent.[38] The Romans saw this as a threat, and after their conquest they made efforts to stamp it out, culminating in a battle and massacre on Anglesey in AD 59. We must assume that the Druid religion recorded by Roman authors arose out of the diverse regional and tribal religions of the Middle Iron Age. This process of amalgamation would have been hastened by the conquest of France (Gaul) by Julius Caesar between 60 and 50 BC. Conquest can provide a strong catalyst for political and other changes, and it would be a mistake to treat the Druidic religion of the half-centuries before and after Christ, as recorded by (hostile) Roman sources, as being wholly representative of what had gone before. Whatever else, the Druidism of the Caesarian period must have become highly politicised.

We're getting very close to the end, and I cannot allow an archaeological book to finish as if it were a political history of early kings and queens. I want to conclude my story with one final object, with a tale to tell. It's not very beautiful – in fact it's hideous. And it doesn't come from south-eastern England, the 'core area' of Late Iron Age times, although it probably has unsavoury connections with that area. It's made of iron, because nothing else would have been strong enough.

The object in question is a gang-chain, or set of slave neck-irons. It's not unique: others are known from the Catuvellaunian kingdom, where the trade in slaves seems to have been based. We cannot say what the social effects of this loathsome traffic were, but they were almost certainly severe. The market was provided by the Roman Empire, and tribes living around the periphery were willing to export people, presumably captives taken in local disputes, for the slave trade.

The slaves' neck-rings are for a gang of four, and they were found during the construction of an airfield runway at Llyn Cerrig Bach, Anglesey, in 1942 and 1943. They formed part of a large votive deposit that had been placed in a lake sometime in the first century BC.[39] The neck-rings are a horrible new element, but many of the other items provide links with more distant times and places, and will be familiar from elsewhere in this book: broken swords – one has actually been bent double; parts of harnesses, including several beautiful horse-bits, pieces taken from carts, and wheels; spearheads; a superbly decorated

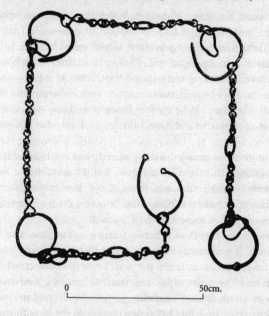

FIG 110   *A set of four neck-irons or slave shackles from a votive deposit in a lake at Llyn Cerrig Bach, Anglesey (first century BC).*

FIG 111   *The slaves' or captives' neck-irons from Llyn Cerrig Bach as they were probably used (first century BC).*

shield; and two large fragments of bronze cauldrons – not to mention a fragment from a bronze trumpet. These extraordinary finds are displayed in the National Museum of Wales, in Cardiff.

The discoveries at Lyn Cerrig Bach were made in wartime, and they included a number of human bones that were not reported at the time – possibly for reasons of morale, or censorship (patterns of thinking which in today's peacetime world are as hard to fathom as the minds of Iron Age warriors). Radiocarbon dates from bone show that the lake was a long-term sacred spot, from at least 500 BC until as late as 100 AD – broadly contemporary with Fiskerton and the later phases of Flag Fen. Mike Parker Pearson reckons that one day a post-built causeway will be found there – and for what it's worth, so do I.[40]

It's more than usually hard to separate the craftsmanship of the neck-rings from their horrible purpose, but it has to be said that they are beautifully made, and well-thought-out too: the chain between each prisoner is passed through the fastening loops, allowing individuals to be added to, or removed from, the gang.

All the components of a heroic warrior culture are here at Llyn Cerrig Bach, from feasting to fighting. But there are other themes that we have encountered earlier: water and the next world, travel and the final journey. The realm of the ancestors still exerts a powerful influence on the daily lives of ordinary people, be they wives, mothers, warriors or children. The careful destruction of the swords and other items suggests that they had been deliberately removed from circulation in this world, a rite that has its origins in the Neolithic, if not earlier. What is an odious object like a set of slaves' neck-rings doing in such company? Nobody has yet provided a satisfactory answer. So let's do what comes naturally to those who study the past – let's use some imagination.

You could say that the capturing of slaves was justified in people's minds as something glorious – a natural part of tribal combat. But it's one thing to outline a general principle, and quite another to recreate an actual event. Archaeologists are good at the former, and tend to fight shy of the latter. I shall go against my instincts.

Try to picture the scene. There's a crowd of about a hundred people standing around the edges of the pond. Out in the shallows, a small party of warriors are placing the broken swords of their slain comrades in the waters, while the village priest, an aged and long-retired blacksmith, offers prayers to the ancestors. The slaves who once wore those neck-rings stand silently by while their shackles are offered to the waters. But then what happened? Perhaps the warriors guarding them stood aside, the priest stepped forward and welcomed them into their new community, and then they joined in the feast. Or perhaps they were released and given a short time to make their escape before a hue-and-cry set out to recapture them. Or perhaps they too were destroyed when their chains entered the waters, and their bodies were then hacked to pieces and disposed of somewhere less sacred.

Maybe the story had a happy ending. The four slaves had been rescued from a dishonourable fate, worse in their eyes than death itself. They belonged to the local tribe, whose ancestral spirits resided in the bogs and lakes of Anglesey. In a daring ambush five days previously, their captors had been slaughtered by a rescue party of their older kinsmen. It was fathers who freed their sons, and when they returned to the village, the celebrations went on late into the night. Now the tribe had gathered to give thanks for their release. They knew well what to do on such occasions. The entire adult community came to their special place, where they offered the hated neck-rings to the shades of the dead heroes who had so successfully guided their sons, grandsons and great-grandsons on their heroic exploit.

Afterword

Britannia: A Province on the Fringes of the Empire

THE BRITISH ATTITUDE to the Roman Conquest of AD 43 has always struck me as odd. Even today, in the twenty-first century, it has been decided that British history as taught in our schools according to the National Curriculum will begin with the arrival of the Romans – an event I regard as a black moment. This extraordinarily myopic decision illustrates a failure to learn from the many discoveries of archaeology over the past fifty years. It's something the Irish, who are proud of their prehistory, would never have considered doing. For reasons I don't fully understand, in Britain the Norman Conquest is usually seen as the 'big' invasion. This is ludicrous, because the Norman conquerors were closely related to the English royal house, and besides, life in the countryside barely changed at all following 1066. Archaeologically speaking, the Norman Conquest is almost undetectable – which cannot possibly be said of the Roman Conquest.

To read most British histories, the events of AD 43 are seen as a more or less unreservedly Good Thing, to use the language of *1066 and All That*. But that is to deny all the achievements of prehistoric British culture, which archaeology has shown were very considerable indeed. Writing as an Englishman, I have to wonder whether this strange state of denial is a side-effect of British attitudes to their own Empire, which after all perpetrated many conquests equal in brutality to those of Ancient Rome. So the British rationalise what happened to them two thousand years ago in the same way that my teachers at school in the 1950s rationalised the Indian Raj. I was taught how the Empire 'gave' the subcontinent a civil service, a common language and cricket, in much the same way that the Romans 'gave' Britain roads, laws, central heating and a disgusting fermented fish sauce known as *garum*.[1] What wasn't introduced into the discussion was the fact that both regimes were economically exploitative, often brutal, and offended against all concepts of natural justice. The British Empire may have been a lot less brutal than many others, both ancient and modern, but that's not the point. Like the Roman Empire long before, it was large, highly successful, and it suppressed the identities of the people it conquered.

It would be churlish to pretend that the influence of the Roman Conquest was wholly negative, and it certainly had positive aspects – the introduction of written laws and so forth. But the conquest of one people by another usually has calamitous, profound and long-term effects. Just read these words from Tacitus' *Agricola* to see what I mean. Tacitus, writing about the changes he believed his father-in-law Gnaeus Julius Agricola made during his time as governor of Britain (AD 78–84), describes how Agricola had to deal with people 'living in isolation and ignorance, and therefore prone to fight; and his object was to accustom them to a life of peace and quiet by the provision of amenities'. He goes on to recount how the Britons adopted Roman customs and dress, and how Agricola provided the sons of tribal chiefs with a liberal education. It's horribly reminiscent of, say, British India, where the sons of Maharajahs were sent off to attend English public schools. The final two sentences of the chapter bring a chill to my heart:

> And so the population was gradually led into the demoralising temptations of arcades, baths, and sumptuous banquets. The unsuspecting Britons spoke of such novelties as 'civilisation', when in fact they were only a feature of their enslavement.[2]

There's still a tendency, when it comes to the Romans, to treat might as right. Indeed, I've heard it said that the Romans 'gave' us civilisation. But as the word 'civilisation' is ultimately itself Latin (via the French *civiliser*), that's hardly surprising. You can't express something if you don't have a word for it. I take the view that there are two sides to this argument. Yes, the Romans did introduce writing and written laws (possibly their greatest contribution to British culture), and they also imported ideas that were ahead of their time, such as the factory production of commodities like pottery. I know of fields outside Peterborough which were major ceramic workshops in Roman times, where the ground over several acres is quite literally crunchy with potsherds. Walking over them is like treading on seashells on the beach. This was production on a truly industrial scale.

By way of contrast to the perceived civilisation and efficiency of Rome, the Ancient Britons have had a poor press. In part this is due to the fact that they were portrayed to the literate world by Roman authors such as Caesar, Tacitus and Dio who had an interest in glorifying the name of Rome and the achievements of her generals. Tacitus wrote about Britain in some detail because he was writing the definitive biography of his father-in-law Gnaeus Julius Agricola, who as we have seen just happened to be governor of the Province of Britain. It is remarkable, however, that the image of the Ancient Britons as naked, woad-painted savages has remained largely unchallenged until recent times and the advent of modern, scientific archaeology. It's as if, as a nation, the British are somehow ashamed of their roots. We see this, for example, in the galleries of the British Museum, which devotes less than 2 per cent of its available space to exhibitions of material from pre-Roman Britain. (Incidentally, even this proportion is very much greater than what one would have seen on a visit to the museum before the last war.)

When the Roman troops arrived in Britain they came to an island of tribal kingdoms whose politics were characterised by a network of complex and constantly changing relationships. To an outsider it must have seemed like turmoil. As I hinted in the previous chapter, we can get some idea of the political machinations that took place in the decades on either side of BC/AD by studying the distribution of the coins that the various tribal leaders or kings produced.[3] Roman military intelligence was good, and the invading forces were able to take advantage of sometimes rather fragile local alliances.

From a technological point of view, the native inhabitants of Britain had been fashioning iron tools and weapons for some seven hundred years. They grew most of the common crops that we see in the modern countryside, and they had possessed sophisticated wheeled vehicles for well over a thousand years. Their clothes were made from brightly dyed woven cloth, and their artists and craftsmen were capable of producing works of art that hold their own alongside the finest creations offered by the ancient world.

It has been said that the Roman army was a highly efficient military machine that drove the expansion of the Empire. That expansion was believed to have been part of a long-term strategy or grand plan. We now realise that this is an overstatement. The fact is that the Roman army in Britain and abroad was often studied by scholars who were themselves well schooled in practical military matters, and regarded the Roman army as a model of military prowess. They were, in other words, predisposed in its favour. What they looked for they found, and the ruthless invincibility of the Roman army became an accepted fact. As a schoolboy I was brought up to regard the Romans as little short of superhuman.

What I learned at school was bolstered by my experiences at home. My father was an officer in British military intelligence during the last war, and he spoke very highly indeed of the late Professor Eric Birley, who was a senior member of the team at the War Office. At the time Birley was the leading British authority on the Roman army, and he applied the tactical principles of their European manoeuvres, some two thousand years ago, to predict – with considerable success, I understand – what the Nazi forces might choose to do next. Birley regarded the Roman army with undisguised admiration, and he was by no means alone.

A more sceptical view of the Roman army has recently been published by the English writer Guy de la Bédoyère, who sees it as a most remarkable, but nonetheless often imperfect, military machine. He attributes much of the traditional, all-conquering, image of the Roman army to the author Josephus, who wrote in detail about the military campaigns in Judea. As Guy says of Josephus: 'his description of the Flavian army on campaign . . . is one of unadulterated order, discipline, effortless control and, above all, homogeneity. This has motivated and excited generals, dictators and archaeologists ever since.'[4]

Guy was also able to draw on a wealth of recent archaeological discoveries in Britain. These most famously include a series of wooden writing tablets found in waterlogged deposits at places such as the Roman fort at Vindolanda,[5] on Hadrian's Wall in Northumberland (excavated, incidentally, by Eric's son Robin Birley).[6] These tablets are the Roman equivalents of letters or postcards, and they provide a truer, less formal account of life at the time than the official inscriptions carved in stone. Taken together with a more critical re-examination of those inscriptions, and of other sources, they paint a rather different view of the ancient military machine. As Guy writes:

> ... the Roman army emerges as a far more complex organisation, perpetually in a state of flux. In this it mirrors the state it represented. The idea of the Empire operating a long-term strategy of conquest and exploitation is difficult to sustain in this respect, and so is the idea that Romanisation was a deliberate policy operated by generations of imperial social strategists.[7]

This picture contrasts with the one we are normally given, which features squabbling and undisciplined armies of Ancient Britons on one side, and a tightly controlled, well-directed, ruthlessly efficient 'military machine' on the other. Of course the various kingdoms of ancient Britain could never have posed a serious threat to the might of the Roman army in a single pitched battle, but it never came to that. As a result, the conquest of Britain was by no means a pushover. Furthermore, during the revolt of Boudica in AD 60/61, just eighteen years after the Conquest, the Roman invaders were very, very nearly driven out of Britain,[8] and large parts of London and Colchester, both major cities, were burnt to the ground. So even after seventeen years of military campaigns, the whole of Britain was by no means effectively subdued. The contest was certainly not entirely one-sided.

Britain was one of the most heavily garrisoned of all Roman provinces, with about sixteen thousand legionaries and an equal number of auxiliary troops – not to mention a huge array of dependants, plus supply and support services. This surely reflects the fact that the native British population was large, well organised and capable of resistance. Britain was seen as something of a feather in the cap of emperors such as Claudius, who launched the invasion of AD 43 and paid a visit to the country very shortly after the Conquest. He was happy to claim credit for victory in Britain, minting gold and silver coins and erecting a triumphal arch in Rome.

There is some dispute about the actual motives that triggered the Roman invasion. Imperial ambition on the part of Claudius was an undoubted factor. The immediate reason – or excuse – for the invasion seems to have been to help an ageing expatriate British prince known as Verica, the son of Commius, who had been leader of the Atrebates, a British kingdom that covered parts of what is now Surrey and Berkshire. Verica seems to have been quite a successful and stable ruler, probably reigning for thirty years between AD 10 and 40, a long spell by the standards of the early first century AD. His reign ended when his territory was overrun by forces of another tribal kingdom, the Catuvellauni (a powerful tribe originally based in Hertfordshire and Essex), that was then being aggressively expansive under its similarly long-lived and successful leader Cunobelin.

Verica fled across the Channel and enlisted the support of the Emperor Claudius, who now had a 'legitimate' reason to invade Britain. From his perspective Britain without Verica and Cunobelin (who as we saw died around AD 40) was in a state of near-turmoil, and he had received a direct appeal for help. As we have seen on numerous occasions in modern times (one thinks of Afghanistan, East Timor, Sierra Leone), foreign military force can be used to prop up or restore 'rightful' leaders – however one defines that word.

Invasions are generally commemorated at their point of landing – for example the Normandy beaches of the last war – or at the first significant battle with the defending forces – as at Battle, near Hastings in 1066. Like many battlefields, both are highly evocative places where processes of profound historical importance were set in motion. Unfortunately, the two key locations in the story of the Claudian conquest of Britain in AD 43 are not stated directly and unambiguously by any contemporary or near-contemporary authority.

There has been a general preference among scholars of the Roman period to favour Richborough in Kent as the equivalent of the Normandy beaches, but until very recently it was hard to be certain. It's also possible to suggest other landing places, on the south coast proper, that would have been within easy reach of Gaul.[9] This imprecision has had the unintentional effect of denying those of us who admire the achievements of prehistoric Britain a focus for our sense of loss. Grief is perhaps too strong a word. A couple of months ago, however, the learned journal *Britannia* published the paper I had been unconsciously awaiting for twenty years. It was written by two of the foremost scholars of Roman Britain, Professors Sheppard Frere and Mike Fulford, and concerns the invasion of AD 43 and its immediate aftermath.[10]

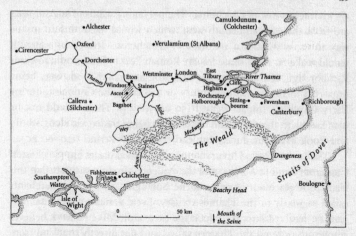

FIG 112   *South-east Britain at the time of the Roman Conquest (AD 43).*

By Roman standards the invasion of Britain was a middle-sized campaign, but it did include a long sea crossing, which made it extremely hazardous. Frere and Fulford argue strongly that the landing place was indeed Richborough. The three divisions of troops, amounting to some forty to forty-five thousand men, were under the overall command of the Roman general Aulus Plautius, who had a distinguished military record. It has been suggested that the landing could have taken place at Chichester, as that would have given better access to what would later be called Calleva Atrebatum, or Silchester, Verica's old capital. But there are problems with this. First, Calleva Atrebatum is forty miles inland, and the intervening territory had recently come under the control of those militarily successful Catuvellaunian forces which would have provided even the Romans with stiff opposition, especially after a long and probably pretty rough crossing.

The invasion had been delayed by morale problems – including a mutiny – and probably took place in the late summer. About two months after the landing, the Roman author Suetonius mentions that the troops for Britain had embarked at Boulogne (the spot from which Napoleon planned to launch his invasion of Britain), which is about

175 kilometres east of Chichester. The prevailing winds of late summer are from the west and south-west, which would make this an insane way to cross what is a notoriously treacherous stretch of water. It would make far more sense for the Roman fleet to head north, towards Richborough. It's worth noting that Roman luxury goods were being imported to Britain in the century or so before the Conquest, during Barry Cunliffe's Impact Period (50 BC–AD 43). These should not be confused with the slaves and other items being traded via Hengistbury and Poole Harbour during the earlier Contact Period (120–60 BC).

The Impact Period luxury items are found at places like Colchester, Canterbury and St Albans, and the evidence strongly suggests that this trade took place out of ports in the Boulogne area, whose merchants sailed regularly to the Thames estuary. Even Verica's old capital, Silchester, received imports, which the excavator, Mike Fulford, believes reached the site via the Thames valley, and not directly overland from the south coast.[11] Presumably the men who captained the merchant vessels could readily have helped the Roman military authorities with guidance, and possibly as pilots too.

Following two skirmishes shortly after landing, which saw off two sets of British warriors under the separate command of the tribal princes Togodumnus and Caratacus – both sons of the greatest warlord of them all, Cunobelin, referred to by Suetonius as *rex Britannorum* (king of the Britons) – there was a more decisive battle at a river. We don't know for certain which river, but Frere and Fulford suggest it was the Medway (supporters of the Chichester landings propose the Hampshire river Avon). The British fighters then crossed the Thames and the marshes on either shore, heading back towards their home territory in Hertfordshire and Essex. This crossing seems to have been between Higham in Kent and East Tilbury in Essex. After further skirmishing, the Roman forces regrouped on top of the high gravel ridge which runs between East Tilbury and Mucking in Essex. I've spent some time excavating on that bitterly cold ridge, and I can vouch for its steepness, which would have been naturally defensive. From here Plautius summoned the Emperor Claudius himself, who he probably met shortly afterwards in London.

Although the actual landing spot has been lost to coastal erosion, there are other strands of evidence to indicate that Richborough was indeed where the three Roman divisions disembarked. For a start, the curve of the surviving Roman earthworks could have been one side of a disembarkation fort, rather than sea defences, as they are usually considered. Second, shortly after the invasion there is evidence for a substantial stores base, used to accommodate the essential supplies of a large military force. These would have included food for the troops, plus fodder for their horses and animals. It's interesting that this major piece of military infrastructure continued in active use through to about AD 85 – after the Boudican revolt, and at a time when the military situation in Britain was becoming less fraught. As if to cap the argument a large monument, now lost, was constructed at Richborough, presumably to celebrate the conquest. Incidentally, no monuments or invasion-period supply bases have been found near Chichester, that other contender for the invasion landing place, or indeed elsewhere along the south coast.

The Emperor Claudius spent only sixteen days in Britain, but he probably commanded the Roman troops in the defeat of Cunobelin's Catuvellaunian capital at Camulodunum, or Colchester. This was an important victory, which in effect secured most of south-eastern England. A younger Catuvellaunian prince, Cogidubnus, was placed in control at Chichester. Cogidubnus had spent time in Rome, perhaps as a hostage, and had been made a Roman citizen by Claudius himself. These events surely demonstrate that the Ancient Britons were far from inconsequential. And of course Claudius was not the only Roman Emperor to take an active interest in the affairs of this far-flung province (one has only to think of Hadrian and his wall).

So that's how it happened. The conquest was nasty, brutish and prolonged. Happily, the Roman presence in Britain lasted barely four centuries, as the withdrawal of troops had been largely completed by the official end-date of the occupation (AD 410), which coincided with the drying-up of funds to pay the few remaining troops. Both Ireland and Scotland escaped largely unscathed, so the native beliefs, traditions and patterns of life were able to resume in post-Roman times, with a bit of help from Iron Age cousins and neighbours from across the North Sea.

One reason why British culture proved so resilient in the face of the greatest politico-military machine of the ancient world is that its roots went back thousands of years. And as any forester or gardener will tell you, deep roots make for strong trees.

Now for one final thought: did Britain's pre-Roman forebears have any effect on modern society? The easy and safe answer would be a simple 'don't know'. But I don't want to think that a lifetime's study of prehistory has proved to be entirely irrelevant to modern life. From a strictly academic perspective it would be both reasonable and sensible to say nothing, largely because there is such a huge span of time between our world and that of prehistory. And of course during that time Britain has received large-scale movements of people from across the North Sea, the best-known being the Anglo-Saxons and the Vikings. But large numbers of new people don't necessarily wipe out indigenous culture. Quite often the original 'native' way of doing things will return after the initial shock of an invasion or migration has worn off.

With such a multitude of imponderables, I'm forced to admit that my thoughts on this matter are intuitive. But my understanding and experience of British prehistory lead me to the view that the Ancient Britons were a resourceful bunch. Their insular society worked well: they seem to have kept their feuding to manageable proportions, and their use of the landscape to raise livestock and grow crops compares well with, if it was not better than, what was happening on the European mainland. British societies were relatively self-contained, and although hierarchies developed from the Bronze Age, these never spawned any sort of super-powerful elite. Society seems, by and large, to have been remarkably egalitarian. Even by the time of Caesar's two visits, the most powerful leaders are best described as warlords, and one must also wonder to what extent they were acknowledged by the bulk of the rural population. The flowering of Late Celtic art in Britain was an indigenous development of a broader, pan-European art style, and it's tempting to see it as, quite simply, Britain's greatest contribution to world art. For these and other reasons, I believe passionately that the story of pre-Roman Britain matters.

But what, if anything, has prehistory contributed to modern British culture? The obvious thing, it seems to me, is a belief in individual freedom. That doesn't mean that the nations of the British Isles have always lived up to this ideal – sadly they have often fallen far short of it. But it is there, and most Britons would defend it to the last gasp. The British passed this ideal on to the United States and the nations of the Commonwealth (with greater or lesser success), where it is generally regarded as an Anglo-Saxon virtue. But is it? Surely the Welsh, Scottish and Irish hold it every bit as dear as the English, the only Anglo-Saxon nation of the British Isles? I would suggest that it has roots that go back much further than either the Anglo-Saxons or the Romans.

That is where I'll leave it. I genuinely believe that the British belief in individual freedom has prehistoric roots. I also believe that it is the mainstay of modern British society, and that it will help the nation cope with the challenges of the future. I get irritated when I hear right-wing politicians and Little Englanders complain that something like the adoption of the euro threatens British culture. That culture took thousands of years to develop, and as a result of this extended period of gestation it is remarkably robust. It would take far more than a handful of new coins, or an army of Brussels bureaucrats, to harm it. If prehistory teaches us anything, it is that we must all learn to think in the long term. One day, maybe in a few centuries' time, our survival, perhaps not just as a nation but as a species, could depend on it.

Many of the places listed below have been discussed in the text. I have also included places which were not mentioned, but which are nonetheless well worth a visit. I have tried to include information on organisations that are actively involved with research into some of the most important sites and regions. Prices of admission have not been quoted, as these may change from one season to another. In common with the main text, I have arranged the list period by period, rather than by location. Dates and times of opening may change, and I strongly suggest making advance contact before travelling any distance. Travel and tourism have been transformed by email and the Internet, and I have not attempted to provide a guide to the numerous and uniquely important archaeological sites of Orkney and Shetland. Instead I have offered information on websites and appropriate archaeological organisations.

Archaeology is constantly changing. For up-to-date information it is well worth subscribing to the excellent popular magazine *Current Archaeology* (9 Nassington Road, London NW3 2TX, tel: 020 7435 7517) which also publishes an annual *Archaeology Handbook*, free to subscribers (available on the web at www.archaeology.co.uk). Membership of the Council for British Archaeology (Bowes Morrell House, 111 Walmgate, York YO1 9WA, tel: 01904 671417) includes the first-rate and accessible magazine *British Archaeology* (the CBA maintains the leading British archaeological website at www.britarch.ac.uk). The CBA also runs the Young Archaeologists Club, for children under sixteen.

Palaeolithic and Mesolithic

CHEDDAR GORGE

Show Caves Museum (and Gough's Cave), Cheddar Gorge, Cheddar, Somerset BS27 3QF

Tel: 01934 742343

Email enquiries: caves@visitcheddar.co.uk
Gough's Cave, discovered by Richard Gough in 1890, is the largest
of the show caves, with nearly half a kilometre of underground
galleries. The museum has a collection of Upper Palaeolithic
artefacts and bones.

CRESWELL CRAGS

Creswell Crags Visitor Centre, Crags Road, Welbeck, Worksop,
Nottinghamshire S80 3LH
Tel: 01909 720378
Email enquiries: info@creswell-crags.org.uk
A World Heritage Site. Recently refurbished, with fine displays that
include artefacts and reproductions.

NATIONAL MUSEUM OF WALES

Cathays Park, Cardiff, South Glamorgan CF1 3NP
Tel: 029 2039 7951
Email enquiries: post@nmgw.ac.uk
Open all year round.
Excellent displays on the Welsh caves and finds from them.

OXFORD UNIVERSITY MUSEUM OF NATURAL HISTORY

Parks Road, Oxford OX1 3PW
Tel: 01865 272950
Email enquiries: info@oum.ox.ac.uk
Material (artefacts and bones) from Paviland Cave.

Neolithic

AVEBURY STONE CIRCLES

Avebury village is eleven kilometres west of Marlborough. Visitor
car park is south of the village, off the A4361. Swindon twenty-five
kilometres. Access to the stone circle is free.
The Alexander Keiller Museum is in the village, and contains
superb collections from the area. Open all year, except at
Christmas and New Year. The old Manor Barn near the museum
has been converted into a new interpretation gallery. Don't forget
to visit sites outside the great circle: Silbury Hill, the West Kennet

Avenue, Windmill Hill, the Sanctuary etc. Allow at least a day, preferably two.

BRÚ NA BÓINNE (BEND OF THE BOYNE)

Brú na Bóinne Visitor Centre, Donore, County Meath
Tel: (353) 41 9880300
Email enquiries: brunaboinne@ealga.ie
South of the River Boyne on the L21, two kilometres west of Donore. The best place to stay is Navan, County Meath.
The Brú na Bóinne visitor centre is the only access point for visits to Newgrange and Knowth.

CÉIDE FIELDS

Belderrig, Ballycastle, County Mayo
Eight kilometres west of Ballycastle on the R314.
Tel: (353) 96 43325
Email enquiries: ceidefields@ealga.ie

WEST KENNET LONG BARROW

Just over one kilometre south-west of West Kennet, off the A4 (Ordnance Survey map 173, grid ref SU 104677). Park in layby off the A4.
Open any reasonable time. Access to the long barrow is free.

WINDMILL HILL CAUSEWAYED ENCLOSURE

Two kilometres north-west of Avebury (Ordnance Survey map 173, grid ref SU 086714).
Open any reasonable time. Access is free.

WOODHENGE

2½ kilometres north of Amesbury, off the A345, just south of Durrington (Ordnance Survey map 184, grid ref SU 151434).
Open any reasonable time. Access is free.

Bronze Age

BRENIG CAIRN FIELD

The Lleyn Brenig Reservoir visitor centre is located at Ordnance Survey Grid Reference SH 967 547.

The monuments (original and partially restored) of the Brenig Cairn Field can be seen by walkers, and a guide leaflet can be obtained at the visitor centre.

DOVER BOAT

Dover Museum, Market Square, Dover, Kent CT16 1PB
Tel: 01304 201066
Email enquiries: museumenquiries@dover.gov.uk
The museum includes the award-winning gallery displaying the Dover Bronze Age boat.

DOWN FARM

Martin Green. Down Farm, Woodcutts, Salisbury SP5 5RY
Tel: 01725 552320
Martin Green has set his farm aside to archaeology. He conducts excavations on mainly Bronze Age and Neolithic sites there, and has set up his own private museum. Very English and very good: a refreshing and personal view of prehistory. His book is essential reading: *A Landscape Revealed: 10,000 Years on a Chalkland Farm* (Tempus Books, Stroud, 2000).

FLAG FEN

Britain's Bronze Age Centre, The Droveway, Northey Road, Peterborough PE6 7QJ
Tel: 01733 313414
Email enquiries: office@flagfen.com
Open all year except for brief period over Christmas.
Preserved waterlogged timbers *in situ*. Also museum of finds and reconstructed dryland settlement, with livestock. Shop etc.

GREAT ORME

Great Orme Mines Ltd, Great Orme, Llandudno LL30 2XG
Tel: 01492 870447

Email enquiries: gomines@greatorme.freeserve.co.uk
Open from 1 February to end of October.
One of the best visitor attractions in British prehistory.
Underground mines, with tours and displays. A must.

STONEHENGE

Three kilometres west of Amesbury at the junction of the A303
and A344/A360.
Tel: 01980 624715
Open all year except Christmas, Boxing Day and New Year's Day.
Perhaps not a good idea to visit during the Summer Solstice.

Iron Age

BUTSER ANCIENT FARM

Horndean, Waterlooville, near Petersfield, Hants
Enquiries: Christine Shaw, Nexus House, Gravel Hill, Waterlooville
PO8 0QE
Tel: 023 9259 8838
Website: www.butser.org.uk
Following the death of the Ancient Farm's founder and director Dr
Peter Reynolds, Butser is adapting to its new circumstances, and is
generally open on weekends only. A number of special events take
place there each summer. Phone first.

CASTELL HENLLYS IRON AGE FORT

Meline, Crymych, Pembrokeshire SA41 3UT
Off the A487 between Cardigan and Newport.
Tel: 01239 891319
Email: enquiries@castellhenllys.pembrokeshire-coast.org.uk
Open Easter to the end of October.
A partially reconstructed Iron Age hill-fort with excellent
roundhouses in a beautiful wooded setting. Shop etc. Numerous
activity days.

COLCHESTER CASTLE MUSEUM
Colchester
Essex CO1 1TJ
Tel: 01206 282931
Collections include material from Camulodunum. For more
information on current excavations in and around the town
contact the Friends of the Colchester Archaeological Trust,
c/o 5 Ashwin Avenue, Copford, Colchester, Essex CO6 1BS.

CORLEA TRACKWAY
Corlea Trackway Visitor Centre, Kenagh, County Longford
Tel: (353) 43 22386
Open April to September.
An eighteen-metre stretch of the timber roadway is preserved in a
specially humidified hall. Be sure not to miss the video film of a
master-craftsman effortlessly splitting a massive oak tree with
nothing but the frailest of wooden wedges.

DANEBURY IRON AGE HILL-FORT
Three kilometres north-west of Stockbridge, off the A30.
Tel: 01962 846737
Guided walks last about two hours.
Must be seen in conjunction with the Museum of the Iron Age,
6 Church Close, Andover, Hants (tel: 01264 366283; open Tuesday
to Saturday), which tells the story of Danebury and includes a
recently discovered Iron Age mirror.

HULL MUSEUM
Hull and East Riding Museum, High Street, Hull HU1 1PS
Tel: 01482 300300
Email enquiries: info@hullcc.gov.uk
Hull Museum contains the immense Iron Age logboat from
Hasholme, together with enigmatic carved wooden figures from
Roos Carr.

MAIDEN CASTLE

Three kilometres south of Dorchester. Access off the A354, north of the bypass (Ordnance Survey map 194, grid ref SY 670885).

Open any reasonable time. Access is free.

The largest and most spectacular hill-fort in Britain. Fine wildflowers, too.

NAVAN FORT

The Navan (Visitor) Centre is not currently open, although it is hoped that this situation will be rectified before too long. For more information contact the Environment and Heritage Service of Northern Ireland, 5–33 Hill Street, Belfast BT11 2LA. Tel: 028 905 43034. Website: www.nics.gov.uk/ehs

PEAT MOORS CENTRE (SOMERSET LEVELS)

Shapwick Road, Westhay, nr Glastonbury, Somerset BA6 9TT
Tel: 01458 860697
Email enquiries: ironage@peatmoors.freeserve.co.uk
An excellent selection of reconstructions, including Iron Age roundhouses based on those found at Glastonbury 'lake village'; also rebuilt prehistoric trackways from the Somerset Levels.

VERULAMIUM MUSEUM

St Michael's Street, St Albans, Herts AL3 4SW.
Tel: 01727 751810
Email enquiries: a.coles@stalbans.gov.uk
The museum is mainly given over to first-rate displays of daily life in Roman Britain.

Multi-Period

THE SHETLAND ISLES

Shetland Amenity Trust, Grantfield, Lerwick, Shetland
ZE1 0NY
Tel: 01595 694688
Email enquiries: shetamenity.trust@zetnet.co.uk
The Shetland Amenity Trust co-ordinates most aspects of the

archaeology of Shetland, which include excavations in the summer
months. Try to plan your trip to coincide with an excavation.
Shetland Museum, Lower Hillhead, Lerwick ZE1 0EL
Tel: 01595 695057
Email enquiries: shetland.museum@zetnet.co.uk
Internet: www.shetland-museum.org.uk
The collections of Shetland Museum draw the rich prehistory of
the Shetland Isles together.

ORKNEY

Friends of Orkney Archaeological Trust, The Janitor's House, Old
Academy, Stromness, Orkney KW16 3AN
Tel: 01856 850285
Email enquiries: oat@lineone.net
Orkney Heritage Society, Langwell Orphir, Orkney KW17 2RF
Tel: 01856 811276
For information on sites and accommodation visit the excellent
website of the Orkney Tourist Board: www.visitorkney.com

NOTES

PREFACE – *'British Peculiarity'*

1 The story broke in June 2002; see the email journal of the Society of Antiquaries of London, SALON, No. 22 (July 2002).

2 'Who Said What', *The Times*, 1 June 2002.

3 E.G. Bowen, *Britain and the Western Seaways* (Thames and Hudson, London, 1972).

4 B.W. Cunliffe, *Facing the Ocean: The Atlantic and its Peoples* (Oxford University Press, 2001).

5 There is a vast literature on connections across the Channel and the North Sea in prehistory. Here are a few of the more important references: J.J. Butler, 'Bronze Age Connections Across the North Sea', *Palaeohistoria*, vol. 9, 1963 (entire issue); Brendan O'Connor, *Cross-Channel Relations in the Later Bronze Age*, 2 vols, British Archaeological Reports International Series No. S91 (Oxford, 1980); L.P. Louwe-Kooijmans, 'A View of the Fens from the Low Countries', *Antiquity*, vol. 62, 1988, pp.377–82.

6 Cyril Fox, *The Personality of Britain: Its Influence on Inhabitant and Invader in Prehistoric and Early Historic Times* (National Museum of Wales, Cardiff, 1932).

CHAPTER ONE – *In the Beginning*

1 Pioneering geologists such as Charles Lyell also played a major part in preparing the world for Darwin's views. See A. Desmond and J. Moore, *Darwin: The Life of a Tormented Evolutionist* (Michael Joseph, London 1991).

2 Robert Foley, 'Parallel Tracks in Time: Human Evolution and Archaeology', in Barry Cunliffe, Wendy Davies and Colin Renfrew (eds), *Archaeology: The Widening Debate* (British Academy, London, 2002), pp.3–42.

3 For more on the rich social and sexual life of the Bonobo see Robin Dunbar and Louise Barrett, *Cousins: Our Primate Relatives* (BBC Worldwide, London, 2000), p.230.

4 Nicholas Barton, *Stone Age Britain* (English Heritage and Batsford Books, London, 1997), p.45.

5 For non-archaeological flint-knapping see A.J. Forrest, *Masters of Flint* (Terence Dalton Ltd., Lavenham, Suffolk, 1983).

6 I use the term 'hominid' in its older sense of man-like creatures. Today, following the results of molecular genetics, it has acquired a more specific definition which includes man and the African apes. A new term, 'hominin', refers to humans and their direct ancestors.

7 This is a slight oversimplification. In point of fact microscopic examination of the cutting edges of some Palaeolithic flakes shows them to have been used as implements. It's the widespread introduction of new flake-based technologies after about forty thousand years ago that is the important point to stress here.

8 I describe the discovery of the Neolithic pit burial in *Seahenge: New Discoveries in Prehistoric Britain* (HarperCollins, London, 2001), pp.53–6.

9 For an illustrated note on the plaque to John Frere see the *Proceedings of the Suffolk Institute of Archaeology and History*, vol. 39, part 4 (2000), pp 541–2.

10 The visit to Hoxne and Finningham is recorded in the *Proceedings of the Suffolk Institute of Archaeology and History*, vol. 39, part 2 (1998), pp.268–9.

11 John Frere, 'Account of flint weapons discovered at Hoxne in Suffolk, in a letter to the Rev. John Brand, Secretary', *Archaeologia*, vol. 13, 1800, pp.204–5.

12 John Wymer, *The Lower Palaeolithic Occupation of Britain*, 2 vols (English Heritage and the Trust for Wessex Archaeology Ltd, Salisbury, 1999).

13 Mark Roberts and Simon Parfitt, *Boxgrove: A Middle Pleistocene Hominid Site at Eartham Quarry, Boxgrove, West Sussex*, English Heritage Archaeological Report 17 (London, 1999).

14 Michael Pitts and Mark Roberts, *Fairweather Eden: Life in Britain Half a Million Years Ago as Revealed by the Excavations at Boxgrove* (Century, London, 1997).

15 Robert Foley, 'Parallel tracks in time: Human evolution and archaeology', in Cunliffe, Davies and Renfrew, *Archaeology: The Widening Debate*, op. cit., p.14.

16 The study of microwear has become a sub-discipline within archaeology. It was instigated by a Soviet archaeologist, S.A. Semenov, whose book *Prehistoric Technology*, translated by M.W. Thompson (Adams and Dart, Bath, 1964), had an enormous influence.

17 Roberts and Parfitt, *Boxgrove*, op. cit., p.378.

18 N. Noe-Nygaard, 'Mesolithic Hunting in Denmark Illustrated by Bone Injuries Caused By Human Weapons', *Journal of Archaeological Science*, vol. 1, 1974, pp.217–48.

19 For the Clacton wooden spearhead see Wymer, *The Lower Palaeolithic Occupation of Britain*, op. cit., plate 15. For the Schöningen spears see H.

Thieme, 'Altpaläolithische Wurfspeere aus Schöningen Niedersachsen: ein Vorbericht', *Archäologisches Korrespondenzblatt*, vol. 26, 1996, pp.377–93. For a more readily obtainable illustration of a Schöningen spear see Barton, *Stone Age Britain*, op. cit., colour plate 7.

20 John Wymer, in Roberts and Parfitt, *Boxgrove*, op. cit., p.xvii.

CHAPTER TWO – *Neanderthals, the Red 'Lady' and Ages of Ice*

1 Wymer, *The Lower Palaeolithic Occupation of Britain*, op. cit., p.41.

2 Don Brothwell, 'Palaeodemography and Earlier British Populations', *World Archaeology*, vol. 4, 1972, pp.75–87.

3 For an excellent modern overview of the Upper Palaeolithic see Nicholas Barton, 'The Lateglacial or Late and Final Palaeolithic Colonization of Britain', in John Hunter and Ian Ralston (eds), *The Archaeology of Britain*, pp.13–34 (Routledge, London, 1999).

4 Derek A. Roe, *The Lower and Middle Palaeolithic Periods in Britain* (Routledge and Kegan Paul, London, 1981); Anthony Stuart, *Life in the Ice Age* (Shire Books, Princes Risborough, 1988); Christopher Smith, *Late Stone Age Hunters of the British Isles* (Routledge, London, 1992); Barton, *Stone Age Britain*, op. cit.

5 The book of the series is superbly illustrated: Douglas Palmer, *Neanderthal* (Channel 4, London, 2000).

6 Erik Trinkaus and Pat Shipman, *The Neanderthals: Changing the Image of Mankind* (Jonathan Cape, London, 1993).

7 Glyn Daniel, *150 Years of Archaeology* (Duckworth, London, 1975); see also Trinkaus and Shipman, op. cit., pp.126–341.

8 Barton, *Stone Age Britain*, op. cit., pp.76–7. Chris Stringer and Clive Gamble, *In Search of the Neanderthals*

(Thames and Hudson, London, 1993).

9 Steven Mithen, 'From Domain Specific to Generalized Intelligence: A Cognitive Interpretation of the Middle/Upper Palaeolithic Transition', in Colin Renfrew and Ezra Zubrow (eds), *The Ancient Mind: Elements of Cognitive Archaeology* (Cambridge University Press, 1994), pp.29–39.

10 I discuss context further in *Seahenge*, op. cit., pp.3–4.

11 This interesting idea is summarised by Barton, *Stone Age Britain*, op. cit., p.76.

12 Paul Pettitt, 'Odd Man Out: Neanderthals and Modern Humans', *British Archaeology*, Feb. 2001, pp.8–13.

13 Stephen Green and Elizabeth Walker, *Ice Age Hunters* (National Museum of Wales, Cardiff, 1991).

14 This extraordinary site has recently been published in interim form: Bill Boismier, 'Lynford Quarry: A Neanderthal Butchery Site', *Current Archaeology*, vol. 182, 2002, pp.53–8.

15 I discuss some of the pitfalls of defining archaeological cultures in *Seahenge*, op. cit., pp.7–8.

16 For an excellent summary of various theoretical approaches see Ian Hodder, *Reading the Past: Current Approaches to Interpretation in Archaeology* (Cambridge University Press, 1986).

17 Ian Hodder, *Symbols in Action: Ethnoarchaeological Studies of Material Culture* (Cambridge University Press, 1982).

18 Pettitt, 'Odd Man Out', op.cit., p.13.

19 Paul Pettitt, 'Neanderthals, Sex and Modern Humans', *British Archaeology*, June 1999, pp.6–7.

20 Chris Stringer and Robin McKie, *African Exodus: The Origins of Modern Humanity* (Jonathan Cape, London, 1996).

21 Bryan Sykes, *The Seven Daughters of Eve* (Bantam Books, London, 2001), p.125.

22 For a short illustrated article on a remarkable site in Norfolk which is currently being excavated, visit the internet 24 Hour Museum for 27 August 2002.

23 Dating the first appearance of modern man is fraught with problems. See Paul Mellars, 'Radiocarbon Dating and the Origins of Anatomically Modern Populations in Europe' in A.F. Harding (ed.), *Experiment and Design: Archaeological Studies in Honour of John Coles* (Oxbow Books, Oxford, 1999), pp.1–12.

24 Chris Stringer and Robin McKie, *African Exodus: The Origins of Modern Humanity* (Jonathan Cape, London, 1996).

25 Daniel, *150 Years of Archaeology*, op. cit., pp.36–7.

26 Stephen Aldhouse-Green (ed.), *Paviland Cave and the 'Red Lady': A Definitive Account* (Western Academic and Specialist Press Ltd, Westbury-on-Trym, Bristol, 2000).

27 Stephen Aldhouse-Green and Paul Pettitt, 'Paviland Cave: Contextualising the "Red Lady" ', *Antiquity*, vol. 72, pp.756–72. See also Stephen Aldhouse-Green, 'Great Sites: Paviland Cave', *British Archaeology*, October 2001, pp.20–4.

28 Aldhouse-Green, 'Great Sites: Paviland Cave', op. cit., p.23.

29 For the inventor, see Richard Burleigh, 'W. F. Libby and the Development of Radiocarbon Dating', *Antiquity*, vol. 55, 1981, pp.96–8. For an excellent introduction to radiocarbon dating, with references, see Colin Renfrew and Paul Bahn, *Archaeology: Theories, Methods and Practice*, 3rd edn (Thames and Hudson, London, 1991), pp.122–9.

30 The Red 'Lady' bones and the ivory rods excavated by Dean Buckland are in the collections of the Oxford University Museum, Parks Road, Oxford. The spatulae and other finds from Goat's Hole Cave are in the National Museum of Wales, Cardiff.

31 J.D. Lewis-Williams, *Believing and Seeing: Symbolic Meanings in Southern San Rock Painting* (Academic Press, London, 1981).

32 For more on the stylised female form in Upper Palaeolithic art, see A. Marshack,

'The Female Image: A "Time-Factored" Symbol. A Study in Style and Aspect of Image Use in the Upper Palaeolithic', *Proceedings of the Prehistoric Society*, vol. 57, 1991, pp.17-31.

33 Richard Bradley, *An Archaeology of Natural Places* (Routledge, London, 2000).

34 For a collection of papers on the archaeological significance of shamanism in general see Neil Price (ed.), *The Archaeology of Shamanism* (Duckworth, London, 2001).

35 The original multi-volumed work should be available at most academic libraries. There is also a large, but abridged, version: Sir James Frazer, *The Golden Bough: A Study in Magic and Religion* (Macmillan, London, 1922).

36 There's a huge literature on the use and abuse of ethnology in archaeology. Three books I have found very useful are: Carole Kramer (ed.), *Ethnoarchaeology: Implications of Ethnography for Archaeology* (Columbia University Press, New York, 1979); Marshall Sahlins, *Stone Age Economics* (Tavistock Publications, London, 1974); Ian Hodder, Glyn Isaac and Norman Hammond (eds), *Pattern of the Past* (Cambridge University Press, 1981).

37 Aldhouse-Green and Pettitt, 'Paviland Cave: Contextualising the "Red Lady" ', op. cit., p.767.

38 Ibid., p.768.

39 Clive Gamble, 'The Social Context for European Palaeolithic Art', *Proceedings of the Prehistoric Society*, vol. 57, 1991, pp.3-15.

40 Perhaps the most accessible book on Stone Age art is Paul Bahn and Jean Vertut, *Images of the Ice Age* (Windward, Leicester, 1988). For a useful shorter summary see Andrew Lawson, *Cave Art* (Shire Books, Princes Risborough, 1991).

41 Gamble, 'The Social Context for European Palaeolithic Art', op. cit., p.3.

CHAPTER THREE – *Hotting up: Hunters at the End of the Ice Age*

1 For the chronology of the Upper Palaeolithic see Barton, 'The Lateglacial or Late and Final Upper Palaeolithic Colonization of Britain', op. cit.

2 A.P. Currant, R.M. Jacobi and C.B. Stringer, 'Excavations at Gough's Cave, Somerset', *Antiquity*, vol. 63, 1989, pp.131-6.

3 Francis Pryor, ' "Look What we've Found": A Case Study in Public Archaeology', *Antiquity*, vol. 63, 1989, pp.51-61.

4 For an excellent popular account of the discoveries in Gough's Cave see Larry Barnham, Philip Priestley and Adrian Targett, *In Search of Cheddar Man* (Tempus Publishing, Stroud 1998).

5 Jill Cook, 'Preliminary Report on Marked Human Bones from the 1986-1987 Excavations at Gough's Cave, Somerset, England', in R.N.E Barton, A.J. Roberts and D.A. Roe (eds), *The Late Glacial in North-West Europe*, Council for British Archaeology, Research Report 77 (London, 1991), pp.160-8.

6 Timothy Taylor, 'The Edible Dead', *British Archaeology*, June 2001, pp.8-12.

7 For an excellent overview of the many ways that death is treated in the archaeological record see Mike Parker Pearson, *The Archaeology of Death and Burial* (Sutton Publishing, Stroud, 1999).

8 R.M. Jacobi, 'The Creswellian, Creswell and Cheddar', in Barton, Roberts and Roe, *The Late Glacial in North-West Europe*, op. cit., pp.128-40.

9 Curt Beck and Stephen Shennan, *Amber in Prehistoric Britain*, Oxbow Monograph 8 (Oxford, 1991).

10 Jill Cook and Roger Jacobi, 'A Reindeer Antler or "Lyngby" Axe from Northamptonshire and its Context in the British Late Glacial', *Proceedings of the Prehistoric Society*, vol. 60, 1994, pp.75-84.

11 Bodil Bratlund, 'A Study of Hunting Lesions Containing Flint Fragments on

Reindeer Bones from Stellmoor, Schleswig-Holstein, Germany', in Barton, Roberts and Roe, *The Late Glacial in North-West Europe*, op. cit., p.199.

12 For a map of these hypothetical migration routes see Barton, *Stone Age Britain*, op. cit., p.134.

13 Richard B. Lee and Irven DeVore (eds), *Man the Hunter* (Aldine, Chicago, 1968).

14 Clive Gamble, *The Palaeolithic Societies of Europe* (Cambridge University Press, 1999).

15 Ibid., pp.424–5.

16 Ibid., p.416.

CHAPTER FOUR – *After the Ice*

1 Barton, 'The Lateglacial or Late and Final Upper Palaeolithic Colonization of Britain', op. cit., p.32.

2 Brian M. Fagan, *Grahame Clark: An Intellectual Biography of an Archaeologist* (Westview Press, Boulder, Colorado).

3 This may reflect the fact that Clark was then in his self-defined 'Typological' or 'Stratigraphical' phases of intellectual development. See J.G.D. Clark, *Star Carr: A Case Study in Bioarchaeology*, Addison-Wesley Module in Anthropology (Reading, Massachusetts), p.1.

4 Grahame Clark, *The Stone Age Hunters* (Thames and Hudson, London, 1967).

5 Smith, *Late Stone Age Hunters of the British Isles*, op. cit.

6 For numerous examples of the effects of waterlogging and acid attack on prehistoric burials see P.V. Glob, *The Mound People: Danish Bronze Age Man Preserved* (Faber and Faber, London, 1970).

7 For meat, see Smith, *Late Stone Age Hunters of the British Isles*, op. cit., p.vii. For greater reliance on plant foods, especially hazelnuts, see David Clarke, 'Mesolithic Europe: The Economic Basis', in G. de G. Sieveking, I.H. Longworth and K.E. Wilson (eds), *Problems in Economic and Social*

Archaeology (Duckworth, London, 1976), pp.449–82.

8 Star Carr has been exhaustively studied by Clark and others. The major report was first published in 1954 and enlarged in 1971: J.G.D. Clark, *Excavations at Star Carr, an Early Mesolithic Site at Seamer, near Scarborough, Yorkshire* (Cambridge University Press). Clark further revised his interpretations in 1972: Clark, *Star Carr: A Case Study in Bioarchaeology*, op. cit.

9 For more on Star Carr after Clark see, for example, A.J. Legge and P.A. Rowley-Conwy, *Star Carr Revisited: A Reanalysis of the Large Mammals*, Centre for Extramural Studies, Birkbeck College (London, 1988); Paul Mellars and Petra Dark, *Star Carr in Context: New Archaeological and Palaeoecological Investigations at the Early Mesolithic Site of Star Carr, North Yorkshire*, McDonald Institute Monograph (Cambridge, 1998); M. Pitts, 'Hides and Antlers: A New Look at the Hunter-Gatherer Site at Star Carr, North Yorkshire, England', *World Archaeology*, vol. 11, 1979, pp.32–42; R.T. Schadla-Hall, 'Recent Investigations of the Early Mesolithic Landscape and Settlements in the Vale of Pickering, North Yorkshire', in P.A. Rowley-Conwy, M. Zvelebil and H.P. Blankholm (eds), *Mesolithic Northwest Europe: Recent Trends* (Department of Archaeology and Prehistory, Sheffield University, 1987), pp.46–54.

10 For stalking and bleeding to death see Noe-Nygaard, 'Mesolithic Hunting in Denmark . . .', op. cit., pp.217–48.

11 Tim Schadla-Hall tells me that at least three Mesolithic dogs are now known from the Lake Flixton area.

12 Alwyne Wheeler, 'Why Were There no Fish Remains at Star Carr?', *Journal of Archaeological Science*, vol. 5, 1978, pp.85–90.

13 Maisie Taylor, 'Identification of the Wood and Evidence for Human Working', in Mellars and Dark, *Star Carr in Context*, op. cit., pp.52–63.

14 However, Bill Boismier tells me that the newly discovered Mousterian site in Norfolk might well prove to be an *in situ* settlement.

15 J.G.D. Clark, *Excavations at Star Carr* . . . , op. cit., p.171.

16 Smith, *Late Stone Age Hunters of the British Isles*, op. cit., pp.114–17.

17 John Wymer, 'Excavations at the Maglemosian Sites at Thatcham, Berkshire, England', *Proceedings of the Prehistoric Society*, vol. 13, 1962, pp.329–61.

18 For more information on the Prehistoric Society contact the Society at University College London, Institute of Archaeology, 31–34 Gordon Square, London WC1H 0PY.

19 D.M. Churchill, 'The Stratigraphy of the Mesolithic Sites III and V at Thatcham, Berkshire, England', *Proceedings of the Prehistoric Society*, vol. 13, 1962, pp.362–70.

20 C. Evans and J. Pollard, 'The Dating of the Storey's Bar Road Fields Reconsidered', in Francis Pryor, *The Flag Fen Basin: Archaeology and Environment of a Fenland Landscape*, English Heritage Archaeological Report (London, 2001), pp.25–6.

21 F. Healy, M. Heaton and S.J. Lobb, 'Excavations of a Mesolithic Site at Thatcham, Berkshire', *Proceedings of the Prehistoric Society*, vol. 58, pp. 41–76.

22 Michael Herity and George Eogan, *Ireland in Prehistory* (Routledge, London, 1977), pp.16–17.

23 Nora Robertson, *Crowned Harp: Memories of the Last Years of the Crown in Ireland* (Figgis, Dublin, 1960).

24 Soren Anderson, 'New Finds of Mesolithic Logboats in Denmark', in Christer Westerdahl (ed.), *Crossroads in Ancient Shipbuilding*, Oxbow Monograph 40 (Oxford, 1994), pp.1–10.

25 Sean McGrail, *Logboats of England and Wales*, 2 vols, British Archaeological Report 51 (Oxford, 1978).

26 The full report is by Peter Woodman, *Excavations at Mount Sandel, 1973–1977,*

Archaeological Research Monographs No. 2 (Belfast, 1985).

27 J.M. Coles and E.S. Higgs, *The Archaeology of Early Man* (Faber and Faber, London, 1969).

28 J.M. Coles and A.F. Harding, *The Bronze Age in Europe* (Methuen, London, 1979).

29 J.M. Coles, 'The Early Settlement of Scotland: Excavations at Morton, Fife', *Proceedings of the Prehistoric Society*, vol. 37, 1971, pp.284–366. See also J.M. Coles, 'Morton Revisited', in A. O'Connor and D.V. Clarke (eds), *From the Stone Age to the 'Forty-Five* (John Donald, Edinburgh, 1982), pp.9–17.

30 For a short account of the site see *British Archaeology*, 60, August 2001, p.4. For a list of the radiocarbon dates see *Discovery and Excavation in Scotland*, vol. 1, 2001, p.124.

31 M.R. Deith, 'Subsistence Strategies at a Mesolithic Camp Site: Evidence from Stable Isotope Analyses of Shells', *Journal of Archaeological Science*, vol. 13, 1986, pp.61–78.

32 Christopher Smith, 'The Population of Late Upper Palaeolithic and Mesolithic Britain', *Proceedings of the Prehistoric Society*, vol. 58, 1992, pp.37–40.

33 It is worth noting that independent authorities accept Christopher Smith's figures. See Steven Mithen, 'Hunter Gatherers of the Mesolithic', in John Hunter and Ian Ralston, *The Archaeology of Britain* (Routledge, London, 1999), p.55.

34 My thoughts on the organisation of Mesolithic society are based on Smith, *Late Stone Age Hunters of the British Isles*, op. cit., Chapter 10.

35 In Scotland the main late to very late Mesolithic culture is known as the Obanian, after sites around Oban Bay (Argyll). For more on the Scottish Mesolithic see T. Pollard and A. Morrison (eds), *The Early Prehistory of Scotland* (Edinburgh University Press, 1996).

36 Smith, *Late Stone Age Hunters of the British Isles*, op. cit., p.5.

CHAPTER FIVE – *DNA and the Adoption of Farming*

1 I. Shennan, K. Lambeck, R. Flather, B. Horton, J. McArthur, J. Innes, J. Lloyd, M. Rutherford and R. Wingfield, 'Modelling Western North Sea Palaeogeographies and Tidal Changes During the Holocene', in I. Shennan and J. Andrews (eds), *Holocene Land–Ocean Interaction and Environment Change around the North Sea*, Royal Geographical Society Special Publications No. 166 (London, 2000), pp.299–319.

2 A very fine book on the archaeology of change by the American archaeologist Fred Plog: *The Study of Prehistoric Change* (Academic Press, London, 1974).

3 Peter J. Ucko and G.W. Dimbleby (eds), *The Domestication of Plants and Animals* (Duckworth, London, 1969).

4 Most books of the 1950s accepted the idea of a 'Neolithic Revolution'. A good example, in plain English, is by Sonia Cole, *The Neolithic Revolution* (British Museum of Natural History, London, 1954).

5 I have based this account of the Leman and Ower 'catch' on that of J.G.D. Clark and H. Godwin, 'A Maglemosian Site at Brandesburton, Holderness, Yorkshire', *Proceedings of the Prehistoric Society*, vol. 22, 1956, pp.6–22.

6 The *Colinda* spearhead is in Norwich Castle Museum.

7 L.P. Louwe-Kooijmans, *The Rhine/ Meuse Delta: Four Studies on its Prehistoric Occupation and Holocene Geology* (E.J. Brill, Leiden, 1974), p.70. See also his paper in the journal of the Dutch State Archaeology Service: 'Mesolithic Bone and Antler Implements from the North Sea and from the Netherlands', *Berichten van de Rijksdienst voor bet Oudheidkundig Bodenmonderz*, vols 20–1, 1970–71, pp.67–73.

8 H.H. Lamb, 'Reconstruction of the Course of Post-Glacial Climate over the World', in A.F. Harding (ed.), *Climate Change in Later Prehistory* (Edinburgh University Press, 1982), pp.11–32.

9 Ian Simmons and Michael Tooley (eds), *The Environment in British Prehistory* (Duckworth, London, 1981). See also John G. Evans, *The Environment of Early Man in the British Isles* (Elek, London, 1975).

10 Although slightly outdated, my favourite book on the British climate is by Gordon Manley, *Climate and the British Scene* (Collins, London, 1952). I also recommend *The Collins Guide to the Weather*, by Gunter D. Roth (Collins, London, 1981).

11 Alasdair Whittle, 'Climate, Grazing and Man: Notes Towards the Definition of a Relationship', in Harding, *Climate Change in Later Prehistory*, op. cit., pp.192–203.

12 In these paragraphs I rely much on Bryan Sykes's inspiring book *The Seven Daughters of Eve*, op. cit.

13 Not being a geneticist myself, I cannot comment on the science of Brian Sykes's work, but it would appear that there may be up to twenty-two female lineages in Europe. See a review of *The Seven Daughters of Eve*, op. cit., by Keri Brown in *British Archaeology*, vol. 66, August 2002, pp.30–1.

14 The 'wave of advance theory' is fully described by A.J. Ammerman and L.L. Cavalli-Sforza, 'A Population Model for the Diffusion of Early Farming in Europe', in Colin Renfrew (ed.), *The Explanation of Culture Change: Models in Prehistory* (Duckworth, London, 1973), pp.343–57.

15 A route known as the 'Carcassonne–Narbonne gap'.

16 Colin Renfrew, *Archaeology and Language: The Puzzle of Indo-European Origins* (Penguin Books, Harmondsworth, 1987).

17 F.R. Hodson, 'Some Pottery from Eastbourne, the "Marnians" and the Pre-Roman Iron Age in Southern England', *Proceedings of the Prehistoric Society*, vol. 28, 1962, pp.140–55; F.R. Hodson, 'Cultural Grouping Within the

British Pre-Roman Iron Age', *Proceedings of the Prehistoric Society*, vol. 30, 1964, pp.99–110.

18 Simon James, *The Atlantic Celts: Ancient People or Modern Invention?* (British Museum Press, London, 1999).

19 David Hall and John Coles, for example, argued strongly for continuity between the Mesolithic and the Neolithic in *Fenland Survey: An Essay in Landscape and Persistence*, English Heritage Archaeological Report No. 1 (London, 1994), p.46.

20 A recent and highly convincing paper links genetic data to the spread of Neolithic culture in the eastern Mediterranean, south-eastern Europe, Italy and southern France: Roy King and Peter A. Underhill, 'Congruent Distributions of Neolithic Painted Pottery and Ceramic Figurines with Y-Chromosome Lineages', *Antiquity*, vol. 76, 2002, pp.707–14.

21 Francis Pryor, *Farmers in Prehistoric Britain* (Tempus Books, Stroud, 1998).

22 G.F. Mitchell, 'The Larnian Culture: A Minimal View', *Proceedings of the Prehistoric Society*, vol. 37, 1971, pp.274–83; P.C. Woodman, 'A Review of the Scottish Mesolithic: A Plea for Normality', *Proceedings of the Society of Antiquaries of Scotland*, vol. 119, pp.1–32.

23 I am not alone in this opinion: Ian Kinnes, 'The Cattleship Potemkin: Reflections on the First Neolithic in Britain', in J.C. Barrett and I.A. Kinnes (eds), *The Archaeology of Context in the Neolithic and Bronze Age: Recent Trends* (Department of Archaeology and Prehistory, University of Sheffield, 1988), pp.2–8.

24 I have discussed the introduction of farming to Britain in greater detail in *Farmers in Prehistoric Britain*, op. cit., pp.23–35.

25 M.R. Jarman, 'Early Animal Husbandry', *Philosophical Transactions of the Royal Society of London*, Series B, vol. 275, pp.85–97.

26 T. Madsen and H.J. Jensen, 'Settlement and Land-Use in Early Neolithic Denmark', *Analecta Praehistorica Leidensia*, vol. 15, pp. 63–86.

27 L.P. Louwe-Kooijmans, 'Wetland Exploitation and Upland Relations of Prehistoric Communities in the Netherlands', in Julie Gardiner (ed.), *Flatlands and Wetlands: Current Themes in East Anglian Archaeology* (Norwich, 1993), East Anglian Archaeology No. 50, pp.71–116.

28 H.P. Blankholm, 'Late Mesolithic Hunter-Gatherers and the Transition to Farming in Southern Scandinavia', in Rowley-Conwy and Zvelebil, *Mesolithic Northwest Europe*, op. cit., pp.155–62.

29 Maisie Taylor has determined, for example, that no fewer than fifty-one bronze axes were used on the timbers at Seahenge. The full report on Seahenge, by Mark Brennand and Maisie Taylor, will appear in a future volume of the *Proceedings of the Prehistoric Society*.

30 Cathy Groves, *Dendrochronological Analysis of a Timber Circle at Holme-next-the-Sea, Norfolk*, English Heritage Centre for Archaeology Report 6/2002 (Portsmouth, 2002).

31 Richard Bradley, *The Prehistoric Settlement of Britain* (Routledge, London, 1978).

32 The Somerset Levels Project is one of the longest-running and most successful prehistoric research projects in Britain. Its results were published in a series of annual reports, the *Somerset Levels Papers*, from 1975 (vol. 1), under the auspices of the Departments of Archaeology at Cambridge and Exeter Universities.

33 Bryony and John Coles, *Sweet Track to Glastonbury: The Somerset Levels in Prehistory* (Thames and Hudson, London, 1986), p.38. The Sweet Track is described in Chapter 3 (pp.40–64).

34 John Coles quotes the Californian experiments of Saxton T. Pope: *Experimental Archaeology* (Academic Press, London, 1979), pp.169–72.

35 The leading organisation involved with

all aspects of research into ancient archery is the Society of Archer-Antiquaries, 36 Myrtledene Road, Abbey Wood, London SE2 0EZ.

36 Figures taken from notes on a lecture to the Society of Antiquaries of London on 10 January 2001 by Robert Hardy. Source: the Society of Antiquaries online bulletin SALON, No. 1, 14 January 2001.

37 J.G.D. Clark, 'Neolithic Bows from Somerset, England and the Prehistory of Archery in Northwest Europe', *Proceedings of the Prehistoric Society*, vol. 29, 1963, pp.50–98.

38 We know of at least seven longbows from Britain and Ireland dating from Neolithic to Bronze Ages times. Alison Sheridan, 'A Longbow from Rotten Bottom, Dumfriesshire, Scotland', *NewsWARP*, No. 12, 1992, pp.13–15.

39 John Coles, Bryony Orme, A.C. Bishop and A.R. Woolley, 'A Jade Axe from the Somerset Levels', *Antiquity*, vol. 48, 1974, pp.216–20.

40 Bradley, *An Archaeology of Natural Places*, op. cit., pp.133–4.

41 For an excellent overview of tree-ring dating see M.G.L. Baillie, *A Slice Through Time: Dendrochronology and Precision Dating* (Batsford, London, 1995).

42 J. Hillam, C.M. Groves, D.M. Brown, M.G.L. Baillie, J.M. Coles and B.J. Coles, 'Dendrochronology of the English Neolithic', *Antiquity*, vol. 64, 1990, pp.210–20.

CHAPTER SIX – *The Earlier Neolithic (4200–3000 BC). Part 1: The Daily Round*

1 Mark Edmonds, *Ancestral Geographies of the Neolithic: Landscapes, Monuments and Memory* (Routledge, London, 1999).

2 It has been enlarged and revised in a second edition: Julian Thomas, *Understanding the Neolithic* (Routledge, London, 1999).

3 Seamus Caulfield, 'Neolithic Fields: The Irish Evidence', in H.C. Bowen and P.J. Fowler (eds), *Early Land Allotment*, British Archaeological Reports No. 48 (Oxford, 1978), pp.137–44.

4 Gabriel Cooney, 'Images of Settlement and the Landscape in the Neolithic', in Peter Topping (ed.), *Neolithic Landscapes*, Oxbow Monograph No. 86 (Oxford, 1997), pp.23–31.

5 Alex Bayliss and Francis Pryor, 'Radiocarbon and Absolute Chronology', in Pryor, *The Flag Fen Basin*, op. cit., pp.390–9.

6 Francis Pryor, 'Sheep Stockyards and Field Systems: Bronze Age Livestock in Eastern England', *Antiquity*, vol. 70, 1996, pp.313–24.

7 Stuart Needham and Mark G. Macklin (eds), *Alluvial Archaeology in Britain*, Oxbow Monograph No. 27 (Oxford, 1992).

8 For a good summary of early Neolithic farming villages in Europe see Alasdair Whittle, *Neolithic Europe: A Survey* (Cambridge University Press, 1985), pp.76–87.

9 See papers by Timothy Darvill, Eoin Grogan and Gordon J. Barclay in Timothy Darvill and Julian Thomas (eds), *Neolithic Houses in Northwest Europe and Beyond*, Oxbow Monograph No. 57 (Oxford, 1996).

10 Francis Pryor, *Excavation at Fengate, Peterborough, England: The First Report*, Royal Ontario Museum Archaeology Monograph No. 3 (Toronto, 1974), pp.6–14.

11 J.G.D. Clark, 'A Neolithic House at Haldon, Devon', *Proceedings of the Prehistoric Society*, vol. 4, 1938, pp.222–3.

12 I came clean about my change of mind in 1988: 'Earlier Neolithic Organized Landscapes and Ceremonial in Lowland Britain', in Barrett and Kinnes, *The Archaeology of Context in the Neolithic and Bronze Age*, op. cit., pp.63–72. I have also written more extensively about how I rethought my ideas on the 'house' in *Seahenge*, op. cit., pp.57–65.

13 Julian Thomas, 'Neolithic Houses in Mainland Britain and Ireland: A

Sceptical View', in Darvill and Thomas, *Neolithic Houses in Northwest Europe and Beyond*, op. cit., pp.1–12.

14 Daryl Garton, 'Buxton', *Current Archaeology*, vol. 103, 1987, pp.250–3.

15 E.H. Willcock, 'A Neolithic Site on Haldon', *Proceedings of the Devon Archaeological Exploration Society*, vol. 2, 1936, pp.244–63.

16 F.M. Griffith, 'Recent Work on Neolithic Enclosures in Devon', in Timothy Darvill and Julian Thomas (eds), *Neolithic Enclosures in Atlantic Northwest Europe* (Oxbow Books, Oxford, 2001), pp.66–77.

17 Eoin Grogan, 'Neolithic Houses in Ireland: A Broader Perspective', *Antiquity*, vol. 76, 2002, pp.517–25.

18 Derek Simpson, 'Ballygalley Houses, Co. Antrim, Ireland', in Darvill and Thomas, *Neolithic Houses in Northwest Europe and Beyond*, op. cit., pp.123–32; Derek Simpson and Andrew Selkirk, 'Ballygalley', *Current Archaeology*, vol. 134, 1993, pp.60–2.

19 Fishing was very important in the Mesolithic of Ireland. See Peter Woodman, 'Getting Back to Basics: Transitions to Farming in Ireland and Britain', in T. Douglas Price (ed.), *Europe's First Farmers* (Cambridge University Press, 2000), pp.219–59.

20 There is a vast literature on surface flint scatters. Three good examples: R. Holgate, *Neolithic Settlement of the Thames Basin*, British Archaeological Reports No. 194 (Oxford, 1988); Hall and Coles, *Fenland Survey*, op. cit., pp.55–64; John Schofield, *Managing Lithic Scatters: Archaeological Guidance for Planning Authorities and Developers* (English Heritage, London, 2000).

21 M.R. Edmonds, 'Rocks and Risk: Problems with Lithic Procurement Strategies', in A.G. Brown and M.R. Edmonds (eds), *Lithic Analysis and Later Prehistory*, British Archaeological Reports No. 162 (Oxford, 1987), p.174.

22 F.M.M. Pryor, *Excavation at Fengate, Peterborough England: The Second Report*, Royal Ontario Museum Archaeology Monograph 5 (Toronto, 1978).

23 See Table 21 in Maisie Taylor, 'Wood and Bark from the Enclosure Ditch', in Francis Pryor, *Etton: Excavations at a Neolithic Causewayed Enclosure near Maxey, Cambridgeshire, 1982–7*, English Heritage Archaeological Report No. 18 (London, 1998), pp.115–59.

24 Thomas, *Understanding the Neolithic*, op. cit., p.78.

25 Finds along the river Thames are constantly being monitored by the Thames Archaeological Survey. To take part contact the City of London Archaeological Society (website: www.colas.org.uk).

26 Roy Adkins and Ralph Jackson, *Neolithic Stone and Flint Axes from the River Thames*, Department of Prehistoric and Romano-British Antiquities No. 1 (British Museum, London, 1978).

27 W.A. Cummins, 'The Neolithic Stone Axe Trade in Britain', *Antiquity*, vol. 48, 1974, pp.201–5.

28 The standard modern account of the Neolithic 'axe trade' is Richard Bradley and Mark Edmonds, *Interpreting the Axe Trade: Production and Exchange in Neolithic Britain* (Cambridge University Press, 1993).

29 Bradley, *An Archaeology of Natural Places*, op. cit.

30 One is known in Northern Ireland and two in Scotland. All are far smaller than the southern English examples.

31 Martyn Barber, David Field and Peter Topping, *The Neolithic Flint Mines of England*, Royal Commission on the Historical Monuments of England (English Heritage, Swindon, 1999).

32 For an excellent account of Pull's achievements, mostly using his own sources and fine photos, see Miles Russell (ed.), *Rough Quarries, Rocks and Hills: John Pull and the Neolithic Flint Mines of Sussex*, Bournemouth University School of Conservation Sciences Occasional Paper No. 6 (Oxbow Books, Oxford, 2001).

33 Richard Bradley, *Altering the Earth: The Origin of Monuments in Britain and Continental Europe* (Society of Antiquaries of Scotland, Edinburgh, 1993).

34 Richard Bradley, 'Neolithic Expectations'. Manuscript awaiting publication (2002).

35 Richard Bradley, 'In the Dutch Mountains: The Ritualization of Domestic Life in Neolithic Society'. Manuscript awaiting publication (2002).

36 Survival of the physical remains of the last war in Britain has been monitored by the Council for British Archaeology's Defence of Britain Project (DoB), which was successfully completed in March 2002. Airfield control towers may be taken as an example of destruction: of the many hundreds built, only two survive even relatively intact. Only 1.6 per cent of those false airfields and towns known as bombing decoys survive at all complete, and 67 per cent have vanished entirely. The archive of the DoB is stored at the Imperial War Museum, London. The DoB website is at http//:www.britarch.ac.uk/projects/ dob. The database may be visited at http://ads.ahds.ac.uk/catalogue/ resources.html/dob.

CHAPTER SEVEN – *The Earlier Neolithic (4200–3000 BC). Part 2: Monuments and Pathways*

1 Thomas, *Understanding the Neolithic*, op. cit., p.23. For an accessible account of the serpent mound builders and the Hopewell culture see Brian M. Fagan, *Kingdoms of Gold, Kingdoms of Jade: The Americas Before Columbus* (Thames and Hudson, London, 1991).

2 For an accessible introduction see R.J. Mercer, *Causewayed Enclosures* (Shire Publications, Princes Risborough, 1990).

3 Pryor, *Etton*, op. cit.

4 Niels H. Andersen, *Sarup Vol. 1: The Sarup Enclosures* (Aarhus University Press, Denmark, 1997).

5 R. Palmer, 'Interrupted Ditch Enclosures in Britain: The Use of Aerial Photography for Comparative Studies', *Proceedings of the Prehistoric Society*, vol. 42, 1976, pp.161–86; D.R. Wilson, ' "Causewayed Camps" and "Interrupted Ditch Systems" ', *Antiquity*, vol. 49, 1975, pp.178–86.

6 For a general discussion of the coincidence of causewayed enclosures and flint mines see A. Oswald, C. Dyer and M. Barber, *The Creation of Monuments: Neolithic Causewayed Enclosures in the British Isles*, Royal Commission on the Historical Monuments of England (English Heritage, Swindon, 2001), p.117.

7 Isobel Smith, *Windmill Hill and Avebury: Excavations by Alexander Keiller 1925–1939* (Oxford University Press, 1965), p.19.

8 Mark Edmonds, *Ancestral Geographies of the Neolithic: Landscapes, Monuments and Memory* (Routledge, London, 1999), pp.118–19.

9 Pryor, *Seahenge*, op. cit., pp.79–108.

10 Oswald, Dyer and Barber, *The Creation of Monuments*, op. cit., p.107.

11 A.J. Walker and R.L. Otlet, 'Briar Hill: The Carbon 14 Measurements', in Helen M. Bamford, *Briar Hill: Excavation 1974–1987*, Archaeological Monograph No. 3 (Northampton Development Corporation, 1985), pp.126–8.

12 R.J.C. Atkinson, *Stonehenge: Archaeology and Interpretation*, 3rd edn (Penguin Books, Harmondsworth, 1979).

13 R.M.J. Cleal, K.E. Walker and R. Montague, *Stonehenge in its Landscape: Twentieth Century Excavations*, English Heritage Archaeological Report No. 10 (London, 1995).

14 For tree-throw pits see P.B. Kooi, 'De Orkaan van 13 November 1972 en het Onstaan van "Hoefijzervormige" Grondsporen', *Helinium*, vol. 14, 1974, pp.57–65.

15 Mike Pitts tells me that the Stonehenge Mesolithic posts aren't unique in southern Britain. A handful of others are known, but they are usually found

to be isolated – and often on much later sites.

16 Julian Richards, *The Stonehenge Environs Project*, English Heritage Archaeological Report No. 16 (London, 1990).

17 A few examples. First, northern England: A. Harding, 'Excavations in the Prehistoric Ritual Complex near Milfield, Northumberland', *Proceedings of the Prehistoric Society*, vol. 47, 1981, pp.87–135. Scotland: S. Piggott, 'The Excavations at Cairnpapple Hill, West Lothian, 1947–8', *Proceedings of the Society of Antiquaries of Scotland*, vol. 82, 1947–8, pp.68–123; G.J. Barclay and C.J. Russell-White, 'Excavations in the Ceremonial Complex of the Fourth to Second Millennium BC at Balfarg/Balbirnie, Glenrothes, Fife', *Proceedings of the Society of Antiquaries of Scotland*, vol. 123, 1993, pp.43–210.

18 Humphrey Case, 'A Ritual Site in North-East Ireland', in Glyn Daniel and Poul Kjaerum (eds), *Megalithic Graves and Ritual: Papers Presented at the III Atlantic Colloquium, Moesgard 1969*, Jutland Archaeological Society Publications No. 11 (Copenhagen, 1973), pp.173–96.

19 Francis Pryor, 'The Welland Valley as a Cultural Boundary Zone: An Example of Long-Term History', in Tom Lane and John Coles (eds), *Through Wet and Dry: Essays in Honour of David Hall*, Lincolnshire Archaeology and Heritage Reports No. 5 (Heckington, 2002), pp.18–32.

20 For a fine recent example see papers by McAvoy, Malim, Evans and Knight in Mike Dawson (ed.), *Prehistoric, Roman, and Post-Roman Landscapes of the Great Ouse Valley*, Council for British Archaeology Research Report No. 119 (York, 2000).

21 Contemporary droveways or field boundary ditches, for instance, are often absent (see, for example, the paper by Tim Malim cited in the previous note).

22 Cursuses are the subject of an important recent collection of essays:

Alistair Barclay and Jan Harding (eds), *Pathways and Ceremonies: The Cursus Monuments of Britain and Ireland*, Neolithic Studies Group Seminar Papers No. 4 (Oxbow, Oxford, 1999).

23 I discussed and illustrated the Maxey ritual landscape in *Seahenge*, op. cit., pp.109–85. That account is based on the original report: Francis Pryor and Charles French, *Archaeology and Environment in the Lower Welland Valley*, 2 vols, East Anglian Archaeology Report No. 27 (Cambridge, 1985).

24 Kenneth Brophy, 'The Cursus Monuments of Scotland', in Barclay and Harding, *Pathways and Ceremonies*, op. cit., pp.119–29.

25 Julian Thomas, 'The Holywood Cursus Complex, Dumfries: An Interim Account 1997', in ibid., pp.107–15.

26 Christopher Tilley, *A Phenomenology of Landscape: Places, Paths and Monuments* (Berg, London, 1994).

27 D.G. Buckley, J.D. Hedges and N.Brown, 'Excavations at a Neolithic Cursus, Springfield, Essex, 1979–85', *Proceedings of the Prehistoric Society*, vol. 67, 2001, pp.101–62.

28 John Barrett, Richard Bradley and Martin Green, *Landscape, Monuments and Society: The Prehistory of Cranborne Chase* (Cambridge University Press, 1991), p.56.

CHAPTER EIGHT – *The Archaeology of Death in the Neolithic*

1 I write this with painful memories of a close friend, the excavation supervisor at Maxey, Mark Gregson, who was killed in a car accident in 1982, at the age of only twenty-four. His friends published a tribute to him: Keith Ray (ed.), *Young Archaeologist: Collected Unpublished Papers, Contributions to Archaeological Thinking and Practice from Mark S. Gregson* (privately printed, Cambridge, 1982).

2 Thomas, *Understanding the Neolithic*, op. cit., p.129.

3 Alan Saville, *Hazleton North: The Excavation of a Neolithic Long Cairn of the Cotswold-Severn Group*, English Heritage Archaeological Report No. 13 (London, 1990).

4 Glyn Daniel's *The Megalithic Builders of Western Europe* (Penguin Books, Harmondsworth, 1962) is the best account of this outdated view of megalithic 'cultures'. It lost credence with the publication of the first radiocarbon dates, which demonstrated that many of the connections between different areas of the supposed 'culture' could not have happened. The radiocarbon evidence was summarised by Colin Renfrew, *Before Civilization: The Radiocarbon Revolution and Prehistoric Europe* (Jonathan Cape, London, 1973).

5 J.G. Evans, 'Habitat Change on the Calcareous Soils of Britain: The Impact of Neolithic Man', in D.D.A. Simpson (ed.), *Economy and Settlement in Neolithic and Early Bronze Age Britain and Europe* (Leicester University Press, 1971), pp.27–74.

6 At Maxey, for example, our soil scientist, Charles French, was able to prove the deliberate deturfing of the ground below a small oval barrow: Charles French, 'Soil, Sediment and Molluscan Analyses of Excavated Features', in Francis Pryor, Charles French et al., *The Fenland Project No. 1: The Lower Welland Valley*, vol. 1, East Anglian Archaeology No. 27 (Cambridge, 1985), pp.205–9

7 Saville, *Hazleton North*, op. cit., p.179.

8 J.G. Evans and D.D.A. Simpson, 'Giants' Hills 2 Long Barrow, Skendleby, Lincolnshire', *Archaeologia*, vol. 109, 1991, pp.1–46.

9 Michael Shanks and Christopher Tilley, 'Ideology, Symbolic Power and Ritual Communication: A Reinterpretation of Neolithic Mortuary Practices', in Ian Hodder (ed.), *Symbolic and Structural Archaeology* (Cambridge University Press, 1982), pp.129–54.

10 Stuart Piggott, *The West Kennet Long Barrow, Excavations 1955–56*, Ministry of Works Archaeological Reports No. 4 (HMSO, London, 1962).

11 Ibid., p.6.

12 I.J. Thorpe, 'Ritual, Power and Ideology: A Reconstruction of Earlier Neolithic Rituals in Wessex', in Richard Bradley and Julie Gardiner (eds), *Neolithic Studies: A Review of Some Current Research*, British Archaeological Reports No. 133 (Oxford, 1984), p.49.

13 B.E. Vyner, 'The Excavation of a Neolithic Cairn at Street House, Loftus, Cleveland', *Proceedings of the Prehistoric Society*, vol. 50, 1984, pp.151–95.

14 Hall and Coles, *Fenland Survey*, op. cit.

15 Ian Hodder and Paul Shand, 'The Haddenham Long Barrow: An Interim Statement', *Antiquity*, vol. 62, 1988, pp.349–53.

16 The trend towards articulation is discussed by Thorpe, 'Ritual, Power and Ideology', op. cit., pp.51–4.

17 Pryor, *Seahenge*, op. cit., Chapter 6.

18 Mike Pitts, *Hengeworld* (Arrow Books, London, 2001).

19 Alistair Barclay and Claire Halpin, *Excavations at Barrow Hills, Radley, Oxfordshire. Volume 1: The Neolithic and Bronze Age Monument Complex*, Oxford Archaeological Unit Thames Valley Landscapes Vol. 11 (Oxford, 1999).

20 Barrow Hills is a sorry tale, because most of the destruction, especially of the causewayed enclosure, took place before modern planning controls came into effect. See Don Benson and David Miles, *The Upper Thames Valley: An Archaeological Survey of the River Gravels*, Oxfordshire Archaeological Unit Survey No. 2 (Oxford, 1974), pp.87–90.

21 I have stayed with Richard Bradley's original phasing for the burial, but this is not in agreement with a subsequent radiocarbon date, which would place it rather later.

22 The phasing is summarised, with radiocarbon dates, in Chapter 9 of Barclay and Halpin, *Excavations at*

Barrow Hills, Radley, Oxfordshire. Volume 1, op. cit.

23 Michael and Claire O'Kelly, 'The Tumulus of Dowth, County Meath', *Proceedings of the Royal Irish Academy*, vol. 83C, 1983, pp.135–90.

24 'At the best, excavation is destruction; and destruction unmitigated by all the resources of contemporary knowledge and accumulated experience cannot be too rigorously impugned' – Sir Mortimer Wheeler, *Archaeology from the Earth* (Penguin Books, Harmondsworth, 1954), p.15.

25 For the justification for the restoration, see Michael O'Kelly, 'The Restoration of Newgrange', *Antiquity*, vol. 53, 1979, pp.205–10. For a critique see P.-R. Giot's review of O'Kelly's book *Newgrange: Archaeology, Art and Legend* (Thames and Hudson, London, 1982), in *Antiquity*, vol. 57, 1979, pp.149–50.

26 The standard reference on megalithic art is by Elizabeth Shee Twohig, *The Megalithic Art of Western Europe* (Oxford University Press, 1981).

27 David P. Sweetman, 'An Earthen Enclosure at Monknewtown, Slane, County Meath', *Proceedings of the Royal Irish Academy*, vol. 76C, 1976, pp.25–72.

28 See papers by Conor Newman, 'Notes on Four Cursus-Like Monuments in County Meath, Ireland' (pp.141–7), and Alistair Barclay and Gill Hey, 'Cattle, Cursus Monuments and the River: The Development of Ritual and Domestic Landscapes in the Upper Thames Valley' (pp.67–76), in Barclay and Harding, *Pathways and Ceremonies*, op. cit.

29 O'Kelly, *Newgrange*, op. cit.; George Eogan, *Knowth and the Passage-Tombs of Ireland* (Thames and Hudson, London, 1986).

30 Both Newgrange and Knowth continued as centres for ritual and settlement after their initial setting-out and use. See, for example: George Eogan, *Excavations at Knowth 1: Smaller Passage-Tombs, Neolithic Occupation and Beaker Activity*, Royal Irish

Academy Monograph in Archaeology No. 1 (Dublin, 1984). See also M.J. O'Kelly, Rose M. Cleary and Daragh Lehan, *Newgrange, County Meath, Ireland: The Late Neolithic/Beaker Period Settlement*, British Archaeological Reports International Series No. 190 (Oxford, 1983).

31 Andrew B. Powell, 'Newgrange: Science or Symbolism?', *Proceedings of the Prehistoric Society*, vol. 60, 1994, pp.85–96.

32 A. and A.S. Thom, *Megalithic Rings: Plans and Data for 229 Monuments in Britain*, British Archaeological Reports No. 81 (Oxford, 1980).

33 A note in *Antiquity*, vol. 28, 1954, pp.231–2.

34 Jeremy Dronfield, 'Entering Alternative Realities: Cognition, Art and Architecture in Irish Passage Tombs', *Cambridge Archaeological Journal*, vol. 6, 1996, pp.37–72.

CHAPTER NINE – *The Age of Stonehenge (the Final Neolithic and Earliest Bronze Age: 2500–1800 BC)*

1 Richard Bradley, *The Social Foundations of Prehistoric Britain: Themes and Variations in the Archaeology of Power* (Longmans, London, 1984).

2 The title of this chapter is borrowed from Colin Burgess, who wrote a superb and accessible book on the British Bronze Age: *The Age of Stonehenge* (Dent, London, reprinted 2002).

3 M. Parker Pearson and Ramilisonina, 'Stonehenge for the Ancestors: The Stones Pass on the Message', *Antiquity*, vol. 72, 1998, pp.308–26; Parker Pearson and Ramilisonina, 'Stonehenge for the Ancestors: Part Two', *Antiquity*, vol. 72, 1998, pp.855–6.

4 M. Parker Pearson and K. Godden, *In Search of the Red Slave: Shipwreck and Captivity in Madagascar* (Sutton Publishing, Stroud, 2002).

5 M. Parker Pearson, 'Ancestors, Bones

and Stones in Neolithic and Early Bronze Age Britain and Ireland', in Anna Ritchie (ed.), *Neolithic Orkney in its European context*, McDonald Institute Monographs (Cambridge, 2000), pp.203–14.

6 Ibid., p.203.

7 G. Wyman Abbott, 'The Discovery of Prehistoric Pits at Peterborough', *Archaeologia*, vol. 62, 1910, pp.332–52.

8 Grooved Ware has been the subject of an excellent collection of recent studies, edited by Rosamund Cleal and Ann MacSween, *Grooved Ware in Britain and Ireland*, Neolithic Studies Group Seminar Papers No. 3 (Oxbow, Oxford, 1999).

9 Pitts, *Hengeworld*, op. cit., pp.310–11.

10 M.E. Cunnington, *Woodhenge* (George Simpson, Devizes, 1929).

11 G.J. Wainwright and I.H. Longworth, *Durrington Walls: Excavations 1966–1968*, Report of the Research Committee of the Society of Antiquaries of London No. 29 (London, 1971).

12 Currently the most accessible source on Stanton Drew, with several references to it, is Pitts, *Hengeworld*, op. cit., pp.15–22.

13 At Stonehenge the 'stone monument' dates to Phase 3 (starting at 2550 BC): R.M.J. Cleal, K.E. Walker and R. Montague, *Stonehenge in its Landscape: Twentieth Century Excavations*, English Heritage Archaeological Report No. 10 (London, 1995), p.167–331. For the transition from timber to stone circles see Alex Gibson, *Stonehenge and Timber Circles* (Tempus Books, Stroud, 1998).

14 For pre-Bronze Age round barrows see I.A. Kinnes, *Round Barrows and Ring-Ditches in the British Neolithic*, British Museum Department of Prehistoric and Romano-British Antiquities Occasional Paper No. 7 (London, 1979).

15 Richards, *The Stonehenge Environs Project*, op. cit., p.243.

16 The Coneybury henge was excavated as part of the Stonehenge Environs Project and is described on pp.123–58 of the report (see previous note).

17 For the Beckhampton Avenue and the new causewayed enclosure in Longstones Field see Mark Gillings, Joshua Pollard and Dave Wheatley, 'Avebury and the Beckhampton Avenue', *Current Archaeology*, vol. 167, 2000, pp.428–33. See also Alasdair Whittle, *Sacred Mound Holy Rings – Silbury Hill and the West Kennet Palisade Enclosures: A Later Neolithic Complex in North Wiltshire*, Oxbow Monograph No. 74 (Oxford, 1997).

18 Peter J. Ucko, Michael Hunter, Alan J. Clark and Andrew David, *Avebury Reconsidered: From the 1660s to the 1990s* (Unwin Hyman, London, 1991), p.223.

19 Robert Bewley, Mark Cole, Andrew David, Roger Featherstone, Andrew Payne and Fiona Small, 'New Features Within the Henge at Avebury, Wiltshire: Aerial and Geophysical Evidence', *Antiquity*, vol. 70, 1996, pp.639–46.

20 See Mike Pitts, 'Return to the Sanctuary', *British Archaeology*, vol. 51, 2000, pp.15–19.

21 Orcadian 'prehistory' is usually extended forwards in time to about AD 1000, to include the Vikings. Two main sources should point you towards the rest of the literature: Colin Renfrew, *Investigations in Orkney*, Report of the Research Committee of the Society of Antiquaries of London No. 38 (London, 1979); and Anna Ritchie (ed.), *Neolithic Orkney in its European Context*, McDonald Institute Monographs (Cambridge, 2000).

22 Anna Ritchie, *Prehistoric Orkney* (Batsford Books, London, 1995).

23 Aaron Watson, 'The Sounds of Transformation: Acoustics, Monuments and Ritual in the British Neolithic', in Price, *The Archaeology of Shamanism*, op. cit., p.185.

24 R. Bradley, T. Phillips, C. Richards and M. Webb, 'Decorating the Houses of the Dead: Incised and Pecked Motifs in Orkney Chambered Tombs', *Cambridge Archaeological Journal*, vol. 11, 2001, pp.45–67.

25 V. Gordon Childe, *Skara Brae: A Pictish Village in Orkney* (Kegan Paul, London, 1931).

26 Colin Richards, 'Barnhouse and Maeshowe', *Current Archaeology*, vol. 131, 1992, pp.444-8.

27 A. Oswald, 'A Doorway on the Past: Practical and Mystic Concerns in the Orientation of Roundhouse Doorways', in Adam Gwilt and Colin Haselgrove (eds), *Reconstructing Iron Age Societies: New Approaches to the British Iron Age*, Oxbow Monograph 71 (Oxford, 1997), p.93.

28 Renfrew, *Investigations in Orkney*, op. cit., pp.44-198.

29 Ibid., pp.31-8.

30 Colin Renfrew, 'Monuments, Mobilization and Social Organization in Neolithic Wessex', in Renfrew, *The Explanation of Culture Change*, op. cit., pp.539-58.

31 Stuart Needham, 'Chronology and Periodisation in the British Bronze Age', *Acta Archaeologica*, vol. 67, 1996, pp.121-40.

32 Joan Taylor, *Bronze Age Goldwork of the British Isles* (Cambridge University Press, 1980), p.46.

33 F.K. Annable and D.D.A. Simpson, *Guide Catalogue of the Neolithic and Bronze Age Collections in Devizes Museum* (Wiltshire Archaeological and Natural History Society, 1964, Devizes), pp.45-6, 99.

34 The Introduction to an excellent exhibition of fine prehistoric objects draws parallels between the Bronze Age and the uniform of modern powerful people, including a traffic warden and the Chief Constable of Lothian and Borders Police! D.V. Clarke, T.G. Cowie and A. Foxon, *Symbols of Power at the Time of Stonehenge* (National Museum of Antiquities of Scotland, Edinburgh, 1985), pp.1-13.

35 I illustrate the Little Cressingham goldwork in *Seahenge*, op. cit.

36 Gwilym Hughes, *The Lockington Gold Hoard: An Early Bronze Age Barrow Cemetery at Lockington, Leicester-shire* (Oxbow Books, Oxford, 2000).

37 Parker Pearson and Ramilisonina, 'Stonehenge for the Ancestors: The Stones Pass on the Message', op. cit., pp.322-3.

38 For a very sane discussion on controlling elites, cosmological alignments and other matters in Neolithic and Bronze Age Orkney see Clive Ruggles and Gordon Barclay, 'Cosmology, Calendars and Society in Neolithic Orkney: A Rejoinder to Euan MacKie', *Antiquity*, vol. 74, 2000, pp.62-74.

39 Parker Pearson, 'Ancestors, Bones and Stones . . .', op. cit., p.212.

40 Renfrew, *Investigations in Orkney*, op. cit., pp.39-43.

41 J.N.G. Ritchie, 'The Stones of Stenness, Orkney', *Proceedings of the Society of Antiquaries of Scotland*, vol. 107, 1976, pp.1-60.

42 Colin Richards, 'Monuments as Landscape: Creating the Centre of the World in Late Neolithic Orkney', *World Archaeology*, vol. 28, 1996, p.206.

43 Irish megalithic tombs have generally been studied as archaeological artefacts, symbols of power or repositories of significant art. They were also important places in other respects, as Gabriel Cooney reminds us in 'Body Politics and Grave Messages: Irish Neolithic Mortuary Practices', in N. Sharples and A. Sheridan (eds), *Vessels for the Ancestors* (Edinburgh University Press, 1992), pp.128-42.

44 George Eogan and Helen Roche, 'Grooved Ware from Brugh na Bóinne and its Wider Context', in Cleal and MacSween, *Grooved Ware in Britain and Ireland*, op. cit., pp.98-111.

45 For a useful summary of the various types of barrow see Leslie V. Grinsell, *Barrows in England and Wales* (Shire Books, Princes Risborough, 1979). This is based on his original study, *The Ancient Burial Mounds of England* (Methuen, London, 1936).

46 For more information on ancient metallurgy contact the Ancient

Metallurgy Research Group, Dept of Archaeological Sciences, Bradford University, Bradford BD7 1DP.

47 For readers with a strong distaste for 'ritual' I can suggest one paper which proposes a different view (with which I disagree on numerous grounds): Colin Pendleton, 'Firstly, Let's Get Rid of Ritual', in Joanna Brück (ed.), *Bronze Age Landscapes: Tradition and Transformation* (Oxbow Books, Oxford, 2001), pp.17–18.

48 Until recently the archaeology of metalworking was viewed from a technological perspective alone. New approaches also take in social and symbolic aspects. See, for example, D.P. Collett, 'Metaphors and Representations Associated with Precolonial Iron-Smelting in Eastern and Southern Africa', in T. Shaw, P. Sinclair, B. Andah and A. Okpoko (eds), *The Archaeology of Africa: Food, Metals and Towns* (Routledge, London, 1963), pp.499–511.

49 Andrew Reid and Rachel MacLean 'Symbolism and the Social Context of Iron Production', *World Archaeology*, vol. 27, 1995, pp.144–61.

50 Aidan O'Sullivan, 'Neolithic, Bronze Age and Iron Age Woodworking Techniques', in Barry Raftery, *Trackway Excavations in the Mountdillon Bogs, County Longford, 1985–1991*, Irish Archaeological Wetland Unit, Transactions, vol. 3 (University College, Dublin, 1996), pp.291–342.

51 A very useful book has appeared on the symbolism of trees in anthropology: Laura Rival (ed.), *The Social Life of Trees: Anthropological Perspectives on Tree Symbolism* (Berg, Oxford, 1998).

52 Bradley, *An Archaeology of Natural Places*, op. cit., p.12.

53 Mark Brennand and Maisie Taylor, 'The Survey and Excavation of a Bronze Age Timber Circle at Holme-next-the-Sea, Norfolk, 1998–99', *Proceedings of the Prehistoric Society*, forthcoming.

54 See Pryor, *Seahenge*, op. cit., pp.228–9.

CHAPTER TEN – *Pathways to Paradise (the Mid- and Later Bronze Age: 1800–700 BC)*

1 I have decided not to use the term 'Celtic' to describe the native population of Iron Age Britain. In this I follow Simon James (*The Atlantic Celts*, op. cit.).

2 Two readily accessible sources of information: Andrew Selkirk (with Tony Hammond), 'The Great Orme Mine', *Current Archaeology*, vol. 130, 1992, pp.404–9; A. Dutton and P.J. Fasham, 'Prehistoric Copper Mining on the Great Orme, Llandudno, Gwynedd', *Proceedings of the Prehistoric Society*, vol. 60, 1994, pp.245–86.

3 Simon Timberlake, 'Mining and Prospection for Metals in Early Bronze Age Britain: Making Claims Within the Archaeological Landscape', in Brück (ed.), *Bronze Age Landscapes*, op. cit., pp.179–92.

4 W. O'Brien, *Bronze Age Copper Mining in Britain and Ireland* (Shire Books, Princes Risborough, 1996).

5 Timberlake, 'Mining and Prospection for Metals in Early Bronze Age Britain', op. cit.

6 W. O'Brien, *Mount Gabriel: Bronze Age Mining in Ireland* (Galway University Press, 1994), pp.207–28.

7 A comprehensive study of the Isleham hoard is currently being prepared by David Coombs. In the meantime we must refer to the initial paper published shortly after the hoard's discovery: Dennis Britton, 'The Isleham Hoard, Cambridgeshire', *Antiquity*, vol. 34, 1960, pp.279–82.

8 Colin Burgess and David Coombs (eds), *Bronze Age Hoards: Some Finds Old and New*, British Archaeological Reports No. 67 (Oxford, 1979); George Eogan, *Hoards of the Irish Later Bronze Age* (University College, Dublin, 1983); Richard Bradley, *The Passage of Arms: An Archaeological Analysis of Prehistoric Hoards and Votive Deposits* (Cambridge University Press, 1990).

9 Francis Pryor, *A Catalogue of British*

and Irish Prehistoric Bronzes in the Royal Ontario Museum (Toronto, 1980), see nos 97–106, pp.46–7.

10 Two excellent books on the subtleties of prehistoric trade and exchange are Marshall Sahlins, *Stone Age Economics* (Tavistock Publications, London, 1972) and Marcel Mauss (trans. Ian Cunnison), *The Gift: Forms and Functions of Exchange in Archaic Societies* (Cohen and West, London, 1969).

11 Pryor, *The Flag Fen Basin*, op. cit.

12 The large report mentioned in the previous note is intended for academic readers. I've written a more accessible account, which is now out of print. It is also outdated in important respects: Francis Pryor, *The English Heritage Book of Flag Fen: Prehistoric Fenland Centre* (Batsford, London, 1991). For a more recent discussion see Pryor, *Seahenge*, op. cit., pp.286–311.

13 I can recommend an excellent and accessible new book on the Peterborough district: David Brandon and John Knight, *Peterborough Past: The City and the Soke* (Phillimore, Chichester, 2001).

14 R.C. Turner and R.G. Scaife (eds), *Bog Bodies: New Discoveries and New Perspectives* (British Museum Press, London, 1995).

15 Pryor, *The Flag Fen Basin*, op. cit., pp.432–4.

16 The site was originally dug by Naomi Field in 1981. Another excavation took place in 2001. A full report is expected to appear in 2002: N. Field and M. Parker Pearson, *Fiskerton: An Iron Age Timber Causeway with Iron Age and Roman Votive Offerings. Volume 1: The 1981 Excavations* (Oxbow Books, Oxford).

17 In fact they were buried complete, but broke in the ground subsequently.

18 Richard Osgood and Sarah Monks, *Bronze Age Warfare* (Sutton Publishing, Stroud, 2000), pp.19–23.

19 See Pryor, *Seahenge*, op. cit., pp.213–15.

20 We should not make the mistake of drawing the simplistic distinction that wet = ritual and dry = domestic. This would imply, for example, that finds of metalwork made on dry land were 'by definition' non-ritual. See Pendleton, 'Firstly, Let's Get Rid of Ritual', op. cit., pp.170–8.

21 Bradley Fen is still being excavated as I write (May 2002). I am deeply indebted to Chris Evans, director of the Cambridge University Archaeological Unit, and to Mark Knight, who is directing the dig, for the provisional plan and for much information on this fascinating site.

22 Both the burnt mounds from the Flag Fen area were recognised, as so often happens in archaeology, after their excavation. The first was described as an 'industrial area' and is covered in one of the Fengate reports: Francis Pryor, *Excavation at Fengate, Peterborough, England: The Third Report*, Combined Royal Ontario Museum Archaeology Monograph 6 and Northamptonshire Archaeological Society Monograph 1 (Northampton and Toronto, 1980), pp.7–14. The second consists of a 'tank' (pit F87) and some other features filled with burnt material. Pryor, *The Flag Fen Basin*, op. cit., pp.70–1.

23 For a useful collection of papers on burnt mounds and related topics see V. Buckley (ed.), *Burnt Offerings: International Contributions to Burnt Mound Archaeology* (Wordwell, Dublin, 1990).

24 Bradley, *The Social Foundations of Prehistoric Britain*, op. cit., p.163.

25 Jacqui Wood is an excellent cook who uses ancient methods, and I have lingered long over her delightful eel stew. Her book *Prehistoric Cooking* (Tempus Books, Stroud, 2002) is also mouthwatering.

26 McGrail, *Logboats of England and Wales*, op. cit.

27 To date we know of three large pieces of plank-built prehistoric boats from Britain (Dover and two from the Humber), plus fragments of another

seven. See also Sean McGrail and Eric Kentley (eds), *Sewn Plank Boats*, British Archaeological Reports, International Series No. 276 (Oxford, 1985).

28 The doyen of boat archaeology in Britain was the late Ted Wright. A book in his honour covers the field admirably: John Coles, Valerie Fenwick and Gillian Hutchinson (eds), *A Spirit of Enquiry: Essays for Ted Wright* (Wetland Archaeological Research Project/Nautical Archaeological Society/National Maritime Museum joint publication, 1993). Dover aside, the Humber area has produced the best evidence for plank boats. For a good summary of these see E.V. Wright, *The North Ferriby Boats* (National Maritime Museum, London, 1972).

29 I have based my account on the unrevised manuscript of the forthcoming definitive report: Peter Clark (ed.), *The Dover Bronze Age Boat*, English Heritage Archaeological Report (London, forthcoming).

30 It has been dated by radiocarbon to 1575–1520 BC. In archaeological terms this date would belong at the beginning of the Middle Bronze Age.

31 Keith Muckleroy, 'Middle Bronze Age Trade Between Britain and Europe: A Maritime Perspective', *Proceedings of the Prehistoric Society*, vol. 47, 1981, pp.275–96.

32 For the bronzes see David Coombs, 'The Dover Harbour Bronze Find: A Bronze Age Wreck?', *Archaeologia Atlantica*, vol. 1, 1976, pp.193–5. For the recovery project see S.P. Needham and M. Dean, 'La Cargaison de Langdon Bay à Douvres: La signification pour les échanges à travers la Manche', in J.-C. Blanchet (ed.), *Les Relations entre la continent et les Isles Britannique à l'Age du Bronze*, supplement to the *Revue Archéologique de Picardie* (Amiens, 1987), pp.119–24.

33 Martin Millett and Sean McGrail, 'The Archaeology of the Hasholme Logboat', *Archaeological Journal*, vol. 44, 1987, pp.69–155.

34 N. Nayling and A. Caseldine, *Excavations at Caldicote, Gwent: Bronze Age Palaeochannels in the Lower Nedern Valley*, Council for British Archaeology Research Report No. 108 (York, 1997). Since the Caldicote find further Bronze Age boat planks have been found in the Severn estuary: S. Johnson, S. McGrail and R. Morgan, 'Boat Planks of c.1170 BC', in M. Bell, A. Caseldine and H. Neumann, *Prehistoric Intertidal Archaeology in the Welsh Severn Estuary*, Council for British Archaeology Research Report No. 120 (York, 2000), pp.74–82.

35 There is a huge body of research into the prehistory of the Somerset Levels. A useful way in is via J.M. and B.J. Coles, *Prehistory of the Somerset Levels*, Somerset Levels Project (Exeter, 1989).

36 Martin Bell, 'Trackways and Other Linear Structures at Goldcliff', in Bell, Caseldine and Neumann, *Prehistoric Intertidal Archaeology in the Welsh Severn Estuary*, op. cit., pp.136–58.

37 The full report is still in preparation, but for pictures and a short description see Pryor, *Seahenge*, op. cit., p.227.

38 Several sizeable hoards containing large numbers of cart and harness fittings were found from the earliest Iron Age, in the sixth and seventh centuries BC. Many of these were imported from the Continent. See B.W. Cunliffe, *Iron Age Communities in Britain: An Account of England, Scotland and Wales from the Seventh Century BC Until the Roman Conquest*, 3rd edn (Routledge, London, 1991), pp.414–15.

39 Although now a little dated, this masterly review is still the last word on the subject: Stuart Piggott, *The Earliest Wheeled Transport, from the Atlantic Coast to the Caspian Sea* (Thames and Hudson, London, 1983). Stuart Piggott also published a more recent study on much the same subject: *Wagon, Chariot and Carriage: Symbol and Status in the History of Transport* (Thames and Hudson, London, 1992).

40 Pryor, *Seahenge*, op. cit., pp.222–3.

41 Details of the site (Code: CHT 009) may be found in the Suffolk County Council Sites and Monuments Record at County Hall, Ipswich.

42 A tripartite Bronze Age wheel has recently been found in the southern fens: Christopher Evans, 'Sampling Settlements: Investigations at Lingwood Farm, Cottenham and Eye Hill Farm, Soham', *Fenland Research*, vol. 8, 1993, pp.26–30. For Ireland: A.T. Lucas, 'Prehistoric Block-Wheels from Doogarymore, County Roscommon, and Timahoe, East County Kildare', *Journal of the Royal Society of Antiquaries of Ireland*, vol. 102, 1972, pp.19–48. For the continent: Hajo Hayen, 'Zwei in Holz erhalten gebliebene Reste von Wagenrädern aus Olympia', *Die Kunde*, vol. 31/32, 1980/81, pp.135–91.

43 J.D. van der Waals, 'Neolithic Disc Wheels in the Netherlands', *Palaeohistoria*, vol. 10, 1962, pp.103–46.

44 There is now a large literature on the principles behind the orientation and arrangement of prehistoric landscapes. A formative book is Christopher Tilley, *A Phenomenolgy of Landscape*, op. cit. The influence of the natural form of the landscape is superbly dealt with by Mark Edmunds and Tim Seaborne, *Prehistory in the Peak* (Tempus Books, Stroud, 2001). See also Chapter 10 (pp.145–64) of Richard Bradley, *The Significance of Monuments: On the Shaping of Human Experience in Neolithic and Bronze Age Europe* (Routledge, London, 1998).

45 The best-known example of such a layout is the parishes around Marshland in north-west Norfolk: Bob Sylvester, 'Some Early Maps of the Fens', in Lane and Coles, *Through Wet and Dry*, op. cit.

46 In upland areas the removal of rocks from field surfaces has traditionally been seen as simply an agricultural process. But there is increasing evidence to suggest that such 'clearance cairns' also played a symbolic role within the landscape. See for example Robert Johnston, ' "Breaking New Ground": Land Tenure and Fieldstone Clearance During the Bronze Age', in Brück, *Bronze Age Landscapes*, op. cit., pp.99–109.

47 The most up-to-date and accessible account of Barleycroft is Christopher Evans and Mark Knight, 'The "Community of Builders": The Barleycroft Post Alignments', in ibid., pp.83–98.

48 The main site of this period is at Welland Bank: Francis Pryor, 'Welland Bank Quarry, South Lincolnshire', *Current Archaeology*, vol. 160, 1998, pp.139–45.

49 David Thomas Yates, 'Bronze Age Field Systems in the Thames Valley', *Oxford Journal of Archaeology*, vol. 18, 1999, pp.157–70; D.T. Yates, 'Bronze Age Agricultural Intensification in the Thames Valley and Estuary', in Brück, *Bronze Age Landscapes*, op. cit., pp.65–82.

50 J. Moore and D. Jennings, *Reading Business Park: A Bronze Age Landscape*, Oxford Archaeological Unit (Oxford, 1992).

51 Francis Pryor, 'Sheep, Stockyards and Field Systems: Bronze Age Livestock Populations in the Fenlands of Eastern England', *Antiquity*, vol. 70, 1996, pp.313–24.

52 Andrew J. Lawson, *Potterne 1982–5: Animal Husbandry in Later Prehistoric Wiltshire*, Wessex Archaeology Report No. 17 (Salisbury, 2000).

53 Stuart P. Needham, *Excavation and Salvage at Runnymede Bridge 1978* (British Museum Press, London, 1991).

54 David Coombs, 'Metalwork', Chapter 10 of Pryor, *The Flag Fen Basin*, op. cit., pp.288–9.

55 David McOmish, David Field and Graham Brown, *The Field Archaeology of the Salisbury Plain Training Area* (English Heritage, Swindon, 2002).

56 Andrew Fleming, *The Dartmoor Reaves: Investigating Prehistoric Land Divisions* (Batsford, London, 1988).

57 Lynchets are banks of soil that accumulate down-slope against a field boundary after ploughing. They build up slowly, but can become very large indeed. See for example H.C. Bowen, *Ancient Fields* (S.R. Publishers, Wakefield, reprinted 1970); Christopher Taylor, *Fields in the English Landscape* (Dent, London, 1975); S. Wade-Martins, *Farms and Fields* (Batsford, London, 1995).

58 Cunliffe, *Facing the Ocean*, op. cit., pp.311–64.

CHAPTER ELEVEN – *Men of Iron (the Early Iron Age: 700–150 BC)*

1 Peter Reynolds died on 26 September 2001. Mick Aston's obituary in the *Guardian* (5 October 2001) is a fitting tribute.

2 Peter J. Reynolds, *Iron Age Farm: The Butser Experiment* (Colonnade Books, London, 1979).

3 D.W. Harding and I.M. Blake, 'An Early Iron Age Settlement in Dorset', *Antiquity*, vol. 37, 1963, pp.63–4.

4 For other large Iron Age roundhouses see Cunliffe, *Iron Age Communities in Britain*, 3rd edn, op. cit., p.244.

5 Problems associated with the concept of agency are well discussed in Chapter 3 of Bradley, *The Significance of Monuments*, op. cit., pp.36–50.

6 Timothy Darvill (ed.), *The Concise Oxford Dictionary of Archaeology* (Oxford University Press, 2002).

7 Eogan, *Knowth and the Passage-Tombs of Ireland*, op. cit., pp.198–9.

8 Helen M. Bamford, *Beaker Domestic Sites in the Fen Edge and East Anglia*, East Anglian Archaeology No. 16 (Dereham, 1982).

9 Drains filled with brushwood, known as 'brush drains', were used as land drains in the fens until the 1920s, when they were replaced by fired clay pipes.

10 Oswald, 'A Doorway on the Past', op. cit., pp.87–95.

11 Mike Parker Pearson, 'Food, Fertility and Front Doors in the First Millennium BC', in T.C. Champion and J.R. Collis (eds), *The Iron Age in Britain and Ireland: Recent Trends* (J.R. Collis Publications, Department of Archaeology and Prehistory, Sheffield University, 1996), pp.117–32.

12 Mike Parker Pearson, 'Food, Sex and Death: Cosmologies in the British Iron Age with Particular Reference to East Yorkshire', *Cambridge Archaeological Journal*, vol. 9, 1999, pp.43–69.

13 Sonia Chadwick, 'Early Iron Age Enclosure on Longbridge Deverill Cow Down, Wiltshire', in S.S. Frere (ed.), *Problems of the Iron Age in Southern Britain* (Institute of Archaeology, London University, 1958), pp.18–20.

14 I have used Stuart Needham's chronology here. See Needham, 'Chronology and Periodisation in the British Bronze Age', op. cit., p.137.

15 W.H. Manning, 'Ironwork Hoards in Iron Age and Roman Britain', *Britannia*, vol. 3, 1972, pp.224–50.

16 For references to Llyn Fawr see Cunliffe, *Iron Age Communities in Britain*, 3rd edn, op. cit., p.617. As a matter of interest, an iron-socketed axe was also found during recent excavations by Jim Rylett at the Fiskerton causeway.

17 A good regional study of iron-working is Chris Salter and Robert Ehrenreich, 'Iron Age Iron Metallurgy in Central Southern Britain', in Barry Cunliffe and David Miles (eds), *Aspects of the Iron Age in Central Southern England*, University of Oxford Committee for Archaeology Monograph No. 2 (Oxford, 1984), pp.146–61.

18 Richard Hingley, 'Iron, Ironworking and Regeneration: A Study of the Symbolic Meaning of Metalworking in Iron Age Britain', in Gwilt and Haselgrove, *Reconstructing Iron Age Societies*, op. cit., pp.9–18.

19 Peter Northover, 'Iron Age Bronze Metallurgy in Central Southern England', in Cunliffe and Miles, *Aspects of the Iron Age in Central Southern England*, op. cit., pp.126–45.

20 Mansel G. Spratling, 'The Debris of Metal Working', in G.J. Wainwright, *Gussage All Saints: An Iron Age Settlement in Dorset*, Department of the Environment Archaeological Reports No. 10 (HMSO, London, 1979), pp.125–49; Jennifer Foster, *The Iron Age Moulds from Gussage All Saints*, British Museum Occasional Paper No. 2 (London, 1980).

21 In Ireland the prehistoric period is considered to end in the fifth century AD with the rise of early Christian Ireland and the spread of late Roman and Anglo-Saxon influences from Britain and the Continent. See, for example, M. Herity and G. Eogan, *Ireland in Prehistory* (Routledge, Lomdon, 1977), pp.248–9.

22 The process began in the Early Iron Age. See Mike Seager Thomas, 'Two Early First Millennium BC Wells at Selsey, West Sussex and their Wider Significance', *Antiquaries Journal*, vol. 81, 2001, pp.15–50.

23 Cunliffe, *Iron Age Communities in Britain*, 3rd edn, op. cit.

24 B.W. Cunliffe, *Iron Age Communities in Britain*, 1st edn (Routledge, London, 1974), p.xvii.

25 Three refreshing collections of essays that take a new look at the period are: Champion and Collis, *The Iron Age in Britain and Ireland*, op. cit.; Gwilt and Haselgrove, *Reconstructing Iron Age Societies*, op. cit.; Simon James and Martin Millett (eds), *Britons and Romans: Advancing an Archaeological Agenda*, Council for British Archaeology Research Report No. 125 (York, 2001).

26 Gerald A. Wait, *Ritual and Religion in Iron Age Britain*, 2 vols, British Archaeological Reports No. 149 (Oxford, 1985). See also V. Kruta, O.H. Frey, B. Raftery and M. Szabó (eds), *The Celts* (Thames and Hudson, London, 1991).

27 *The Ordnance Survey Map of Southern Britain in the Iron Age* (Chessington, 1962) is a splendid source of useful information, such as the distribution of hill-forts.

28 J.F. Dyer, 'Dray's Ditches, Bedfordshire, and Early Iron Age Territorial Boundaries in the Eastern Chilterns', *Antiquaries Journal*, vol. 41, 1961, pp.32–43.

29 C.A.I. French and F.M.M. Pryor, *The South-West Fen Dyke Survey Project, 1982–86*, East Anglian Archaeology Report No. 59 (Peterborough, 1993), pp.68–76.

30 See Parker Pearson, 'Food, Fertility and Front Doors in the First Millennium BC', op. cit., p.118.

31 Andrew Fitzpatrick, 'The Deposition of La Tène Iron Age Metalwork in Watery Contexts in Southern England', in Cunliffe and Miles, *Aspects of the Iron Age in Central Southern England*, op. cit., pp.178–90.

32 E.M. Jope, 'Daggers of the Early Iron Age in Britain', *Proceedings of the Prehistoric Society*, vol. 27, 1961, pp.307–43.

33 I.M. Stead, *The Arras Culture*, Yorkshire Philosophical Society (York, 1979). More technical, but up-to-date and easier to find, is I.M. Stead, *Iron Age Cemeteries in East Yorkshire*, English Heritage Archaeological Report No. 22 (London, 1991).

34 I.M. Stead, 'A Distinctive Form of La Tène Barrow in Eastern Yorkshire and on the Continent', *Antiquaries Journal*, vol. 61, 1961, pp.44–62.

35 Recently an Arras-style cart burial (but lacking a barrow) was found at Newbridge, west of Edinburgh. See Stephen Carter and Fraser Hunter, 'The Newbridge Chariot', *Current Archaeology*, vol. 178, 2002, pp.413–15.

36 Although outdated, the most comprehensive assessment of Iron Age funerary practices is still Rowan Whimster, *Burial Practices in Iron Age Britain: A Discussion and Gazetteer of the Evidence c.700 BC–AD 43*, 2 vols, British Archaeological Reports No. 90 (Oxford, 1981).

37 Parker Pearson, 'Food, Sex and Death', op. cit., pp.43–69.

38 For a 'typical' Arras cemetery, at Wetwang Slack, see John S. Dent, 'Cemeteries and Settlement Patterns of the Iron Age on the Yorkshire Wolds', *Proceedings of the Prehistoric Society*, vol. 48, 1982, pp.437–58.

39 J. Musty and A.G. MacCormick, 'An Early Iron Age Wheel from Holme Pierrepont, Notts.', *Antiquaries Journal*, vol. 53, 1973, pp.275–7.

40 See Maisie Taylor, *Wood in Archaeology* (Shire Publications, Princes Risborough, 1981).

41 The sixth-century BC princely burial at Eberdingen-Hochdorf (Baden-Württemberg, Germany) contains a four-wheeled wagon and a bronze couch which would not look out of place in the Prince Regent's Pavilion in Brighton. See J. Biel, 'The Late Hallstatt Chieftain's Grave at Hochdorf', *Antiquity*, vol. 55, pp.16–18. For colour illustrations of the finds, plus other princely burials in the region, see J. Biel, 'The Celtic Princes of Hohenasperg (Baden-Württemberg)', in Kruta, Frey, Raftery and Szabó, *The Celts*, op. cit., pp.108–13.

42 Euan W. MacKie has argued for religious specialists as early as the Neolithic period: see *Science and Society in Prehistoric Britain* (Paul Elek, London, 1977).

43 J.D. Hill, 'Wetwang Chariot Burial', *Current Archaeology*, vol. 178, 2002, pp.410–12.

44 Maisie Taylor, 'The Wood', in Pryor, *The Flag Fen Basin*, op. cit., pp.216–18.

45 I base my account of Mr Hurford's carriage on a report by Robin Young in *The Times*, 19 February 2002, p.11.

46 There is a mountainous pile of publications on hill-forts. The following are useful, if rather dated, collections: J. Forde-Johnston, *Hillforts of the Iron Age in England and Wales* (Liverpool University Press, 1976); Margaret Jesson and David Hill (eds), *The Iron Age and its Hillforts: Papers Presented to Sir Mortimer Wheeler* (Southampton University Archaeological Society, 1971); D.W. Harding, *Hillforts: Later Prehistoric Earthworks in Britain and Ireland* (Academic Press, London, 1976).

47 Cunliffe, *Iron Age Communities in Britain*, 3rd edn, op. cit., pp.491–3.

48 An excellent popular account of Danebury is Barry Cunliffe, *Danebury: The Anatomy of an Iron Age Hillfort* (Batsford, London, 1983). Three of the key academic publications on Danebury are: Barry Cunliffe, *Danebury, An Iron Age Hillfort in Hampshire, Vol. 6: A Hillfort Community in Perspective*, Council for British Archaeology Research Report No. 102 (York, 1995); Barry Cunliffe, *The Danebury Environs Programme, the Prehistory of a Wessex Landscape, Volume 1: Introduction*, English Heritage and Oxford University Committee for Archaeology Monograph No. 48 (Institute of Archaeology, Oxford, 2000); R. Palmer, *Danebury, an Iron Age Hillfort in Hampshire: An Aerial Photographic Interpretation of its Environs*, Royal Commission on Historical Monuments (England), Supplementary Series No. 6 (London, 1984).

49 R.E.M. Wheeler, *Maiden Castle Dorset*, Report of the Research Committee of the Society of Antiquaries of London No. 12 (London, 1943), plates 52–63.

50 N.M. Sharples, *Maiden Castle: Excavations and Field Survey, 1985–6*, English Heritage Archaeological Report No. 19 (London, 1991), pp.100–1.

51 Cunliffe, *Danebury, an Iron Age Hillfort in Hampshire, Vol. 6*, op. cit., p.97.

52 For Maiden Castle see notes 49 and 50, above. South Cadbury is famous for being a possible post-Roman 'Camelot'. Archaeologically it is more important as a Late Bronze Age and Iron Age centre, and is the subject of a major recent publication: John C. Barrett, P.W.M. Freeman and Ann Woodward, *Cadbury Castle Somerset: The Later Prehistoric and Early Historic Archaeology*, English

Heritage Archaeological Report No. 20 (London, 2000).

53 George Williams, 'Recent Work on Rural Settlement in Later Prehistoric and Early Historic Dyfed', *Antiquaries Journal*, vol. 68, 1988, pp.30–54.

54 See, for example, Colin Renfrew and John F. Cherry (eds), *Peer Polity Interaction and Socio-Political Change* (Cambridge University Press, 1986); Colin Renfrew and Stephen Shennan (eds), *Ranking, Resource and Exchange: Aspects of the Archaeology of Early European Society* (Cambridge University Press, 1982).

55 See chapters on Goldcliff in Bell, Caseldine and Neumann, *Prehistoric Intertidal Archaeology in the Welsh Severn Estuary*, op. cit.

CHAPTER TWELVE – *Glimpses of Vanished Ways (the Later Iron Age: 200 BC–AD 43, and After)*

1 For more information on sites and monuments in Northern Ireland, visit the Department of the Environment for Northern Ireland's Environment and Heritage Service website at www.ehsni.gov.uk.

2 For a succinct summary of Tara, with references and radiocarbon dates, see Elizabeth Shee Twohig, *The Megalithic Art of Western Europe* (Oxford University Press, 1981), p.220.

3 For a useful look at modern Irish Iron Age studies see Barry Raftery, 'Iron Age Studies in Ireland: Some Recent Developments', in Champion and Collis, *The Iron Age in Britain and Ireland*, op. cit., pp.155–61.

4 *The Cattle Raid of Cooley* is translated by Thomas Kinsella as *The Tain* (Oxford University Press, 2002).

5 St Patrick converted Ulster to Christianity after his arrival there in AD 405. He founded a missionary centre at Armagh and died c.463.

6 An excellent interim report appeared in *Current Archaeology*, vol. 22, 1970, pp.304–8. This was followed by an

updated version, which included new material based on Celtic sources, in *Current Archaeology*, vol. 134, 1993, pp.44–9.

7 D.M. Waterman, *Excavations at Navan Fort 1961–71*, Northern Ireland Archaeological Monographs No. 3 (The Stationery Office, Belfast, 1997).

8 A. Selkirk (after Chris Lynn), 'Navan Fort: New Light on the Irish Epics', *Current Archaeology*, vol. 134, 1993, p.46.

9 See for example Pryor, *Seahenge*, op. cit., p.181, or C.A.I. French, *Excavation of the Deeping St Nicholas Barrow Complex, South Lincolnshire*, Lincolnshire Archaeology and Heritage Report Series No. 1 (Heckington, 1994), pp.34–42.

10 Raftery, *Trackway Excavations in the Mountdillon Bogs, County Longford, 1985–1991*, vol. 3, op. cit.

11 Humour is rare in academic reports, and connoisseurs of the genre have a lean time of it, but Dr Paul Halstead managed to slip one past me in his report on the animal bones found at Flag Fen: '. . . at least one of these dogs was male (on the evidence of a baculum perceptively labelled by the excavator as a "bone tool"!)'. Pryor, *The Flag Fen Basin*, op. cit., p.349.

12 W.A. Casparie and A. Moloney, 'Corlea 1: Paleo-Environmental Aspects of the Trackway', in Raftery, *Trackway Excavations in the Mountdillon Bogs, County Longford, 1985–1991*, vol. 3, op. cit., p.374.

13 Dáithí Ó hÓgáin, 'The Road and the Literature', in ibid., p.359.

14 Many Bronze Age crannogs are, however, known. For an excellent recent review of prehistoric and historic Irish crannogs see Aidan O'Sullivan, *The Archaeology of Lake Settlement in Ireland*, Discovery Programme Monographs No. 4 (Royal Irish Academy, Dublin, 1998).

15 Euan W. MacKie, 'The Origin and Development of the Broch and Wheelhouse Building Cultures of the Scottish Iron Age', *Proceedings of the*

Prehistoric Society, vol. 31, 1965, pp.93–146.

16 Mike Parker Pearson and Niall Sharples, *Between Land and Sea: Excavations at Dun Vulan, South Uist*, Sheffield Environmental and Archaeological Research Campaign in the Hebrides No. 3 (Academic Press, Sheffield, 1999).

17 There is a lively debate on the roles of brochs, wheelhouses and other buildings of the Iron Age. See, for example, three papers by Ian Armit vs Niall Sharples and Mike Parker Pearson in Gwilt and Haselgrove, *Reconstructing Iron Age Societies*, op. cit., pp.248–69. For a synopsis of the alternative view see Ian Armit, 'Broch Building in Northern Scotland: The Context of Innovation', *World Archaeology*, vol. 21, 1990, pp.435–45.

18 His earlier work was summarised much later: O. Blundell, 'On Further Examination of Artificial Islands in the Beauly Firth, Loch Bruiach, Loch Moy, Loch Garry, Loch Lundy, Loch Oich, Loch Lochy and Loch Treig', *Proceedings of the Society of Antiquaries of Scotland*, vol. 44, 1910, pp.12–33.

19 The Archaeological Diving Unit of the University of St Andrews, Fife, KY16 9AJ, specialises in underwater research. Their website: www.adu.org.uk.

20 For a well-written and -illustrated account of modern research see Ian Morrison, *Landscape with Lake Dwellings: The Crannogs of Scotland* (Edinburgh University Press, 1985). For something more recent: Nicholas Dixon and Barrie Andrian, 'Underwater Archaeology in Scotland', *Scottish Archaeological Review*, vols 9 and 10, 1995, pp.26–35.

21 J.W. Barber and B.A. Crone, 'Crannogs: A Diminishing Resource? A Survey of the Crannogs of Southwest Scotland and Excavations at Buiston Crannog', *Antiquity*, vol. 67, 1993, pp.520–33.

22 John Coles, Armynell Goodall and Stephen Minnitt, *Arthur Bulleid and the Glastonbury Lake Village 1892–1992*, Somerset Levels Project and Somerset

County Council Museums Service (Exeter, 1992).

23 M.W. Thompson, *General Pitt Rivers: Evolution and Archaeology in the Nineteenth Century* (Moonraker Press, Bradford-on-Avon, 1977).

24 John Coles and Stephen Minnitt, *Industrious and Fairly Civilized: The Glastonbury Lake Village*, Somerset Levels Project and Somerset County Council Museums Service (Exeter, 1995). The same authors and publishers also produced a smaller, popular account, *The Lake Villages of Somerset* (1996).

25 The original and most influential study is that by Paul Jacobsthal, *Early Celtic Art*, 2 vols (Oxford University Press, 1944). But see also Sir Cyril Fox, *Pattern and Purpose: A Survey of Early Celtic Art in Britain* (National Museum of Wales, Cardiff, 1958). For northern Britain see Morna MacGregor, *Early Celtic Art in North Britain*, 2 vols (Leicester University Press, 1976). And for the wider picture, J.V.S. Megaw, *Art of the European Iron Age: A Study of the Elusive Image* (Adams and Dart, Bath, 1970).

26 Ian Stead, *Celtic Art* (British Museum Publications, London, 1985).

27 P.R. Lowery, R.D.A. Savage and R.L. Wilkins, 'A Technical Study of the Designs on the British Mirror Series', *Archaeologia*, vol. 105, 1976, pp.99–126.

28 John Brailsford, *Early Celtic Masterpieces from Britain in the British Museum* (British Museum Publications, London, 1975), pp.62–7.

29 Tony Gregory, *Excavations in Thetford, 1980–1982, Fison Way*, 2 vols, East Anglian Archaeology No. 53 (Norwich, 1991). Like most people in archaeology I was very fond of Tony, and it was good that he was able to dig such a wonderfully exciting site before his tragically early death in 1991.

30 In order to obtain an up-to-date consensus I have consulted a recognised book of reference: John Cannon (ed.), *The Oxford Dictionary of British History*

(Oxford University Press, 2001), pp.518–19.

31 Iron Age Silchester is the only British town which shows evidence for a gridiron arrangement. M.G. Fulford, 'Silchester: The Early Development of a Civitas Capital', in S.J. Greep (ed.), *Roman Towns: The Wheeler Inheritance*, Council for British Archaeology Research Report No. 93 (York, 1993), pp.16–33.

32 A.L.F. Rivet, *Town and Country in Roman Britain* (Hutchinson, London, 1964), p.66.

33 John Peter Wild, 'Roman Settlement in the Lower Nene Valley', *Archaeological Journal*, vol. 131, 1974, pp.140–70; D.F. Mackreth, 'Durobrivae, Chesterton, Cambridgeshire', in A.E. Brown (ed.), *Roman Small Towns in Eastern England and Beyond*, Oxbow Monograph No. 52 (Oxford, 1995), pp.145–55.

34 There is a vast literature on the archaeology of Verulamium and its Iron Age antecedents. The best-known report is Sir Mortimer Wheeler, *Verulamium, A Belgic and Two Roman Cities*, Report of the Research Committee of the Society of Antiquaries of London No. 11 (London, 1936). For a modern report that pulls the various strands together, see I.M. Stead and V. Rigby, *Verulamium: The King Harry Lane Site*, English Heritage Archaeological Report No. 12 (London, 1989).

35 Colin Haselgrove and Martin Millett, 'Verlamion Reconsidered', in Gwilt and Haselgrove, *Reconstructing Iron Age Societies*, op. cit., pp.282–96.

36 Cunliffe, *Iron Age Communities in Britain*, op. cit., pp.541–3.

37 James, *The Atlantic Celts*, op. cit.

38 For a useful summary account of the Druids see Cunliffe, *Iron Age Communities in Britain*, op. cit., pp.518–20.

39 Cyril Fox, *A Find of the Early Iron Age from Llyn Cerrig Bach, Anglesey* (National Museum of Wales, Cardiff, 1946). See also H.N. Savory, *Guide Catalogue of the Early Iron Age Collections* (National Museum of Wales, Cardiff, 1976).

40 Mike Parker Pearson, 'Great Sites: Lyn Cerrig Bach', *British Archaeology*, vol. 53, 2000, pp.8–11.

AFTERWORD – *Britannia: A Province on the Fringes of the Empire*

1 For the full horrors of *garum*, or *liquamen*, see Jane Grigson, *Fish Cookery* (Penguin Books, Harmondsworth, 1975), p.369. Six storage tanks dating to the second century AD, that may have been used to produce the stuff, have recently been found at Pompeii by a team from Bradford University (see *History Today*, April 2002, p.9).

2 Tacitus (trans. Harold Mattingly, revised by S.A. Handford), *The Agricola and the Germania* (Penguin Books, Harmondsworth, 1970), p.73.

3 There is a large literature on the coinage of pre-Roman Britain. The standard modern catalogue is R.D. Van Arsdell, *Celtic Coinage of Britain* (Spink, London, 1989).

4 Guy de la Bédoyère, *Eagles Over Britannia: The Roman Army in Britain* (Tempus Publications, Stroud, 2001), p.12.

5 Alan K. Bowman, *The Roman Writing Tablets from Vindolanda* (British Museum Press, London, 1983).

6 For a recent report on the fort, with full references, see Paul T. Bidwell, *The Roman Fort of Vindolanda, at Chesterholm, Northumberland*, Historic Buildings and Monuments Commission for England Archaeological Report No. 1 (London, 1985).

7 De la Bédoyère, *Eagles Over Britannia*, op. cit., p.12.

8 Graham Webster, *Boudica: The British Revolt Against Rome AD 60* (Batsford, London, 1978). See also de la Bédoyère, *Eagles Over Britannia*, op. cit.

9 D.G. Bird, 'The Claudian Invasion Campaign Reconsidered', *Oxford*

Journal of Archaeology, vol. 19, 2000, pp.91–104.

10 S.S. Frere and M. G. Fulford, 'The Roman Invasion of AD 43', *Britannia*, vol. 32, 2001, pp.45–56.

11 M.G. Fulford and J. Timby, *Late Iron Age and Roman Silchester: Excavations at the Site of the Forum-Basilica 1977, 1980–86*, Britannia Monograph No. 15 (London, 2000).

INDEX

P.S.

Ideas,
interviews
& features ...

Portrait

by Josh Lacey

A FEW YEARS AGO, Francis Pryor went to a funeral of a close friend in Manchester. After the ceremony, he got hopelessly lost and wandered through the streets, trying to locate a familiar landmark. Just as the occasional raindrops threatened to turn into a storm, a cab stopped. Pryor got inside. The driver glanced in his rear-view mirror, and said, 'You're that the bloke from the telly, aren't you?' When Pryor admitted that he was, the driver grinned and started asking questions. He had noticed an inconsistency between two of the *Time Team* programmes, and had been waiting for a chance to discover the explanation. For the next thirty minutes, as they drove round Manchester, Pryor and the driver had an involved discussion about the philosophy and practice of archaeology. The driver had no training, no degree, and no formal education, but his archaeological knowledge was astonishing, as was his enthusiasm for the subject.

If Francis Pryor is ever wondering who might read his books, or why he is writing them, he remembers that man, navigating Manchester in his minicab, thinking about archaeology. These are Pryor's ideal audience – people who might have become archaeologists if they had not been failed by our educational system or distracted by other opportunities; people whose lives have been enriched by knowing about the past. He thinks of men and women who, without any formal training or professional interest, understand and interpret some aspects of their own existence through archaeology.

Not only is Pryor passionate about his subject, but he also feels a duty to share his expertise and experience. Archaeology gives him, he is sure, 'a unique perspective on the present', and he constantly uses the present and the past to illuminate one another. Part of his method is a refusal to see anything in isolation. He makes connections. He searches for context. He uses his own emotions and experiences to help interpret the past, and uses the past to understand the present. To gain a better understanding of prehistoric farmers, for instance, he decided to keep sheep. Now, he and his wife own a flock of 120, and devote a significant proportion of their lives to working as farmers. During the lambing season, his archaeological work just has to wait. This means, of course, that he lives an enviably balanced life. Most writers retreat inside their heads and forget their bodies. When Pryor is writing, he spends the morning secluded inside his house, sitting at a desk and staring at a computer screen, thinking and typing. In the afternoons, he works outside in the fresh air, herding the sheep or digging the soil, using his body as much as his brain.

Pryor has a straightforward explanation for why he and so many others are fascinated by archaeology. He quotes the first line of L. P. Hartley's *The Go-between* – 'The past is another country' – and adds a refinement of his own: the past is 'unreachable, but there'. He has devoted his life to imaginative ▶

> ❛He has devoted his life to imaginative reconstructions of a country that he can walk over and touch, even smell or taste, but never actually inhabit.❜

Portrait *(continued)*

◀ reconstructions of a country that he can
walk over and touch, even smell or taste, but
never actually inhabit. He offers a similarly
neat paradox to express the difference
between prehistoric humanity and ourselves:
he describes the inhabitants of the Bronze
Age as 'a different species which is identical
to ours'. Over the past few thousand years,
human thought and culture has changed
completely – and yet, in some sense, humans
have not changed at all.

If people from the Bronze Age were
suddenly transported into the twenty-first
century, once they had overcome their
amazement at the physical differences
between our lives and theirs, Francis Pryor
is convinced that they would be astonished
by one thing above all others: the short-
termism of modern life. Pryor is passionate
about the wastefulness of modern society.
Whether we're consuming junk food,
burying disposable nappies, or driving gas-
guzzling cars, we seem to be determined to
use up the world's resources as quickly as
possible. Looking around, Pryor is depressed
by our lust for immediate gratification and
the destruction that we leave in our wake. Of
course, he appreciates that such wastefulness
might be useful to his colleagues. A few
thousand years from now, one of his
descendants may be searching through the
debris, unpicking our rubbish, looking for
clues to the way we lived. ■

Top Ten
Favourite Books

1. **Tristram Shandy**
   Laurence Sterne

2. **The Diary of a Nobody**
   George and Weedon Grossmith

3. **The Diary of Samuel Pepys**

4. **The Life of Samuel Johnson**
   James Boswell

5. **Ulysses**
   James Joyce

6. **The Seven Pillars of Wisdom**
   T.E. Lawrence

7. **Pride and Prejudice**
   Jane Austen

8. **Vanity Fair**
   William Makepeace Thackeray

9. **Look Homeward, Angel**
   Thomas Wolfe

10. **At Swim-Two-Birds**
    Flann O'Brien

A Visit to Flag Fen

by Josh Lacey

FORTY-FIVE MINUTES on the train from
London, followed by a brief drive through
the suburbs of Peterborough, and I'm
standing inside a Bronze Age roundhouse,
smelling the scent of recently burnt timbers.
Blackened logs lie in the middle of the floor.
Benches line the walls. Skulls hang from
posts. I can hear no sound except the chatter
of bickering ducks. In the darkness and the
cool air, sitting on a soft sheepskin, I forget
the day, the year, the decade, the millennium.
In the shadows, I notice some movement,
and realize that two small eyes are watching
me. They inspect me for a moment. We stare
at one another. Her eyes are black, intense,
and suspicious. I don't move. Abruptly, she
turns her head away, deciding that I am not
a threat. She bounces across the floor, then
flies through the doorway.

I follow the wren out of the roundhouse
and into the sunshine. The incongruous sight
of some picnic tables is the only reminder
that I am in the twenty-first century. Walking
around Flag Fen, I notice a few other signs
of modern life. An occasional small plane
flies overhead. On the horizon, I can see
Peterborough Cathedral and the outline of
a local factory. But as I stroll along a low,
grassy path, surrounded by beds of reeds,
and watch a pair of coots bustle around their
five tiny chicks, it is easy to imagine that I
have been transported several thousand years
into the past.

Flag Fen has a small museum, showing
what has been found on the site: knives,

jars, axe handles, a sword, a wheel, and so on. In the surrounding fields, you can wander through Bronze Age and Iron Age roundhouses, sniff a Roman herb garden, investigate a cross-section of a Roman road, or hurry along a prehistoric droveway. There is even a natural amphitheatre where you can see occasional performances ranging from touring theatre companies to gladiatorial contests. But, for me, the highlight is a dark, chilly hut filled with a few old timbers.

It is called the Preservation Hall and is a brick building containing Bronze Age timbers preserved just as they were found at Flag Fen. Constantly sprayed with water to prevent decay, the line of dark wooden posts has been surrounded by a large mural painted by a local artist, Rob Fuller. Each of the four walls shows a different season, and the whole effect is wonderfully evocative. Gazing across the timbers, you have the illusion that you are staring at the landscape as it might have looked in 1000 BC. Here, you can see the lush colours and plentiful flowers of summer. There, you see the stark wastes of winter. A kingfisher perches on one of the wooden posts, and a heron wades through the weeds. In the distance, a couple of shepherds stroll through the grass, guarding their animals.

As I leave the Preservation Hall and walk outside into the sunshine, three sheep look up, startled, and bolt. Their long, curled horns would provide excellent protection against any attack, but they still seem ▶

> ❝ Prehistoric animals are permanent residents of Flag Fen. ❞

A Visit to Flag Fen *(continued)*

◄ nervous. Prehistoric animals are permanent residents of Flag Fen. There is a flock of Soay sheep, a Bronze Age breed that have managed to remain uncontaminated by modern life by surviving on the St Kilda islands, accompanied by Mouflon, wild sheep from Corsica and Sardinia. Alongside these animals, only appropriate trees, shrubs, and flowers have been planted at Flag Fen – including lots of flag irises, from which the fen takes its name.

Francis Pryor and his wife, Maisie Taylor, have devoted decades of their life to this one site. Much of their archaeological expertise comes from the sheer amount of time they have spent here, getting to know the landscape and its context. When Maisie Taylor gave me a lift from Peterborough Station to Flag Fen, she pointed out particular factories and warehouses along the route and described digging in the soil before any of the foundations had been laid. Over the past few decades, they have seen immense changes wrought on the landscape. Without their efforts, even more of this fenland might have been buried under tarmac and bricks, and its archaeological treasures would have been lost.

After walking round the site, I stop in the café for a cup of tea with Francis Pryor. A woman and a child arrive with a brochure and apologetically ask for his autograph. Pryor brushes their apologies aside and chats about their visit. Have they enjoyed themselves? (Yes.) Is this their first visit? (No.) Will they come again? (Definitely.)

> ❝ Without their efforts, even more of this fenland might have been buried under tarmac and bricks, and its archaeological treasures would have been lost. ❞

Their enthusiasm is a small sign of how intimately Flag Fen is connected with the neighbouring population, the residents of Peterborough, and the surrounding countryside. Volunteers staff the visitor centre. Local enthusiasm has provided vital help during tricky financial patches. More than anything, Flag Fen has fostered an extraordinary bond between the current residents of this area and their predecessors, connecting the double-glazing and fast cars of modern suburbs with the thatched roofs and wooden wheels of several thousand years ago. It's an almost magical connection between the past and the present, linking groups of people who have been inhabiting the same piece of land for millennia. ∎

❛Flag Fen has fostered an extraordinary bond between the current residents of this area and their predecessors. ❜

A Critical Eye

LIVING HISTORY WAS impressed by the range and depth of *Britain BC*, concluding that 'you'll be hard-pressed to find a more convincing and readable introduction to the subject than this'. Writing in the **TLS**, the archaeologist Christopher Chippendale agreed: 'Pryor has given us a remarkable, imaginative and persuasive account ... Its enthusiastic and confident approach deserves to be very influential.' It is, he concluded, 'a splendid book'. In **New Scientist**, Barry Cunliffe was struck by the 'vivid vignettes' that create 'a compulsive narrative intertwining prehistory, the excitement of discovery and personalities'. In the **Telegraph**, Tom Holland praised the 'engagingly anecdotal touch' of 'Pryor's immensely readable new book'. **British Archaeology**'s critic Peter Drewett gave a surprisingly candid view of the book and its rivals: 'Much has been written about British Prehistory that is unintelligible, dull or just plain bad. What a delight therefore to review a book that is the exact opposite, beautifully written, exciting and extremely good.' ■

Have You Read?

Britain AD: A Quest for Arthur, England and the Anglo-Saxons
In his latest book, published in September 2004 and accompanied by a Channel 4 series, Francis Pryor traces the story of King Arthur and Camelot back to its Bronze Age origins. Investigating the British landscape from Edinburgh to Cornwall, he suggests that the legend has its roots in pre-Roman British culture.

Seahenge
In this fascinating book Francis Pryor charts the recent discovery and excavation of one of Britain's most enigmatic Bronze Age sites. 'One of the finest accounts of how archaeologists think and go about their work that I have ever read . . . a tour de force.' Professor Brian Fagan.

Farmers in Prehistoric Britain
Drawing on his personal experience as both an archaeologist and a sheep farmer, Francis Pryor investigates the lives and methods of prehistoric farmers. He discusses intensive farming, the use of dogs, and the surprising sophistication of Bronze Age farmers.

If You Loved This,
You'll Like ...

Bronze Age Britain
Michael Parker Pearson
This well-illustrated book shows the
transformation of the British landscape over
the four thousand years from the beginning
of farming to the Iron Age.

*The Significance of Monuments: On the
Shaping of Human Experience in Neolithic
and Bronze Age Europe*
Richard Bradley
In this book, Bradley describes the locations
and possible significances of Neolithic and
Bronze Age burial mounds, henges, stone
circles and barrows.

*The Atlantic Celts: Ancient people or
modern invention?*
Simon James
Arguments rage over the Celts. Do they hold
a vital place in our national heritage? Or did
they never actually exist? Simon James asks
whether the obsession with so-called Celtic
identity is a misinformed romanticization. ∎